ANALYSIS FOR FINANCIAL MANAGEMENT

ANALYSIS FOR FINANCIAL MANAGEMENT

Third Edition

Robert C. Higgins
The University of Washington

IRWIN
Homewood, IL 60430
Boston, MA 02116

*In memory of Alex Robichek,
teacher, colleague, and friend.*

 This symbol indicates that the paper in
this book is made from recycled paper. Its
fiber content exceeds the recommended
minimum of 50% waste paper fibers as
specified by the EPA.

© RICHARD D. IRWIN, INC., 1983, 1989, and 1992
A professional edition of this book is available through
BUSINESS ONE IRWIN

Sponsoring editor: Michael W. Junior
Project editor: Paula Buschman
Production manager: Ann Cassady
Cover designer: Lori Fox
Compositor: Graphic Sciences Corporation
Typeface: 11/13 Century Schoolbook
Printer: R. R. Donnelley & Sons Company

Library of Congress Cataloging-in-Publication Data

Higgins, Robert C.
    Analysis for financial management / Robert C. Higgins. — 3rd ed.
      p. cm.
    Includes bibliographical references and index.
    ISBN 0-256-09234-6   ISBN 1-55623-549-6
    1. Corporations—Finance. I. Title
HG4026.H496 1992b
658.15′1—dc20   91-28341

Printed in the United States of America
2 3 4 5 6 7 8 9 0 DOC 8 7 6 5 4 3 2

PREFACE

Like its predecessors, the third edition of *Analysis for Financial Management* is written for nonfinancial executives and business students interested in the practice of financial management. Its purpose is to introduce standard techniques and recent developments in a practical, intuitive way. The book assumes no prior background beyond a rudimentary and perhaps rusty familiarity with financial statements—although a healthy curiosity about what makes business tick is also useful. Emphasis throughout is on the managerial implications of financial analysis.

Analysis for Financial Management should prove valuable to individuals interested in sharpening their own managerial skills and to participants in executive programs. The book has also found a home in university classrooms as the sole text in applied finance courses, as a companion text in case-oriented courses, and as a supplementary piece in more theoretical finance courses.

Analysis for Financial Management is my attempt to translate into another medium the enjoyment and stimulation I have experienced over the past two decades working with executives and college students. From this experience I have become convinced that financial techniques and concepts need not be abstract or obtuse; that recent developments in the field such as market signaling, market efficiency, and capital asset pricing are important to practitioners; and that finance has much to say about the broader aspects of company management. I also believe that any activity in which so much money changes hands so quickly cannot fail to be interesting.

The story begins in Part I with a look at the management of existing resources, including the use of financial statements to assess a company's financial health, its strengths, weaknesses, recent performance, and future prospects. A recurring theme is that a business must be viewed as an integrated whole, and that effective financial management is possible only within the context of a company's broader operating characteristics and strategies.

The rest of the book deals in one way or another with the acquisition and management of new resources. Part II looks at financial forecasting and planning, with particular emphasis on managing growth and decline. Part III considers the financing of company operations, including a review of the principal security types, the markets in which they trade, and the proper choice of security type by the issuing company. The latter requires a close look at financial leverage, and its impact on the firm and its shareholders.

Evaluation of investment opportunities is the topic of Part IV. Included here are the use of discounted cash flow techniques—such as the net present value and the internal rate of return—to estimate an investment's merit and a look at the difficult task of incorporating risk into decision making. The book concludes with an examination of corporate restructuring within the context of the ongoing battle between shareholders and incumbent managers for control of the corporation.

CHANGES IN THE THIRD EDITION

In addition to the usual updates and expansions endemic to new editions, those familiar with the evolution of *Analysis for Financial Management* will note several changes in the third edition. First, as a belated concession to reality, I have internationalized the text. Rather than tack an international chapter onto the end of the book—the one you never have time to cover—I have woven the subject throughout existing chapters. Among the international topics examined are assessing the performance of international subsidiaries, comparing interest rates across differing currencies, discussing Eurodollar markets, and managing foreign exchange exposure. Second, I have replaced the appendix on convertible securities with one on the use of option and forward markets to manage financial risks. Third, I have revised the treatment of a number of topics, including an expanded discussion of cash flow statements, a greatly simplified derivation of the sustainable growth equation, an expanded treatment of the pitfalls of discounted cash flow analysis in capital budgeting, and an acknowledgment that the era of the corporate raider is at an end. Fourth, as an aid to readers, I have included suggested answers to all chapter problems at the end of the book.

A word of caution: *Analysis for Financial Management* emphasizes the application and interpretation of analytic techniques in decision making. These techniques have proved useful for putting financial problems into perspective and for helping managers anticipate the consequences of their actions. But techniques do not substitute for thought. Even with the best technique it is still necessary to define and prioritize issues, to modify analysis to fit specific circumstances, to strike the proper balance between quantitative analysis and more qualitative considerations, and to evaluate alternatives insightfully and creatively. Mastery of technique is only the necessary first step toward effective management.

I want to thank Bill Alberts, Dave Dubofsky, George Parker, Megan Partch, Alan Shapiro, and Nik Varaiya for insightful help and comments on this and prior editions. I also want to thank my wife for tolerating an often distracted spouse these past months, and my students and colleagues at the University of Washington, the Pacific Coast Banking School, the University of Hawaii Advanced Management Program, Bank of America, and Hawaiian Electric Industries, among others, for stimulating my continuing interest in financial management.

Robert C. Higgins

CONTENTS

APPENDIXES

PART 1

ASSESSING THE FINANCIAL HEALTH OF A FIRM

CHAPTER 1

INTERPRETING FINANCIAL STATEMENTS

*Financial statements are
like fine perfume; to be
sniffed but not swallowed.*
Abraham Brilloff

Accounting is the scorecard of business. It translates the diverse activities of a company into a set of objective numbers that provide information about the firm's performance, problems, and prospects. Finance involves the interpretation of these accounting numbers for the assessment of performance and the planning of future actions.

The skills of financial analysis are important to a wide range of people, including investors, creditors, and regulators. Nowhere are they more important than within the company. Regardless of functional speciality or company size, managers who possess these skills are able to diagnose their firm's ills, prescribe useful remedies, and anticipate the financial consequences of their actions. Like a ball player who cannot keep score, an operating manager who does not fully understand accounting and finance works under an unnecessary handicap.

This chapter and the following one look at the use of accounting information for the assessment of financial health. We begin with an overview of the accounting principles governing financial statements and a discussion of one of the most abused and confused notions in all of finance—cash flow. In Chapter 2, we will look at measures of financial performance and ratio analysis.

THE CASH FLOW CYCLE

Finance can seem arcane and complex to the uninitiated. There are, however, a comparatively few basic principles that should guide your thinking. One is that *a company's finances and its operations are integrally connected.* A company's activities, method of operation, and competitive strategy all fundamentally shape its financial structure. The reverse is also true. Decisions that appear to be primarily financial in nature can significantly affect company operations. For example, the way a company finances its assets can affect the nature of the investments it is able to undertake in future years.

The cash flow–production cycle appearing in Figure 1–1 illustrates the close interplay between company operations and finances. For simplicity, suppose the company shown is a new one

FIGURE 1–1
The Cash Flow–Production Cycle

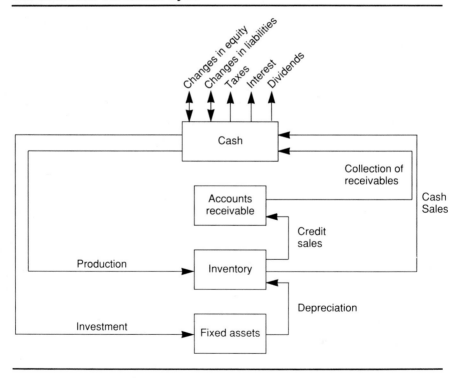

that has raised money from owners and creditors, has purchased productive assets, and is now ready to begin operations. To do so, the company uses cash to purchase raw materials and hire laborers; they make the product and store it temporarily in inventory. What began as cash is now physical inventory. When the company sells an item, the physical inventory changes once again into cash. If the sale is for cash, this occurs immediately; otherwise, cash is not realized until some time later when the account receivable is collected.

This simple movement of cash to inventory, to accounts receivable, and back to cash is the firm's *operating, or working capital cycle.* Another ongoing activity represented in Figure 1–1 is investment. Over a period of time, the company's fixed assets are consumed, or worn out, in the creation of products. It is as if every item passing through the business takes with it a small portion of the value of fixed assets. The accountant recognizes this process by continually reducing the accounting value of fixed assets and increasing the value of merchandise flowing into inventory by an amount known as depreciation. To maintain productive capacity, the company must invest part of its newly received cash in new fixed assets. The object of the exercise, of course, is to ensure that the cash returning from the working capital cycle and the investment cycle exceeds the amount that started the journey.

We could complicate Figure 1–1 further by including accounts payable and by expanding on the use of debt and equity to generate cash, but the figure already demonstrates two basic principles. First, *financial statements are an important window on reality.* A company's operating policies, production techniques, and inventory and credit-control systems fundamentally determine its financial profile. If, for example, a company requires prompter payment on credit sales, its financial statements will reveal a reduced investment in accounts receivable and possibly a change in its revenues and profits. This linkage between a company's operations and its finances is our rationale for studying financial statements. We seek to understand company operations and to predict the financial consequences of changing operations.

The second principle illustrated in Figure 1–1 is that *profits do not equal cash flow.* Cash—and the timely conversion of cash into inventories, accounts receivable, and back to cash—is the lifeblood of any company. If this cash flow is severed or significantly interrupted, insolvency can occur. Yet the fact that a company is profitable is no assurance that its cash flow will be sufficient to maintain solvency. To illustrate, suppose a company loses control of its accounts receivable by allowing customers an increasingly long time to pay, or suppose the company consistently makes more merchandise than it sells. Then, even though the company is selling merchandise at a profit in the eyes of an accountant, its sales may not be generating enough cash soon enough to replenish the cash outflows required for production and investment. When a company has insufficient cash to pay its maturing obligations, it is insolvent. Here is another example. Suppose the company is managing its inventory and receivables carefully, but that rapid sales growth is forcing an ever-larger investment in these assets. Then, despite the fact that the company is profitable, it may have too little cash to meet its obligations. The company will literally be "growing broke." These brief examples illustrate why a manager must be concerned at least as much with cash flows as with profits.

We will return to these themes repeatedly in later chapters and will consider cash flow analysis in a few pages. But first it is necessary to review the basics of financial statements. If this is your first look at financial accounting, buckle up because we will be moving quickly; if the pace is too quick, you might consider referring to one of the accounting texts recommended at the end of the chapter.

THE BALANCE SHEET

The most important source of information for evaluating the financial health of a company is its financial statements, consisting principally of a balance sheet, an income statement, and a cash flow statement. Let us look at each briefly in turn.

A balance sheet is a financial snapshot, taken at a point in time, of all the assets owned by the company and all the claims against those assets. The basic relationship is:

$$\text{Assets} = \text{Liabilities} + \text{Shareholders' equity}$$

It is as if a herd (flock? covey?) of auditors run through the business on the appointed day, making a list of everything the company owns, and assigning each item a value. Having tabulated the firm's assets, the auditors next make a list of all outstanding company liabilities, where a liability is just any form of an IOU. Having thus toted up what the company *owns* and what it *owes,* the auditors call the difference between the two shareholders' equity. Shareholders' equity is the accountant's estimate of the value of the shareholders' investment in the firm. It is analogous to the situation of a homeowner, whose equity equals the value of the home, less the mortgage outstanding against it. Shareholders' equity is also known as *owners' equity, stockholders' equity, net worth,* or simply *equity.*

To illustrate the techniques and concepts presented throughout this book, I will refer whenever possible to Russell Corporation—a designer, manufacturer, and marketer of leisure apparel, athletic uniforms, and woven fabrics—headquartered in Alexander City, Alabama. You probably have a Russell sweatshirt or two in your closet. Tables 1–1 and 1–2 present Russell's balance sheet and income statement for 1988 and 1989. If the precise meaning of every asset and liability category appearing in Table 1–1 is not immediately apparent, be patient. We will discuss many of them in the following pages.[1]

Referring to 1989, Russell's basic balance sheet equation is

Assets	=	Liabilities	+	Shareholders' equity
$720.8 million	=	$318.6 million	+	$402.2 million

Current Assets and Liabilities

Accountants customarily define any asset or liability that will be converted into cash within one year as current; all other assets or liabilities are long-term. Inventory is a current asset be-

---

[1]Accountants usually classify preferred stock as part of equity. I have not done so in Table 1–1 because the company does not and because, like creditors, Russell's preferred shareholders can force the company to redeem the shares. See Chapter 5 for a more complete look at preferred stock.

TABLE 1–1
Russell Corporation Balance Sheets ($ millions)

	December 31		Change in Account
	1988	1989	
Assets			
Current assets:			
Cash	$ 2.2	$ 2.8	$ 0.6
Temporary investments	10.3	72.8	62.5
Accounts receivable	99.9	133.3	33.4
Inventories	94.4	108.8	14.4
Prepaid expenses and other current assets	1.5	6.9	5.4
Future income tax benefits	1.6	2.4	0.8
Total current assets	209.9	327.0	
Property, plant, and equipment			
Land	2.9	2.6	
Buildings	126.6	135.4	
Machinery and equipment	362.1	438.7	
Construction in progress	18.5	6.3	
Less allowance for depreciation	(188.3)	(222.1)	
Net property, plant, & equipment	321.8	360.9	39.1
Other long-term assets	29.1	32.9	3.8
Total assets	$560.8	$720.8	
Liabilities and shareholders' equity			
Current liabilities:			
Commercial paper	$ 30.5	$ 0.0	($ 30.5)
Notes payable	0.0	5.4	5.4
Accounts payable	33.2	26.9	(6.3)
Accrued wages and expenses	12.0	17.2	5.2
Accrued taxes	5.5	6.4	0.9
Current maturities on long-term debt	4.5	3.9	(0.6)
Total current liabilities	85.7	59.8	
Long-term debt	84.3	204.8	120.5
Deferred taxes	37.1	43.6	6.5
Accrued liabilities	3.1	4.7	1.6
Preferred stock	5.7	5.7	
Total liabilities	215.9	318.6	
Shareholders' equity:			
Common stock	0.4	0.4	
Paid-in capital	48.7	49.0	
Retained earnings	315.0	367.8	
Unrealized loss on noncurrent investment	(3.3)	0.0	
Treasury stock	(15.7)	(15.2)	
Currency translation adjustment	0.0	0.2	
Total shareholders' equity	345.1	402.2	57.1
Total liabilities and shareholders' equity	$561.0	$720.8	

TABLE 1–2
Russell Corporation Income Statements ($ millions)

	December 31,	
	1988	1989
Net sales	$531.1	$688.0
Cost of sales	344.1	457.9
Gross profit	187.0	230.1
Selling, general, and administrative expenses	91.3	109.7
Operating income	95.7	120.4
Nonoperating income (expense):		
Interest	(8.8)	(15.6)
Other	(1.1)	(2.0)
Income before taxes	85.8	102.8
Provision for taxes	32.0	38.0
Net income	53.8	64.8
Preferred dividends		0.6
Net income available for common shareholders	$ 53.8	$ 64.2

cause it is reasonable to assume it will be sold and will generate cash within the year. Accounts payable are short-term liabilities because they must be paid within the year. Note that, even though Russell is a manufacturing firm, almost one half of its assets are current. We will have more to say about this in the next chapter.

Shareholders' Equity

One common source of confusion is the large number of accounts appearing in the shareholders' equity portion of the balance sheet. Russell has six, beginning with common stock and ending with currency translation adjustment. Unless forced to do otherwise, my advice is to forget these distinctions. They keep accountants and attorneys employed, but do not often make much practical difference. Just add up everything that is not an IOU and call it shareholders' equity.

A Word to the Unwary

Nothing puts a damper on a good financial discussion (if such exists) faster than the suggestion that if a company is short of cash, it can always spend some of its shareholders' equity. Shareholders' equity is on the liabilities side of the balance sheet, not the asset side. It represents owners' claims against existing assets. In other words, that money has already been spent.

THE INCOME STATEMENT

A balance sheet is a snapshot at a point in time. An income statement, on the other hand, records the flow of resources over time. The basic relationship is

$$\text{Net sales} - \text{Cost of sales} - \text{Operating expenses} + \text{Nonoperating income (expense)} - \text{Taxes} = \text{Earnings}$$

$$\$688.0 - \$457.9 - \$109.7 - \$17.6 - \$38.0 = \$64.8$$

Earnings measure the extent to which revenues generated during the accounting period exceeded expenses incurred in producing the revenues. For variety, earnings are also commonly referred to as *profits* or *income,* frequently with the word "net" stuck in front of them; and net sales are frequently known as *revenues,* or *net revenues.* I have never found a meaningful distinction between these terms.

Income statements are commonly divided into operating and nonoperating segments. As the names imply, the operating segment reports the results of the company's major, ongoing activities, while the nonoperating segment summarizes all secondary activities of the firm. In 1989 Russell reported operating income of $120.4 million and nonoperating expense—mainly interest—of $17.6 million.

Measuring Earnings

This is not the place for a detailed discussion of accounting. Because earnings, or lack of same, are a critical indicator of financial health, however, several technical aspects of earnings measurement deserve mention.

Accrual Accounting

The measurement of accounting earnings involves two steps: (1) Identify revenues for the period and (2) match the corresponding costs to revenues. Looking at the first step, it is important to recognize that revenue is not the same as cash received. According to the *accrual principle* (a cruel principle?) of accounting, revenue is recognized as soon as the effort required to generate the sale is substantially complete and there is a reasonable certainty that payment will be received. The accountant sees the timing of the actual cash receipts as only a technicality. For credit sales, the accrual principle means that revenue is recognized at the time of sale, not when the customer pays. This can result in a significant time lag between the generation of revenue and the receipt of cash. Looking at Russell, for instance, we see that revenue in 1989 was $688 million, but that accounts receivable increased $33.4 million over the year. We conclude that the cash received from sales during 1989 was only $654.6 million ($688 million − $33.4 million). The other $33.4 million still awaits collection.

Depreciation

Fixed assets, and associated depreciation, present the accountant with a particularly thorny problem in matching. Suppose in 1990 a company constructs for $50 million a new facility that has an expected productive life of 10 years. If the accountant assigns the entire cost of the facility to expenses in 1990, operating income in that year will clearly plunge and operating income in the following nine years will get a free ride in the sense that the new facility will contribute to revenue but will not add to expenses. Accounting for the cost of the new machine in this manner clearly distorts the company's reported profitability over time.

The preferred approach is to spread the cost of the facility over its expected useful life in the form of depreciation. Because the only cash outlay associated with the facility occurs in 1990, the annual depreciation listed as a cost on the company's income statement is not a cash outflow. It is a *noncash charge* used to match the 1990 expenditure with resulting revenue. Said differently, depreciation is the allocation of past expenditures to future time periods so as to match revenues and expenses. Although the precise numbers cannot be confirmed from Russell's income statement or balance sheet, you will see momentarily that the company acquired $79.6 million of property, plant, and equipment in 1989 and included a $45.6 million charge for depreciation in cost of goods sold.

To determine the amount of depreciation to be taken on a particular asset, three estimates are required: the asset's useful life, its salvage value, and the method of allocation to be employed. All of these estimates should be based on economic and engineering information, experience, and any other objective data about the asset's likely performance. Broadly speaking, there are two methods of allocating an asset's cost over its useful life. Under the *straight-line* method, the accountant depreciates the asset by a uniform amount each year. If an asset costs $50 million, has an expected useful life of 10 years, and an estimated salvage value of $10 million, straight-line depreciation would be $4 million per year [($50 million − $10 million)/10].

The second method of cost allocation is really a family of methods known as *accelerated depreciation*. Each technique charges more depreciation in the early years of the asset's life and correspondingly less in later years. Accelerated depreciation does not enable a company to take more depreciation in total; instead it alters the timing of the recognition. While the specifics of the various accelerated techniques need not detain us here, you should recognize that the life expectancy, the salvage value, and the allocation method used by a company can fundamentally affect reported earnings. In general, if a company is conservative and depreciates its assets rapidly, it will tend to understate current earnings, and vice versa.

Taxes

A second noteworthy feature of depreciation accounting involves taxes. Most companies, except the very small, keep at least two sets of financial records: one for managing the company and reporting to shareholders and another for determining its tax bill. The objective of the first set is, or should be, to portray accurately the financial performance of the company. The objective of the second is much simpler: to minimize taxes. Forget objectivity and minimize taxes. These differing objectives mean that the accounting principles used to construct the two sets of books differ substantially. Depreciation accounting is a case in point. Regardless of the method used for reporting to shareholders, company tax books will minimize current taxes by employing the most rapid method of depreciation over the shortest useful life allowed by the tax authorities.

This dual reporting creates some complications on a company's published financial statements. To illustrate, the provision for taxes of $38 million appearing on Russell's 1989 income statement are the taxes due according to the accounting techniques used to construct Russell's published statements. Since Russell used different accounting techniques for reporting to the tax authorities—techniques intended to defer the recognition of tax liabilities until future years—$38 million is not the amount actually paid by Russell in 1989. To confirm this, note the following changes in tax accounts on Russell's balance sheet during 1989: (1) Deferred taxes, a long-term liability, rose $6.5 million, (2) accrued taxes, a short-term liability, rose $0.9 million, and (3) future income tax benefits, a short-term asset, rose $0.8 million. Here's what happened. Using legal tax-deferral techniques, Russell was able to delay payment on $7.4 million of tax liabilities from 1989 to future years; $0.9 million of this amount is due in 1990 and $6.5 million in subsequent years. Russell has also either prepaid another $0.8 million of taxes or increased the tax credit it can claim against future liabilities by this amount. So as shown below, Russell's cash disbursement for taxes was not $38 million but only $31.4 million.

Provision for taxes	$38.0
− Increase in deferred taxes	(6.5)
− Increase in accrued taxes	(0.9)
+ Increase in future income tax benefits	0.8
Taxes paid	$31.4 million

Because these taxes are only postponed, not eliminated, they appear as an increase in liabilities on Russell's 1989 balance sheet. In the meantime, Russell has use of the money. In essence, tax-deferral techniques create the equivalent of an interest-free loan from the government.

CASH FLOW STATEMENT

Until 1988, the third component of financial statements, in addition to an income statement and a balance sheet, was a creature known as the statement of changes in financial position. Once described as "a random collection of pluses and minuses," the statement of changes in financial position was so confusing that even accountants were not certain of its intended purpose.

Fortunately, the accounting profession has largely remedied this situation by abandoning the statement of changes in financial position in favor of a cash flow statement. But just to keep life interesting, two presentation formats are permitted. The *direct method* is a straightforward statement of cash received and disbursed, while the *indirect method* arrives at the same result but only after a tortuous conversion of income statement numbers to a cash basis. From the user's perspective, the direct method is much superior, but because it is also more costly to prepare, most companies—including Russell—use the much more obtuse indirect format. (See the accompanying discussion, Direct versus Indirect Presentation Formats, for a more detailed look at the differences between the two.)

Much of the information contained in a cash flow statement can be gleaned from careful study of a company's income statement and balance sheet. The statement nonetheless has three principal virtues. First, accounting neophytes, and those who never have trusted accrual accounting, have at least some hope of understanding it; second, it provides more accurate information about certain cash flows than can be inferred from income statements and balance sheets alone; and third, it casts a welcome light on the issue of firm solvency. By noting how a company spends its money and where the money comes from, one can gain useful insights into the firm's operating strategies and the viability of these strategies over time.

Table 1–3 presents Russell Corporation's 1989 cash flow statement. Regardless of which presentation format a company uses, the basic relationship is

>Cash flows from operating activities
>+ Cash flows from investing activities
>+ Cash flows from financing activities

+ Net effect of exchange rate changes on cash
= Net increase (or decrease) in cash.

In most instances, the numbers appearing in a company's cash flow statement are straightforward combinations of balance sheet and income statement data. Thus, changes in accounts receivable should equal the difference between 1989 and 1988 receivables, as shown on the balance sheet. Because Russell acquired a small company during 1989, its cash flow statement does not conform to this expectation, although the differences are modest. For instance, the change in accounts receivable on Russell's cash flow statement is $31.5 million, compared to an indicated change on its balance sheets of $33.4 million. Such is the price one pays for using real-world data instead of concocted examples.

Cash Flow Statements: Direct versus Indirect Presentation Formats

The most important differences between the direct and the indirect methods of presenting a cash flow statement occur under the first heading, *cash flows from operating activities*. Below are the cash flows from operating activities for a typical business using first the direct, and then the indirect, format. See how simple the direct method is. The company put $10,700 in the till as a result of operations, paid $7,750 out of the till, and has $2,950 left. All vestiges of accrual accounting are removed so that even accounting-phobes can understand what the company is up to.

Now look at the indirect method. It comes to the same conclusion, but by a much more circuitous route. Beginning with net income, an accrual accounting number, the indirect method makes a series of adjustments intended to transform net income into cash flows from operations.

The adjustments to net income are of three types: Expenses not involving cash outflows are added back, cash outflows not treated as expenses are subtracted, and revenues not involving cash inflows are subtracted as well. Depreciation, deferred taxes, increased accounts payable, and increased accrued interest payable are all expenses that did not involve cash outflows during the period. Hence, they must be added back to net income to put it on a

---

(continued)

Cash Flow Statements: Direct versus Indirect Presentation Formats (concluded)

cash basis. Increases in inventory correspond to cash outflows not recorded as expenses, and so must be subtracted from net income. And finally, increased accounts receivable, increased accrued interest earned, and gain on sale of property are all revenues that did not generate cash during the period, and so must be subtracted.

Incidentally, whatever cash was generated by the sale of property will appear on the cash flow statement as proceeds from the sale of property under the heading *cash flows from investing activities*. The *gain* on sale of property is the difference between the property's selling price and its balance sheet value when sold. Because this gain is already part of the proceeds from sale of property, showing it also as part of cash flows from operating activities would amount to double-counting.

The Direct Method

Cash flows from operating activities:		
Cash received from customers	$10,000	
Dividends received	700	
Cash provided by operating activities		$10,700
Cash paid to suppliers and employees	$ 6,000	
Interest and taxes paid	1,750	
Cash disbursed for operating activities		7,750
Net cash flows from operations		$ 2,950

The Indirect Method

Cash flows from operating activities:	
Net income as reported on income statement	$ 3,000
Adjustments to reconcile net income to net cash provided by operating activities:	
Depreciation	1,500
Deferred taxes	150
Net increase in receivables, inventory, and payables	(850)
Increase in accrued interest earned	(350)
Increase in accrued interest payable	100
Gain on sale of property	(600)
Net cash flows from operations	$ 2,950

TABLE 1–3
Russell Corporation Cash Flow Statement ($ millions)

Cash flows from operating activities	1989
Net income	$ 64.7
Adjustment to reconcile net income to net cash provided by operating activities:	
Depreciation	45.6
Deferred income taxes and taxes payable	7.1
Loss on sale of equipment and investment	3.4
Changes in assets and liabilities:	
Accounts receivable	(31.5)
Inventories	(10.8)
Accounts payable accrued liabilities and accrued expenses	(9.9)
Net cash flows from operations	68.8
Cash flows from investing activities	
(Increase) decrease in temporary investments	(62.4)
Acquisitions (net of cash acquired)	(9.3)
Purchase of property, plant, and equipment	(79.6)
Proceeds from sale of equipment and investment	10.2
Investment in noncurrent assets	(2.7)
Net cash used in investing activities	(143.8)
Cash flows from financing activities	
Distribution of treasury shares	0.9
Long-term borrowings	94.6
Payments on long-term debt and notes payable	(8.1)
Dividends on preferred stock	(0.4)
Dividends on common stock	(11.3)
Net cash from financing activities	75.5
Effect of exchange rate changes on cash	0.0
Net increase in cash	0.6
Cash balance at beginning of year	2.2
Cash balance at end of year	$ 2.8

Reviewing Russell's cash flow statement, note that although the company's reported net income for 1989 was only $64.8 million, cash flows from operating activities were almost $70 million. Note too that the company invested almost $80 million in new property, plant, and equipment, and still had enough cash to squirrel away over $60 million in temporary investments. Where did all this money come from? The principal source was a hefty $95 million increase in long-term debt. The picture then is one of a company generating substantial cash from operations but using this cash, and more, to pay for increased productive capacity. The additional required cash in 1989 came from long-term borrowing, an entirely appropriate source provided that long-term debt does not grow out of proportion to net income and total assets. We will take a more detailed look at these relationships in later chapters.

One potentially confusing entry is "Effect of exchange rate changes on cash" toward the bottom of the cash flow statement. It arises as follows. Companies engaged in international business commonly hold cash balances in foreign countries, balances denominated in foreign currencies. When the value of the U.S. dollar changes relative to other currencies, the dollar value of these foreign-denominated cash balances changes as well. For example, if a U.S. company has 1 million German marks in German banks and the exchange rate changes over the year from one mark costs 50 cents to one mark costs 25 cents, the dollar value of the German deposits will fall from $500,000 to $250,000. This $250,000 decline will appear on the cash flow statement under the heading "Effect of exchange rate changes on cash." Such changes were not material to Russell in 1989.

Sources and Uses Statement

A sources and uses statement can be thought of as a poor man's cash flow statement. Although what it reveals about a company can be somewhat impressionistic, a sources and uses statement is easy to make and is often preferred by operating managers to a more formal cash flow statement. We will review this common tool here because knowledge of its construction will cement your understanding of cash flow statements, and will further illustrate the ties between a company's operations and its finances.

Constructing a sources and uses statement entails two very simple steps. First, place two company balance sheets for different dates side-by-side and note all changes occurring. The right column of Table 1–1 contains the requisite changes for Russell during 1989. Second, segregate the changes into those that generated cash and those that consumed cash. The result is a sources and uses statement.

Here are the rules for deciding which balance sheet changes are sources of cash and which are uses.

A company generates cash in two ways: by reducing an asset or by increasing a liability. The sale of used equipment, the liquidation of inventories, and the reduction of accounts receivable are all reductions in asset accounts and are all sources of cash to the company. On the liabilities side of the balance sheet, an increase in a bank loan or the sale of common stock are increases in liabilities, which again generate cash.

A company also uses cash in two ways: to increase an asset account or to reduce a liability account. Adding to inventories or accounts receivable or building a new plant all increase assets and all use cash. Conversely, the repayment of a bank loan, the reduction of accounts payable, and an operating loss all reduce liabilities and all use cash.

Naturally, total uses of cash over an accounting period must equal total sources; otherwise, the company would be spending money it didn't have.

Table 1–4 presents a sources and uses statement for Russell covering 1989. The two largest sources of cash were a $120.5 million increase in long-term debt and a $57.1 million increase in shareholders' equity, while the two largest uses were a $62.5 million increase in temporary investments and a $39.1 million increase in net property, plant, and equipment. The increase in shareholders' equity reflects Russell's retention of earnings, while the increase in net property, plant, and equipment shows the combined effect of new investment, less depreciation. As with Russell's cash flow statement, we see a profitable, growing company borrowing money to invest in more productive capacity. Notice that although the cash flow statement and the sources and uses statement tell a similar tale, the cash flow statement is considerably more detailed.

TABLE 1–4

Russell Corporation Sources and Uses Statement 1989 ($ millions)

Sources:

Increase in notes payable	$ 5.4
Increase in accrued wages and expenses	5.2
Increase in accrued taxes	0.9
Increase in long-term debt	120.5
Increase in deferred taxes	6.5
Increase in accrued liabilities	1.6
Increase in total shareholders' equity	57.1
Total sources	$197.2

Uses:

Increase in cash	$ 0.6
Increase in temporary investments	62.5
Increase in accounts receivable	33.4
Increase in inventory	14.4
Increase in prepaid and other current assets	5.4
Increase in future income tax benefits	0.8
Increase in net property, plant, and equipment	39.1
Increase in other long-term assets	3.8
Reduction in commercial paper	30.5
Reduction in accounts payable	6.3
Reduction in current maturities on long-term debt	0.6
Total uses	$197.6

Totals may not add due to rounding

One potential source of confusion in Table 1–4 is that the increase in cash during 1989 appears as a use of cash to Russell. How can an increase in cash be a use of cash? It is the same as when you add money to your checking account: You increase your bank balance, but have less cash in hand to spend. Conversely, a withdrawal from your bank account reduces your balance but provides a source of spendable cash.

FINANCIAL STATEMENTS AND THE VALUE PROBLEM

To this point we have reviewed the basics of financial statements and grappled with the distinctions between earnings and cash flow. As a further perspective and in anticipation of later materials, I want to conclude by examining a recurring problem in the use of accounting data for financial decision making.

Market Value versus Book Value

Part of what I will call the value problem involves the distinction between the market value and the book value of shareholders' equity. Russell's 1989 balance sheet states that the value of shareholders' equity is $402.2 million. This is known as the *book value* of Russell's equity. However, Russell is not worth $402.2 million to its shareholders or to anyone else, for that matter. There are two reasons why. One is that financial statements are *transactions based*. If a company purchased an asset in 1950 for $1 million, this transaction provides an objective measure of the asset's value, which becomes the value of the asset on the company's balance sheet. Unfortunately, it is a 1950 value that may or may not have much

---

Cash Flow from Operations

A frequently used term in finance is cash flow from operations, defined as

Cash flow from operations = Earnings + or − Noncash items

Cash flow from operations is intended to measure the cash a business generates, as distinct from the earnings—a laudable objective. Applying this formula to Russell, cash flow from operations in 1989 was $117.5 million, composed of $64.8 million in earnings plus $45.6 million in depreciation and $7.1 million in deferred taxes.

A problem with cash flow from operations is that it implicitly assumes that the firm's working capital accounts are either unrelated to operations or do not change over time. In Russell's case the cash flow statement reveals that large increases in accounts receivable and inventories, and a reduction in accounts payable, reduced actual cash generated by operating activities to only $68.8 million. The attempt by Russell's management to spend its presumed $117.5 million cash flow from operations would quickly reveal that almost one half of this amount has already been spent on increases in working capital. When using the above definition of cash flow from operations, proceed with caution.

Quoth the Banker, "Watch Cash Flow"

Once upon a midnight dreary as I pondered weak and weary
Over many a quaint and curious volume of accounting lore,
Seeking gimmicks (without scruple) to squeeze through some new
  tax loophole,
Suddenly I heard a knock upon my door,
  Only this, and nothing more.

Then I felt a queasy tingling and I heard the cash a-jingling
As a fearsome banker entered whom I'd often seen before.
His face was money-green and in his eyes there could be seen
Dollar-signs that seemed to glitter as he reckoned up the score.
  "Cash flow," the banker said, and nothing more.

I had always thought it fine to show a jet black bottom line,
But the banker sounded a resounding, "No,
Your receivables are high, mounting upward toward the sky;
Write-offs loom. What matters is cash flow."
  He repeated, "Watch cash flow."

Then I tried to tell the story of our lovely inventory
Which, though large, is full of most delightful stuff.
But the banker saw its growth, and with a mighty oath

relevance today. Moreover, to further confound things, the accountant attempts to reflect the gradual deterioration of an asset over time by periodically subtracting depreciation from its balance sheet value. This practice makes sense as far as it goes, but depreciation is the only change in value recognized by the accountant. The $1 million asset purchased in 1950 may be technologically obsolete and therefore virtually worthless today; or due to inflation, its current value may be much higher than its original purchase price. This is especially true of land, which can have a current value many times its original cost.

It is tempting to argue that accountants should forget the original cost of long-term assets and provide a more meaningful current value. The problem, however, is that objectively determinable current values of many assets do not exist. Faced with a trade-off between relevant, but subjective current values, and irrelevant,

Quoth the Banker, "Watch Cash Flow" (concluded)

He waved his arms and shouted, "Stop! Enough!
 Pay the interest, and don't give me any guff!"

Next I looked for non-cash items which could add ad infinitum
To replace the ever-outward flow of cash,
But to keep my statement black I'd held depreciation back,
And my banker said that I'd done something rash.
 He quivered, and his teeth began to gnash.

When I asked him for a loan, he responded, with a groan,
That the interest rate would be just prime plus eight,
And to guarantee my purity he'd insist on some security—
All my assets plus the scalp upon my pate.
 Only this, a standard rate.

Though my bottom line is black, I am flat upon my back,
My cash flows out and customers pay slow.
The growth of my receivables is almost unbelievable;
The result is certain—unremitting woe!
And I hear the banker utter an ominous low mutter,
 "Watch cash flow."

Herbert S. Bailey, Jr.

Source: Reprinted from *Publishers Weekly,* January 13, 1975, published by R. R. Bowker Company. Copyright © 1975 by Xerox Corporation.

but objective historical costs, accountants have opted for irrelevant historical costs. This means that it is the user's responsibility to make any adjustments to historical-cost asset values she deems appropriate.

Prodded by the Securities and Exchange Commission, the Financial Accounting Standards Board, accounting's principal rule-making fraternity, has recently begun consideration of whether certain assets and liabilities should appear on financial statements at their market value instead of at historical cost. Such "marking to market" would apply to all assets and liabilities that trade actively in markets, including many common stocks and bonds. The proposal has been greeted with howls of protest by commercial bankers, among others, who fear that the move will increase the apparent volatility of earnings, and more menacingly, will reveal many banks to be insolvent. The appearance of benign stability is apparently more appealing to these critics than the hint of an ugly reality.

To understand the second, more fundamental reason Russell is not worth $402.2 million, we need to recall that equity investors buy shares for the future income they hope to receive, not for the value of the firm's assets. Indeed, if all goes according to plan, most of the firm's existing assets will be consumed in generating future income. The problem with the accountant's measure of shareholders' equity is that it bears little relation to future income. The chief reason is that companies have many assets and liabilities that do not appear on their balance sheets, but that, nonetheless, affect future income. Examples of unrecorded assets include patents and trademarks limiting competition for the firm's products, loyal customers fostered by a reputation for quality and service, entrenched market position created by effective advertising or superior technology, and, of course, better management. It is said that in many companies the most valuable assets go home to their spouses in the evening. Examples of unrecorded liabilities include pending lawsuits, inferior management, and obsolete production processes. The accountant's inability to measure assets and liabilities such as these means that book value is customarily a highly inaccurate measure of the value seen by shareholders.

For a publicly traded company, it is a simple matter to calculate the value of equity as seen by shareholders: just multiply the number of common shares outstanding by the market price per share. On the last day of 1989, Russell's common shares closed on the New York Stock Exchange at $26.12 per share. With 40.4 million shares outstanding, this yields a value of $1,055 million, or more than 2.6 times the book value ($1,055 million/$402.2 million). This figure is known as the *market value* of equity.

Table 1–5 presents the market and book values of equity for nine representative companies. It demonstrates clearly that book value is a poor proxy for market value.

Economic Income versus Accounting Income

A second dimension of the value problem is rooted in the accountant's distinction between *realized* and *unrealized* income. To an economist, income is what you could spend during the period to

TABLE 1–5
The Book Value of Equity Is a Poor Proxy for the Market Value of Equity
December 31, 1989

Company	Value of Equity ($ millions)		Ratio, Market Value to Book Value
	Book	*Market*	
Abbott Labs	$2,726	$15,044	5.5
Bethlehem Steel	2,003	1,392	0.7
Glenfed, Inc.	1,147	491	0.4
Hewlett-Packard	5,446	11,228	2.1
J. P. Morgan	4,495	8,085	1.8
Russell Corporation	408	1,056	2.6
Sun Microsystems	662	1,448	2.2
Valley National Corp.	447	254	0.6
Wal-Mart Stores	3,966	25,406	6.4

end up as well off at the end as you were at the start. For example, suppose a woman's assets, net of liabilities, are worth $100,000 at the start of the year and rise to $120,000 by the end of the year. Suppose further that she received $30,000 in wages during the year, all of which she spent. The economist would say this individual's income for the year was $50,000 ($30,000 wages + $20,000 increase in net assets).

The accountant, on the other hand, would say the individual's income was only $30,000. The accountant would not recognize the $20,000 increase in the market value of assets as income because the gain was not *realized* by the sale of the assets. Because the market value of the assets could fluctuate in either direction before the assets are sold, the gain is only on paper; and accountants generally do not recognize paper gains or losses (of course, money is *only* paper as well). Accountants consider *realization* the necessary objective evidence required to record the gain.

It is easy to criticize accountants' conservatism when measuring income. Certainly the amount the woman could spend, ignoring inflation, and be as well off as at the start of the year is the economist's $50,000, not the accountant's $30,000. Moreover, if the woman were to sell her assets for $120,000 and immediately repurchase them for the same price, the $20,000 gain would become realized in the accountant's eyes, and he would include it as part of income. That income could depend upon a sham transaction like this is enough to raise suspicions about the accountant's definition.

However, two points should be noted in the accountant's defense. First, if the woman described above holds her assets for several years before selling them, the gain or loss recognized by the accountant on the sale date will just equal the sum of the annual gains and losses recognized by the economist. So it's really not total income that is at issue here but just the timing of its recognition. A second point in the accountant's favor is that it is extremely difficult to measure the periodic change in the value of many assets unless they are actively traded. So even if an accountant wanted to include paper gains and losses in income, he would often have great difficulty doing so. In the corporate setting, this means the accountant must be content to measure realized rather than economic income.

Imputed Costs
A similar but more subtle problem exists on the cost side of the income statement. It involves the cost of equity capital. Russell's auditors acknowledge that in 1989 the company had use of $402.2 million of shareholders' money, measured at book value. They would further acknowledge that Russell could not have operated without this money and that this money is not free. Just as creditors earn interest on loans, equity investors expect a return on their investment. Yet if you look again at Russell's income statement, Table 1–2, you will find no mention of the cost of this equity—interest expense appears but no comparable cost for equity.

While acknowledging that equity capital has a cost, the accountant does not record it on the income statement because the cost must be imputed—that is, estimated. Because there is no piece of paper stating the amount of money Russell is obligated to pay owners, the accountant refuses to recognize any cost of equity capital. As before, the accountant would rather be reliably wrong than make a potentially inaccurate estimate. The result has been serious confusion in the minds of less knowledgeable observers and continuing "image" problems for corporations.

Below is the bottom portion of Russell's 1989 income statement as prepared by its accountants and as it might be prepared by an economist. Observe that while the accountant shows earnings of $64.8 million for the year, the economist records a profit of only $4.5 million. These numbers differ because the economist includes a $60.3 million cost of equity capital, while the accountant shows no cost. (We will consider ways to estimate a company's cost of equity capital in Chapter 8. Here I have assumed a 15 percent equity cost and applied it to the book value of Russell's equity [$60.3 million $= 15\% \times \$402.2$ million].)

Russell Corporation's 1989 Income as Seen by an Accountant and by an Economist ($ millions)

	Accountant	Economist
Operating income	$120.4	$120.4
Interest expense	(15.6)	(15.6)
Cost of Equity		(60.3)
Nonoperating expense	(2.0)	(2.0)
Income before tax	102.8	42.5
Provision for taxes	38.0	38.0
Accounting earnings	$ 64.8	
Economic earnings		$ 4.5

The distinction between accounting earnings and economic earnings might be only a curiosity if everyone understood that positive accounting earnings were not necessarily a sign of superior, or even commendable, performance. But when many labor unions and politicians view accounting profits as evidence that a company can afford higher wages or higher taxes or more onerous regulation, and when most managements view such profits as justification for distributing handsome performance bonuses, the distinction can be an important one. Keep in mind, therefore, that the right of equity investors to expect a competitive return on their investment is every bit as legitimate as a creditor's right to interest and an employee's right to wages. They all voluntarily contribute scarce resources, and they all are justified in expecting compensation. Remember too that a company is not shooting par unless its *economic* profits are zero or above. By this criterion Russell had a good, but not a great, year in 1989. On close inspection many companies reporting apparently large earnings are really performing like weekend duffers when the cost of equity is included.

To summarize, the value problem means that financial statements will customarily provide distorted information about company earnings and market value. This limits their applicability for many important managerial decisions. However, financial statements are frequently the best information available, and if their limitations are borne in mind, they can be a useful starting point for analysis. In the next chapter, we consider the use of accounting data for evaluating financial performance.

APPENDIX

INFLATION AND THE ASSESSMENT OF COMPANY PERFORMANCE

'Tis the night before Christmas
and all through the nation
your bonus means nothing
because of Inflation
Mad Magazine

Assessing the financial performance of a company during inflation is like measuring the width of a table with a rubber band: The size of the yardstick keeps changing. Here we will consider briefly the ways in which inflation distorts historical-cost financial statements and the accounting techniques available to minimize these distortions.

Inflation and Company Profits

Inflation distorts a company's income statement in three distinct ways. One involves historical-cost depreciation, another the valuation of inventory, and the third, accounting for interest expense. The first two sources of distortion are well known, while the third is less well known and frequently misunderstood.

Historical-Cost Depreciation

Because depreciation expense under historical-cost accounting must be based on the original cost of the asset, the annual amount charged against income during inflation understates the true decline in the value of assets. Or said differently, historical-cost depreciation is not sufficient to maintain the value of company assets during inflation. This understatement of annual depreciation causes an overstatement of reported earnings and an increase in corporate taxes due.

Inventory Valuation

An analogous problem arises with inventories. The two most widely used methods of inventory accounting in the United States are first-in, first-out (FIFO) and last-in, first-out (LIFO). In an inflationary environment, a company's reported earnings and its tax bill depend on which method it uses. To illustrate, suppose a company manufactures and sells boxes and that it keeps its inventory of finished boxes in a stack, as shown in the figure below. Each time a new box is completed, it is added to the top of the pile. The dollar amounts to the left of the boxes are the cost incurred by the company in making each box. Since prices are rising, the cost of each successive box is higher, starting with the oldest box in inventory at $1 and rising to the most recently produced box at $1.50.

When the company sells a box for, say, $2.00, the accountant must match the cost of the box sold against the revenue. If the company uses FIFO, the assigned cost of goods sold will be $1; while if LIFO accounting is employed, the cost of goods sold will be $1.50. (Here, we ignore all practical problems associated with removing a box from the bottom of the stack.) As shown in the figure, the choice of the inventory valuation method significantly affects the company's tax liability and its reported earnings. In our numerical example, FIFO accounting produces earnings and taxes of $0.50 as opposed to $0.25 for LIFO accounting.

Which earnings figure is correct? Since the current cost of manufacturing one box is much closer to $1.50 than to $1.00, the LIFO earnings figure is the more accurate measure of true earnings under inflation. Yet for reasons we need not go into here, a great many corporations use FIFO accounting. For these companies, inflation again causes an overstatement of reported earnings and an increase in taxes.

Gains to Net Debtors

The third distortion to a company's income statement under inflation involves the way accountants measure interest expense on a loan. Suppose you borrow $100 from a bank for one year. In the absence of inflation, the banker might be content for you to repay $104 at year end—$100 in principal and $4 in interest. But in an environment of, say, 50 percent inflation, $104 will no longer be sufficient. The banker now will want his $100 principal back *plus* enough to maintain the purchasing power of the prin-

Inventory Valuation, Taxes, and Earnings under Inflation

Cost of production	Finished boxes		FIFO accounting	LIFO accounting
$1.50		Selling price	$2.00	$2.00
1.40		Cost of goods sold	1.00	1.50
1.30		Taxable income	1.00	0.50
1.20		Tax @ 50%	0.50	0.25
1.10		Earnings after tax	$ 0.50	$ 0.25
1.00				

cipal, or $50. In addition, he will want a return on the loan of $4 *plus* enough to maintain the purchasing power of the return, or $2. So in total you will be asked to repay $156 in one year. You and the banker both know that $150 of this amount is really the repayment of principal and only $6 represents interest on the loan. But the accountant, whether she knows the truth or not, does not report the transaction this way. Instead, she reasons that because you borrowed $100, this by definition is the principal, and the rest must be interest expense. This overstatement of interest expense causes an understatement of reported earnings and a reduction of taxes due. Of course, these effects apply only to companies that are "net debtors," that is, companies that have more IOUs outstanding than "you-owe-mes."

The Net Effect
The overstatement of reported earnings caused by historical-cost depreciation and FIFO inventory accounting is well known. Indeed, for a number of years U.S. national income accounts have included adjustments to aggregate corporate income required to remove these distortions. They are known as the inventory valuation adjustment (IVA) and the capital consumption adjustment (CCA).

However, the understatement of reported earnings caused by the mislabeling of interest expense is not known precisely. One study suggests that on *average* the understatement of company earnings due to the mislabeling of interest is about equal in magnitude, but opposite in sign, to the *total* overstatement due to FIFO accounting and historical-cost depreciation.[2] This means that for the economy as a whole the three distor-

[2]F. Modigliani and R. Cohn, "Inflation, Rational Valuation and the Market," *Financial Analysts Journal* (March/April 1979).

tions to reported income approximately offset one another, leaving reported earnings about equal to true earnings. This, of course, does not suggest that such a conclusion applies to every company. Depending on the particular company's degree of capital intensity, accounting conventions, and capital structure, reported earnings can differ substantially from true earnings.

Inflation and Company Balance Sheets

The distortions to a company's balance sheet caused by inflation are the direct result of the three biases already discussed. Thus, historical-cost accounting tends to understate the balance sheet value of long-term assets. Similarly, a look back at the figure summarizing FIFO and LIFO·inventory accounting will convince you that LIFO accounting understates the balance sheet value of company inventories. Indeed, after the sale of one box in our example, finished goods inventory would be $6.50 under FIFO but only $6.00 under LIFO.

Finally, the accounting treatment of liabilities under inflation tends to overstate their balance sheet values. Consistent with the idea that borrowers repay debts with cheaper dollars during inflation, the true value of many liabilities declines during inflationary periods. However, this de-

---

Inflation Biases Company Earnings

During a period of rapid inflation, Companies A and B both report earnings of $100 million. Company A uses LIFO accounting, has primarily current assets, and makes extensive use of debt financing. Company B uses FIFO accounting, has primarily fixed assets, and is very conservatively financed. Which company, in truth, is probably the more profitable?

Answer: Company A. FIFO accounting and historical-cost accounting cause reported earnings to exceed true earnings during inflation. Company A suffers comparatively little from these biases. Debt financing and the resulting misstatement of interest expense cause reported earnings to understate true earnings. Company A does suffer from this bias. Hence, true earnings are probably above $100 million. By the same reasoning, Company B's true earnings are probably below $100 million.

cline is ignored by the accountant, with the result that the apparent in-debtedness of a company overstates reality.

Let me caution: I am not saying it is necessarily good to be a debtor during inflation. The true value of liabilities does decline, but if the infla-tion is anticipated, the interest rate rises to offset the decline. The ac-countant's error is that she includes the higher interest rate but ignores the fall in the value of the liabilities.

Inflation Accounting

In the late 1970s and early 1980s, as the U.S. inflation rate headed toward the moon, the accounting profession made a half-hearted attempt to remedy the problems cited here by requiring large corporations to report some of the effects of inflation on their historical-cost financial state-ments. However, the information was relegated to a footnote, was pre-sented in a confusing format, and did not include gains to net debtors. Not surprisingly, it was seldom used, and as soon as the inflation rate dipped to a tolerable level, the reporting requirement was eliminated entirely.

The intent here is *not* to ridicule historical-cost financial statements but simply to remind you that historical-cost statements are especially misleading under inflation. At the same time, it must be admitted that in-flation accounting is still new and controversial. One debate involves the extent to which it is proper to write up fixed assets under inflation, while another surrounds the question of whether gains to net debtors should appear on the income statement. Until these and related controversies are resolved, and as long as inflation remains low, many executives are prepared to acknowledge that inflation distorts historical-cost state-ments, while remaining skeptical about the objectivity and usefulness of available remedies.

CHAPTER SUMMARY

1. The purpose of this chapter has been to review the accounting principles governing financial statements and to describe the re-lationship between earnings and cash flow.
2. A company's finances and its business operations are integrally related. We study a company's financial statements because they are a window on its operations.
3. Earnings are not cash flow. The financial executive watches both.

4. A balance sheet is a snapshot of a company's assets and liabilities at a point in time. An income statement records sales, related expenses, and earnings over a period. Both documents are transactions based and use the accrual principle. Because accounting statements are transactions based, long-term assets and depreciation are listed at historical cost, and paper gains and losses are ignored. Use of the accrual principle means that revenues and expenses do not always coincide with cash inflows and outflows.
5. A cash flow statement presents a company's cash receipts and disbursements over the accounting period.
6. Two steps are required to create a sources and uses statement: (*a*) calculate changes in balance sheet accounts over the accounting period and (*b*) segregate the sources from the uses.
7. There are two recurring problems in the use of accounting statements for financial analysis: (*a*) accounting book values seldom equal market values and (*b*) the accountant's refusal to recognize unrealized gains and losses and imputed costs makes accounting income differ from economic income.

ADDITIONAL READING

Anthony, Robert N. *Essentials of Accounting.* 4th ed. Reading, Mass.: Addison-Wesley, 1988.

By a distinguished emeritus Harvard professor. A very popular programmed text with over 500,000 copies in print. A great way to review or pick up the basics of financial accounting on your own. Available in paperback.

Callard, Charles G., and David C. Kleinman. "Inflation-Adjusted Accounting: Does It Really Matter?" *Financial Analysts Journal* (May–June 1985), pp. 51–59.

An empirical study of the relation between stock prices and accounting information. The authors conclude that inflation-adjusted accounting data correlate more closely with stock prices than do historical-cost data. They also point out the dangers to investors and managers of using less accurate historical-cost information.

Davidson, Sidney, Clyde P. Stickney, and Roman L. Weil. *Financial Accounting: An Introduction to Concepts, Methods, and Uses.* 5th ed. Chicago: The Dryden Press, 1988. 800 pages.

A clearly written introduction to financial accounting. Part Two, Accounting Concepts and Methods, provides a solid treatment of financial statements in about 200 pages.

Downes, John, and Jordan Elliot Goodman. *Dictionary of Finance and Investment Terms.* 2nd ed. New York: Barron's Educational Services, Inc., 1987. 495 pages.

Over 2,500 terms clearly defined. Available in paperback for about $8.95.

Merrill Lynch, Pierce, Fenner & Smith, Inc. "How to Read a Financial Report," 6th ed. 1990. 28 pages.

First published in 1973, this brief pamphlet offers a clear, straighforward introduction to finàncial statements and their interpretation. See your nearest Merrill Lynch representative for a complimentary copy.

CHAPTER PROBLEMS

1. Why do you suppose financial statements are constructed on an accrual basis rather than a cash basis when cash accounting is so much easier to understand?
2. Selected information about the Walters Company for 1990 and 1991 appear below. Use this information to
   a. Fill in the blanks in the company's 1991 data.
   b. Show that the increase in cash from operations (i.e., the cash flow from operations) in 1991 is the same whether it is calculated from the reporting books or the tax books.

	1990 Books of Account	
	Reporting Purposes	Tax Purposes
Accrued taxes	$ 200	$ 0
Gross fixed assets	1,600	1,600
Accumulated depreciation	200	500

	1991 Books of Account	
	Reporting Purposes	Tax Purposes
Net sales	$2,000	$2,000
Cost of goods sold	1,000	1,000
Gross profit		
General, selling, and administrative expenses	400	400
Depreciation	20	80
Operating income		
Nonoperating expense	100	100
Income before tax		
Provision for taxes @ 40%	Taxes due @ 40%	
Net income	$	$
Accrued taxes		
Gross fixed assets	1,600	1,600
Accumulated depreciation		
Net fixed assets	$	$

3. Use the following information to estimate APL Corporation's net cash flows from operations as it would appear on the company's 1991 cash flow statement.

	1990	1991
Net sales	$300	$400
Cost of goods sold	160	200
Gross income	140	200
Depreciation	30	40
General, selling expenses	20	20
Income before tax	90	140
Provision for taxes @ 40%	36	56
Income after tax	54	84
Cash	100	50
Accounts receivable	50	100
Inventory	60	40
Accrued taxes	100	120
Accrued wages	60	30
Accounts payable	30	40

4. Table 3–1 in Chapter 3 presents financial statements over the period 1987–1990 for R&E Supplies, Inc.
   a. Construct a sources and uses statement for the company from 1987 through 1990 (one statement for all three years).
   b. What insights, if any, does the sources and uses statement give you about the financial position of R&E Supplies?
5. Explain briefly how each of the following transactions would affect a company's balance sheet, income statement, and cash flow statement.
   a. Purchase of a new building for $1 million cash.
   b. Purchase of a new $1 million building, financed 60 percent with a bank loan and 40 percent with cash.
   c. Receipt of $100,000 payment from customer on account receivable.
   d. Repurchase of $10 million of company stock for cash.
6. You are responsible for labor relations in your company. During heated labor negotiations, the General Secretary of your largest union exclaims, "Look, this company has $1 billion worth of assets, $500 million worth of equity, and made a profit last year of $40 million—due largely to the effort of union employees. So don't tell me you can't afford our wage demands." How would you respond?

7. Below are summary cash flow statements for three roughly equal-size companies.

Company	($ millions)		
	A	B	C
Net cash flows from operations	$(10)	$(10)	$10
Net cash used in investing activities	(30)	(1)	(3)
Net cash from financing activities	40	7	(8)
Cash balance at beginning of year	5	5	5

a. Calculate each company's cash balance at the end of the year.
b. Explain what might cause company C's net cash from financing activities to be negative.
c. Looking at companies A and B, which company would you prefer to own? Why?
d. Is company C's cash flow statement cause for any concern on the part of C's management or shareholders? Why or why not?

CHAPTER 2

EVALUATING FINANCIAL PERFORMANCE

You can't manage what you can't measure
William Hewlett

The cockpit of a 747 airliner, if you have never seen one, looks like a three-dimensional video game. It is a sizable room crammed with meters, switches, lights, and dials requiring the full attention of three highly trained pilots. When compared to the cockpit of a Piper Cub, it is tempting to conclude that the two planes are different species rather than distant cousins. Yet, at a more fundamental level, the similarities probably exceed the differences. Despite the complexity and the technology, the 747 pilot controls his plane in the same way as the Piper Cub pilot: with a stick, a throttle, and flaps. And if either pilot wants to change the altitude of his plane, he does so by making simultaneous adjustments to the same few levers he has for controlling the plane.

Much the same is true of companies. Once you strip away the facade of apparent complexity, the levers by which managers affect the financial performance of their firm are comparatively few and are similar among firms. The executive's job is to control these levers to ensure a safe and efficient flight. And, like the pilot, he or she must remember that the levers are interrelated; one cannot change the business equivalent of the flaps without also adjusting the stick and the throttle.

THE LEVERS OF FINANCIAL PERFORMANCE

Our goal in this chapter will be to analyze financial statements for the purpose of evaluating performance and for understanding the levers of management control. We begin by studying the ties between a company's operating decisions—such as pricing policy, inventory control practices, and financing strategies—and its financial performance. These operating decisions are the levers by which management controls financial performance. Then we will broaden the discussion to consider the uses and limitations of ratio analysis as a tool for evaluating performance. To retain a practical perspective, we will again use the financial statements for Russell Corporation, presented in Tables 1–1, 1–2, and 1–3 of the last chapter, to illustrate the techniques. The chapter will conclude with an evaluation of Russell's financial performance relative to its competition.

RETURN ON EQUITY

By far the most popular yardstick of financial performance among investors and senior managers is the return on equity (ROE), defined as:

$$\text{Return on equity} = \frac{\text{Earnings available for common shareholders}}{\text{Shareholders' equity}}$$

Referring to Tables 1–1 and 1–2 in the last chapter, Russell's ROE for 1989 was:

$$\text{ROE} = \frac{\$64.2}{\$402.2} = 16.0\%$$

It is not an exaggeration to say that the careers of many senior executives rise and fall in harmony with their firm's ROE. ROE is accorded such importance because it is a measure of the *efficiency* with which the firm employs owners' capital. It is an estimate of the earnings per dollar of invested equity capital, or alternatively, the percentage return to owners on their investment in the firm. In short, it measures bang per buck.

Later in this chapter we will consider some significant problems with ROE as a measure of financial performance, but for now let us accept it provisionally as at least widely used and see what we can learn.

Three Determinants of ROE

To see how a company can increase its ROE, let us use some simple algebra to restate the ratio in terms of its three principal components.

$$\text{ROE} = \frac{\text{Earnings to common}}{\text{Shareholders' equity}}$$

$$= \frac{\text{Earnings to common}}{\text{Sales}} \times \frac{\text{Sales}}{\text{Assets}} \times \frac{\text{Assets}}{\text{Shareholders' equity}}$$

In words,

$$\frac{\text{Return on}}{\text{equity}} = \frac{\text{Profit}}{\text{margin}} \times \frac{\text{Asset}}{\text{turnover}} \times \frac{\text{Financial}}{\text{leverage}}$$

We find that Russell's ROE in 1989 was generated as follows:

$$\frac{\$64.2}{\$402.2} = \frac{64.2}{688} \times \frac{688}{720.8} \times \frac{720.8}{402.2}$$

$$16.0\% = 9.3\% \times 1.0 \times 1.8$$

This expression says that management has three levers for controlling ROE. They are (1) the earnings squeezed out of each dollar of sales, or the *profit margin*, (2) the sales generated from each dollar of assets employed, or the *asset turnover*, and (3) the amount of debt used to finance the assets, or the *financial leverage*. With limited exception, whatever management does to increase these ratios increases ROE.

Note too the close correspondence between the levers of performance and company financial statements. The profit margin summarizes a company's income statement performance, while asset turnover and financial leverage do the same for the left side and the right side of the balance sheet, respectively. This is reassuring evidence that, despite their simplicity, the three levers do capture the major elements of a company's financial performance.

Table 2–1 presents ROE decomposed into its three principal components for 10 widely diverse companies. It shows clearly that there are many paths to heaven: The ROEs of the companies are

TABLE 2–1
ROE and the Levers of Performance for 10 Diverse Firms (1989)

	Return on Equity (ROE) (percent)	=	Profit Margin (P) (percent)	×	Asset Turnover (A) (times)	×	Financial Leverage (T) (times)	Returns on Assets (ROA) (percent)
Boeing Company	11.0%	=	3.3%	×	1.53	×	2.17	5.1%
Delta Airlines	17.6	=	5.7	×	1.25	×	2.47	7.1
Hewlett-Packard	15.2	=	7.0	×	1.18	×	1.85	8.2
Kmart Corporation	16.0	=	2.9	×	2.27	×	2.42	6.6
Mobil Corporation	11.7	=	3.6	×	1.29	×	2.53	4.6
Norfolk Southern Railroad	11.7	=	13.4	×	0.44	×	1.98	5.9
Pacific Gas & Electric	12.1	=	10.5	×	0.40	×	2.86	4.2
Russell Corporation	16.0	=	9.3	×	0.95	×	1.79	9.0
Security Pacific Bank	16.0	=	7.4	×	0.12	×	18.10	0.9
Winn-Dixie Stores	17.3	=	1.5	×	5.81	×	2.01	8.6

quite similar, but the combinations of profit margin, asset turnover, and financial leverage which produce this end result vary widely. Thus ROE ranges from a high of 17.6 percent for Delta Airlines to a low of 11 percent for Boeing Company, while the range for the profit margin, to take one example, is from a low of 1.5 percent for Winn-Dixie supermarkets to a high of 13.4 percent for the Norfolk Southern Railroad. ROE differs by about 50 percent from low to high, while the profit margin differs by a factor of almost 10 to 1.

Why are ROEs similar across firms while profit margins, asset turns, and financial leverage differ dramatically? The answer in a word is competition. Attainment of an unusually high ROE by one company acts as a magnet attracting rivals anxious to emulate such performance. And over time the resulting heightened competition drives the successful company's ROE back toward the average. Conversely, unusually low ROEs force some companies to fail or to leave a market, and they repel potential new competitors, so that over time ROEs of surviving firms rise toward the average.

To understand how managerial decisions and a company's competitive environment combine to affect ROE, we will examine each of the levers of performance in more detail. In anticipation of the discussion of ratio analysis to follow, we will also consider related commonly used financial ratios.

The Profit Margin

The profit margin measures the portion of each dollar of sales that trickles down through the income statement to profits. The ratio is of particular importance to operating managers because it reflects the company's pricing strategy and its ability to control operating costs. As Table 2–1 indicates, profit margins differ greatly among industries and companies within an industry, depending on the nature of the product sold and the company's competitive strategy.

Note too that profit margin and asset turnover tend to vary inversely. Companies with high profit margins tend to have low asset turns, and vice versa. This is no accident. In the manufacturing sector, companies like Hewlett-Packard, with unique products, or companies that add significant value to a product, can demand high profit margins. However, because maintaining unique products and adding significant value to a product usually require lots of assets, these same firms tend to have lower asset turns. Much the same is true at the retail level. Grocery stores such as Winn-Dixie, which add little to product value, have very low profit margins but high asset turns. At the other extreme, jewelry stores which carry expensive inventories and spend heavily on display and selling have low asset turns but much higher profit margins. It should be apparent, therefore, that a high profit margin is not necessarily better than a low profit margin, for it all depends on the combined effect of the profit margin and the asset turnover.

Return on Assets
For a look at the combined effect of margins and turns, we can calculate the *return on assets* (ROA).

$$\text{ROA} = \frac{\text{Profit}}{\text{margin}} \times \frac{\text{Asset}}{\text{turnover}}$$

$$= \frac{\text{Earnings to common}}{\text{Sales}} \times \frac{\text{Sales}}{\text{Assets}}$$

$$= \frac{\text{Earnings to common}}{\text{Assets}}$$

Russell's ROA in 1989 was:

$$\text{ROA} = \frac{64.2}{720.8} = 8.9\%$$

This means that Russell earned an average of 8.9 cents on each dollar invested.

ROA is a basic measure of the efficiency with which a company allocates and manages its resources. It differs from ROE in that ROA measures profit as a percent of total assets as opposed to profit as a percent of shareholders' equity only.

Some companies, such as PG&E and Norfolk Southern, produce their ROAs by combining a high profit margin with a moderate asset turn, while others, such as Winn-Dixie and Kmart, adopt the reverse strategy. A high profit margin *and* a high asset turn are ideal, but can be expected to attract considerable competition. Conversely, a low profit margin and a low asset turn will attract only bankruptcy lawyers.

Gross Margin

When analyzing a company's profit margin, it is often useful to distinguish between variable costs and fixed costs. Variable costs are those that change as sales vary, while fixed costs remain constant. Companies with a high proportion of fixed costs are more vulnerable to sales declines than other firms because they cannot reduce fixed cost as sales fall. This means that falling sales will produce major profit declines in high fixed-cost businesses.

The accountant unfortunately does not differentiate between fixed and variable costs when constructing an income statement. However, it is usually safe to assume that most expenses in cost of goods sold are variable, while most of the other operating costs are fixed. The gross margin enables us to distinguish, insofar as possible, between fixed and variable costs. It is defined as

$$\text{Gross margin} = \frac{\text{Gross profit}}{\text{Sales}} = \frac{\$230.1}{\$688} = 33.4\%$$

Roughly speaking then, 33.4 percent of Russell's sales dollar is a *contribution to fixed cost and profits;* 33.4 cents of every sales dollar is available to pay for fixed costs and to add to profits.

Asset Turnover

The second principal determinant of ROE is the sales generated by each dollar of assets, or the asset turnover. Russell's asset turnover of 1.0 means that Russell generated $1.00 of sales for each dollar invested in assets. This ratio is a measure of capital intensity, with a low asset turnover signifying a capital-intensive business and a high turnover the reverse.

The nature of a company's products and its competitive strategy are major determinants of a company's asset turnover. But the process is not a mechanical one. Management diligence and creativity in controlling assets is also vital. When product technology is similar among competitors, control of assets is often the margin between success and failure.

Control of current assets is especially critical. It might appear at first glance that distinguishing between current and fixed assets based solely on whether the asset will revert to cash within one year is artificial. But there is more involved than this. Current assets, especially accounts receivable and inventory, have several unique properties that should be recognized. One is that if something goes wrong—if sales decline unexpectedly, if customers delay payment, or if a critical part fails to arrive—a company's investment in current assets can grow very rapidly. When even manufacturing companies routinely invest one half or more of their money in current assets, it is easy to appreciate that even modest alterations in the management of these assets can significantly affect company finances.

A second distinction is that, unlike fixed assets, current assets can become a source of cash during business downturns. As sales decline, a company's investment in accounts receivable and inventory should decline as well, thereby freeing cash for other uses. The fact that in a well-run company current assets move in accordionlike fashion with sales is appealing to creditors. They know that during the upswing of a business cycle rising current assets will require loans, while during a downswing falling current assets will provide the cash to repay the loans. In bankers' jargon such a loan is said to be *self-liquidating* in the sense that the use to which the money is put creates the source of repayment.

Because control of current assets is so important in generating an acceptable ROE, it is useful to be able to analyze each type of asset individually. This gives rise to what are known as *control ratios*. Although the form in which each ratio is expressed may vary, every control ratio is really just an asset turnover for a particular type of asset. In each instance, the firm's investment in the asset is compared to net sales, or a closely related figure.

Why compare current assets to sales? The fact that a company's investment in, say, inventories has risen over time could be due to two forces: (1) Perhaps sales have risen and simply dragged inventories along, or (2) management may have slackened its control of inventories, allowing excess quantities to accumulate. Relating inventory to sales in a control ratio adjusts for changes in sales, enabling the analyst to concentrate on the more important effects of changing management control. Thus the control ratio distinguishes between sales-induced changes in investment and other, perhaps more sinister, causes. A number of standard control ratios follow.

Inventory Turnover
The inventory turnover ratio is defined as

$$\text{Inventory turnover} = \frac{\text{Cost of goods sold}}{\text{Ending inventory}} = \frac{\$457.9}{\$108.8} = 4.2 \text{ times}$$

An inventory turn of 4.2 times means that an average item in Russell's inventory turns over 4.2 times per year or, said differently, the average item sits in inventory almost three months before being sold (12 months/4.2 times = 2.9 months).

Several alternative definitions of the inventory turnover ratio exist, including sales divided by ending inventory, and cost of goods sold divided by average inventory. Cost of goods sold is a more appropriate numerator than sales because sales include a profit markup that is absent from inventory. But beyond this, there is little to choose from among the various definitions.

The Collection Period
The collection period reflects a company's management of accounts receivable. It is defined as

$$\text{Collection period} = \frac{\text{Accounts receivable}}{\text{Credit sales per day}} = \frac{\$133.3}{\$688/365} = 70.7 \text{ days}$$

Credit sales rather than net sales are used here because only credit sales generate accounts receivable. I assume here that all of Russell's sales are on credit, so we can use net sales in place of credit sales in this instance. Credit sales per day is defined as credit sales for the accounting period divided by the number of days in the accounting period. Using Russell's annual statements, the divisor is 365 days.

Two interpretations of Russell's 70.7-day collection period are possible. We can say that Russell has an average of 70.7 days' worth of credit sales tied up in accounts receivable, or we can say that the average time lag between sale and receipt of cash from the sale is 70.7 days.

If we liked, we could define a simpler asset turnover ratio for accounts receivable as credit sales/accounts receivable. However, the collection-period format is more informative because it is possible to compare a company's collection period with its terms of sale. Thus, if Russell sells on 60-day terms, a collection period of 70.7 days may not be too bad, but if the terms of sale are 30 days, our interpretation would be quite different.

Days' Sales in Cash

This ratio is defined as

$$\text{Days' sales in cash} = \frac{\text{Cash and securities}}{\text{Net sales per day}} = \frac{\$2.8 + \$72.8}{\$688/365} = 40.1 \text{ days}$$

Russell has 40.1 days' worth of sales in cash and securities. It is difficult to generalize about whether this amount is appropriate for Russell or not. Companies require modest amounts of cash to facilitate transactions and are often required to carry substantially larger amounts as compensating balances for bank loans. In addition, marketable securities can be an important source of liquidity to a firm, obviating the need to maintain backup borrowing facilities with banks. So the question of how much cash a company should carry is often closely related to broader financial policies. Nonetheless, over 40 days' sales in cash and securities appears

---

A Word of Warning on Seasonal Companies

Interpreting many ratios of companies with *seasonal sales* can be quite difficult. For example, suppose a company's sales are seasonal, with a large peak at the end of the year. The sales peak will result in a high year-end accounts receivable balance. Yet in calculating credit sales per day, using annual financial statements, this peak will be averaged with periods of low sales. The result will be an apparently very high collection period. To avoid being misled, a better way to calculate the collection period for a seasonal company is to relate end-of-year accounts receivable to credit sales per day, based on the prior 60 to 90 days' sales. This matches the accounts receivable to the credit sales that actually generated the receivables.

---

more than ample, especially when we note that the comparable figure in 1988 was only 8.6 days (($2.2 + $10.3)/$531.1/365).

Payables Period

The payables period is a control ratio for a liability. It is just the collection period applied to accounts payable.

$$\frac{\text{Payables}}{\text{period}} = \frac{\text{Accounts payable}}{\text{Credit purchases per day}} = \frac{\$26.9}{\$457.9/365} = 21.4 \text{ days}$$

The proper definition of the payables period is in terms of credit purchases because this is what generates accounts payable. However, credit purchases are seldom available to the outside analyst, so it is frequently necessary to settle for the closest approximation—cost of goods sold. This is what I have done in the above figures for Russell—$457.9 million is Russell's cost of goods sold, not its credit purchases. Cost of goods sold can differ from credit purchases for two reasons. First, the company is producing, and hence purchasing material, at a rate that differs from its sales rate; and second, the company adds labor and depreciation to material in the production process, thereby making cost of goods sold larger than purchases. Because of these differences, it is not meaningful to compare a manufacturing company's payables period, based on cost of goods sold, to its purchase terms.

Fixed Asset Turnover

Fixed asset turnover reflects the capital intensity of a business. Changes in the ratio over time provide information about whether management is becoming more or less efficient in its utilization of fixed assets. It is defined as

$$\frac{\text{Fixed asset}}{\text{turnover}} = \frac{\text{Sales}}{\text{Net fixed assets}} = \frac{\$688}{\$360.9} = 1.9 \text{ times}$$

where $360.9 million is the book value of Russell's net property, plant, and equipment.

Financial Leverage

The third lever by which management affects ROE is financial leverage. A company increases its financial leverage when it raises the proportion of debt relative to equity used to finance the business. Unlike the profit margin and the asset turnover ratio, where more is generally preferred to less, financial leverage is not something management necessarily wants to maximize, even when doing so might increase ROE. Instead, the challenge of financial leverage is to strike a prudent balance between the benefits of debt financing and the costs. We will later devote a full chapter to this important financial decision. For now it is sufficient to recognize that, while companies have considerable latitude in their choice of how much financial leverage to employ, there are economic and institutional constraints on their discretion.

As Table 2–1 suggests, the nature of a company's business and its assets influence the financial leverage it can employ. In general, businesses with highly predictable and stable operating cash flows, such as PG&E, can safely undertake more financial leverage than firms facing a high degree of market uncertainty, such as Hewlett-Packard. In addition, enterprises such as commercial banks, which have a diversified portfolio of liquid assets, can also safely use more financial leverage than the typical firm. By *liquid assets,* I refer to assets which can be readily sold without significant loss of value.

Another pattern evident in Table 2–1 is that ROA and financial leverage tend to be inversely related. Companies with low ROA generally employ more debt financing, and vice versa. This is consistent with the previous paragraph. Safe, stable, liquid investments tend to generate low returns but substantial borrowing capacity. Commercial banks are extreme examples of this pattern. Security Pacific, as an example, combines what by manufacturing standards would be a horrible ROA of 0.9 percent with an astronomic leverage ratio of 18.1 to generate an attractive ROE of 16 percent. The key to this pairing is the safe, liquid nature of Security Pacific's assets. The bank's loans to Arizona real estate speculators are, of course, another story—one the bank would just as soon forget.

In following paragraphs we will discuss the more common ways to measure financial leverage and the related concept of liquidity. These ratios are useful to managers and creditors in appraising a company's debt capacity.

Balance Sheet Ratios

The most common measure of financial leverage compares the book value of a company's liabilities to the book value of its assets or of its shareholders' equity. This gives rise to the debt-to-assets ratio and the debt-to-equity ratio, defined as

$$\text{Debt-to-assets ratio} = \frac{\text{Total liabilities}}{\text{Total assets}} = \frac{\$318.6}{\$720.8} = 44.2\%$$

$$\text{Debt-to-equity ratio} = \frac{\text{Total liabilities}}{\text{Shareholders' equity}} = \frac{\$318.6}{\$402.2} = 79.2\%$$

The first ratio says that 44.2 percent of Russell's assets, in book-value terms, come from creditors of one kind or another. The second ratio says the same thing in a slightly different way: Creditors supply Russell with 79.2 cents for every dollar supplied by shareholders.[1]

---

[1]The leverage ratio used earlier, Assets/Shareholders' equity, is just the debt-to-equity ratio plus one:

$$\frac{\text{Assets}}{\text{Equity}} = \frac{\text{Liabilities} + \text{Equity}}{\text{Equity}} = \frac{\text{Liabilities}}{\text{Equity}} + 1$$

For Russell, $1.8 = 79.2\% + 1$

Coverage Ratios

There exist a number of variations on these balance sheet measures of financial leverage. There is conceptually no reason to prefer one to another, however, for they all focus on the balance sheet value of liabilities and, hence, all suffer from the same weakness. The financial burden imposed on a company by the use of debt financing ultimately depends not on the size of the liabilities relative to assets or to equity but on the ability of the company to meet the annual cash payments required by the debt. A simple example will illustrate the distinction. Suppose two companies have the same debt-to-assets ratio, but one is very profitable, while the other is losing money. The money-losing company will probably have difficulty meeting the annual interest and principal payments required by its loans; yet the profitable company with the same debt-to-assets ratio may have no such difficulties. We conclude that balance sheet ratios are of primary interest only in liquidation when the proceeds of asset sales are to be distributed to creditors and owners. In all other instances, we should be more interested in comparing the annual burden imposed by the debt to the cash flow available for debt service.

To measure the annual financial burden placed on a company by its use of leverage, it is useful to calculate what are known as *coverage ratios*. The two most common coverage ratios, *times interest earned* and *times burden covered,* are defined as

$$\text{Times interest earned} = \frac{\text{Earnings before interest and taxes}}{\text{Interest expense}}$$

$$= \frac{\$118.4}{\$15.6} = 7.6 \text{ times}$$

$$\text{Times burden covered} = \frac{\text{Earnings before interest and taxes}}{\text{Interest} + \left(\dfrac{\text{Principal repayment}}{1 - \text{Tax rate}} \right)}$$

$$= \frac{\$118.4}{\$15.6 + \left(\dfrac{\$4.5}{1 - 0.37} \right)} = 5.2 \text{ times}$$

Both ratios compare income available for debt service to some annual measure of financial obligation. For both ratios the income available is *earnings before interest and taxes* (EBIT). This is the earnings generated by the company that can be used to make interest payments. EBIT is before tax because interest payments are a before-tax expenditure and we want to compare like quantities. Russell's 1989 EBIT is income before tax, $102.7 million, plus interest expense of $15.6 million, or $118.4 million. The resulting times-interest-earned ratio of 7.6 means that the company earned its interest obligation 7.6 times over in 1989; EBIT was 7.6 times as large as interest.

The times-burden-covered ratio expands the definition of annual financial obligation to include debt principal repayments as well as interest. If a company fails to make a principal repayment when due, the outcome is just as if it had failed to make an interest payment. In both cases, the company is in default and creditors can force it into bankruptcy. When including principal repayment as part of the company's financial burden, we must remember to express the figure on a before-tax basis comparable to interest and EBIT. Unlike interest payments, principal repayments are not a tax-deductible expense. This means that if a company is in, say, the 50 percent tax bracket, it must earn $2 before taxes to have $1 after taxes to pay creditors. The other dollar goes to the tax collector. For other tax brackets, the before-tax burden of a principal repayment is found by dividing the repayment by one minus the company's tax rate. Adjusting the principal repayment in this manner to its before-tax equivalent is known in the trade as "grossing up" the principal—about as gross as finance ever gets.

Russell's 1989 principal payment equals the 1988 value of current maturities on long-term debt, or $4.5 million. I estimated Russell's average tax rate as provision for taxes divided by income before tax, or 37 percent ($38 million/$102.8 million). The times-burden-covered ratio of 5.2 times indicates that in 1989 Russell earned its interest and principal burden 5.2 times over.

An often-asked question is, Which of these coverage ratios is more meaningful? The answer is that both are important. If a company could always roll over its maturing obligations by taking out new loans as it repaid old ones, the *net* burden of the debt would be just the interest expense, and times-interest-earned would be the more important ratio. The problem with this logic is that the replacement of maturing debt with new debt is not an automatic feature of capital markets. In some instances, when capital markets are unsettled or the fortunes of a company decline, creditors may refuse to renew maturing obligations. In these cases, the burden of the debt is interest plus principal payments, and the times-burden-covered ratio becomes critical. This is what happened to Burmah Oil, a large British company, in 1974. Burmah took out a large, short-term Eurodollar loan to finance acquisition of Signal Oil Company in the United States, thinking they could roll over the maturing short-term debt into more permanent financing as it came due. However, before Burmah was able to roll over the debt, Herstatt Bank in Germany failed, creditors became very conservative, and no one was willing to lend money to Burmah. A crisis was averted only when the British government bailed Burmah out by purchasing for cash a large block of British Petroleum stock owned by Burmah. In sum, it is fair to conclude that the times-burden-covered ratio is too conservative, assuming the company will pay its existing loans down to zero; but the times-interest-earned ratio is too liberal, assuming the company will roll over all its obligations as they mature.

Another frequent question is, How much coverage is enough? This question cannot be answered precisely, but several generalizations are possible. If a company has ready access to cash in the form of unused borrowing capacity or sizable cash balances or readily salable assets, it can operate safely with lower coverage ratios than competitors without such reserves. The ready access to cash gives the company a means of payment it can use whenever operating earnings are insufficient to cover financial obligations. A second generalization is that coverage should increase with the *business risk* faced by the firm. For example, Hewlett-Packard operates in a dynamic environment characterized by rapid technological change and high rates of product obsolescence. In view of this high business risk, HP would be ill-advised to take on the added financial risk that accompanies low coverage ratios. Said another way, an electric utility that has very stable, predictable cash flows can operate safely with much lower coverage ratios than a company such as HP, which has trouble forecasting more than three or four years into the future.

Liquidity Ratios
As noted earlier, one determinant of a company's debt capacity is the liquidity of its assets. An asset is liquid if it can be readily con-

verted to cash, while a liability is liquid if it must be repaid in the near future. As the Burmah Oil debacle illustrates, it is risky to finance illiquid assets, such as fixed plant and equipment, with liquid, short-term liabilities because the liabilities will come due before the assets generate enough cash to pay them. A company that mismatches the maturity of its assets and liabilities in this manner must roll over, or refinance, maturing liabilities to avoid insolvency.

Two common ratios intended to measure the liquidity of a company's assets relative to its liabilities are the *current ratio* and the *acid test,* defined as

$$\text{Current ratio} = \frac{\text{Current assets}}{\text{Current liabilities}}$$

$$= \frac{\$327}{\$59.8} = 5.5 \text{ times}$$

$$\text{Acid test} = \frac{\text{Current assets} - \text{Inventory}}{\text{Current liabilities}}$$

$$= \frac{\$327 - \$108.8}{\$59.8} = 3.6 \text{ times}$$

The current ratio compares the assets that will turn into cash within the year to the liabilities that must be paid within the year. A company with a low current ratio lacks liquidity in the sense that it cannot reduce its current asset investments to supply cash to meet maturing obligations. It must rely instead on operating income and outside financing.

You should recognize that these ratios are rather crude measures of liquidity for at least two reasons. First, rolling over some obligations, such as accounts payable, involves virtually no insolvency risk provided the company is at least marginally profitable; second, the size of a company's investment in current assets and its ability to reduce this investment to pay its bills are two different things. Unless sales decline, cuts in accounts receivable and inventory will usually hurt profits, sales, and production efficiency. Except in liquidation, companies do not customarily sell off large portions of their current assets to meet maturing obligations.

The acid-test ratio, or what is sometimes called the quick ratio, is identical to the current ratio except that the numerator is reduced by the value of inventory. Inventory is subtracted because it is frequently illiquid. Under distress conditions, a company or its creditors may not be able to realize much cash from the sale of inventory. In liquidation sales, sellers typically receive 40 percent or less of the book value of inventory.

IS ROE A RELIABLE FINANCIAL YARDSTICK?

Until now we have assumed that management wants to increase its ROE, and we have analyzed three important levers of financial performance: profit margin, asset turnover, and financial leverage. We concluded that whether a company is General Motors or the corner drugstore, careful management of these levers can positively affect ROE. We also saw that determining and maintaining appropriate values of the levers is a challenging managerial task, involving an understanding of the nature of the company's business, the way it competes, and the interdependencies among the levers themselves.

It is time now to ask how reliable ROE is as a measure of financial performance. If Company A has a higher ROE than Company B, is its financial performance necessarily superior? If Company C increases its ROE, is this unequivocal evidence of improved financial performance?

As a measure of financial performance, ROE is prone to three problems: a timing problem, a risk problem, and a value problem. Seen in proper perspective, these problems mean that ROE is seldom an unambiguous measure of performance. ROE remains a useful and important indicator, but it must be interpreted in light of its limitations and no analyst should mechanistically infer that a higher ROE is always better than a lower one.

The Timing Problem

Many business opportunities require the sacrifice of present earnings in anticipation of enhanced future earnings. This is true when a company introduces a new product involving heavy start-up costs. If we calculate the company's ROE just after introduction of the new product, it will appear depressed. But rather than suggesting poor performance, the low ROE is just the result of the company's new product introduction. Because ROE necessarily includes earnings for only one year, it frequently fails to capture the full impact of longer-term decisions.

The Risk Problem

Business decisions commonly involve the classic "eat well-sleep well" dilemma. If you want to eat well, you had best be prepared to take risks in search of higher returns. If you want to sleep well, you will likely have to forgo high returns in search of safety. Seldom will you find high returns and safety. (And when you do, please give me a call.)

The problem with ROE in this regard is that it says nothing about what risks a company has taken to generate its ROE. Here is a simple example. Take-a-Risk, Inc., earns an ROA of 6 percent from wildcat oil exploration in South Africa, which it combines with an assets-to-equity ratio of 5.0 to produce an ROE of 30 percent (6% × 5.0). Never-Dare, Ltd., meanwhile, has an ROA of 10 percent on its investment in government securities, which it finances with equal portions of debt and equity to produce an ROE of 20 percent (10% × 2.0). Which company is the better performer? My answer is Never-Dare. Take-a-Risk's ROE is high, but its high business risk and extreme financial leverage make it a very uncertain enterprise. I would prefer the more modest but eminently safer ROE of Never-Dare. Even if I preferred eating well to sleeping well, I would still choose Never-Dare and finance my purchase with a little personal borrowing to lever my return on the investment. In sum, because ROE looks only at return while ignoring risk, it can be an inaccurate yardstick of financial performance.

Return on Invested Capital

To circumvent the distorting effects of financial risk on ROE and ROA, I recommend calculating return on invested capital, also known as return on net assets (RONA).

$$\text{ROIC} = \frac{\text{EBIT} (1 - \text{Tax rate})}{\text{Debt} + \text{Equity}}$$

Russell's 1989 ROIC was

$$\frac{\$118.4\ (1 - 38/102.7)}{\$5.4 + \$3.9 + \$204.8 + \$5.7 + \$402.2} = 12.0\%$$

The numerator of this ratio is the earnings the firm would report if it were all-equity financed, while the denominator is the sum of all company capital on which a return must be earned. Thus, while accounts payable is a source of capital to the firm, it is excluded because it carries no explicit cost. In essence, ROIC is the rate of return earned on the total capital invested in the firm without regard to whether that capital is called debt or equity.

To see the virtue of ROIC, consider the following example. Companies A and B are identical in all respects except that A is highly levered and B is all-equity financed. Because the two companies are identical except for capital structure, we would like a return measure that reflects this fundamental similarity. The figures below show that ROE, and for that matter ROA, fails this test. Reflecting its extensive use of financial leverage, A's ROE is 18 percent, while B's zero-leverage position generates a lower, but better quality, ROE of 7.2 percent. ROA goes to the other extreme, punishing company A for its extensive use of debt and leaving B unaffected. Only ROIC is independent of the differing financing schemes employed by the two companies, showing a 7.2 percent return for both firms. ROIC thus reflects the fundamental earning power of the company before it is confounded by differences in financing strategies.

	A	B
Debt @ 10% interest	$ 900	$ 0
Equity	100	1,000
Total assets	$1,000	$1,000
EBIT	$ 120	$ 120
− Interest expense	90	0
Earnings before tax	30	120
− Tax @ 40%	12	48
Earnings after tax	$ 18	$ 72
ROE	18.0%	7.2%
ROA	1.8%	7.2%
ROIC	7.2%	7.2%

The Value Problem

ROE measures the return on shareholders' investment; however, the investment figure used is the *book value* of shareholders' equity, not the *market value*. This distinction is an important one. Russell's ROE in 1989 was 16.0 percent and, indeed, this is the annual return you could have earned had you been able to buy Russell's equity for its book value of $402.2 million. But that would have been impossible, for as noted in the previous chapter, the market value of Russell's equity was $1,055 million. At this price, your annual return would have been only 6.0 percent, not 16.0 percent ($64.2/$1,055 = 6.0%). The market value of equity is more significant to shareholders because it measures the current, realizable worth of the shares, while book value is only history. We conclude that, because of possible divergence between the market value of equity and its book value, a high ROE may not be synonymous with a high return on investment to shareholders.

The Earnings Yield and the P/E Ratio
It might appear that we can circumvent the value problem by just replacing the book value of equity with its market value in the ROE. Such a ratio is known as the *earnings yield*.

$$\text{Earnings yield} = \frac{\text{Earnings to common}}{\text{Market value of shareholders' equity}}$$

$$= \frac{\text{Earnings per share}}{\text{Price per share}} = \frac{\$1.57}{\$26.12}$$

$$= 6.0\%$$

Is it logical to say that earnings yield is a useful measure of performance and that managers should try to increase their earnings yield? No! The difficulty with earnings yield as a performance measure is that a company's stock price is very sensitive to investor expectations about the future. A share of stock entitles its owner to a portion of *future* earnings as well as present earnings. Naturally, the higher the investor's expectations of future earnings, the more he will be willing to pay for the stock. This means that a bright future, a high stock price, and a *low* earnings yield go together. Clearly, a high earnings yield is not an indicator of superior performance. Said another way, the earnings yield suffers from a severe timing problem of its own that invalidates it as a performance measure.

Turning the earnings yield on its head produces the price-to-earnings ratio, or the P/E ratio.

$$\text{Price to earnings ratio} = \text{P/E ratio}$$

$$= \frac{\text{Price per share}}{\text{Earnings per share}} = \frac{\$26.12}{\$1.57}$$

$$= 16.6 \text{ times}$$

The P/E ratio adds little to our discussion of performance measures, but its wide usage among investors deserves comment. The P/E ratio measures the amount of money investors are willing to pay for one dollar of current earnings, and is a means of standardizing stock prices to facilitate comparison among companies with different earnings. In December 1989, investors were paying $16.60 for each dollar of Russell earnings. Speaking broadly, a company's P/E ratio depends on two things: its future earnings prospects and the risk associated with those earnings. As already noted, stock price, and hence the P/E ratio, rises as a company's prospects for future growth improve. Risk has the opposite effect. A high degree of uncertainty about a company's future earnings prospects reduces a company's P/E ratio. In general, the P/E ratio tells you little about a company's current financial performance, but it does indicate what investors feel about the company's future prospects.

ROE or Market Price?

For years academicians and practitioners have been at odds over the proper measure of financial performance. Academicians criticize ROE for the reasons cited above and argue that the correct measure of financial performance is the firm's stock price. Moreover, they contend that management's goal should be to maximize stock price. Their logic is persuasive: Stock price represents the value of the owners' investment in the firm. Assuming that the objective of managers is to further the interest of owners, managers should take actions that increase value to owners. Indeed, the notion of "value creation" has become a central theme in the writings of many academicians and consultants.

Practitioners acknowledge the logic of this reasoning but are concerned about its applicability. One problem is the difficulty of specifying precisely how operating decisions affect stock price. If we are not certain what impact a change in, say, the business strategy of one division will have on a company's stock price, the goal of increasing price cannot guide decision making. A second problem is that managers typically know more about their company than outside investors, or at least think they do. Why then should managers consider the assessments of less-informed investors when making business decisions? Yet another practical problem with stock price as a performance measure is that it depends on a whole array of factors outside the company's control. One can never be certain whether an increase in stock price reflects improving company performance or an improving external economic environment. For these reasons, practitioners continue to rely on ROE as an admittedly imperfect measure of financial performance. Academicians and financial consultants, meanwhile, continue to make value creation a more practical financial objective.

RATIO ANALYSIS

In the course of our discussion of the levers of financial performance, we defined a number of financial ratios. It is time now to broaden the discussion to consider the systematic use of such ratios to analyze financial performance. This involves nothing more than calculating a number of diverse ratios and comparing them to certain standards, in search of insights into the company's operations and its financial health.

Ratio analysis is widely used by managers, creditors, regulators, and investors. Used with care and imagination, the technique can reveal much about a company and its operations. But there are a few things to bear in mind about ratios. First, a ratio is just one number divided by another, so it is unreasonable to expect that the mechanical calculation of one ratio, or even several ratios, will automatically yield important insights into anything as complex as a modern corporation. It is useful to think of ratios as clues in a detective story. One or even several ratios might be misleading, but when combined with other knowledge of a company's management

Can ROE Substitute for Share Price?

The accompanying graphs (Figures 2–1 and 2–2) suggest that the gulf between academicians and practitioners over the proper measure of financial performance may not be as wide as might be supposed. The graphs plot the market value of equity divided by book value of equity against ROE for two representative industries. ROE is measured as a weighted average of the past five years' ROEs. The smooth line in each figure is a regression line indicating the general relation between the two variables. The strong positive relationship visible in both graphs suggests that high-ROE firms tend to have high stock prices relative to book value, and vice versa. Hence, working to increase ROE in these industries is largely consistent with working to increase stock price.

The proximity of the company dots to the fitted regression lines is also interesting. It shows the importance of factors other than ROE in determining a company's market-to-book ratio. As we should expect, these other factors play a significant role in determining the market value of a specific firm's shares.

For interest, I have indicated the position of several companies on the graphs. Note in Figure 2–1 that Russell is somewhat above the regression line, indicating that, based purely on historical ROEs, Russell's stock price is a little rich compared to other apparel companies. Note too that Oshkosh B'Gosh and Liz Claiborne have lofty ROEs of 26.4 percent and 27.5 percent, respectively, and are accorded the highest market-to-book ratios of 4.7 and 3.5.

In Figure 2–2, Zondervan Corporation is an example of "hope springs eternal." Although their ROE does not exceed 3 percent over the last four years examined, investors are still willing to pay well above book value for their shares.

To summarize, these graphs offer tantalizing evidence that, despite its weaknesses, ROE may be a useful proxy for share price in measuring financial performance.

and economic circumstances, ratio analysis can tell a revealing story.

A second point to bear in mind is that there is no single correct value for a ratio. Like Goldilocks and the three bears, the observation that the value of a particular ratio is too high, too low, or just right depends on the perspective of the analyst and on the company's competitive strategy. As an example, consider the current ratio. From the perspective of a short-term creditor, a high current ratio is a positive sign because it suggests ample liquidity and a high likelihood of repayment. Yet an owner of the company might look on the same current ratio as a negative sign suggesting that the company's assets are too conservatively deployed. Moreover, from an operating perspective, a high current ratio could be a sign of conservative management or it could be the natural result of a competitive strategy that emphasizes liberal credit terms and sizable inventories. In this case, the important question is not whether the current ratio is too high, but whether the chosen strategy is best for the company.

Using Ratios Effectively

Now that we have calculated a number of ratios, what shall we do with them? If there are no universally correct values for ratios, how do you interpret them? How do you decide whether a company

FIGURE 2–1.

The Market Value to Book Value of Equity Ratio versus Return on Equity in the Apparel Industry

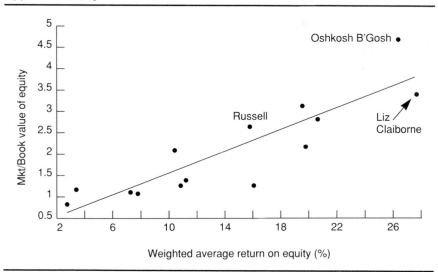

Sources: *Value Line Investment Survey* (November 30, 1990); Copyright © 1991 By Value Line Publishing, Inc.; used by permission. For subscription information to the *Value Line Investment Survey* please call (800) 634-3583.

FIGURE 2–2.
The Market Value to Book Value of Equity Ratio versus Return on Equity in the Publishing Industry

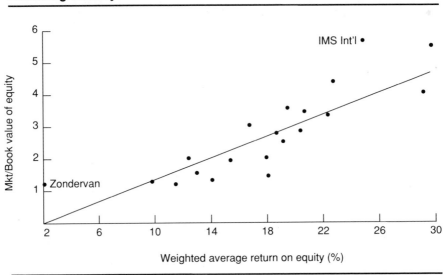

is healthy or sick? There are three approaches: compare the ratios to rules of thumb, compare them to industry averages, or look for changes in the ratios over time. Comparing a company's ratios to rules of thumb has the virtue of simplicity, but has little to recommend it conceptually. The appropriate values of ratios for a company depend too much on the analyst's perspective and on the company's specific circumstances for rules of thumb to be very useful. The most positive thing to be said in their support is that, over the years, companies conforming to these rules of thumb tend to go bankrupt somewhat less frequently than those that do not.

Comparing a company's ratios to industry ratios provides a useful feel for how the company measures up to its competitors. But it is still true that company-specific differences can result in entirely justifiable deviations from industry norms. There is also no guarantee that the industry as a whole knows what it is doing. The knowledge that one railroad was much like its competitors was cold comfort in the depression of the 1930s, when virtually all railroads got into financial difficulties.

The most useful way to evaluate ratios involves trend analysis. Calculate ratios for a company over several years and take note of how they change over time. Trend analysis avoids cross-company and cross-industry comparisons, enabling the analyst to draw firmer conclusions about the firm's financial health and its variation over time.

Moreover, the levers of performance suggest one logical approach to trend analysis. Instead of calculating ratios at random, hoping to stumble across one that might be meaningful, take advantage of the structure implicit in the levers. As illustrated in Figure 2–3, the levers of performance organize ratios into three tiers. At the top, ROE looks at the performance of the enterprise as a whole; in the middle, the levers of performance indicate how three important segments of the business contributed to ROE; and on the bottom, many of the other ratios discussed reveal how the management of individual income statement and balance sheet accounts contributed to the observed levers. To take advantage of this structure, begin at the top by noting the trend in ROE over

FIGURE 2–3
The Levers of Performance Suggest One Roadmap for Ratio Analysis

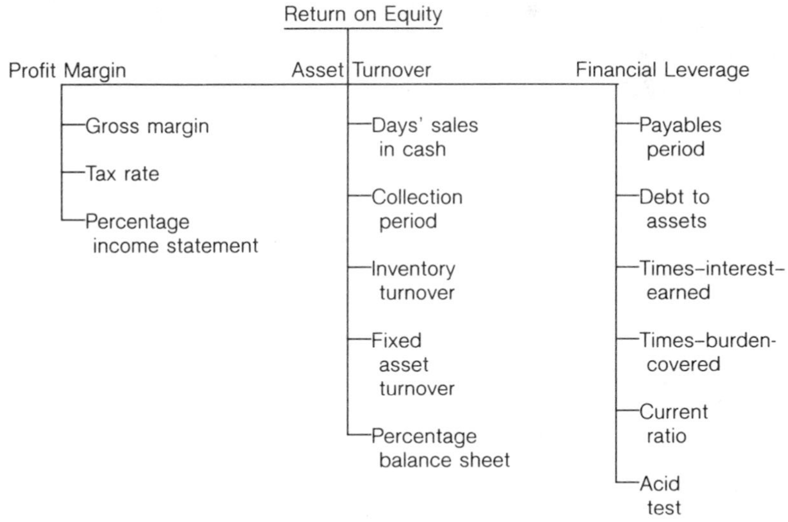

Return on Equity

Profit Margin   Asset Turnover   Financial Leverage

—Gross margin   —Days' sales in cash   —Payables period
—Tax rate   —Collection period   —Debt to assets
—Percentage income statement   —Inventory turnover   —Times–interest–earned
                  —Fixed asset turnover   —Times–burden–covered
                  —Percentage balance sheet   —Current ratio
                                           —Acid test

time; then narrow your focus and ask what changes in the three levers account for the observed ROE pattern; and finally, get out your microscope and study individual accounts in search of explanations for the observed changes in the levers. For example, if ROE has plunged while the profit margin and financial leverage have remained constant, examine the control of individual asset accounts in search of the culprit, or culprits.

Ratio Analysis of Russell Corporation

As a practical demonstration of ratio analysis, let us see what the technique can tell us about Russell Corporation. Table 2–2 presents 18 previously discussed ratios for Russell over the years 1985 to 1989 and, where possible, industry average ratios for 1989. The comparison industry consists of the five firms from the Textile-Apparel Manufacturers industry represented in the Standard & Poor's 500 stock averages.[2] As a further example of readily available industry data, Table 2–4, at the end of the chapter, presents similar ratios for other representative industries, including median, upper quartile, and lower quartile values for the represented ratios.[3]

Beginning with Russell's return on equity, we see that the number has been reasonably stable at around 16 percent for the past three years. This is a healthy figure relative to the average American corporation, but is noticeably below the industry average of 19.8 percent.[4] Looking next at Russell's levers of perform-

---

[2]The companies represented are Hartmarx Corp., Liz Claiborne, Inc., Oshkosh B'Gosh, Russell Corp., and V F Corp. The fact that Russell is itself a member of the industry averages attenuates the differences observed between Russell and the industry. Figures for a broader cross section of firms are available; however, they appear to be dominated by much smaller companies. Despite the small number of firms represented, the sample chosen appears to provide the most relevant comparison with Russell.

[3]For any ratio, if we were to array all of the values for the companies in the industry from the highest to the lowest, the figure falling in the middle of the series is the *median;* the ratio halfway between the highest value and the median is the *upper quartile;* while the ratio halfway between the lowest value and the median is the *lower quartile.* Data are from *Industry Norms and Key Business Ratios: Desk-Top Edition 1989–90,* Dun & Bradstreet Information Services, 1990.

[4]According to *Business Week,* March 19, 1990, p. 67, the 1989, all-industry composite return on equity for 900 U.S. companies was 13.2 percent. The composite return on equity for 16 firms comprising the apparel industry, including Russell, was 20.3 percent.

TABLE 2-2
Ratio Analysis of Russell Corporation 1985–1989 and Industry Averages for 1989

	1985	1986	1987	1988	1989	Industry Average*
Profitability ratios:						
Return on equity (%)	13.5	17.4	16.6	15.6	16.0	19.8
Return on assets (%)	9.2	12.3	10.4	9.6	8.9	10.2
Return on invested capital (%)	12.0	15.6	13.3	12.6	12.0	14.1
Profit margin (%)	7.7	9.9	9.7	10.1	9.3	7.4
Gross margin (%)	30.2	34.9	34.0	35.2	33.4	NA
Price to earnings (x)	12.8	15.8	16.1	11.9	16.6	13.6
Leverage and liquidity ratios:						
Assets to equity (x)	1.5	1.4	1.6	1.6	1.8	2.0
Debt to assets (%)	31.8	29.2	37.2	38.5	44.2	48.7
Debt to equity (%)	46.6	41.3	59.2	62.6	79.2	95.1
Times interest earned (x)	14.7	21.1	12.6	10.7	7.6	8.9
Times burden covered (x)		7.5	6.5	1.9	5.2	NA
Current ratio (x)	5.4	5.6	3.9	2.4	5.5	3.1
Acid test (x)	3.3	3.5	2.7	1.3	3.6	1.5
Turnover-control ratios:						
Asset turnover (x)	1.2	1.2	1.1	0.9	1.0	1.4
Fixed asset turnover (x)	2.5	2.6	2.2	1.6	1.9	5.1
Inventory turnover (x)	4.2	4.1	4.5	3.6	4.2	NA
Collection period (days)	65.3	63.9	67.5	68.7	70.7	47.8
Days sales in cash (days)	31.7	28.4	44.4	8.6	40.1	NA
Payables period (days)	22.4	19.3	20.2	35.2	21.4	NA

NA = Not available.

*Source: *Standard & Poor's Analysts Handbook: Official Series: 1990 Annual Edition,* p. 269, and *Monthly Supplement* (November 1990), p. 30. Copyright Standard & Poor's Corporation. All rights reserved. Sample consists of five firms in the S&P 500 stock index from the Textile-Apparel Manufacturers industry. The companies are Hartmarx Corp., Liz Claiborne, Inc., Oshkosh B'Gosh, Russell Corp., and V F Corp.

ance, the profit margin has been steady at about 9 to 10 percent for four years and exceeds the industry average by a healthy margin. Russell appears to have few problems on its income statement. The asset turnover, on the other hand, has sagged from a high of 1.2 times to 1.0 in 1989, and is noticeably below the industry average of 1.4. A below-average asset turnover is not necessarily bad, for it may only reflect a greater capital intensity on Russell's part. Indeed, this explanation is consistent with Russell's ability to command higher profit margins than its rivals. However, the downward trend in the ratio is more worrisome. To put the decline in perspective, had Russell's asset turnover been 1.2 in 1989—its 1986 value—ROE would have been 20 percent higher. Looking at the third lever of performance, Russell has offset its declining asset turnover by increasing financial leverage. The assets-to-equity ratio is up from a 1986 low of 1.4 times to a high of 1.8 in 1989; still below the industry but rising steadily. Similarly, the 1989 times-interest-earned ratio is at a five-year low and below the industry average. Security analysts would argue that, although Russell's ROE may be roughly constant, rising leverage has reduced its quality by forcing shareholders to bear more financial risk.

Our look at Russell's ROE and levers of performance reveals two offsetting trends: falling asset turns and rising leverage. Digging a little deeper into these broad trends, it appears that the company's asset turns are falling for several reasons. Most importantly, the turnover of fixed assets, although up in 1989 to 1.9 times, is well below its 1986 peak of 2.6, and is little more than *one-third* the industry average. Russell is either much more capital intensive than competitors or very inefficient in its use of fixed assets. Given the company's healthy earnings, I am inclined to believe the former. The collection period shows the same pattern, lengthening almost seven days from its 1986 low to almost twice the industry average. Why tie up so much money in accounts receivable? Is a collection period of over 70 days necessary to generate sales, or have collection efforts become too lax? Finally, the days' sales in cash ratio shows substantial year-to-year variability. The ratio is high in 1989, apparently because Russell raised more cash from a long-term debt issue than immediately required, and parked the excess temporarily in securities. The excess cash suggests that Russell is anticipating continued high investment requirements or, possibly, an acquisition in the near future. The combined effect of slower turning fixed assets and receivables is apparent in Russell's return on assets and return on invested capital, both of which have fallen over 20 percent from their 1986 highs. The basic efficiency with which Russell manages its assets has fallen over the past four years.

Russell's leverage and liquidity ratios show rising indebtedness, although still below industry averages, and very ample liquidity. The high liquidity in 1989 appears to be due principally to the increase in temporary investments, for the current ratio and the acid test were actually somewhat below average the prior year.

Table 2–3 presents what are known as common-size financial statements for Russell over the period 1985 to 1989, as well as industry averages for 1989. A common-size balance sheet simply presents each asset and liability as a percent of total assets. A common-size income statement is analogous except that all items are scaled in proportion to net sales instead of total assets. The motivation for scaling financial statements in this fashion is to concentrate on underlying trends by abstracting from changes in the dollar figures caused by growth or decline. In addition, common-size statements are useful in removing simple scale effects when comparing companies of differing size.

Looking first at the balance sheet, note that although Russell is a capital-intensive manufacturer, almost one half of its assets are short-term—primarily accounts receivable and inventories. Moreover, this proportion is low relative to the industry, where over 60 percent of assets are current. These numbers again highlight the importance of working-capital management to most businesses. When 50 to 60 percent of a company's investment is in assets as volatile as inventory and accounts receivable, that investment bears close watching. In this light, note Russell's careful management of inventories, which constitute only 15.1 percent of assets compared to over 30 percent for the industry. But the big difference between Russell and its rivals on the asset side of the balance sheet is Russell's huge investment in fixed assets. Net property, plant, and equipment account for over one half of Russell's assets, while the comparable industry figure is only about 27 percent. This again reflects Russell's greater capital intensity, and gives cause to wonder whether Russell might be more vulnerable to economic downturns than its rivals.

The story on the liabilities side of the balance sheet, especially in 1989, is Russell's modest reliance on short-term liabilities. The company is supporting only 8.3 percent of its assets in 1989 with short-term liabilities, compared to almost 20 percent for competitors. Of particular note is the low percentage for trade credit. We know from Table 2–2 that Russell's payables period in 1989 was only 21.4 days. Is the company passing up low-cost financing, or do

TABLE 2–3

Common-Size Financial Statements, 1985–1989, and Industry Averages for 1989

	1985	1986	1987	1988	1989	Industry Average*
			ASSETS			
Current assets:						
Cash	0.3%	0.4%	0.4%	0.4%	0.4%	NA
Temporary investments	10.1	9.3	12.7	1.8	10.1	NA
Accounts receivable	21.4	21.8	19.9	17.8	18.5	18.1%
Inventories	19.7	19.7	15.8	16.8	15.1	30.4
Other current assets	0.2	0.2	0.3	0.6	1.3	1.6
Total current assets	51.7	51.4	49.2	37.4	45.4	60.9
Net property, plant, and equipment	47.9	48.1	49.3	57.4	50.1	26.8
Other long-term assets	0.4	0.5	1.5	5.2	4.6	12.3
Total assets	100.0%	100.0%	100.0%	100.0%	100.0%	100.0%
		LIABILITIES AND SHAREHOLDERS' EQUITY				
Current liabilities:						
Short-term debt				5.4%	0.7%	4.3%
Accounts payable	5.1%	4.3%	3.9%	5.9	3.7	6.1
Accrued wages and expenses	2.2	2.5	2.0	2.1	2.4	7.0
Accrued taxes	1.1	1.2	1.1	1.0	0.9	1.8
Current maturities on long-term debt	1.2	1.1	5.6	0.8	0.5	0.5
Total current liabilities	9.7	9.1	12.6	15.3	8.3	19.8
Long-term debt	13.0	10.8	16.5	15.0	28.4	25.0
Deferred taxes	8.8	9.0	7.6	6.6	6.0	3.0
Accrued liabilities	0.4	0.3	0.4	0.6	0.7	0.8
Preferred stock	0.0	0.0	0.0	1.0	0.8	0.1
Total liabilities	31.8	29.2	37.2	38.5	44.2	48.7
Shareholders' equity	68.2	70.7	62.8	61.5	55.8	51.3
Total liabilities and shareholders' equity	100.0%	100.0%	100.0%	100.0%	100.0%	100.0%

suppliers' prompt payment discounts justify the low payables period?

Russell's common-size income statement is the picture of stability. Margins are high relative to the industry and are admirably steady. One general observation: Although small percentage changes on an income statement may appear inconsequential,

TABLE 2–3 (concluded)
Common-Size Financial Statements, 1985–1989, and Industry Averages for 1989)

	1985	1986	1987	1988	1989	Industry Average*
Net sales	100.0%	100.0%	100.0%	100.0%	100.0%	100.0%
Cost of sales	69.8	65.1	66.0	64.8	66.6	___
Gross profit	30.2	34.9	34.0	35.2	33.4	
Selling, general, and administrative expenses	15.9	15.6	16.3	17.2	15.9	
Operating income	14.3	19.2	17.7	18.0	17.5	12.6
Interest expense	1.0	0.9	1.4	1.7	2.3	1.5
Other income (expense)	0.1	0.0	0.5	(0.2)	(0.3)	0.9
Income before taxes	13.5	18.4	16.7	16.2	14.9	12.0
Provision for taxes	5.8	8.5	7.0	6.0	5.5	4.6
Net income	7.7	9.9	9.7	10.1	9.4	7.4
Preferred dividends				0.0	0.1	0.1
Net income available for common shareholders	7.7%	9.9%	9.7%	10.1%	9.3%	7.4%

NA = Not available.

they seldom are. For example, Russell's interest expense rises a mere 1.3 percentage points from 1985 to 1989. But when we compare the increase to net income rather than sales, the increase takes on more significance. Because net income is only about 10 percent of sales, the increase in interest expense equals a healthy 13 percent of what really matters. When only five to 10 cents of every sales dollar make their way to earnings, even apparently small setbacks along the way are important.

In sum, ratio analysis of Russell reveals a solid, stable, conservatively managed company. The high and rising collection period, the falling turnover of fixed assets, the growing indebtedness, and the modest payables period are possible sources of concern, as is the high degree of capital intensity in an historical cyclical business. But all in all, Russell management can take pleasure in a job well done.

TABLE 2–4
Selected Ratios for Representative Industries 1989 (Upper quartile, median, and lower quartile values)

Lines of Business and Number of Firms Reporting	Current Ratio (times)	Total Liabilities to Net Worth	Collection Period (days)	Net Sales to Inventory (times)	Total Assets to Net sales	Profit Margin	Return on Assets	Return on Equity
Agriculture, construction, and mining:								
Dairy farms (303)	6.1	18.3%	13.1	15.0	69.8%	12.8%	9.8%	32.3%
	1.9	56.0	23.9	6.6	127.2	6.4	4.6	7.0
	1.0	118.4	34.1	2.3	241.9	0.9	0.9	1.5
Drilling oil and gas wells (547)	4.2	18.3	29.2	57.8	51.1	9.7	8.5	15.6
	1.7	44.6	54.8	19.6	86.4	1.1	0.7	1.9
	1.0	146.9	85.1	7.3	209.0	(9.3)	(7.4)	(11.0)
Single family housing construction (2,145)	3.9	32.8	7.3	90.4	17.0	10.6	29.1	69.4
	1.7	92.6	22.3	22.0	30.7	4.6	10.3	28.1
	1.1	215.4	47.5	6.5	58.0	1.3	2.2	7.8
Manufacturing:								
Men's and boys' shirts (303)	3.5	39.0	18.4	9.8	29.5	6.3	11.6	28.0
	2.1	99.6	40.2	6.0	42.2	2.7	6.0	13.0
	1.5	217.4	77.8	4.1	58.0	0.9	2.0	5.3
Wood household furniture (928)	3.8	34.2	14.7	20.7	21.9	9.0	16.5	41.8
	2.0	89.6	30.3	10.3	34.4	4.5	8.1	17.9
	1.3	210.7	46.7	5.8	56.1	1.4	2.7	7.4
Semiconductors and related devices (584)	3.8	31.9	37.0	12.7	39.8	11.5	12.5	26.3
	2.2	80.6	54.3	7.0	63.9	4.3	5.4	10.8
	1.4	173.9	69.4	4.6	98.6	0.5	0.1	0.6
Motor vehicle parts and accessories (1,237)	3.7	32.3	24.5	14.4	32.1	8.5	15.1	34.3
	2.0	94.0	39.8	7.7	44.7	3.8	6.0	15.7
	1.3	228.8	55.1	5.0	66.5	0.8	1.3	4.8

Retailing:

	1	2	3	4	5	6	7	8
Department stores (1,892)	6.3	17.2	6.2	6.2	37.4	3.9	7.6	15.7
	3.7	55.1	24.1	4.5	49.2	1.7	3.3	6.6
	2.1	146.3	52.6	3.2	69.0	0.3	0.6	1.2
Grocery stores (2,183)	4.3	32.0	1.1	25.2	12.4	2.9	12.2	28.3
	2.2	83.2	2.3	17.3	18.0	1.4	6.0	13.1
	1.3	197.8	6.2	11.8	28.2	0.4	1.7	4.5
Jewelry stores (2,319)	7.3	19.1	9.0	4.0	45.9	11.7	14.2	30.3
	3.3	57.8	23.4	2.5	65.4	5.0	6.5	12.0
	1.9	145.1	51.8	1.7	96.1	1.5	2.0	4.4

Services:

	1	2	3	4	5	6	7	8
Passenger car rental (547)	2.9	97.0	9.9	106.4	66.8	12.1	7.9	37.2
	1.2	257.6	21.5	21.2	120.1	5.4	3.7	17.0
	0.5	504.0	42.7	2.6	177.1	1.5	1.0	5.9
Colleges and universities (1,978)	4.9	11.3	7.3	125.2	152.2	8.8	4.9	7.0
	2.1	24.7	15.0	75.3	210.5	2.3	1.4	2.0
	1.1	51.6	30.8	48.8	283.2	0.2	0.1	0.2

Wholesaling:

	1	2	3	4	5	6	7	8
Sporting and recreational goods (1,647)	4.0	39.7	15.3	9.6	26.4	6.6	13.4	33.9
	2.1	105.5	29.2	5.7	36.9	2.7	5.5	13.9
	1.4	232.0	46.5	3.6	54.7	0.9	1.9	5.0
Electrical appliances, television, and radio (1,726)	3.3	44.1	18.5	13.3	21.1	4.9	11.4	28.6
	1.8	122.4	30.3	7.8	31.9	2.2	5.5	13.6
	1.3	270.5	44.9	5.0	45.3	0.7	1.9	5.8

Source: *Industry Norms and Key Business Ratios: Desk-Top Edition 1989–90*, Dun & Bradstreet Information Services, 1990. Copyright 1990, Dun & Bradstreet Information Services. All rights reserved. Reprinted with permission.

APPENDIX

EVALUATING DIVISIONAL PERFORMANCE

*Bureaucracy: A device for converting energy into solid
  waste.*
Anonymous

During the question and answer period following a presentation to MBA
students at Stanford University, George Schultz—former dean of the
University of Chicago business school, former Secretary of the Treasury,
future Secretary of State, and then President of Bechtel Engineering—
was asked what he saw as the major difference between managing in the
public sector and in the private sector. After a long pause, he responded,
"Let me put it this way. As president of Bechtel Engineering, when I call a
subordinate into my office with a task I want him to perform, I find I have
to explain the task to him *very* carefully, because I realize when he leaves
my office, he may actually do it."

As Schultz suggests, the particular genius of a competitive economy
is its ability to energize large corporate bureaucracies in the pursuit of
common goals—something distinctly lacking in most governmental and
socialistic organizations. The source of this discipline among firms is apparent. When a company strays too far from the path of maximizing market value, or return on equity, rivals are only too glad to elbow it out of the
market. In a capitalistic economy the rewards of success and the penalties
of failure are large enough to capture the attention of even the most distracted chief executive.

But in large companies how does management communicate the
competitive pressures felt so keenly at the top to all parts of the organization, so that even the clerk in the mailroom sees himself as a competitor,
not a bureaucrat? The now-standard answer, first used by General Motors and the Du Pont Company around the turn of the century, is to de-
centralize. Carve the corporation into a number of quasi-independent
businesses and measure the performance of each as if it were a stand-
alone entity.

The pervasiveness of decentralization in large corporations means
that operating managers typically spend much more time assessing the
financial performance of profit centers within their own company than
they do evaluating other firms. To appreciate the magnitude of such "internal financial analysis," it is instructive to note that ITT once had 250
separate profit centers, each reporting its financial performance to top
management on at least a quarterly basis. It is therefore of interest to ask

whether the techniques already presented for analyzing entire companies are also appropriate for assessing the financial health of individual divisions within a company. You will be heartened to learn that the techniques are indeed appropriate—but with several important provisos.

Management has at least three objectives in mind when evaluating division performance: to learn which divisions need help and what type of help is required, to learn which divisions are doing exceptionally well so that investment in these activities can be increased, and to learn which division managers are doing well so their superior achievement can be rewarded.

The evaluation of division performance is obviously closely related to the topics already discussed in this chapter. Both a company and a division invest resources in pursuit of profits, and the challenge is to measure their success in this activity. There are, however, some differences. One is that divisions seldom have debt or equity of their own. Instead, all financing is done at the corporate level, so it is impossible to define an ROE for a division. Another difference is that the prices applicable to transactions among sister divisions within the same company are often difficult to determine objectively. The resulting need to rely on what are known as *transfer prices* can obscure the assessment of divisional performance and can lead to poor management decision making. A third difference is that in divisional performance appraisal, the managerial incentives created by the evaluation are usually as important as the objective results of the appraisal itself.

Return on Investment

To see the logic of the most common yardstick for measuring the financial performance of a division, recall the levers of performance equation.

$$\text{ROE} = \underbrace{\frac{\text{Profit}}{\text{margin}} \times \frac{\text{Asset}}{\text{turnover}}}_{\substack{\text{Divisional} \\ \text{responsibility}}} \times \underbrace{\frac{\text{Financial}}{\text{leverage}}}_{\substack{\text{Headquarters'} \\ \text{responsibility}}}$$

Top management, of course, uses all three levers in pursuit of a competitive return on equity. One level removed from top management, division managers manipulate the first two performance levers within their division, but not the third. This gives rise to an important division of labor in decentralized companies, according to which operating managers are collectively responsible for generating healthy profit margins and asset turns, while headquarters people worry about how best to finance the assets.

Given this separation of duties, the logical yardstick for measuring division performance is the product of the first two levers of control, or the division's return on assets, ROA.

$$\text{ROA} = \frac{\text{Earnings}}{\text{Sales}} \times \frac{\text{Sales}}{\text{Assets}} = \frac{\text{Earnings}}{\text{Assets}}$$

When applied to a division, ROA is also commonly referred to as the division's return on investment, or ROI, and we will follow that custom here.

$$\text{ROI} = \frac{\text{Division earnings}}{\text{Division assets}}$$

In practical application, companies frequently customize ROA in various ways. Tektronix Inc., a large manufacturer of sophisticated electronic equipment headquartered in Beaverton, Oregon, calculates what they call "return on operations," or ROO, defined as division operating income before tax divided by division assets. Jardine Fleming, a large Hong Kong-based company, uses a similar quantity they call "return on operating funds," or ROOF, and reminds managers of its importance with the homily "A house without a ROOF provides no shelter."

Companies use variants of ROA rather than ROA itself for several largely technical reasons. First, operating executives frequently do not control all of the assets assigned to their unit. Cash, for example, is usually centrally managed and, hence, removed from the asset base on which the manager is evaluated. Second, as noted during our discussion of return on invested capital, ROA and financial leverage are not truly independent of one another. Indeed, increasing interest expense causes ROA to decline as leverage rises. Use of ROA in performance appraisal would thus suggest that operating managers had performed poorly whenever leverage increased. Customized versions of ROA get around this problem by using income before interest expense in the numerator.

ROI as a Measure of Division Performance

Just as with ROE, ROI suffers from timing, risk, and value problems when used as a performance measure. The timing problem is especially critical because it encourages managers to take a short-run focus. If you anticipate being a division manager for only five years, the natural incentive is to do whatever you can to boost near-term ROI and to ignore everything beyond this horizon. American industry has received considerable criticism of late for just such a myopia, and perhaps an over-reliance on ROI is one of the root causes of this problem.

Residual Profits

A second incentive problem with ROI involves new investment. Suppose division managers are rewarded according to their divisions' ROI and that division A has an ROI of 25 percent, while division B's is only 5 percent. Now assume that each division is presented with an opportunity to invest in a project yielding a 20 percent return.

Although 20 percent is a rather attractive return, the manager of division A will likely reject the investment because it will reduce his ROI, while the manager of B will jump at the chance to make the investment because it will increase his ROI. In fact, he'll undertake any investment promising more than 5 percent. The net effect of this distortion is that successful divisions will tend to underinvest and unsuccessful ones will overinvest.

There is no simple way to circumvent the timing, risk, and value problems inherent in the use of accounting ratios, but it is possible to eliminate the distortion described above by using what is known as residual profits rather than ROI as the performance measure. It is defined as

$$\frac{\text{Residual}}{\text{profits}} = \frac{\text{Division}}{\text{earnings}} - \left(K \times \frac{\text{Division}}{\text{assets}} \right)$$

where K is a percentage number representing the minimum acceptable rate of return on investment in the profit center, as defined by senior management. In later chapters we will refer to K as the cost of capital and will explain how it can be estimated.

To illustrate the use of residual profits, consider again divisions A and B faced with an investment promising a 20 percent return. If both divisions have assets of $100 and if K equals 15 percent, then residual profits are

Division A	*Division B*
$\dfrac{\text{Residual}}{\text{profits}} = \$25 - 15\% \times 100$	$\dfrac{\text{Residual}}{\text{profits}} = \$5 - 15\% \times 100$
$= \$10$	$= -\$10$

Then, supposing the new 20 percent investment costs $50, its contribution to residual profits will be +$2.50 regardless of which division makes the investment ($2.50 = 20\% \times \$50 - 15\% \times \$50$). Now, both division managers will want to make any investment promising a return greater than 15 percent regardless of their existing ROI or residual profits.

Transfer Pricing

The Achilles heel of decentralized performance appraisal is transfer pricing. Virtually all large, decentralized businesses use transfer prices and virtually none are satisfied with the results. When one division supplies a sister division in the same company with a good or a service, the transfer must be priced in order to measure the profits of the two divisions. The price for such intracompany transactions is known as a *transfer price.*

In the absence of an objectively determined market price for such intracompany transactions, management must set a transfer price that accurately measures the value of the resources transferred and that properly motivates the division managers involved. Too high a price encourages the selling division to overproduce and the buying division to underconsume, while too low a price produces opposite effects.

How should transfer prices be set? There is no universally applicable, ideal answer to this question, but here are four possibilities in decending order of preference. (If you are seriously interested in this topic, take a look at *The Transfer Pricing Problem: A Theory for Practice.*[5]) Whenever possible the best approach is to use a competitively determined market price for the same, or a highly similar, product. If division A sells unbleached wheat to division B, use the published current, or spot, price for wheat on the Chicago Commodities Exhange, possibly adjusted for differences in quality and location.

When a market price is not available, perhaps because the product is highly proprietary, the next best approach is usually to simulate a competitive price by allowing buyer and seller to bargain. However, you should know that companies using this approach report two difficulties. One is that by putting buyer and seller in an adversarial relationship, bargaining undermines a possibly critical spirit of teamwork among the divisions. The manager of division A will probably not exert himself to develop a new product for division B if he is still miffed about the last price negotiations.

The second difficulty is that effective bargaining usually requires that both parties have credible alternatives, meaning that each must have the ability to take his business elsewhere if a satisfactory price cannot be negotiated. But, of course, taking one's business elsewhere implies losing profits on work that could just as easily have been done in-house—

---

[5]R. G. Eccles, *The Transfer Pricing Problem: A Theory for Practice* (Lexington, Mass.: Lexington Books, 1985).

something some senior executives find too high a price to pay for un-
tainted transfer prices.

A third approach to setting transfer prices is for senior management
simply to dictate a price, or pricing formula, based on standard manufacturing costs and typical profit margins. Despite its appealing simplicity,
any familiarity with the history of cost-plus pricing on military contracts
and the infamous $600 toilets will convince you that this approach is a
landmine of analytical and motivational problems. Companies are well
advised to use formula-based transfer prices only as a last resort.

The fourth approach is to avoid the whole problem by merging buyer
and seller into one larger division, so that the transfer pricing problem
disappears into the bureaucracy. The fact that such a merger runs precisely counter to the philosophy of decentralization qualifies this approach for last place on the list of options.

International Performance Appraisal

The growing internationalization of business makes the assessment of
foreign and cross-border activities increasingly important. The following
paragraphs highlight the major differences between domestic and international performance appraisal and note some of the pitfalls in the assessment of international operations. To those readers who are inclined
to think of a weekend in Toronto as an exotic, foreign adventure, a word
of warning before we begin: This topic is a challenging, rapidly evolving
one with few simple answers, so do not be surprised if the following observations are a bit impressionistic.

Single-Country Foreign Subsidiaries

Let us begin with the simple case of a foreign division operating entirely
within a single country. As an example, suppose a U.S. company wants to
assess the performance of its wholly owned Brazilian division, and assume that all of the division's revenues, costs, and assets are denominated in cruzeiros, the currency of Brazil. (For legal reasons unrelated to
our analysis, the Brazilian operation will most likely be organized as a
subsidiary, and we will refer to it as such.)

A useful starting point for our analysis is to write an expression for
the subsidiary's dollar earnings. Ignoring fixed costs for simplicity,

$$\text{Subsidiary earnings (in dollars)} = S\,[(P_c - VC_c)Q]$$

where S is the current dollar-cruzeiro exchange rate, stated as the number of dollars required to purchase one cruzeiro, P_c is price per item, VC_c is cost per item, and Q is the number of items sold. The subscript c indicates that the subscripted quantities are denominated in cruzeiros rather than dollars. As a reality check, this equation says that a subsidiary selling 100 items costing 40 cruzeiros each for 90 cruzeiros records a profit of 5,000 cruzeiros $((90 - 40) \times 100)$. The quantity in brackets is thus the subsidiary's earnings in cruzeiros. If the exchange rate is one cruzeiro costs 10 cents, the subsidiary's dollar earnings are $500 ($0.10 \times 5,000$).

This equation says that the Brazilian subsidiary's dollar earnings depend on two things: its cruzeiro earnings and the exchange rate used to translate these earnings into dollars. Note that while subsidiary management can influence cruzeiro earnings, it has no control whatsoever over the exchange rate. Consequently, management might find itself striving valiantly all year to increase local currency earnings only to lose it all to an unexpected plunge in the exchange rate. Conversely, an increase in the exchange rate can just as easily turn a bad year for dollar earnings into a good one.

Subsidiary performance appears less random when we look at return on investment.

$$\text{ROI}_\$ = \frac{S\ [(P_c - VC_c)Q]}{S \times \text{Subsidiary assets}_c} = \frac{[(P_c - VC_c)]Q}{\text{Subsidiary assets}_c} = \text{ROI}_c$$

where the subscript $ indicates that the subscripted variable is denominated in dollars. The equation indicates that the subsidiary's ROI is independent of the exchange rate and has the same value whether measured in dollars or cruzeiros. It is appropriate, therefore, to hold subsidiary management responsible for its local currency ROI, and to measure financial performance according to the same yardstick. Moreover, subsidiary ROIs are comparable across countries and across currencies, regardless of exchange rates or inflation rates.

One practical word of warning: Beware of historical cost accounting when inflation is high, for in the presence of rapid inflation, a ratio consisting of this year's earnings divided by the depreciated, historical cost of old assets can produce ludicrously high ROIs. Be sure to write up the assets to some measure of their current value before calculating the subsidiary's return on investment.

Cross-Border Subsidiaries

Unfortunately, single-country subsidiaries are the exception, not the rule. More commonly, a subsidiary generates revenues and costs that are denominated in several currencies. For a brief look at the evaluation of such cross-border subsidiaries, suppose our Brazilian subsidiary is the marketing arm of its U.S. parent, that it imports everything it sells from the parent, and that it sells everything in Brazil. Assume too that the parent wants to be paid in dollars, while the subsidiary prices its sales in cruzeiros. Then, ignoring fixed costs, and writing an expression for the subsidiary's dollar earnings as before,

$$\text{Subsidiary earnings (in dollars)} = S\left[\left(P_c - \frac{VC_{\$}}{S}\right)Q\right]$$

where all the terms are as previously defined. This equation says simply that the subsidiary's dollar earnings equal the exchange rate times its cruzeiro earnings, where the latter is revenues, $(P_c \times Q)$, minus costs, $(VC_{\$} \times Q/S)$. To confirm the cost expression, when the parent sells the subsidiary $100,000 of merchandise and one cruzeiro costs 10 cents, the subsidiary's cruzeiro costs are 1 million cruzeiros (100,000/0.10).

The above equation reveals that our problem is now more complicated. When a subsidiary operates in a single country, the exchange rate disappears from ROI, and life is pretty simple. But when the subsidiary's cash flows are denominated in more than one currency, the effect of the exchange rate is more pervasive. In our two-country example, the exchange rate affects dollar earnings in two distinct ways. It translates the subsidiary's cruzeiro earnings into dollars, as in the single-country case. And it affects the subsidiary's cost of goods sold. The latter is known as the *competitive effect* of exchange rates because a change in costs directly affects the subsidiary's competitive position relative to rivals. Thus a fall in the dollar price of the cruzeiro from 10 cents to, say, 5 cents will double the subsidiary's cost of goods sold, an event which could severely affect earnings and market share. On the other hand, a rise in price of the cruzeiro would have just the opposite competitive effects.

The implications of this competitive effect for a subsidiary's earnings and ROI are difficult to assess and can range from major to trivial, depending on the subsidiary's ability to respond to changing costs. If the subsidiary faces intense local competition and cannot increase prices when costs rise, the full adverse effect of a cheaper cruzeiro will be felt in earnings and ROI. Conversely, an ability to pass the full extent of cost increases on to customers in the form of higher prices immunizes the subsidiary's earnings and ROI from a weak cruzeiro.

So what does this imply for international performance appraisal? It may appear that a foreign subsidiary's earnings are so dependent on inexplicable changes in exchange rates that objective performance evaluation is almost impossible. But the situation is not quite so bleak, for at least two reasons. First, exchange-rate movements are not entirely capricious. Some movements are quite appropriate economically and tend to simplify international performance appraisal, not complicate it. Second, there is reason to believe that the random elements of exchange rate movements tend to offset one another over time, so that long-run performance is less subject to chance than year-to-year figures would suggest.

This is not the place for a detailed study of exchange rates; nonetheless, a brief look at the stabilizing nature of some rate movements will prove instructive. Let's assume for the moment that exchange rates move in opposition to inflation rates, so that countries experiencing rapid inflation have depreciating currencies, and vice versa. Table 2A–1 shows the implications of this relationship for our subsidiary when Brazilian prices double. Observe in column two of the table that a doubling of Brazilian prices will enable the subsidiary to increase its cruzeiro prices and, because its costs are in dollars, this will tend to increase earnings as long as the exchange rate stays constant. In fact, a doubling of the Brazilian price level will cause dollar earnings to jump sixfold if the exchange rate does not change. But when high inflation engenders a weak currency as conjectured, the falling cruzeiro will raise the subsidiary's costs and prevent earnings from increasing. This is confirmed in column three of the table by the fact that the subsidiary's dollar earnings are unchanged from last year when the cruzeiro falls by half. Clearly, exchange-rate movements in opposition to inflation rates are stabilizing, not destabilizing.

TABLE 2A–1
Performance of Brazilian Subsidiary When Brazilian Prices Double

		This Year	
	Last Year	Exchange Rate Constant	Exchange Rate Halves
Exchange rate (S)	$0.10	0.10	0.05
Price per unit (P_c)	crz100	200	200
Cost per unit ($C_\$$)	$8	8	8
Units sold (Q)	1,000	1,000	1,000
Earnings in cruzeiros:			
Revenues	crz100,000	200,000	200,000
Costs	crz80,000	80,000	160,000
Earnings	crz20,000	120,000	40,000
Earnings in dollars	$2,000	12,000	2,000

The same is also true in reverse. High U.S. inflation coupled with a stable exchange rate increases costs and reduces earnings; but this time a strengthening cruzeiro again keeps dollar earnings constant. We conclude that as long as exchange rates move in opposition to inflation rates, they stabilize subsidiary income and ROI. Such "warranted" changes in exchange rates act as economic "shock absorbers," protecting subsidiary earnings and ROIs from the effects of differing inflation rates among countries.

Purchasing Power Parity.   Why might exchange rates move in opposition to inflation rates? The answer is *purchasing power parity,* or PPP to its friends, which says—quite plausibly—that exchange rates should adjust so that a dollar buys about the same amount of merchandise in one country as in another. If a dollar buys six ounces of beef in America, it should buy about the same amount in Brazil or England or Malaysia. Moreover, the theory goes on to argue that large deviations of exchange rates from their PPP values carry the seeds of their own destruction; as the deviations grow, speculators will find it increasingly profitable to buy goods in low-price countries for immediate resale in high-price ones, thereby driving prices and exchange rates back toward parity.

Using PPP to relate the price of beef in the U.S. to that in Brazil,

$$\frac{\$ \text{ price}}{\text{of beef}} = S \left(\frac{\text{crz price}}{\text{of beef}} \right)$$

which implies that if six ounces of beef costs a dollar in America and, say, 10 cruzeiros in Brazil, the exchange rate, S, should equal 10 cents. Finally, looking at the tie between exchange rates and inflation, the equation indicates that if Brazilian prices were to double, so that six ounces of beef now costs 20 cruzeiros, the exchange rate should fall by half, to 5 cents. According to PPP, exchange rates will move in opposition to inflation rates.

If exchange rates moved only according to the dictates of purchasing power parity, the world would be a better place—or at least a simpler one. For then exchange rate changes would eliminate the distorting effects of differing inflation rates among countries; foreign subsidiary earnings, measured in dollars, and ROIs would not depend on exchange rates or foreign inflation rates; and assessing the performance of foreign operations would pose no special challenges. Regrettably, exchange rates diverge frequently and widely from their PPP values, injecting considerable volatility into cross-border activities and considerable ambiguity into the evaluation of foreign subsidiary performance.

For a look at just how widely exchange rates depart from their parity values, Table 2A–2 presents part of what *The Economist*—that fine weekly magazine of world affairs and business—calls its Big Mac index, published with tongue only partly in cheek since 1986. Big Mac hamburgers are sold throughout the world, contain a variety of basic, locally produced commodities, and are virtually identical from one country to the next. If PPP holds, the dollar cost of a Big Mac should be the same around the world. Conversely, the extent to which the dollar cost differs among countries is a measure of the divergence of exchange rates from parity. For instance, the table indicates that the mean price of a Big Mac in four U.S. cities in early 1991 was $2.25, while the price in Germany was DM 4.30; so an exchange rate of $1 = DM 1.91 would render the dollar price of a Big Mac the same in both countries (1.91 = 4.30/2.25). The fact that the actual exchange rate was only $1 = DM 1.67 suggests that the dollar was undervalued relative to Big Mac parity by 13 percent ([1.67 − 1.91]/1.91).

As the Big Mac index and other more somber studies of exchange rate behavior suggest, exchange rates might best be thought of as connected to their PPP values by a lengthy rubber band. Rates are free to wander about their parity values by as much as ± 30 to 35 percent before the rubber tether begins to pull them back toward parity. Moreover, vagrant rates can wander away from their parity values for as long as five years before the rubber band begins to pull them back toward PPP.

TABLE 2A–2
The Big Mac Index of Foreign Exchange Rates (April 1991)

Currency	Hamburger Prices in Local Currency	Implied PPP+ of the Dollar	Actual Exchange Rate 4/09/91	% Over (+) or Under (−) Valuation of the Dollar
Australia	A$2.45	1.09	1.27	+17
Britain	£1.67	0.74	0.56	−24
Canada	C$2.35	1.04	1.15	+11
France	FFr18.00	8.00	5.65	−29
Germany	DM4.30	1.91	1.67	−13
Japan	¥380	169.00	135.00	−20
S. Korea	won2,100	933.00	721.00	−23
United States	$2.25	—	—	—

+PPP = foreign currency price of Big Mac/$ price of Big Mac.

Source: *The Economist*, "Big MacCurrencies," April 13–19, 1991, p. 78. Copyright 1991, The Economist Newspaper, Ltd. Reprinted with permission.

Given this pattern of exchange-rate movements, here is some practical advice for managers charged with assessing the performance of international operations. First, recognize the complexity of the task and be suspicious of simple solutions. Unwarranted and unanticipated changes in exchange rates can significantly affect international performance and performance measurement. Second, when evaluating an international manager's performance, take note of the extent to which the currencies involved appear to be above or below their PPP values, and how these deviations might color the observed performance. Third, when making long-term international decisions, such as investment or disinvestment in a country, do not attach undue importance to current exchange rates. Base your decision more on the analysis of alternatives, assuming exchange rates are at their PPP values. Long-run, actual performance can be expected to approximate your PPP results, with substantial year-to-year variations as exchange rates wander about their PPP values.

A closing comment regarding the evaluation of profit center performance: U.S. managers appear to be relearning an important lesson these days. It is short-sighted to manage anything strictly by the numbers. Executives need to take a broader, more qualitative view of the evaluation process, even when such a perspective reduces objectivity and dilutes incentives. Corporations are too complicated to allow the substitution of mechanical rules for creative thought. Numerical measures of performance are valuable tools, but their use must be kept in perspective.

SOURCES FOR BUSINESS RATIOS

Check your library for:

Dun & Bradstreet Information Services. *Industry Norms and Key Business Ratios.* New York, published annually. Percentage balance sheets and 14 ratios for over one million U.S. corporations, partnerships, and proprietorships, both public and private, representing 800 lines of business as defined by SIC codes. Median-, upper-, and lower-quartile values.

Robert Morris Associates. *Annual Statement Studies.* Philadelphia, published annually. Common-size financial statements and widely used ratios in many business lines. Ratios broken out into six size ranges by sales and by assets. Also contains comparative historical data. One limitation is that only companies with assets of $250 million or less are included. Excellent bibliography entitled "Sources of Composite Financial Data."

Standard & Poor's. *Analysts Handbook.* Income statement, balance sheet, and share price data by industry for all companies in S & P 500 stock averages. Published annually with monthly supplements.

CHAPTER SUMMARY

1. Although a major corporation and the corner drugstore may seem vastly different, the levers by which managers in both firms affect performance are similar and few in number. The purpose of this chapter has been to study the ties between these levers and the firm's financial performance.
2. Return on equity is the most popular single yardstick of financial performance, although it does suffer from timing, risk, and value problems.
3. The primary components of return on equity are the profit margin, the asset turnover ratio, and financial leverage. The profit margin summarizes income statement performance; the asset turnover ratio focuses on the left side of the balance sheet and indicates how efficiently management has used the firm's assets; financial leverage looks at the right side of the balance sheet and how the company has financed its assets.
4. Turnover-control ratios are very important for operating managers. They indicate the efficiency with which the company uses a specific type of asset, such as accounts receivable or inventories.
5. More financial leverage is not always better than less. Financial leverage can be measured by using balance sheet ratios or coverage ratios. The latter are usually superior for long-term debt.
6. Ratio analysis is the systematic examination of a number of company ratios in search of insights into the firm's operations and its financial vitality. Used creatively, ratios are useful tools; but they can be misleading if applied mechanically.

ADDITIONAL READING

Bernstein, Leopold A. *Financial Statement Analysis: Theory, Application, and Interpretation.* 4th ed. Homewood, Ill.: Richard D. Irwin, 1988.
   A detailed examination of financial statements and their uses from an accounting perspective. Not what I would call exciting reading, but particularly levelheaded and thorough.

Eccles, Robert G. "The Performance Measurement Manifesto." *Harvard Business Review* (January/February 1991), pp. 131–37.

A purple-passioned plea for inclusion of nonfinancial performance measures in performance appraisal that, nonetheless, offers useful insights into the reasons performance measures have remained so finance-bound, the weaknesses of financial measures of performance, and the steps necessary to implement a broader performance measurement system.

Gallinger, George W. *Liquidity Analysis and Management.* 2nd ed. Reading, Mass.: Addison-Wesley, 1991, 642 pages.

A textbook on the management of current assets and liabilities. Topics covered include cash flow analysis; off-balance sheet financing; international cash management; hedging with futures, options, and swaps; and asset-based financing. Intended for advanced finance students and practicing professionals. A thorough look at an important, but neglected topic.

CHAPTER PROBLEMS

1. In 1990, Natural Selection, a nationwide computer dating service, had $80 million of assets and $50 million of liabilities. Earnings before interest and taxes were $10 million, interest expense was $5 million, the tax rate was 40 percent, sinking fund requirements were $2 million, and annual dividends were 40 cents per share on 5 million shares outstanding.
   a. Calculate:
      (1) Natural Selection's liabilities-to-equity ratio,
      (2) assets-to-equity ratio,
      (3) liabilities-to-assets ratio,
      (4) times interest earned,
      (5) times burden covered.
   b. What percentage decline in earnings before interest and taxes could Natural Selection have sustained before failing to cover
      (1) sinking fund requirements,
      (2) common dividend payments?
2. A company's assets-to-equity ratio is 250 percent. Show that its liabilities-to-equity ratio is 150 percent.
3. XYZ Corporation earns a 12 percent profit margin on sale of its high-technology electronic calibrators. The manager of the calibrator division strongly opposes introduction of a new mass-market calibrator because its anticipated profit margin is only 6 percent. She argues that the new calibrator can only lower division returns. Do you believe this is a valid argument against introduction of the new calibrator? Why, or why not?
4. An executive argues against acquiring another business because the acquisition will reduce his company's ROE. Do you find this argument convincing? Why, or why not?
5. a. Calculate ABC Corporation's ROE, ROA, and ROIC given the following information:

Earnings before interest and tax	$100
Interest expense	10
Earnings before tax	90
Tax @ 40%	36
Earnings after tax	$ 54
Assets = $500; Equity = $400	

b. ABC management intends to raise $300 in debt, with an interest rate of 10 percent, and to repurchase its own shares so as to reduce equity to $100. Assuming EBIT remains constant, calculate ROE, ROA, and ROIC after this recapitalization.

c. After recapitalization is ABC Corporation a better company because ROE is higher? Is it worse because ROA is lower? What do you make of the fact that ROIC does not change?

6. Given the following facts, complete the balance sheet below.

Payables period	10 days
Liabilities to assets	60 percent
Inventory turnover	5.0 times
Current ratio	2.0 times
Days' sales in cash	12 days
Collection period	40 days

(You may assume that all sales are credit sales, ratios are based on a 365-day year, and the payables period is based on cost of goods sold.)

Assets

Cash	$ 100,000
Accounts receivable	
Inventory	400,000
Total current assets	
Net fixed assets	
Total assets	$1,000,000

Liabilities and Owners' Equity

Accounts payable	$
Short-term debt	
Total current liabilities	
Long-term debt	
Shareholders' equity	
Total liabilities & equity	$

PART 2

PLANNING FUTURE FINANCIAL PERFORMANCE

CHAPTER 3

FINANCIAL FORECASTING

Planning is the substitution of error for chaos.
Anonymous

To this point we have looked at the *past,* evaluating existing financial statements and assessing past performance. It is time now to look to the *future.* We begin in this chapter with an examination of the principal techniques of financial forecasting and a brief overview of planning and budgeting as practiced by modern, large corporations. The following chapter will look at planning problems unique to the management of company growth. Throughout this chapter our emphasis will be on the *techniques* of forecasting and planning; so as a counterweight, it will be important for you to bear in mind that proper technique is only a part of effective planning. At least as critical is the development of creative market strategies and operating policies which underlie the financial plans.

PRO FORMA STATEMENTS

Finance is central to a company's planning activities for at least two reasons. First, much of the language of forecasting and planning is financial. Plans are stated in terms of financial statements, and many of the measures used to evaluate the plan are financial. Second, and more important, the financial executive is responsible for a critical resource: money. Because virtually every corporate action has financial implications, a critical part of any plan is the determination of whether it is attainable, given the company's limited resources.

Companies typically prepare a wide array of plans and budgets. Some, such as production plans and staff budgets, focus on a particular aspect of the firm, while others, such as pro forma statements, are much broader in scope. Our strategy here will be to begin with the broader techniques and to talk briefly about more specialized procedures later when addressing planning in large corporations.

The preparation of pro forma financial statements is the most widely used technique for financial forecasting. A pro forma statement is nothing more than a prediction of what a company's financial statements will look like at the end of the forecast period. These predictions may be the culmination of intensive, detailed operating plans and budgets or nothing more than rough, back-of-the-envelope projections. Either way, the pro forma format displays the information in a logical, internally consistent manner. A major use of pro forma forecasts, as will become apparent below, is to estimate the company's future need for external financing.

Percent-of-Sales Forecasting

One simple, yet effective way to project company financial performance is to tie many of the income statement and balance sheet figures to future sales. The rationale for this percent-of-sales approach is the tendency, noted earlier, for all variable costs and most current assets and current liabilities to vary directly with sales. Obviously, this will not be true for all of the entries in a company's financial statements, and certainly some independent forecasts of individual items will be required. Nonetheless, the percent-of-sales method does provide simple, logical estimates of many important variables.

The first step in a percent-of-sales forecast should be an examination of historical data to determine which financial statement items have varied in proportion to sales in the past. This will enable the forecaster to decide which items can safely be estimated as a percent of sales and which must be forecast by using other information. The second step is to forecast sales. Because so many other items will be linked mechanically to the sales forecast, it is critically important to estimate sales as accurately as possible. Also, once the pro forma statements are completed, it is a good idea to test the sensitivity of the results to reasonable variations in the sales forecast. The final step in the percent-of-sales forecast is to estimate individual financial statement items by extrapolating the historical patterns to the newly estimated sales. For instance, if inventories have historically been about 20 percent of sales, and if next year's sales are forecasted to be $10 million, we would expect inventories to be $2 million. It's that simple.

To illustrate the use of the percent-of-sales method, consider the problem faced by Suburban National Bank. R&E Supplies, Inc., a modest-sized wholesaler of plumbing and electrical supplies, has been a customer of the bank for a number of years. The company has maintained average deposits of approximately $30,000 and has had a $50,000 short-term, renewable loan for five years. The company has prospered, and the loan has been renewed annually with only cursory analysis.

In late 1990, the president of R&E Supplies visited the bank and requested an increase in the short-term loan for 1991 to $500,000. The president explained that despite the company's growth, accounts payable had increased steadily and cash balances had declined. A number of suppliers had recently threatened to put the company on COD for future purchases unless payments were received more promptly. When asked why he was requesting $500,000, the president replied that this amount seemed "about right" and that it would enable him to pay off his most insistent creditors and to rebuild his cash balances.

Knowing that the bank's credit committee would never approve a loan request of this magnitude without careful financial projections, the lending officer suggested that he and the president prepare pro forma financial statements for 1991. He explained that these statements would provide a more accurate indication of R&E's credit needs.

The first step in preparing the pro forma projections was to examine the company's financial statements for the years 1987 to 1990, shown in Table 3–1, in search of stable patterns. The results of this ratio analysis appear in Table 3–2. The president's concern about declining liquidity and increasing trade payables is well founded; cash and securities have fallen from 6 percent of sales to 2 percent, while accounts payable have risen from 9 to 16 percent. In terms of the payables period, defined as accounts payable divided by cost of goods sold per day, the increase has been from 39 days to 66 days. Another worrisome trend is the increase in cost of goods

TABLE 3-1

Financial Statements for R&E Supplies, Inc. December 31, 1987–1990 ($000)

Income Statements	1987	1988	1989	1990*
Net sales	$11,190	$13,764	$16,104	$20,613
Cost of goods sold	9,400	11,699	13,688	17,727
Gross profit	1,790	2,065	2,416	2,886
Expenses:				
General, selling, and administrative expenses	1,019	1,239	1,610	2,267
Net interest expense	100	103	110	90
Earnings before tax	671	723	696	529
Tax	302	325	313	238
Earnings after tax	$ 369	$ 398	$ 383	$ 291

Balance Sheets

Assets

	1987	1988	1989	1990*
Current assets:				
Cash and securities	$ 671	$ 551	$ 644	$ 412
Accounts receivable	1,343	1,789	2,094	2,886
Inventories	1,119	1,376	1,932	2,267
Prepaid expenses	14	12	15	18
Total current assets	3,147	3,728	4,685	5,583
Net fixed assets	128	124	295	287
Total assets	$3,275	$3,852	$4,980	$5,870

Liabilities and owners' equity

	1987	1988	1989	1990*
Current liabilities:				
Bank loan	$ 50	$ 50	$ 50	$ 50
Accounts payable	1,007	1,443	2,426	3,212
Current portion long-term debt	60	50	50	100
Accrued wages	5	7	10	18
Total current liabilities	1,122	1,550	2,536	3,380
Long-term debt	960	910	860	760
Common stock	150	150	150	150
Retained earnings	1,043	1,242	1,434	1,580
Total liabilities and owners' equity	$3,275	$3,852	$4,980	$5,870

*Estimate.

TABLE 3–2
Selected Financial Statement Items as a Percentage
of Sales for R&E Supplies, Inc., 1987– 1991

	1987	1988	1989	1990*	1991†
Annual increase in sales	—	23%	17%	28%	25%
Percent of sales:					
Cost of goods sold	84	85	85	86	86
General, selling, and					
administrative expenses	9	9	10	11	12
Cash and securities	6	4	4	2	5
Accounts receivable	12	13	13	14	14
Inventories	10	10	12	11	10
Accounts payable	9	10	15	16	14
Tax/Earnings before tax‡	0.45	0.45	0.45	0.45	0.45
Dividends/Earnings after tax	0.50	0.50	0.50	0.50	0.50

*Estimate.
†Forecast.
‡Including state and local taxes.

sold and general, selling, and administrative expenses in proportion to sales. Earnings clearly are not keeping pace with sales.

The last column in Table 3–2 contains the projections agreed to by R&E's president and the lending officer. In line with recent experience, sales are predicted to increase 25 percent over 1990. General, selling, and administrative expenses will continue to rise as a result of an unfavorable labor settlement. The president feels that cash and securities should rise to at least 5 percent of sales, or 18 days' sales. Since much of this money will sit in his bank, the lending officer concurs. The president also feels that accounts payable should decline to no more than 14 percent of sales, giving the company a payables period of 59 days.[1] The tax rate and the dividends-to-earnings ratio are expected to stay constant.

The resulting pro forma financial statements appear in Table 3–3. Looking first at the income statement, the implication of the above assumptions is that earnings after tax will decline to

---

[1]

$$\text{Payables period} = \frac{\text{Accounts payable}}{\text{Cost of goods sold per day}} = \frac{14\% \text{ Sales}}{86\% \text{ Sales}/365} = 59 \text{ days}$$

TABLE 3–3
Pro Forma Financial Statements for R&E Supplies, Inc.
December 31, 1991 ($000)

Income Statement

	1991	*Comments*
Net sales	$25,766	25% increase
Cost of goods sold	22,159	86% of sales
Gross profit	3,607	
Expenses:		
General, selling, and		
administrative expenses	3,092	12% of sales
Net interest expense	90	Initially constant
Earnings before tax	425	
Tax	191	At 45% tax rate
Earnings after tax	$ 234	

Balance Sheet

Assets

Current assets:		
Cash and securities............	$ 1,288	5% of sales
Accounts receivable	3,607	14% of sales
Inventories	2,577	10% of sales
Prepaid expenses	20	Rough estimate
Total current assets	7,492	
Net fixed assets.................	280	See text discussion
Total assets	$ 7,772	

Liabilities and owners' equity

Current liabilities:		
Bank loan	PLUG	
Accounts payable	$ 3,607	14% of sales
Current portion long-term debt	100	See text discussion
Accrued wages	22	Rough estimate
Total current liabilities	3,729	+ PLUG
Long-term debt	660	
Common stock..................	150	
Retained earnings	1,697	See text discussion
Total liabilities and owners' equity ..	$ 6,236	+ PLUG

$234,000, down 20 percent from the prior year. The only entry on this statement requiring further comment is net interest expense. Net interest expense will clearly depend on the size of the loan required by the company. However, because we do not know this yet, net interest expense has initially been assumed to equal last year's value with the understanding that this assumption may have to be modified later.

Estimating the Plug

To most operating executives, a company's income statement is more interesting than its balance sheet because the income statement measures profitability. The reverse is true for the financial executive. When the object of the exercise is to estimate future financing requirements, the income statement is interesting only insofar as it affects the balance sheet. To the financial executive, the balance sheet is key.

The first entry on R&E's pro forma balance sheet (Table 3–3) requiring comment is prepaid expenses. Like accrued wages, prepaid expenses is a small item that increases erratically with sales. Since the amounts are small and a high degree of precision in the forecast is not required, rough estimates will suffice.

When asked about new fixed assets, the president indicated that a $43,000 capital budget had already been approved for 1991. Further, depreciation for the year would be $50,000, so net fixed assets would decline $7,000 to $280,000 ($280,000 = $287,000 + $43,000 − $50,000).

Note that the bank loan is labeled PLUG. We will calculate the bank loan that must be "plugged" into the balance sheet to make total assets equal liabilities and owners' equity. Continuing down the balance sheet, "current portion of long-term debt" is just the principal repayment due in 1992. It is a contractual commitment specified in the loan agreement. As this required payment becomes a current liability, the accountant shifts it from long-term debt to current portion long-term debt.

The last entry in need of explanation is retained earnings. Since the company does not plan to sell new equity in 1991, common stock remains constant. Retained earnings are determined as follows:

$$\frac{\text{Retained}}{\text{earnings}}\text{'91} = \frac{\text{Retained}}{\text{earnings}}\text{'90} + \frac{\text{Earnings}}{\text{after tax}}\text{'91} - \text{Dividends '91}$$

$$\$1,697,000 \quad = \$1,580,000 \quad + \$234,000 \quad - \$117,000$$

In words, when a business earns a profit larger than its dividend, the excess adds to retained earnings. The retained earnings account is the principal bridge between a company's income statement and its balance sheet, so that as profits rise, retained earnings grow, and loan needs decline. Sometimes companies will complicate this equation by charging nonrecurring gains or losses directly to retained earnings. But this is not a problem here.

The final step in constructing R&E's pro formas is to determine the size of the plug. We know from the principles of double-entry bookkeeping that

$$\text{Total assets} = \text{Liabilities} + \text{Owners' equity}$$

Using the forecasted amounts, this means that

$$\$7,772,000 = \$6,236,000 + \text{PLUG}$$
$$\text{PLUG} = \$1,536,000$$

According to our forecast, R&E Supplies needs not $500,000 but *over $1.5 million* to achieve the president's objectives.

The lending officer for Suburban National Bank is apt to be of two minds about this result. On one hand, R&E has a projected 1991 accounts receivable balance in excess of $3.5 million, which would probably provide excellent security for a $1.5 million loan. On the other hand, R&E's cavalier attitude toward financial planning and the president's obvious lack of knowledge about where his company is headed are definite negatives.

PRO FORMA STATEMENTS AND FINANCIAL PLANNING

To this point R&E's pro forma statements have just displayed the financial implications of the company's operating plans. This is the forecasting half of the exercise. Now R&E management is ready to begin financial planning. This involves review of the forecasts and consideration of whether the operating plans should be modified. The first step is to decide whether the initial pro formas are satisfactory. This involves assessment of the financial health of the company as revealed in the pro formas, with special attention devoted to whether the estimated plug is too large. If the answer is yes, either because R&E does not want to borrow $1.5 million or because the bank is unwilling to grant such a large loan, management must modify its plans to conform to the financial realities. This is where operating plans and financial plans merge to create a coherent strategy.

To illustrate, suppose R&E management wants to reduce the size of the plug. It might then decide to test the following revisions in its operating plans for their impact on the company's external financing needs: (1) moderate the buildup in liquidity so that cash and securities are only 4 percent of sales instead of 5, (2) tighten up collection of accounts receivable so that receivables are 12 percent of sales rather than 14 percent, and (3) settle for a more modest improvement in trade payables so that payables equal 15 percent of sales rather than 14 percent. In combination, these reductions in assets and increases in liabilities would reduce R&E's plug by just under $1 million [(3 percent reduction in assets + 1 percent increase in liabilities) × net sales = $1 million].

Although each of these actions reduces R&E's need for external financing, each clearly has some offsetting disadvantages, so we cannot say for certain that the revised operating plan is necessarily better than the original one. It should be evident, however, that the pro forma format is useful for evaluating the financial dimensions of alternative operating strategies.

Sensitivity Analysis

Sensitivity analysis is the formal name for "what if" questions: What if R&E's sales grow by 15 percent instead of 25 percent? What if cost of goods sold is 84 percent of sales instead of 86 percent? It involves systematically changing one of the assumptions on which the pro forma statements are based and observing how the forecast responds. The exercise is useful in at least two ways. First, it provides information about the range of possible outcomes. For example, suppose sensitivity analysis reveals that, depending on the future sales volume attained, a company's need for external financing could vary between $1.5 and $2 million. This tells management that it had better have enough flexibility in its financing plans to add an extra $500,000 in new debt as the future unfolds. A second use of sensitivity analysis involves management by exception. Sensitivity analysis enables managers to determine which assumptions most strongly affect the forecast and which are secondary. This enables management to concentrate their data-gathering and forecasting efforts on the most critical assumptions. Subsequently, during implementation of the plan, the same information enables management to focus their attention on those factors most critical to the success of the plan.

Personal computers and financial spreadsheets have greatly increased the popularity of sensitivity analysis in business decisions. Once the basic pro forma forecast is complete, additional trials based on revised assumptions can be spun out in seconds. But be forewarned: A properly executed sensitivity analysis is not always as simple as it might appear. To illustrate, suppose we want to estimate R&E Supplies' loan needs assuming sales fall 15 percent below expectations. One approach is simply to cut forecasted sales 15 percent and recalculate R&E's plug, resulting in an apparent reduced loan need. The problem with this approach is that it implicitly assumes the shortfall in sales will not affect any of the other estimates underlying the forecast. Thus, if the proper assumption is that inventories will initially rise when sales fall below expectations, failure to include this relationship will cause an underestimate of the plug. The moral is that testing the sensitivity of R&E's plug to changes in sales requires more than just changing sales. It requires a careful rethink of each of the variables that depend on sales to either reaffirm the original assumption or to substitute a new one.

Simulation

Simulation is an elaborate, computer-assisted extension of sensitivity analysis. To perform a simulation we begin by assigning a probability distribution to each uncertain element in the forecast. The distribution describes the possible values that the variable could conceivably take on, and it states the probability of each value occurring. The next step is to ask a computer to pick at random a value for each uncertain variable consistent with the assigned probability distribution and to generate a set of pro forma statements based on the selected values. This creates one *trial*. Performing the last step many times produces a large number of trials. The output from a simulation is a table, or a graph, summarizing the results of many trials. For example, the output from a simulation study of R&E's loan needs for 1991 involving 1,000 trials might be the following.

Projected Loan Need	Number of Trials Occurring	Percent of Trials Occurring
$ 751,000–$1,000,000	150	15%
1,001,000– 1,250,000	200	20
1,251,000– 1,500,000	300	30
1,501,000– 1,750,000	200	20
1,751,000– 2,000,000	100	10
More than $2,000,000	50	5
Total	1,000	100%

These results suggest that there is a 30 percent chance R&E's plug will be in the $1.25 to $1.50 million range, but that there is a 5 percent chance it will top $2 million.

The principal advantage of simulation over sensitivity analysis is that all of the uncertain input variables are allowed to vary at once. The principal disadvantage of simulation, in my experience, is that the results are often hard to interpret. One reason is that few executives are used to thinking about future events in terms of a range of possible outcomes or probabilities of outcomes. In terms of the above chart, should the company be prepared to raise in excess of $2 million, or is the 5 percent chance of this need occurring too remote to warrant concern? What is a reasonable maximum loan need the company should be prepared to meet?

A second reason simulation is less useful than sensitivity analysis in practice recalls President Eisenhower's dictum that "It's not the plans, but the planning that matters." With simulation much of the "planning" occurs inside a computer, and management sees only the results. Consequently management does not develop the depth of insight into the company and its future prospects that occurs when simpler techniques are used.

Interest Expense

One thing that bothers attentive novices about pro forma forecasting is the circularity involving interest expense and indebtedness. As noted above, interest expense cannot be estimated accurately until the plug has been determined. Yet because the plug depends in part on the amount of interest expense, it would appear one cannot be accurately estimated without the other.

There are two ways around this dilemma. One is to define a set of simultaneous equations to solve for interest expense and the plug together. If you are using a computer spreadsheet, this is equivalent to asking the computer to work through the statements several times, with each pass coming closer to the simultaneous solution. The other more pragmatic approach is to forget the whole problem with the expectation that the first-pass solution will be close enough. Given the likely errors in predicting sales and other variables, the additional error caused by a failure to determine interest expense accurately is usually not all that important.

To illustrate, R&E Supplies' first-pass pro formas assumed a net interest expense of $90,000, whereas the balance sheet indicates total interest-bearing debt of over $2.2 million. At an assumed interest rate of 10 percent, this volume of debt implies an interest expense of $220,000, not $90,000. If we subtract, say, $20,000 for the higher cash balances the firm is expected to carry in 1991, net interest expense should be about $200,000, or $110,000 higher than our first-pass estimate. But think what happens as we trace the impact of a $110,000 addition to interest expense through the income statement. As shown below, the increase in net interest expense reduces the addition to retained earnings by only $31,000 and increases the plug by the like amount. But when the plug is already over $1.5 million, what's another $31,000 among friends? Granted, increased interest expense has a noticeable percentage impact on earnings, but by the time the increase filters through taxes and dividend payments, the impact on the plug is quite modest.

	Original	Revised	Difference
Gross profit	$3,607	$3,607	
General, selling,			
administrative expenses	3,092	3,092	
Net interest expense	90	200	+110
Earnings before tax	425	315	−110
Tax	191	142	−49
Earnings after tax	234	173	−61
Dividend at 50%	117	87	−30
Addition to retained earnings	$ 117	$ 86	−$31

Seasonality

A more serious potential problem with pro forma statements and, indeed, all of the forecasting techniques mentioned in this chapter, is that the results are applicable only on the forecast date. The pro formas in Table 3–3 present an estimate of R&E Supplies' loan requirements on December 31, 1991. They say nothing about the company's need for financing on any other date before or after December 31. If a company has seasonal financing requirements, knowledge of year-end loan needs may be of little use in financial planning, since the year end may bear no relation whatever to the date of the company's peak financing need. To protect against this, you should make monthly or quarterly forecasts rather than annual ones. Alternatively, if the date of peak borrowing need is known, you can simply make this date the forecast horizon.

CASH FLOW FORECASTS

A cash flow forecast is just a listing of all anticipated sources of cash to the company and uses of cash by the company over the forecast period. The difference between forecasted sources and forecasted uses is the plug, which must be financed externally. Table 3–4 shows a 1991 cash flow forecast for R&E Supplies. The assumptions underlying the forecast are the same as those used to construct R&E's pro forma statements.

Cash flow forecasts are quite straightforward and easily understood. Their principal weakness compared to pro forma statements is that they are less informative. R&E's pro forma state-

TABLE 3–4
Cash Flow Forecast for R&E Supplies, Inc., 1991 ($000)

Sources of Cash	
Net income	$ 234
Depreciation	50
Decreases in assets or increases in liabilities:	
Increase in accounts payable	395
Increase in accrued wages	4
Total sources of cash	$ 683
Uses of Cash	
Dividends	$ 117
Increases in assets or decreases in liabilities:	
Increase in cash and securities	876
Increase in accounts receivable	721
Increase in inventories	310
Increase in prepaid expenses	2
Investment in fixed assets	43
Decrease in long-term debt	100
Decrease in short-term debt	50
Total uses of cash	$2,219

Determination of PLUG:

$$\text{Total sources} + \text{PLUG} = \text{Total uses}$$
$$\$683,000 + \text{PLUG} = \$2,219,000$$
$$\text{PLUG} = \$1,536,000$$

ments not only indicate the size of the loan required, they also provide information that is useful for evaluating the company's creditworthiness. Thus, the loan officer can assess the company's future financial position by analyzing the pro forma statements. Because the cash flow forecast presents only *changes* in the quantities represented, a similar analysis using cash flow forecasts would be much more difficult.

CASH BUDGETS

A cash budget is a list of all anticipated receipts of cash and disbursements of cash over the forecast period. It can be thought of as a detailed cash flow forecast in which all traces of accrual accounting have been eliminated.

Table 3–5 presents a monthly cash budget of TransInternational Manufacturing (TIM) for the third quarter of 1990. To purge the accounting data of all accrual effects, it is necessary to remember that a period of time elapses between a credit sale or a credit purchase and the receipt or disbursement of the associated cash. In TIM's case, a 60-day collection period on accounts receivable means there is an average lag of 60 days between a credit sale and the receipt of cash. Consequently, cash collections in any

TABLE 3–5
Cash Budget for TransInternational Manufacturing, 3rd Quarter, 1990 ($000)

	Actual		Forecast		
	May	June	July	August	September
		Raw Data			
Credit sales	$10,000	$14,000	$16,000	$19,000	$15,000
Credit purchases	$ 5,000	$ 6,000	$ 5,000	$12,000	$ 6,000
		Cash Budget			
Cash receipts:					
Sales for cash			$ 1,000	$ 1,000	$ 1,000
Collections from credit sales			10,000	14,000	16,000
(assumes 60-day lag, sale to collection)					
Sale of used machinery				19,000	
Total cash receipts			11,000	34,000	17,000
Cash disbursements:					
Purchases for cash			1,000	1,000	2,000
Payments for credit purchases			6,000	5,000	12,000
(assumes 30-day lag, purchase to payment)					
Wages and salaries			4,000	4,000	4,000
Interest payments					12,000
Principal payments					26,000
Dividends					8,000
Tax payments			3,000		
Total cash disbursements			14,000	10,000	64,000
Net cash receipts (disbursements)			($3,000)	$24,000	($47,000)
Determination of cash needs:					
Beginning cash			$15,000	$12,000	$36,000
Net receipts (disbursements)			(3,000)	24,000	(47,000)
Ending cash			12,000	36,000	(11,000)
Minimum cash desired (assumed)			10,000	10,000	10,000
Cash surplus (deficit)			$ 2,000	$26,000	($21,000)

month equal credit sales two months prior. The analogous lag for credit purchases is one month. Note that depreciation does not appear on a cash budget because it is not a disbursement of cash.

The bottom portion of TIM's cash budget illustrates the determination of cash needs. Observe that the ending cash balance for one month becomes the beginning balance for the next month. Comparing the ending cash balance to the desired minimum balance, as determined by management, yields an estimate of TIM's monthly cash surplus or deficit. The deficit corresponds to the plug in a pro forma forecast; it is the amount of money that must be raised on the forecast date to cover disbursements and to leave ending cash at the desired minimum. A forecasted cash surplus means that the company will have excess cash on that date and that ending cash will exceed the desired minimum by the forecasted amount.

Because a cash budget focuses so narrowly on the cash account, it is seldom used by operating executives as a general forecasting tool. Its principal application is by treasury specialists for managing the company's cash balances. TIM's cash budget suggests that surplus cash will be available for investment in July and August but that the investments chosen had better be liquid, because all of the excess cash, plus $21 million from other sources, will be required in September.

THE TECHNIQUES COMPARED

Although the formats differ, it should come as a relief to learn that all of the forecasting techniques considered in this chapter produce the same results. As long as the assumptions are the same and no arithmetic or accounting mistakes are made, all of the techniques will produce the same plug. Moreover, if your accounting skills are up to the task, it is possible to reconcile one format with another.

A second reassuring fact is that, regardless of which forecasting technique is used, the resulting estimate of new financing needs is not biased by inflation. Consequently, there is no need to resort to elaborate inflation adjustments when making financial forecasts in an inflationary environment. This is not to say that the need for new financing is independent of the inflation rate. Indeed, as will become apparent in the next chapter, the financing needs of most companies rise with inflation. Rather, we are saying that direct application of the previously described forecasting techniques will correctly indicate the need for external financing even in the presence of inflation.

Mechanically, then, the three forecasting techniques are equivalent, and the choice of which to use can depend on the purpose of the forecast. For most planning purposes and for credit analysis, I recommend pro forma statements because they present the information in a form suitable for additional financial analysis. For short-term forecasting and the management of cash, the cash budget is appropriate. A cash flow forecast is somewhere between the other two. It presents a broader picture of company operations than a cash budget and is easier to construct and more accessible to accounting novices than pro formas, but is also less informative than pro formas.

PLANNING IN LARGE COMPANIES

In a well-run company, financial forecasts are only the tip of the planning iceberg. Executives throughout the organization devote substantial time and effort toward developing strategic and operating plans that eventually become the basis for the company's financial plans. This formalized planning process is especially important in large, multidivision corporations because it is frequently a key means of coordination, communication, and motivation within the organization.

Effective planning in a large company usually involves three formal stages that recur on an annual cycle. In broad perspective, these stages can be viewed as a progressive narrowing of the strategic choices under consideration. In the first stage, headquarters executives and division managers hammer out a corporate strategy. This involves a broad-ranging analysis of the market threats and opportunities facing the company, an assessment of the company's own strengths and weaknesses, and a determination of the performance goals to be sought by each of the company's business

A Problem with Depreciation

XYZ Corporation is forecasting its financing needs for next year. The original forecast shows a plug of $10 million. On reviewing the forecast, the production manager, having just returned from an accounting seminar, recommends increasing depreciation next year—for reporting purposes only, not for tax purposes—by $1 million. He explains, rather condescendingly, that this will reduce net fixed assets $1 million, and because a reduction of an asset is a source of cash, this will reduce the plug by a like amount. Explain why the production manager is incorrect.

Answer: Increasing depreciation will reduce net fixed assets. However, it will also reduce provision for taxes and earnings after tax by the same amount. Since both are liability accounts and reduction of a liability is a use of cash, the whole exercise is a wash with respect to the size of the plug. This is consistent with cash budgeting, which ignores depreciation entirely. Here is a numerical example.

	Original Depreciation	Increase Depreciation	Change in Liability Account
Operating income	$10,000	$10,000	
Depreciation	4,000	5,000	
Earnings before tax	6,000	5,000	
Provision for tax @ 40%	2,400	2,000	−400
Earnings after tax	3,600	3,000	
Dividends	1,000	1,000	
Additions to retained earnings	$ 2,600	$ 2,000	−$ 600
Total change in liabilities			−$1,000

units. At this initial stage, the process is creative and largely qualitative. The role of financial forecasts is limited to outlining in general terms the resource constraints faced by the company and to testing the financial feasibility of alternative strategies.

In the second stage, division managers and department personnel translate the qualitative, market-oriented goals established in stage one into a set of internal division activities that is deemed necessary to achieve the agreed-upon goals. For example, if a stage-one goal is to increase product X's market share by at least 2 percent in the next 18 months, the stage-two plans define what division management must do to achieve this objective. At this point, top management will likely have indicated, in general terms, the resources to be allocated to each division, although no specific spending plans will have been authorized. So division management will find it necessary to prepare at least rough financial forecasts to make certain their plans are generally consistent with senior management's resource commitments.

In the third stage of the planning process, department personnel develop a set of quantitative plans and budgets based on the activities defined in stage two. This essentially involves putting a price tag on the agreed-upon division activities. The price tag appears in two forms: operating budgets and capital budgets. Although each company has its own definition of which expenditures are to appear on which budget, capital budgets customarily include expenditures on costly, long-lived assets, whereas operating budgets include recurring expenditures, such as materials, salaries, and so on.

The integration of these detailed divisional budgets at headquarters produces the corporation's financial forecast. If management has been realistic about available resources throughout the planning process, the forecast will contain few surprises. If not, headquarters executives may discover that in aggregate the spending plans of the divisions exceed available resources and that some revisions in division budgets will be necessary.

Chapters 7 and 8 will consider the financial analysis of investment opportunities in some detail. For now it is sufficient to acknowledge that corporate investment decisions are not made in a vacuum but rather are an integral part of the planning process described. This means, among other things, that even though a capital expenditure opportunity may appear to be financially attractive, it is likely to be rejected by senior management unless it furthers the attainment of agreed-upon corporate objectives. The proper perspective with regard to investment analysis, therefore, is that a company's strategic plans should create an umbrella under which operating and capital budgeting take place.

CHAPTER SUMMARY

1. This chapter has presented the principal techniques of financial forecasting and planning.
2. Pro forma statements are the best all-around means of financial forecasting. They are a projection of the company's income statement and balance sheet at the end of the forecast period.
3. Percent-of-sales forecasting is a simple but useful technique in which most income statement and many balance sheet entries are assumed to change in proportion to sales.
4. Most operating managers are concerned chiefly with the income statement. When the goal is forecasting the need for outside financing, the income statement is of interest only insofar as income affects the balance sheet.
5. Financial forecasting involves the extrapolation of past trends and agreed-upon changes into the future. Financial planning occurs when management evaluates the forecasts and considers possible modifications.
6. A cash budget is a less general way to forecast than pro forma statements. It consists of a list of anticipated cash receipts and disbursements and their net effects on the firm's cash balances. Done correctly and using the same assumptions, cash budgets and pro forma statements generate the same estimated need for outside financing.
7. Planning in most large companies involves three continuing cycles: (a) a strategic planning cycle in which senior management is most active, (b) an operational cycle in which divisional managers translate qualitative strategic goals into concrete plans, and (c) a budgeting cycle that essentially puts a price tag on the operational plans. Financial forecasting and planning are increasingly important in each succeeding stage of the process.

ADDITIONAL READING

McLaughlin, Hugh S., and J. Russell Boulding. *Financial Management with Lotus 1-2-3*. Englewood Cliffs, N.J.: Prentice Hall, 1986, 224 pages.

Personal computers are playing an increasingly important role in financial analysis. Here's a how-to book for constructing your own programs to take much of the drudgery out of the calculations recommended in this and following chapters.

CHAPTER PROBLEMS

1. The treasurer of Raycore Drilling, a wholesale distributor of well drilling and pumping gear, wants to estimate her company's cash balances for the last three months of 1991.

   Use the following information to construct a monthly cash budget for Raycore for October through December 1991. Does it appear from your results that the treasurer should concern herself with where to invest excess cash or with where to borrow money?

Sales (20 percent for cash, the rest on 30-day credit terms):

August actual	$140,000
September actual	400,000
October forecast	200,000
November forecast	80,000
December forecast	80,000

Purchases (all on 60-day terms):

August actual	180,000
September actual	400,000
October forecast	100,000
November forecast	40,000
December forecast	40,000
Wages payable monthly	60,000
Principal payment due in December	70,000
Interest due in December	30,000
Dividend payable in December	100,000
Taxes payable in November	60,000
Cash balance on October 1	100,000
Minimum desired cash balance	50,000

---

2. Continuing problem 1, Raycore Drilling's income statement and balance sheet for September 30, 1991, appear below. Additional information about Raycore's accounting methods and the treasurer's expectations for the 4th quarter 1991 is contained in the footnotes.

Raycore Drilling
Income Statement
9 months ending September 30, 1991 ($ 000s)

Net sales	$2,000
Cost of goods sold[1]	1,300
Gross profits	700
Selling and administrative expenses[2]	540
Interest	30
Depreciation[3]	30
Net profits before tax	100
Tax @ 33%	33
Net profits after tax	67

Balance Sheet
September 30, 1991
($ 000s)

Assets

Cash		100
Accounts receivable		320
Inventory		600
Total current assets		$1,020
Gross fixed assets	$300	
Accumulated depreciation	50	
Net fixed assets		250
Total assets		$1,270

Liabilities

Bank loan		$ 0
Accounts payable		580
Miscellaneous accruals[4]		20
Current portion long-term debt[5]		70
Taxes payable		100
Total current liabilities		$ 770
Long-term debt		330
Shareholders' equity		170
Total liabilities and shareholders' equity		$1,270

[1]Cost of goods sold consists entirely of purchase costs and is expected to continue to equal 65 percent of net sales.
[2]Selling and administrative expenses consist entirely of wages.
[3]Depreciation is at the rate of $10,000 per quarter.
[4]Miscellaneous accruals are not expected to change in the 4th quarter.
[5]1992 principal payments on long-term debt will be $50,000.

    a. Using this information and information in question 1, construct a pro forma income statement for the 4th quarter of 1991 and a pro forma balance sheet for December 31, 1991. Use the bank loan as your plug.

    b. Does the December 31, 1991, loan need you estimated in question 1 above equal your plug? Should they be equal?

    c. Do your pro forma forecasts tell you more than your cash budget about Raycore's financial prospects? In particular, do you think Raycore should reconsider its December dividend?

3. Based on your answer to question 2, construct a 4th quarter cash flow forecast for Raycore Drilling.

4. How would you interpret a negative plug?

5. Below are 1990 financial statements of L.M. Wilson, Inc. For 1991 assume

    (a) Sales will increase 20 percent.

    (b) Investment in fixed assets will be $20 million.

    (c) Cost of goods sold, accounts receivable, inventories, and accounts payable will rise in proportion to sales.

    (d) Dividends will equal 50 percent of profit after tax.

    (e) General selling expenses, depreciation, tax rate, long-term debt, and common stock will not change.

    a. If the company wants to maintain a minimum cash balance of at least $4 million, how large a bank loan will be required at year-end 1991? Please ignore any increases in interest expense.

    b. How large a loan will Wilson need if its inventory turnover ratio falls to 2.4 times?

    c. How large a loan will Wilson need if its inventory turnover ratio falls to 2.4 *and* the company eliminates its dividend?

L.M. Wilson, Inc.
Income Statement and Balance Sheet
December 31, 1990 ($ millions)

Net sales		$100
Cost of goods sold		70
Gross profit		$ 30
General selling expenses		5
Depreciation		5
Interest expense		5
Profit before tax		15
Tax at 34%		5
Profit after tax		10
Dividends paid		5
Additions to retained earnings		$ 5
Assets		
Cash		$ 10
Accounts receivable		20
Inventories		25
Total current assets		$ 55
Gross fixed assets	$150	
Accumulated depreciation	70	
Net fixed assets		80
Total assets		$135
Liabilities and shareholders' equity		
Accounts payable		$ 5
Bank loan		25
Total current liabilities		$ 30
Long-term debt		50
Common stock		20
Retained earnings		35
Total liabilities and shareholders' equity		$135

CHAPTER 4

MANAGING GROWTH

Alas, the road to success is always under repair.
Anonymous

Growth and the management of growth present special problems in financial planning, in part because many executives see growth as something to be maximized. Their reasoning is simply that, as growth increases, the firm's market share and profits should rise as well. From a financial perspective, however, growth is not always a blessing. Rapid growth can put considerable strain on a company's resources, and unless management is aware of this effect and takes active steps to control it, rapid growth can lead to bankruptcy. Companies can literally grow broke. It is a sad truth that almost as many companies go bankrupt because they grow too fast as do those who grow too slowly. It is doubly sad to realize that those companies that grew too fast met the market test by providing a product people wanted and failed only because they lacked the financial acumen to manage their growth properly.

At the other end of the spectrum, companies that grow too slowly have a different, but no less pressing, set of financial concerns. As will become apparent, if these companies fail to appreciate the financial implications of slow growth, they become potential candidates for takeover by more perceptive raiders. In either case, the financial management of growth is a topic worthy of inspection.

We begin our look at the financial dimensions of growth by defining a company's *sustainable growth rate*. This is the maximum rate at which company sales can increase without depleting financial resources. Then we will look at the options open to management when a company's target growth rate exceeds its sustainable growth rate and, conversely, when growth falls below sustainable levels. An important conclusion will be that growth is not necessarily something to be maximized. In many companies, it may be necessary to limit growth to conserve financial strength. This is a hard lesson for operating managers used to thinking that more is better; it is a critical one, however, because nonfinancial managers bear major responsibility for managing growth.

SUSTAINABLE GROWTH

It is possible to think of successful companies as passing through a predictable life cycle. The cycle begins with a start-up phase, in which the company loses money while developing products and establishing a foothold in the market. This is followed by a rapid-growth phase, in which the company is profitable but is growing so rapidly it needs regular infusions of outside financing. The third phase is maturity, characterized by a decline in growth and a switch from absorbing outside financing to generating more cash than the firm can profitably reinvest. The last phase is decline, during which the company is perhaps marginally profitable, generates more cash than it can reinvest internally, and suffers declining sales. Mature and declining companies frequently devote considerable time and money to seeking investment opportunities in new products or firms that are still in their growth phase.

Our discussion will begin by looking at the growth phase, when financing needs are most pressing. Later we will consider the growth problems of mature and declining firms. Central to our discussion is the notion of sustainable growth. Intuitively, sustainable growth is just a formalization of the old adage, "It takes money to make money." Increased sales require more assets of all types, which must be paid for. Retained profits and the accompanying new borrowing generate some cash but only in limited amounts. Unless the company is prepared to sell common stock, this limit puts a ceiling on the growth a company can achieve without straining its resources. This is the firm's sustainable growth rate.

The Sustainable Growth Equation

Let's begin by writing a simple equation to express the dependence of growth on financial resources. For this purpose, assume:

1. The company wants to grow as rapidly as market conditions permit.
2. Management is unable or unwilling to sell new equity.
3. The company has a target capital structure and a target dividend policy that it wants to maintain.

I will say more about these assumptions in a few pages. For now it is enough to realize that although they are certainly not appropriate for all firms, the assumptions are descriptive of a great many.

Figure 4–1 shows the rapidly growing company's plight. It represents the firm's balance sheet as two rectangles, one for assets, the other for liabilities and owners' equity. The two long, unshaded rectangles represent the balance sheet at the beginning of the year. The rectangles are, of course, the same height because assets must equal liabilities plus owners' equity. Now, if the company wants to increase sales during the coming year, it must also increase assets, such as inventory, accounts receivable, and productive capacity.

FIGURE 4–1
New Sales Require New Assets, which Must Be Financed

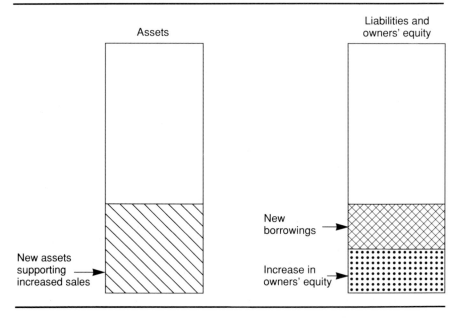

The cross-hatched area on the left of the figure represents the value of new assets necessary to support the increased sales. Because the company will not be selling equity, by assumption, the cash required to pay for this increase in assets must come from retained profits and increased liabilities.

We want to know what limits the rate at which the company in Figure 4–1 can increase sales. Assuming in effect that all parts of a business expand in strict proportion—like a balloon—what limits the rate of this expansion? To find out, start in the lower-right corner of the figure with owners' equity. As equity grows, liabilities can increase proportionately without altering the capital structure; and together the growth of liabilities and equity determines the rate at which assets expand. This, in turn, limits the growth rate in sales. So after all the dust settles, the thing that limits the growth rate in sales is the rate at which owners' equity expands. A company's sustainable growth rate, therefore, is nothing more than its growth rate in equity.

Letting g^* represent the sustainable growth rate,

$$g^* = \frac{\text{Change in equity}}{\text{Beginning-of-period equity}}$$

With the help of a little algebra as shown below,[1] we can rewrite this expression more informatively as

$$g^* = P \; R \; A \; \hat{T}$$

---

[1] Assuming the firm issues no new equity, the numerator in the above equation, Change in equity, equals (R) Earnings, where R is the firm's retention rate, defined as the proportion of earnings retained in the business. Thus,

$$g^* = \frac{(R)\text{Earnings}}{\text{Equity}_{\text{bop}}}$$

where bop denotes beginning-of-period. Representing Earnings/Equity$_{\text{bop}}$ as $RO\hat{E}$

$$g^* = (R)RO\hat{E}$$

where the hat denotes beginning-of-period equity. Finally recalling from Chapter 2 that

$$\text{ROE} = \frac{\text{Profit}}{\text{margin}} \times \frac{\text{Asset}}{\text{turnover}} \times \frac{\text{Financial}}{\text{leverage}}$$

$$g^* = P \; R \; A \; \hat{T}$$

where $\hat{T}$ is assets divided by beginning-of-period equity.

where P, A, and $\hat{T}$ are our old friends from Chapter 2, the levers of performance. Recall that P is the profit margin, A the asset turnover ratio, and $\hat{T}$ the assets-to-equity ratio. The assets-to-equity ratio wears a hat here as a reminder that it is assets divided by *beginning-of-period* equity, instead of end-of-period as defined in Chapter 2. The fourth ratio, R, is the firm's retention rate, defined as the fraction of earnings retained in the business. If a company distributes 30 percent of its earnings as dividends, its retention rate is 70 percent. Alternatively, the retention rate is 1.00 minus the firm's dividend payout ratio.

This is the sustainable growth equation.[2] Let's see what it tells us. Given the assumptions noted above, the equation says that a company's sustainable growth rate in sales, g^*, must equal the product of four ratios, P, R, A, and $\hat{T}$. Two of these ratios, P and A, summarize the operating performance of the business, while the other two describe the firm's principal financial policies. Thus management's attitudes toward the distribution of dividends are captured in the retention rate, R, and its policies regarding financial leverage are reflected in the assets-to-equity ratio, $\hat{T}$.

An important implication of the sustainable growth equation is that g^* *is the only growth rate in sales that is consistent with stable values of the four ratios.* If a company increases sales at any rate other than g^*, one or more of the ratios *must* change. This means that when a company grows at a rate in excess of its sustainable growth rate, it had better improve operations (represented by an increase in the profit margin or the asset turnover ratio), or prepare to alter its financial policies (represented by increasing its retention ratio or its financial leverage).

TOO MUCH GROWTH

This is the crux of the sustainable growth problem for rapidly expanding firms: Because increasing operating efficiency is not always possible and altering financial policies is not always wise, we see that it is entirely possible for a company to grow too fast for its

---

[2] I shall refrain from admonishing you to avoid "prat" falls.

own good. This is particularly true among smaller companies, which may do too little financial planning. Such companies see sales growth as something to be maximized and think too little of the financial consequences. They do not realize that rapid growth has them on a treadmill; the faster they grow, the more cash they need, even if they are profitable. They can meet this need for a time by increasing leverage, but eventually the company will reach its debt capacity, lenders will refuse additional credit requests, and the company will find itself without the cash to pay its bills. All of this can be prevented if managers understand that growth above the company's sustainable rate creates financial problems that must be anticipated and solved. We will return to strategies for managing growth after looking at a numerical example.

R&E Supplies' Sustainable Growth Rate

To illustrate the growth-management problems of a rapidly expanding enterprise, let's look again at R&E Supplies, the wholesale distributor discussed in the last chapter. Table 4–1 presents R&E's actual and sustainable annual growth rates in sales for the period 1988 to 1991. For each year, the sustainable growth rate was calculated by plugging the four required ratios for that year into the sustainable growth equation. (R&E's historical and pro forma financial statements appear in Tables 3–1 and 3–3 of the preceding chapter.) Table 4–1 shows that R&E's sustainable growth rate has declined steadily over the years, and that the gap between the company's actual growth rate and its sustainable growth rate is steadily widening. For example, at year-end 1988, the sustainable growth equation says the company could maintain a 16.7 percent growth rate in sales without needing to improve operations or alter financial policies. R&E's actual 1989 growth rate of 17.0 percent was not far above this mark. But by year-end 1990, the company's sustainable growth rate is only 9.1 percent, and it contemplates growing 25.0 percent in 1991.

R&E's sustainable growth rate has fallen primarily because the company's profit margin is down to less than one third of its 1987 value. The combination of a falling profit margin and growth in excess of the firm's sustainable rate has forced an increasing reliance on debt financing. This is reflected in the assets-to-equity

TABLE 4–1
R&E Supplies, Inc., Sustainable Growth Calculations

	1987	1988	1989	1990	Pro Forma 1991
Required ratios:					
Profit margin (*P*) (%)	3.3	2.9	2.4	1.4	0.9
Retention ratio (*R*) (%)	50.0	50.0	50.0	50.0	50.0
Asset turnover (*A*) (times)	3.4	3.6	3.2	3.5	3.3
Financial leverage ($\hat{T}$) (times)	N.A.	3.2	3.6	3.7	4.5
R&E's sustainable growth rate (*g**) (%)	—	16.7	13.8	9.1	6.7
R&E's actual growth rate (*g*) (%)	—	23.0	17.0	28.0	25.0

What if?

	Profit Margin 1.9%	Retention Ratio 80%	Asset Turnover 4.0 times	All of These Occur
R&E's sustainable growth rate in 1991	14.1%	10.7%	8.1%	27.4%

ratio, which has increased from 3.2 times in 1988 to a pro forma 1991 figure of 4.5. As noted in the last chapter, the pro forma bank loan required for 1991 may be possible to obtain, but the trend is a very unhealthy one. In the near future, R&E will reach its debt capacity and will be unable to raise added debt without a significant increase in equity. At this juncture, R&E will be without the money necessary to pay for added growth. If R&E and its creditors realize what is happening in the near future, remedial action is possible; if not, the probable outcome will be bankruptcy.

"What If" Questions

Once management realizes that it has sustainable growth problems, the sustainable growth equation can be useful in searching for solutions. This is done through a series of "what if" questions, as shown in the bottom portion of Table 4–1. We see, for example, that if R&E Supplies can increase its profit margin by one percentage point, its sustainable growth rate in 1991 will rise from 6.7 percent to 14.1 percent. Similarly, an increase in the retention ratio to 80 percent, holding everything else constant, increases sustainable growth to 10.7 percent, while raising the asset turnover to four times increases sustainable growth only marginally to 8.1 percent. If R&E did all of these things at the same time, sustainable growth would rise to 27.4 percent, thereby solving its sustainable growth problems.

WHAT TO DO WHEN ACTUAL GROWTH EXCEEDS SUSTAINABLE GROWTH

We have now developed the sustainable growth equation and illustrated its use for rapidly growing businesses. The next question is, What should management do when actual growth exceeds sustainable growth? The first step is to determine how long the situation will continue. If the company's growth rate is likely to decline in the near future as the firm reaches maturity, the problem is only a transitory one that probably can be solved by further borrowing. Then in the future, when the actual growth rate falls below the sustainable rate, the company will switch from an absorber of cash to a generator of cash, and the loans can be repaid. For longer-term sustainable growth problems some combination of the strategies described below will be necessary.

Sell New Equity

If a company is willing and able to raise new equity capital by selling shares, its sustainable growth problems vanish. The increased equity, plus whatever added borrowing is possible as a result of the increased equity, is a source of cash with which to finance further growth.

The problem with this strategy is that it is not available to many companies and unattractive to many others. In most countries throughout the world, equity markets are poorly developed or nonexistent. To sell equity in these countries, companies must go through the laborious and expensive task of seeking out investors directly to buy the new shares. This is a difficult undertaking because, without active stock market trading of the shares, new investors will become minority owners of illiquid securities. Consequently, those investors interested in buying the new shares will be limited largely to friends and acquaintances of existing owners.

Even in countries with well-developed stock markets, such as the United States, many companies find it very difficult to raise new equity. This is particularly true of smaller concerns which, unless they have a glamorous product, find it difficult to secure the services of an investment banker to help them sell the shares. Without such help, the firms might just as well be in a country without developed markets, for a lack of trading in the stock will again restrict potential buyers largely to friends and acquaintances.

Finally, even many companies that are able to raise new equity prefer not to do so. This is evidenced in Table 4–2, which shows the sources of capital to U.S. nonfinancial corporations over the period 1965 to 1989. Observe that internal sources, depreciation and increases in retained earnings, were by far the most important sources of corporate capital over this period, accounting for about 60 percent of the total. At the other extreme, *new equity has not been a source of capital at all, but a use,* meaning that American corporations retired more stock on average over this period than they issued.

Figure 4–2 shows the value of new equity issues, net of share repurchases and retirements, on a year-by-year basis. The highest figure reached was about $28 billion in 1983, while in more recent years, new equity has been a very large *use* of capital. Indeed, in

TABLE 4–2
Sources of Capital to U.S. Nonfinancial Corporations, 1965–1989

Internal		
Retained profits	15.34%	
Depreciation	47.06	
Subtotal		62.39%
External		
Increased liabilities	40.12%	
New equity issues	–2.52	
Subtotal		37.61
TOTAL		100.00%

Sources: Federal Reserve System, *Flow of Funds Accounts 1949–78,* and *Flow of Funds Accounts,* various issues.

FIGURE 4–2
Net New Equity Issues, 1965–1989

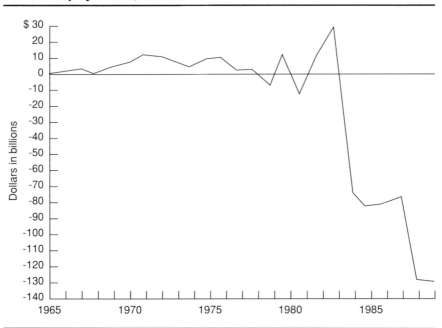

Sources: Federal Reserve System, *Flow of Funds Accounts, 1949–78,* and *Flow of Funds Accounts,* various issues.

1989 stock repurchases and retirements by corporations exceeded new issues by $131 billion. Year-end figures for 1990 are not yet available, but preliminary indications are that the number will again be negative, although not as dramatically large as in recent years. Companies reduce common stock outstanding in two ways: by repurchasing their own stock, or by acquiring the stock of another firm for cash. Figure 4–2 attests to the huge wave of share repurchases and acquisitions in the latter half of the 1980s.

Ironically, companies' reliance on new equity appears to have varied *inversely* with stock prices. In direct opposition to the old buy low-sell high strategy, companies sold very few shares during the late 1960s when stock prices were high, relied more heavily on new equity in the early 1970s as prices fell, and then in the mid-1980s massively repurchased shares during one of the strongest bull markets in history. This does not speak well of executives' ability to time new equity issues.

Like the fellow who drowned crossing the stream because he had heard it was only five feet deep on average, it is important to remember that the equity figures presented are the *net* result of new issues and retirements. Figure 4–3 shows the gross proceeds from new common stock sales, including limited partnerships, from 1970 to 1988. The 19-year average is $24.9 billion, and the peak is almost $70 billion in 1986. Of the almost $70 billion, about half was raised by real estate and financial companies, much of it undoubtedly in the form of real estate limited partnerships. To put these numbers in perspective, gross proceeds from new stock issues equaled 7.8 percent of total sources of capital to corporations over the period. If one were to exclude public utilities (because the regulatory process appears to encourage new equity issues) and real estate and financial enterprises (because their numbers are dominated by limited partnerships), the figure would fall to 3.9 percent.

The appropriate conclusion appears to be that in aggregate the stock market is not an important source of capital to corporate

FIGURE 4–3
Gross New Equity Issues, 1970–1988

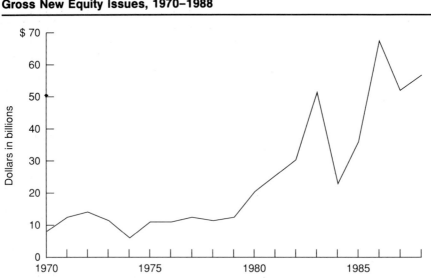

Source: Federal Reserve System, *Annual Statistical Digest,* various issues.
Note: New equity includes limited partnerships, preferred stock, and other equity.

America, but that it is quite significant to some companies. Those making extensive use of the new equity market tend to be companies with what brokers call "story paper," high-growth enterprises with a particular product or concept brokers can hype to stimulate investor enthusiasm. R&E Supplies would definitely not be among such firms.

Why Don't U.S. Corporations Issue More Equity?

There are a number of reasons. We will consider several here and will return to the topic in Chapter 6 when reviewing financing decisions in more detail. First, it appears that in recent years companies in the aggregate simply have not needed new equity. Retained profits and new borrowing have been sufficient. Second, equity is expensive to issue. Issue costs commonly run in the neighborhood of 5 to 10 percent of the amount raised, with the percentage even higher on small issues. This is at least twice as high as the issue costs for a comparable-size debt issue. On the other hand, the equity is outstanding forever, so its effective annualized cost is modest. Third, many managers, especially U.S. managers, have a fixation on earnings per share (EPS). They translate a complicated world into the simple notion that whatever increases EPS must be good, and whatever reduces EPS must be bad. In this view, a new equity issue is bad because, at least initially, the number of shares outstanding rises but earnings do not. EPS is said to have been *diluted.* Later, as the company makes productive use of the money it raised, earnings should increase, but in the meantime EPS has suffered. Moreover, as we will see in a later chapter, EPS is almost always higher when debt financing is used in favor of equity.

A fourth reason companies do not raise more equity is what might be called the "market doesn't appreciate us" syndrome. When a company's stock is selling for $10 a share, management has a tendency to think that the price will be a little higher in the future as soon as the current strategy begins to bear fruit. When the price rises to $15, management begins to believe this is just the beginning and that the price will be even higher in the near future. An inherent enthusiasm on the part of managers for their company's prospects produces a feeling that the firm's shares are undervalued at whatever price they currently command, and it creates a bias toward forever postponing new equity issues. This syndrome is borne out by a 1984 Louis Harris poll of top executives from more than 600 firms. Fewer than one third thought the stock market correctly valued their stock, and only 2 percent felt their stock was overvalued, while fully 60 percent felt it was undervalued.[3]

A fifth reason managers appear to shy away from new equity issues is the feeling that the stock market is basically an unreliable funding source. In addition to uncertainty about the price a company can get for new shares, managers also face the possibility that during some future periods the stock market will not be receptive to new equity issues on any reasonable terms. In finance jargon, the "window" is said to be shut at these times. Naturally, executives are reluctant to develop a growth strategy that is dependent on such an unreliable source of capital. Rather, the philosophy is to formulate growth plans that can be financed from retained profits and accompanying borrowing, and to relegate new equity financing to a minor backup role. More on this topic in later chapters.

Increase Leverage

If selling new equity is not a solution to a company's sustainable growth problems, two other financial remedies are possible. One is to cut the dividend payout ratio, and the other is to increase leverage. A cut in the payout ratio raises sustainable growth by increasing the proportion of earnings retained in the business, while increasing leverage raises the amount of debt the company can add for each dollar of retained profits.

We will have considerably more to say about leverage in the next two chapters. It should be apparent already, however, that there are limits to the use of debt financing. As previously noted, all companies have a creditor-imposed debt capacity that restricts the amount of leverage the firm can employ. Moreover, as leverage increases, the risks borne by owners and creditors rise, as do the costs of securing additional capital.

---

[3]As reported in Alfred Rappaport, "Stock Market Signals to Managers," *Harvard Business Review,* November/December 1987, p. 57.

Reduce the Payout Ratio

Just as there is an upper limit to leverage, there is a lower limit of zero to a company's dividend payout ratio. In general, owners' interest in dividend payments varies inversely with their perceptions of the company's investment opportunities. If owners believe that the retained profits can be put to productive use earning attractive rates of return, they will be willing to forgo current dividends in favor of higher future ones. If the investment opportunities do not promise attractive returns, a reduction in current dividends or in the payout ratio will cause a decline in stock price. An added concern for closely held companies is the impact of changing dividends on the owners' income and tax liabilities.

Profitable Pruning

Beyond modifications in financial policy, there are several operating adjustments a company can make to manage rapid growth. One is called "profitable pruning." During much of the 1960s and early 1970s, some financial experts emphasized the merits of product diversification. The idea was that companies could reduce risk by combining the income streams of businesses in different product markets. As long as these income streams were not affected in exactly the same way by economic events, the thought was that the variability inherent in each stream would "average out" when combined with others. We now recognize two problems with this conglomerate diversification strategy. One is that although it may reduce the risks seen by management, it does nothing for the shareholders. If shareholders want diversification, they can get it on their own by just purchasing shares of different independent companies. The second problem with conglomerate diversification is that because companies have limited resources, they cannot be important competitors in a large number of product markets at the same time. Instead, they are apt to be followers in many markets, holding small shares and unable to compete effectively with the dominant firms.

Profitable pruning is the opposite of conglomerate merger. It recognizes that when a company spreads its resources across too many products, it may not be able to compete effectively in any.

Better to sell off marginal operations and plow the money back into remaining businesses.

Profitable pruning reduces sustainable growth problems in two ways: It generates cash directly through the sale of marginal businesses, and it reduces actual sales growth by eliminating some of the sources of the growth. This strategy was successfully used by Cooper Industries, a large Texas company, in the mid-1970s. Cooper sold several of its divisions during this time, not because they were unprofitable, but rather because Cooper did not believe it had the resources to become a dominant factor in the markets involved.

Profitable pruning is also possible for a single-product company. Here, the idea is to prune out slow-paying customers or slow-turning inventory. This lessens sustainable growth problems in three ways. It frees up cash, which can be used to support new growth; it increases asset turnover; and it reduces sales. The strategy will reduce sales because tightening credit terms and reducing inventory selection will drive away some customers.

Sourcing

Sourcing involves the decision of whether to perform an activity in-house or to purchase it from an outside vendor. A company can increase its sustainable growth rate by sourcing more and doing less in-house. When a company sources, it releases assets that would otherwise be tied up in performing the activity, and it increases its asset turnover. Both diminish growth problems. An extreme example of this strategy is a franchiser who sources out virtually all of the company's capital-intensive activities to franchisees and who, as a result, has very little investment.

The key to effective sourcing is determining where the company's unique abilities lie. If a clear distinctive competence can be identified and if peripheral activities are not critical to the maintenance of this competitive edge, they can be sourced.

Pricing

An obvious inverse relationship exists between price and revenue. When sales growth is too high relative to a company's financing capabilities, it may be necessary to raise prices to reduce the growth. If higher prices increase the profit margin, the price increase will also raise the sustainable growth rate.

Looking again at R&E Supplies' growth problem, it is possible that R&E has been, in effect, buying sales by underpricing competition. This is consistent with the rapid sales growth and the declining profit margin. A price increase might establish a proper balance between sales growth and profitability.

Is Merger the Answer?

When all else fails, it may be necessary to look for a partner. Two types of companies are capable of supplying the needed cash. One is a mature company, known in the trade as a "cash cow," looking for profitable investments for its excess cash flow. The other is a conservatively financed company that would bring liquidity and borrowing capacity to the marriage. Acquiring another company or being acquired by another company is a drastic solution to growth problems. But it is better to merge when a company is still financially strong than to wait until excessive growth forces the issue.

TOO LITTLE GROWTH

From the preceding discussion, it may appear that only rapidly expanding companies have growth problems, but this is not the case. Slow-growth firms—those for which the sustainable growth rate exceeds actual growth—have problems too, but they are of a different kind. Rather than struggling continually for fresh cash to stoke the fires of growth, slow-growth companies face the dilemma of what to do with profits in excess of company needs. This might appear to be a trivial or even enviable problem, but to an increasing number of enterprises it is a very real and occasionally frightening one.

To look more closely at the difficulties created by insufficient growth, Table 4–3 presents a six-year, sustainable growth analysis of Deb Shops, Inc., a chain of junior-sized women's apparel stores headquartered in Philadelphia. Over the period 1985 to 1990, Deb Shops' actual growth rate in sales has fallen precipitously, while its sustainable growth rate has remained comparatively stable, and at a high level. The predictable result of this growing mismatch is idle

TABLE 4–3
Deb Shops, Inc. Sustainable Growth Calculations, 1985–1989

	1985	*1986*	*1987*	*1988*	*1989*	*1990*
Required ratios:						
Profit margin (*P*) (%)	7.0	7.0	6.0	7.1	8.7	8.6
Retention ratio (*R*) (%)	86.0	83.0	74.0	77.0	82.0	82.2
Asset turnover ratio						
(*A*) (times)	2.5	2.5	2.5	2.1	1.9	1.9
Financial leverage						
(*T̂*) (times)	2.0	1.9	1.6	1.5	1.5	1.5
Deb Shops' sustainable						
growth rate (*g**) (%)	30.1	27.6	17.8	17.2	20.3	20.5
Deb Shops' actual						
growth rate (*g*) (%)	22.2	23.3	9.4	–2.2	4.0	4.5

resources. Indeed, Deb Shops is veritably bulging at the seams with excess cash. By year-end 1990, the company had eliminated virtually all of its interest-bearing liabilities and had built up a cash and securities hoard equal to almost *one half of total assets*—banks should be so lucky. These trends are reflected in Table 4–3 by continuing declines in the company's assets-to-equity ratio and its asset turnover ratio. The asset turnover is falling, not because company operations are becoming less efficient, but because its cash balances are rising much more rapidly than sales. Indeed, the asset turnover, omitting cash and securities, has actually risen since 1985. Deb Shops' problem in 1991 is to rekindle growth, or failing that, to find other productive uses for its idle resources.

WHAT TO DO WHEN SUSTAINABLE GROWTH EXCEEDS ACTUAL GROWTH

The first step in addressing problems of inadequate growth is to decide whether the situation is temporary or longer-term. If temporary, management can simply continue accumulating resources in anticipation of future growth.

When the difficulty is longer-term, the issue becomes whether the lack of growth is industrywide—the natural result of a maturing market—or unique to the company. If the latter, the reasons for inadequate growth, and possible sources of new growth, are to be found within the firm. In this event, management must look carefully at its own performance in order to identify and remove the internal constraints on company growth, a potentially painful process involving organizational changes as well as increased developmental expenses. The nerve-wracking aspect of such soul-searching is that the strategies initiated to enhance growth must bear fruit within a few years, or management will be forced to seek other, often more drastic, solutions.

When a company is unable to generate sufficient growth from within, it has three options: ignore the problem, return the money to shareholders, or buy growth. Let us consider each briefly in turn.

Ignore the Problem

This response comes in two forms. Management can continue investing in its core businesses despite the lack of attractive returns, or it can simply sit on an ever-larger pile of idle resources. The difficulty with either response is that, like dogs to a fire hydrant, underutilized resources attract raiders. Poorly utilized resources depress a company's stock price and make it feasible and attractive for a raider to strike. If she has done her sums correctly, the raider can redeploy the firm's resources more productively, and earn a substantial profit in the process. And among the first resources to be redeployed in such a raid is incumbent management, who find themselves suddenly reading help wanted ads.

Deb Shops, Inc., might well be vulnerable to such a hostile raid were it not for the fact that the firm's top two officers own 42 percent of the stock and a third investor owns an additional 18 percent. When management owns the dice, it can play the game virtually any way it pleases, and there is little that you, I, or Carl Ichan can do about it.

Return the Money to Shareholders

The most direct solution to the problem of idle resources is just to return the money to owners by increasing dividends or repurchasing shares. This appears not to be the strategy of choice among many American managers, however, and for several reasons. One is that, unlike the practice in many other countries, the U.S. tax code encourages earnings retention by fully taxing dividends at the corporate level and again at the personal level, so that even mediocre investments by corporations can be more attractive to shareholders than increased dividends.

More importantly, many executives appear to have a bias in favor of growth, even when the growth has little or no effect on earnings. At the personal level, many managers resist paying large dividends because the practice hints of failure. Shareholders entrust managers with the task of profitably investing their capital, and for management to return the money suggests an inability to perform a basic managerial function. A cruder way to say the same thing is that dividends reduce the size of management's empire, an act counter to basic human nature.

Gordon Donaldson and others also document a bias toward growth at the organizational level.[4] In a carefully researched review and synthesis of the decision-making behavior of senior executives in a dozen large companies, Donaldson noted that executives commonly opt for growth, even uneconomic growth, out of concern for the long-run viability of their organization. As seen by senior managers, growth contributes importantly to company morale by fostering stimulating career opportunities for employees throughout the organization. And when growth slackens, the enterprise risks losing many of its best people.

Buy Growth

This leads naturally to the third strategy. Motivated by pride in their ability as managers, concern for retaining key employees, and fear of raiders, managers commonly respond to excess cash flow by attempting to diversify into other businesses. Management systematically searches for worthwhile growth opportunities in other, more vibrant industries. And because time is a factor, this usually involves acquiring existing businesses rather than starting new ones from scratch.

---

[4]Gordon Donaldson, *Managing Corporate Wealth* (New York: Praeger Publishers, 1984).

The proper design and implementation of a corporate acquisition program is a complex and challenging task which need not detain us here. Two points, however, are worth noting. First, in many important respects the growth management problems of mature or declining companies are just the mirror image of those faced by rapidly growing firms. In particular, slow-growth businesses are generally seeking productive uses for their excess cash, while rapidly growing ones are in search of additional cash to finance their unsustainably rapid growth. It is natural, therefore, that high- and low-growth companies will frequently solve their respective growth-management problems by merging, so that the excess cash generated by one organization can finance the rapid growth of the other. Second, after a flurry of optimism in the 1960s and early 1970s, accumulating evidence increasingly suggests that, from the shareholders' perspective, buying growth is distinctly inferior to returning the money to owners. More often than not, the superior growth prospects of potential acquisitions are fully reflected in the target's stock price, so that after paying a substantial premium to acquire another firm, the buyer is left with a mediocre investment, or worse. The conflict between managers and owners in this regard will be considered in more detail in Chapter 9.

SUSTAINABLE GROWTH AND INFLATION

Growth comes from two sources: increasing volume and increasing prices. Unfortunately, the amount of money a company must invest to support a dollar of inflationary growth is about the same as the investment required to support a dollar of real growth. Imagine a company that has no real growth—it makes and sells the same number of items every year—but is experiencing 10 percent inflationary growth. Then even though it has the same number of units in inventory, each unit will cost more in nominal terms to build, so the total investment in inventory will be higher. The same is true with accounts receivable. The same volume of customers will purchase the same number of units, but because each unit has a higher nominal selling price, the total investment in accounts receivable will be higher.

A company's investment in fixed assets behaves similarly under inflation but with a delay. When the inflation rate increases, there is no immediate need for more fixed assets. The existing fixed assets can produce the same number of units. As the existing assets wear out and are replaced at higher prices, however, the company's investment in fixed assets rises.

This inflationary increase in assets must be financed just as if it were real growth. It is fair to say then that inflation worsens a rapidly expanding company's growth-management problems. The degree to which this occurs depends primarily on the extent to which management and creditors understand the impact of inflation on company financial statements.

Inflation does at least two things to company financial statements. First, it increases the amount of external financing required, and second, in the absence of new equity financing, it increases the company's debt-to-equity ratio when *measured on its historical-cost financial statements.* This combination can spell trouble. If management or creditors require that the company's historical-cost debt-to-equity ratio stay constant over time, inflation will lower the company's real sustainable growth rate. If the sustainable growth rate is 15 percent without inflation, the real sustainable growth rate will fall to about 5 percent when the inflation rate is 10 percent. Intuitively, under inflation, cash that would otherwise support real growth must be used to finance inflationary growth.

If managers and creditors understand the effects of inflation, this inverse relation between inflation and the sustainable growth rate need not exist. It is true that the amount of external financing required does rise with the inflation rate, but because the real value of company liabilities is declining as companies are able to repay their loans with depreciated dollars, the *net* increase in external financing may be little affected.

In sum, with historical-cost financial statements, inflationary growth appears to substitute for real growth on almost a one-for-one basis—each one percentage point increase in inflation appears to reduce the real sustainable growth rate by the same amount. More accurate, inflation-adjusted financial statements show, however, that inflation turns out to have relatively little effect on sustainable growth. Let us hope that executives can convince their bankers of this fact.

SUSTAINABLE GROWTH AND PRO FORMA FORECASTS

It is important to keep the material presented here in perspective. I find that comparison of a company's actual and sustainable growth rates reveals a great deal about the principal financial concerns confronting senior management. When actual growth exceeds sustainable growth, management's focus will be on getting the cash to fund expansion; conversely, when actual growth falls below sustainable growth, the financial agenda will swing 180 degrees to one of productively spending the excess cash flow. The sustainable growth equation also appears to describe the way many top executives view their jobs: Avoid external equity financing and work to balance operating strategies, growth targets, and financial policies so that actual and sustainable growth are about equal. Finally, for nonfinancial types the sustainable growth equation is useful for highlighting the tie between a company's growth rate and its financial resources.

The sustainable growth equation, however, is essentially just a simplification of pro forma statements. If you really want to study a company's growth management problems in detail, therefore, I recommend you take the time to construct pro forma financial statements. The sustainable growth equation may be great for looking at the forest, but is considerably less helpful for studying an individual tree.

CHAPTER SUMMARY

1. The purpose of this chapter has been to study the financial management of growth and decline.
2. Unless a company is willing and able to raise new equity, more growth is not always a blessing. Without careful financial planning, companies can literally grow broke.
3. A company's sustainable growth rate is the maximum rate at which it can grow without depleting financial resources. More precisely, it equals the product of four ratios: the profit margin, the retention ratio, the asset turnover ratio, and financial leverage, defined here as assets divided by beginning-of-period equity. Alternatively, it equals the retention rate times the return on beginning-of-period equity. If a company's sales expand at any

rate other than the sustainable rate, one or some combination of the four ratios must change.

4. If a company's actual growth rate *temporarily* exceeds its sustainable rate, the required capital can likely be provided by increased borrowing.

5. When actual growth exceeds sustainable growth for longer periods, management must formulate a financial strategy from among the following options: sell new equity, permanently increase financial leverage, reduce dividends, liquidate marginal operations, source more activities, increase prices, or find a merger partner with deep pockets.

6. For a variety of reasons, some of which are yet to be discussed, most businesses are reluctant to sell new equity. Indeed, since 1985 corporations have repurchased far more shares in terms of market value than they have issued.

7. When actual growth is less than the sustainable growth rate, management's principal financial problem is finding productive uses for excess cash flows. The options are to increase dividends, reduce liabilities, increase liquid assets, repurchase common shares, or acquire other firms for their growth potential.

8. If managers and creditors base decisions on historical-cost financial statements, inflation reduces a company's sustainable growth rate. If they adjust for the effects of inflation, inflation has comparatively little effect on sustainable growth.

ADDITIONAL READING

Donaldson, Gordon. *Managing Corporate Wealth.* New York: Praeger Publishers, 1984. 199 pages.

This book is the result of an ambitious study undertaken by Donaldson and several colleagues at Harvard in which they reviewed the major resource allocation decisions of 12 large corporations over the course of a decade. The collaborators' synthesis of the behavior they observed provides a detailed portrait of how late-20th-century corporations really function, including the important role played by sustainable growth.

Higgins, Robert C. "Sustainable Growth under Inflation." *Financial Management,* Autumn 1981, pp. 36–40.

A look at the dependence of a company's sustainable growth rate on the inflation rate. The paper concludes that inflation will reduce sustainable growth only if an "inflation illusion" exists.

CHAPTER PROBLEMS

1. Below are selected financial data for Jamesway Corporation, a discount department store headquartered in Secaucus, New Jersey.

		1986	1987	1988	1989	1990
Profit margin	(%)	1.77	1.98	1.65	1.24	0.68
Retention ratio	(%)	91	93	90	89	81
Asset turnover	(X)	2.51	2.48	2.35	2.37	2.38
Financial leverage*	(X)	2.36	2.53	2.72	2.78	2.81
Growth rate in sales	(%)	10.04	17.06	14.54	11.56	9.28

*Assets divided by beginning-of-period equity.

a. Calculate Jamesway's sustainable growth rate in each year.
b. Comparing the company's sustainable growth rate to its actual growth rate in sales, what growth problems does Jamesway appear to have faced over this period?
c. How does the company appear to have coped with these problems?
d. During the first half of fiscal 1991, Jamesway repurchased over $1 million of its common equity, apparently because it fell to an irresistibly low price. Comment on this action in light of the company's growth problems.
e. Jamesway opened 12 new stores in the last four years, almost one third of the chain, and has recently indicated they intend to cut the rate of expansion in the future. Comment on this intention in light of the company's growth problems.

139

2. Here are selected financial data for Liz Claiborne Inc., a highly successful designer of women's clothing.

	($ millions)				
	1985	1986	1987	1988	1989
Net sales	$557	$813	$1,053	$1,184	$1,411
Net income	61	86	114	110	165
Total assets	226	336	482	629	849
Stockholders' equity	163	248	357	458	612
Dividends paid	7	10	14	16	17

a. Calculate the company's sustainable growth rate and its actual growth rate in sales for the last four years.

b. Comparing the company's sustainable growth rate to its actual growth rate in sales, what growth problems does the company appear to have faced?

c. How does the company appear to have coped with its growth problems?

PART 3

FINANCING OPERATIONS

CHAPTER 5

FINANCIAL INSTRUMENTS
AND MARKETS

Don't tell mom I'm an investment banker.
She still thinks I play piano in a brothel.
Bruce McKern

A major part of the financial executive's job is raising external capital to finance current operations and future growth. In this capacity, the financial manager acts much like a marketing manager. He or she has a product—claims on the company's future income—that must be packaged and sold to yield the highest price to the company. The financial manager's customers are creditors and investors who put money into the business in anticipation of future income. In return these customers receive a *financial security,* such as a stock certificate or a bond, that describes the nature of their claim on the firm's future income.

In packaging his product, the financial executive must select or design a financial security that meets the needs of the company and is attractive to potential creditors and investors. To do this effectively requires knowledge of financial instruments, of the markets in which they trade, and of the merits of each instrument to the issuing company. In this chapter we consider the first two topics—financial instruments and markets—while the next chapter looks at the proper choice of a financing instrument from the company's perspective.

FINANCIAL INSTRUMENTS

Fortunately, lawyers and regulators have not yet removed all creativity from raising money. When selecting a financial instrument for sale in securities markets, a company is *not* significantly constrained by law or regulation. The company is largely free to select or design any instrument, provided only that it appeals to investors and meets the needs of the company. Securities markets in the United States are regulated by the Securities and Exchange Commission (SEC) and, to a lesser extent, by state authorities. SEC regulation creates a lot of red tape and delay, but the SEC does not pass judgment on the investment merits of a security. It requires only that investors have access to all information relevant to valuing the security and that they have adequate opportunity to evaluate it before purchase. This freedom has given rise to such unusual securities as Foote Minerals' $2.20 cumulative, if earned, convertible preferred stock; Sunshine Mining's silver-indexed bonds; and Arley Merchandising Corporation's common stock with attached "puts." The Arley stock entitles the holder to sell the stock back to the company in two years after the date of issue for cash or an equivalent amount of debt. My favorite international security is a 6 percent bond issued by Hungary in 1983 that, in addition to interest, included a firm promise of telephone service within three years. The usual wait for a phone at the time was said to run up to 20 years.

But do not let the variety of securities obscure the underlying logic. When designing a financial instrument, the financial executive works with three broad variables: the investor's claim on future income, his right to participate in company decisions, and his claim on company assets in liquidation. Below we will describe the more popular security types in terms of these three variables. In reading the descriptions, bear in mind that the characteristics of a specific financial instrument are determined by the terms of the contract between issuer and buyer, not by law or regulation. So the descriptions below should be thought of as indicative of general security types rather than exact definitions of specific securities.

Bonds

A bond, like any other form of indebtedness, is a *fixed-income* security. The holder receives a specified annual interest income and a specified amount at maturity, no more and no less—unless the company goes bankrupt. The difference between a bond and other forms of indebtedness, such as trade credit, bank loans, and private placements, is that bonds are sold to the public in small increments, usually $1,000 per bond. After issue the bonds can be traded by investors on organized security exchanges.

Three variables characterize a bond: its *par value, coupon rate,* and *maturity date.* For example, a typical bond might have a $1,000 par value, a 9 percent coupon rate, and a maturity date of December 31, 2005. The par value is the amount of money the holder will receive on the bond's maturity date. By custom, the par value of bonds issued in the United States is usually $1,000. The coupon rate is the percentage of par value the holder is promised annually as interest income. The preceding bond will pay $90 per year in interest (9 percent × $1,000), usually in two semiannual payments of $45 each. On the maturity date, the company will pay the bondholder $1,000 per bond and will cease further interest payments.

On the issue date, companies usually try to set the coupon rate on the new bond equal to the prevailing interest rate on other bonds of similar maturity and quality. This ensures that the bond's initial market price will about equal its par value. After issue, the market price of a bond can differ substantially from its par value as market interest rates change. As we will see in a later chapter, when interest rates rise, bond prices fall, and vice versa.

Most forms of long-term indebtedness require periodic repayment of principal. This principal repayment is known as a *sinking fund.* Readers who have studied too much accounting will know that, technically, a sinking fund is a sum of money set aside by the company to meet a future obligation, and this is the way bonds used to work, but no more. Today, a bond sinking fund is a direct payment to creditors that reduces principal. Depending on the indebenture agreement, there are several ways a firm can meet its sinking fund obligation. It can repurchase a certain number of bonds in securities markets, or it can retire a certain number of bonds by paying the holders par value. When a company has a choice, it will naturally repurchase bonds if the market price of the bonds is below par value, something that occurs whenever interest rates rise after the bond is issued.

Call Provisions
Virtually all corporate bonds contain a clause giving the issuing company an option to retire the bonds prior to maturity. For exam-

ple, although a bond might mature on December 31, 2001, the company may have the option to call the bonds for retirement prior to maturity. Frequently, the call price for early retirement will be at a modest premium above par. Many bonds have a *delayed call,* meaning the company may not call the bond until it has been outstanding for a specified period, usually 5 or 10 years. An important difference between corporate and U.S. government bonds is that governments do not have call options.

Companies want call options on bonds for two reasons. One is that, if interest rates fall, the company can pay off its existing bonds and issue new ones at a lower interest cost. The other is that the call option gives a company flexibility. If changing market conditions or changing company strategy requires it, the call option enables management to rearrange its capital structure.

At first glance, it may appear that a call option works entirely to the company's advantage. If interest rates fall, the company can call the bonds and refinance at a lower rate; but if rates rise, investors have no similar option. They must either accept the low interest income or sell their bonds at a loss. From the company's perspective, it looks like "Heads I win, tails you lose," but investors are not so stupid. As a general rule, the more attractive the call provisions are to the company, the higher the coupon rate on the bond.

Covenants
Under normal circumstances, no creditors, including bondholders, have a direct voice in company decisions. Bondholders and other long-term creditors exercise control through *protective covenants* specified in the indebenture agreement. Typical covenants include a lower limit on the company's current ratio, an upper limit on its debt-to-equity ratio, and perhaps a requirement that the company not acquire or sell major assets without prior creditor approval. Creditors have no say in company operations as long as the firm is current in its interest and sinking fund payments and no covenants have been violated. If the company falls behind in its payments or violates a covenant, it is in *default,* and creditors gain considerable power. At the extreme, creditors can force the company into bankruptcy, leaving the courts to decide whether the company should be reorganized for the benefit of

creditors or simply be liquidated. In liquidation, the courts will supervise the sale of company assets and distribution of the proceeds to creditors.

Rights in Bankruptcy

The distribution of liquidation proceeds in bankruptcy is determined by the *rights of absolute priority.* At the head of the line are, naturally, the government for past due taxes and the bankruptcy lawyers who wrote the law. Among investors, the first to be repaid are *senior* creditors, then *general* creditors, and finally *subordinated* creditors. Preferred stockholders and common shareholders bring up the rear. Because each class of claimant is paid off in full before the next class receives anything, equity shareholders frequently get nothing in bankruptcy.

Secured Creditors

A secured credit is a form of senior credit in which the loan is collateralized by a specific company asset or group of assets. In liquidation, proceeds from the sale of this asset go only to the secured creditor. If the cash generated from the sale exceeds the debt to the secured creditor, the excess cash goes into the pot for distribution to general creditors. If the cash is too little, the lender becomes a general creditor for the remaining liability.

Bonds as an Investment

For many years, investors thought bonds to be a very low risk. After all, interest income is specified and chances of bankruptcy are remote. However, bonds are a *monetary asset.* Consequently, changes in the rate of inflation have a major effect on real and nominal bond returns. This has led to a growing perception that bonds can be quite risky in an inflationary world.

Table 5–1 presents the rate of return earned by investors in selected securities over the period 1926 to 1990. Looking at long-term corporate bonds, you can see that, had an investor purchased a representative portfolio of corporate bonds in 1926 and held them through 1990 (while reinvesting all interest income and principal payments in similar bonds), his annual return would have been 5.5 percent over the entire 65 years. By comparison, the an-

TABLE 5–1
Rate of Return on Selected Securities, 1926–1990

Security	Return*
Common stocks	12.1%
Long-term corporate bonds	5.5
Long-term government bonds	4.9
Short-term government bills	3.7
Consumer price index	3.2

*Arithmetic mean of annual returns ignoring taxes and assuming reinvestment of all interest and dividend income.

Source: *Stocks, Bonds, Bills and Inflation 1991 Yearbook™,* © Ibbotson Associates, Chicago, p. 32 (annually updates work by Roger G. Ibbotson and Rex A. Sinquefield). All rights reserved.

nual return on an investment in long-term U.S. government bonds would have been 4.9 percent over the same period. We can attribute the 0.6 percent difference to a "risk premium." This is the added return an investor in corporate bonds earns over government bonds to compensate for the risk that corporations might default on their liabilities or deprive investors of attractive returns by calling their bonds prior to maturity.

These returns are *nominal,* meaning they are not adjusted for inflation. The bottom entry in Table 5–1 contains the annual percentage change in the consumer price index over the period. Subtracting the annual inflation rate from 1926 through 1990 of 3.2 percent from these nominal returns yields real, or inflation-adjusted, returns of 2.3 percent for corporates and 1.7 percent for governments. Long-term bonds have done little more than keep pace with inflation over this period.

Bond Ratings

Several companies in the United States analyze the investment qualities of many publicly traded bonds and publish their findings in the form of bond ratings. A bond rating is a letter grade, like AA, assigned to an issue, which reflects the analyst's appraisal of the bond's default risk. These ratings are determined using many of the techniques discussed in earlier chapters, including analysis of the company's balance sheet debt ratios and its coverage ratios relative to competitors. Table 5–2 contains selected debt rating definitions of Standard & Poor's, a major rating firm. Table 6–4 in the next chapter shows the differences in key performance ratios by rating category.

Junk Bonds

The rating a company receives on a new bond issue is important because it affects the interest rate the firm must offer. More importantly, many institutional investors, such as pension funds, are prohibited from investing in bonds that are rated less than "investment" grade, usually defined as BBB− and above. As a result, there have been periods in the past when companies having less

---

When Investing Internationally, What You See Isn't Always What You Get

A 10 percent interest rate on a dollar-denominated bond is not comparable to a 6 percent rate on a yen bond, or a 14 percent rate on a British sterling bond. To see why, let's calculate the rate of return on $1,000 invested today in a one-year British sterling bond yielding 14 percent interest when today's exchange rate is 1£ = $1.50 and the rate in one year is 1£ = $1.35.

$1,000 will buy £666.67 today ($1,000/1.50 = £666.67), and in one year, interest and principal on the sterling bond will total £760 (£666.67[1+.14] = £760). Converting this amount back into dollars yields $1,026 in one year (£760 × 1.35 = $1,026). So the investment's rate of return, measured in dollars, is only 2.6 percent ([$1,026 − $1,000]/$1,000 = 2.6%).

Why is the dollar return so low? Because investing in a foreign asset is really two investments: purchase of a foreign-currency asset, and speculation on future changes in the dollar value of the foreign currency. Here the foreign asset yields a healthy 14 percent, but sterling depreciates 10 percent against the dollar ([$1.50 − $1.35]/$1.50); so the combined return is roughly the difference between the two. The exact relationship is

(1 + return) = (1 + interest rate)(1 + change in exchange rate)
(1 + return) = (1 + 14%)(1 − 10%)
    return = 2.6%

Incidentally, we know that sterling depreciates relative to the dollar because one pound costs less a year from now than it does today.

TABLE 5–2
Selected Standard & Poor's Debt Rating Definitions

A Standard & Poor's corporate or municipal debt rating is a current assessment of the creditworthiness of an obligor with respect to a specific obligation. This assessment may take into consideration obligors such as guarantors, insurers, or lessees.

The debt rating is not a recommendation to purchase, sell, or hold a security, inasmuch as it does not comment as to market price or suitability for a particular investor.

The ratings are based in varying degrees on the following considerations:

(1) Likelihood of default capacity and willingness of the obligor as to the timely payment of interest and repayment of principal in accordance with the terms of the obligation.

(2) Nature of and provisions of the obligation.

(3) Protection afforded to, and relative position of, the obligation in the event of bankruptcy, reorganization, or other arrangement under the laws of bankruptcy and other laws affecting creditors' rights.

AAA Debt rated 'AAA' has the highest rating assigned by Standard & Poor's. Capacity to pay interest and repay principal is extremely strong.

- •
- •
- •

BBB Debt rated 'BBB' is regarded as having an adequate capacity to pay interest and repay principal. Whereas it normally exhibits adequate protection parameters, adverse economic conditions or changing circumstances are more likely to lead to a weakened capacity to pay interest and repay principal for debt in this category than in higher rated categories.

Debt rated 'BB', 'B', 'CCC', 'CC' and 'C' is regarded as having predominantly speculative characteristics with respect to capacity to pay interest and repay principal. 'BB' indicates the least degree of speculation and 'C' the highest degree of speculation. While such debt will likely have some quality and protective characteristics, these are outweighed by large uncertainties or major risk exposures to adverse conditions.

- •
- •
- •

CCC Debt rated 'CCC' has a current identifiable vulnerability to default, and is dependent upon favorable business, financial, and economic conditions to meet timely payment of interest and repayment of principal. In the event of adverse business, financial, or economic conditions, it is not likely to have the capacity to pay interest and repay principal.

- •
- •
- •

D Debt rated 'D' is in default, or is expected to default upon maturity or payment date.

Plus (+) or minus (−): The ratings from 'AA' to 'CCC' may be modified by the addition of a plus or minus sign to show relative standing within the major rating categories.

Source: Standard & Poor's, "Corporate and Municipal Rating Definitions," *Standard Corporation Descriptions*. New York, December 1990, p. 6938. © Standard & Poor's Corporation. All rights reserved.

than a BBB— rating have had extreme difficulty raising debt capital in public markets. Bonds rated below BBB— are known as "speculative"-grade bonds.

A recent phenomenon has been the rise and subsequent collapse of the high-yield or junk bond market, composed of original-issue, speculative-grade bonds. Beginning from a base of just over $10 billion outstanding in 1979, the junk bond market exploded to over $200 billion by late 1989, and then went into a tailspin from which it is yet to recover. A principal factor in the growth of the market was a rethinking on the part of some investors of the risks inherent in speculative-grade bonds. Although interest rate premiums on junk bonds relative to government bonds were as high as five percentage points, accumulating evidence appeared to suggest that premiums of only one to two percentage points were sufficient to compensate for the higher default risk of junk bonds. The resulting investor interest in speculative-grade bonds was a boon to a number of mid-sized companies, which for the first time found the public debt market a viable alternative to traditional bank financing and to corporate raiders and deal makers.

The more recent, highly publicized collapse of the junk bond market can be attributed to a combination of factors, including a rapidly rising junk bond default rate, increasing concern about the economy, new regulations requiring savings and loan associations to sell their huge junk bond portfolios, a spate of ill-conceived and ill-structured junk bond issues, and the legal problems and subsequent demise of the leading proponent of junk bond financing, Drexel Burnham Lambert. Whether the original-issue junk bond market will revive when memories dim and Michael Milken gets out of jail is yet to be seen.

Common Stock

Common stock is a *residual income* security. The stockholder has a claim on any income remaining after the payment of all obligations, including interest on debt. *If the firm prospers, stockholders are the chief beneficiaries; if it falters, they are the chief losers.* The amount of money a stockholder receives annually depends on the dividends the company chooses to pay. The board of directors makes this decision quarterly and is under no obligation to pay any dividend at all.

Shareholder Control

At least in theory, stockholders exercise control over company decisions through their ability to elect the board of directors. In the United States, the wide distribution of share ownership and the laws governing election of the board frequently combine to greatly reduce this authority. In some companies, ownership of as little as 10 percent of the stock is sufficient to control the entire board. In many other firms, there is no dominant shareholder group, and management controls the board, even though they may own little or none of the company.

This does not imply that managers in such companies are free to ignore shareholder interests entirely, for they face at least two potential constraints on their actions. One is created by their need to compete in product markets. If management does not make a product or provide a service efficiently and sell it at a competitive price, the company will lose market share to more aggressive rivals and will eventually be driven from the industry. The actions taken by managers to compete effectively in product markets are consistent with shareholder interests. Securities markets provide a second check on management discretion. If a company wants to raise debt or equity capital in future years, it must maintain its profitability in order to attract money from investors. Moreover, if managers ignore shareholder interests, stock price will suffer, and the firm may become the target of a hostile takeover. This is the subject of Chapter 9.

German and Japanese owners appear to exercise much more control over company managements than do their U.S. or English counterparts. In Germany, the legal ability of banks to hold unlimited equity stakes in industrial companies, combined with the historical insignificance of public financial markets, have led to high concentrations of ownership in many companies. Banks are controlling shareholders of many German businesses, with representation on the board of directors and effective control over the business's access to debt and equity capital. German managers are thus inclined to think twice before ignoring shareholder interests.

Like their American counterparts, Japanese banks are prohibited from owning more than 5 percent of an industrial company's shares. Nonetheless, Japan's *keiretsu* form of organization produces results similar to those in Germany. A *keiretsu* is a group

of companies—usually including a lead bank—that purchase sizable ownership interests in one another as a means of cementing
important business relations. Estimates for the Japanese economy
are that cross-stock holdings of this type account for as much as 60
percent of total shares outstanding.[1] When the majority of a company's stock is in the hands of business partners and associates
through cross shareholdings, managers ignore shareholder interests only at their peril.

Common Stock as an Investment

A common stockholder receives a return on his investment in two
forms: dividends and possible share price appreciation. If d_0 is the
dividends per share during the year and P_0 and P_1 are the
beginning-of-year and end-of-year stock price, the *annual income*
earned by the stockholder is

$$d_0 + P_1 - P_0$$

Dividing by the beginning-of-year stock price, the *annual return* is

$$\frac{\text{Annual}}{\text{return}} = \frac{\text{Dividend}}{\text{yield}} + \frac{\text{Percentage change}}{\text{in share price}}$$

$$= \frac{d_0}{P_0} + \frac{P_1 - P_0}{P_0}$$

Common stocks are an ownership claim against primarily
real, or productive, assets. If companies can maintain profit margins during inflation, real, inflation-adjusted profits should be relatively unaffected by inflation. For years, this reasoning led to the
belief that common stocks are a hedge against inflation, but this
did not prove to be the case during the recent bout of high inflation. Looking at Table 5–1 again, we see that, had an investor purchased a representative portfolio of common stocks in 1926 and
had he reinvested all dividends received in the same portfolio, his
average annual return in 1990, over the entire 65 years, would have

---

[1]Masaru Yoshitomi, "*Keiretsu:* An Insider's Guide to Japan's Conglomerates," *International Economic Insights,* September/October 1990, p. 11.

been 12.1 percent. However, from 1973 through 1981, a period when prices rose an average of 9.2 percent per annum, the average annual return on common stocks was only 5.2 percent.

The common stock return of 12.1 percent from 1926 through 1990 compares with a return of 4.9 percent on government bonds over the same period. The difference between the common stock return and the government bond return of 7.2 percent (12.1 percent − 4.9 percent) can be thought of as a *risk premium.* It is the extra return earned by common stockholders as compensation for the added risks they bore. Comparing the return on common stocks to the annual percentage change in consumer prices, we see that the *real* return to common stock investors over the period was 8.9 percent (12.1 percent − 3.2 percent).

Figure 5–1 presents much the same information more dramatically. It shows an investor's wealth at year-end 1990 had she invested $1 in various assets at year-end 1925. Common stocks are the clear winners here. By 1990 the original $1 investment in the common stock of small companies would have grown to a whopping $1,277.45, while $1 invested in the common stock of companies represented in the Standard & Poor's 500 stock index would have grown to a very respectable $517.50. In contrast, a dollar invested in long-term government bonds would have been worth only $17.99 in 1990. Common stocks, however, have proved to be a much more volatile investment than bonds, as Figure 5–2 attests.

Do Dividends Increase Annual Return?

It may appear from the preceding equation that annual return rises when dividends rise. But the world is not so simple. An increase in current dividends means one of two things: The company will have less money for investment, or it will have to raise more money from external sources to make the same investments. Either way, an increase in current dividends will reduce the stockholders' claim on future income, which will reduce share price appreciation. Depending on which effect dominates, annual returns may or may not increase as dividends rise.

FIGURE 5–1

Wealth Indexes of Investments in the U.S. Capital Markets, 1926–1990
(Assumed initial investment of $1 at year-end 1925; includes reinvestment income)

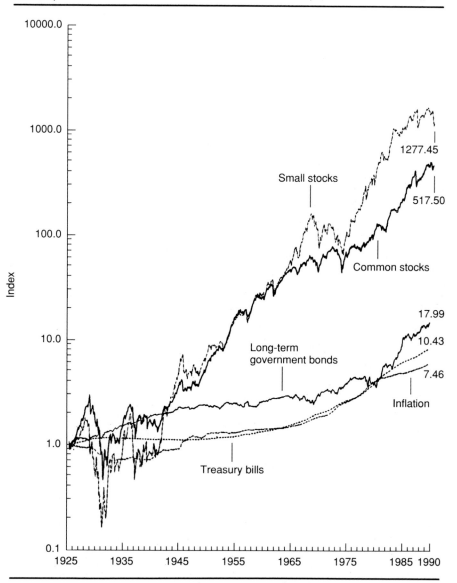

FIGURE 5–2
Volatility of Annual Returns from the U.S. Capital Markets (Common stocks
versus long-term government bonds)

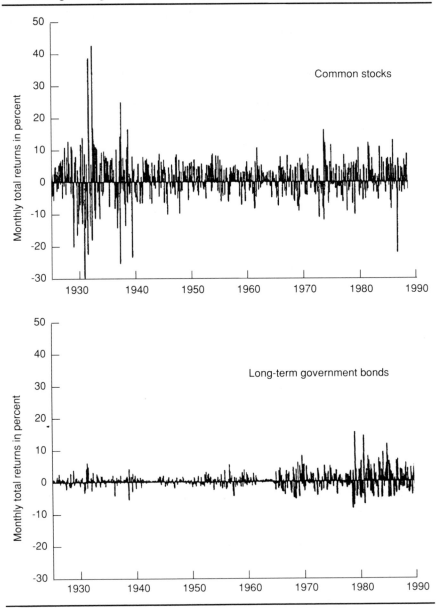

Preferred Stock

Preferred stock is a hybrid security—like debt in some ways, like equity in others. Like debt, preferred stock is a fixed-income security. It promises the investor a fixed dividend annually equal to the security's coupon rate times its par value. Like equity, the board of directors need not distribute this dividend unless it chooses. Also like equity, preferred dividend payments are *not* a deductible expense for corporate tax purposes. For the same coupon rate, this makes the *aftertax* cost of bonds about two-thirds that of preferred shares. Another similarity with equity is that, although preferred stock may have a call option, it frequently has no maturity. The preferred shares are outstanding indefinitely unless the company chooses to call them.

Cumulative Preferred

Company boards of directors have two strong incentives to pay preferred dividends. One is that preferred shareholders have priority over common shareholders as to dividend payments. Common shareholders receive no dividends unless preferred holders are paid in full. Second, virtually all preferred stocks are *cumulative*. If a firm passes a preferred dividend, the arrearage accumulates and must be paid in full before the company can resume common dividend payments.

The control that preferred shareholders have over management decisions varies. In some instances, preferred shareholders' approval is routinely required for major decisions; in others, preferred shareholders have no voice in management unless dividend payments are in arrears.

Preferred stock is not a widely used form of financing. Some persons see preferred stock as *cheap equity*. They see that preferred stock gives management much of the flexibility regarding dividend payments and maturity dates that common equity provides. Yet because preferred shareholders have no right to participate in future growth, they see preferred stock as less expensive than equity. The majority, however, sees preferred stock as *debt with a tax disadvantage*. Because few companies would ever omit a preferred dividend payment unless absolutely forced to, the majority places little value on the flexibility of preferred stock. To them the important fact is that interest payments on bonds are tax deductible, whereas dividend payments on preferred stock are not.

FINANCIAL MARKETS

Having reviewed the basic security types, let us turn now to a look at the markets in which these securities are issued and traded. Of particular interest will be the controversial notion of market efficiency.

Private Placement or Public Issue?

Companies raise money in two broad ways: through private negotiations with banks, insurance companies, pension funds, or other financial institutions, or by selling securities to the public. The former is known as a *private placement;* the latter is a *public issue.* Although private placements of equity are rather rare, private debt placements account for a significant fraction of total corporate debt.

To sell securities to the public, a company must register the issue with the Securities and Exchange Commission. This is an expensive, time-consuming, cumbersome task, but unless registered, securities may not trade on public markets. This is a valuable privilege. It means that the owner of registered securities can sell them by just calling a stockbroker and placing an order. In contrast, when a financial institution wants to liquidate some of its holdings of private placements, it must find another institution willing to purchase a large block of the securities.

A company's choice of whether to raise money via private placement or public issue comes down to this: Private placements are simpler, quicker, and can be tailored more closely to the particular needs of the issuer, but because they are difficult for buyers to resell, private placements carry a higher interest rate than public issues.

In 1989, the SEC relaxed restrictions on the trading of private placements to create, in effect, a quasi-public market for some private placements. Provided the issue is sold only to qualified, large financial institutions, these institutions may now trade the issue freely among themselves after issue. Many market professionals anticipate that this increased liquidity among major large investors will reduce, or eliminate, the interest rate premium on private placements relative to public issues. They also hope that a relaxation of the public disclosure requirements imposed on foreign issuers will improve the attractiveness of the U.S. private placement market relative to its chief rival, the Eurodollar market.

Organized Exchanges and Over-the-Counter Markets

Public issues trade on two types of markets: organized exchanges and over-the-counter markets. Organized exchanges, such as the New York Stock Exchange and the American Stock Exchange, are centralized trading locations that maintain active markets in hundreds of securities. Stockbroker members of the exchange transmit clients' buy-and-sell orders to specialists on the floor of the exchange, who attempt to match buyers with sellers. Specialists may buy or sell securities for their own accounts, but more often they act as agents, pairing buyers with sellers.

Over-the-counter (OTC) markets are much more informal. Any stock brokerage house anywhere in the country can create an OTC market for a security by quoting a *bid* price at which it will buy the security and a higher *asked* price at which it will sell the security. The spread between bid and ask prices is the broker's revenue. In return, the broker must keep an inventory of the security and must frequently trade for her own account to maintain an active market. Most well-known equity securities trade on organized exchanges, whereas the shares of smaller, regional companies and a great many bonds trade on the OTC market.

Eurodollar Markets

From a global perspective, companies can raise money on three types of markets: *domestic, foreign,* and *international.* A domestic market is the market in the company's home country, while foreign markets are the domestic markets of other countries. U.S. financial markets are thus domestic to IBM and General Motors but foreign to Sony Corporation and British Petroleum. Conversely,

Japanese markets are domestic to Sony but foreign to IBM and BP.

Companies find it attractive to raise money in foreign markets for a variety of reasons. When the domestic market is small or poorly developed, a company may find that only foreign markets are large enough to absorb the contemplated issue. Companies may also want liabilities denominated in the foreign currency instead of their own. For example, when Walt Disney expanded into Japan, it sought yen-denominated liabilities as a way to reduce the foreign exchange risk created by its yen-denominated revenues. Finally, issuers may believe that foreign-denominated liabilities will prove cheaper than domestic ones in view of anticipated exchange rate changes.

Access to foreign financial markets has historically been a sometime thing. The Swiss and Japanese have frequently restricted access to their markets by limiting the aggregate amount of money foreigners may raise in a given time period, or by imposing firm-size and credit-quality constraints on foreign issuers. Even U.S. markets, the largest and traditionally most open markets in the world, have not always offered unrestricted access to foreigners. Beginning in the late 1960s and continuing for almost a decade, foreign borrowers in the United States were subject to a surcharge known as the Interest Equalization Tax (IET). The tax was purportedly to compensate for low U.S. interest rates, but was seen by most observers as an attempt to bolster a weak dollar in foreign exchange markets by constraining foreign borrowing.

International financial markets are a free market response to domestic regulation. A transaction is said to occur in the international financial market when the currency employed is outside the control of the issuing monetary authority. A dollar-denominated loan to an American company in London, a German mark loan to a Japanese company in Singapore, and a French franc bond issue by a Dutch company underwritten in Frankfurt are all examples of international financial market transactions. In each instance, the transaction occurs in a locale that is beyond the direct regulatory reach of the issuing monetary authority. Thus, the U.S. Federal Reserve has trouble regulating banking activities in London even when the activities involve American companies and are denominated in dollars, just as the Bundesbank has difficulty regulating German mark activities in Singapore.

International financial markets got their start in London shortly after World War II, and were originally limited to dollar transactions in Europe; hence, the name *Eurodollar*. And while the markets have since grown well beyond dollar transactions in Europe to become truly global, they are still known generically as Eurodollar markets—somehow names like "Japofranc" never caught on.

Euromarket activity has burgeoned in recent years because the markets provide access to large pools of capital, denominated in a number of currencies, at very competitive prices. Moreover, the absence of regulation drives issue costs and reporting requirements to an absolute minimum.

Two important reasons Eurodollar markets can offer lower cost financing than domestic markets are the absence of reserve requirements on Eurodollar deposits and the ability to issue bonds in what is known as *bearer form*. In the United States and many other domestic markets, banks must abide by reserve requirements stipulating that they place a portion of each deposit in a special, noninterest-bearing account at the central bank. Because these reserves tie up resources without yielding a return, domestic loans must carry a higher interest rate than Eurodollar loans to yield the same profit.

The chief appeal of bearer bonds is that they make it easier for investors to avoid paying taxes on interest income. The company issuing a bearer bond never knows its owners and simply makes interest and principal payments to whoever presents the appropriate coupon at the appropriate time. In contrast, the issuer of a registered security maintains records of the owner and the payments made. Because bearer securities facilitate tax avoidance, they are illegal in the United States. Their use in Eurodollar markets means that Eurodollar bonds can carry lower coupon rates than comparable, domestic bonds and still yield the same aftertax returns.

The ability of Eurodollar markets to draw business away from domestic markets has sharply accelerated the deregulation of domestic financial markets. As long as companies and investors can avoid onerous domestic regulations by simply migrating to Eurodollar markets, regulators face a Hobson's choice: They can either remove the offending regulations, or watch Eurodollar markets grow at the expense of domestic markets. The Interest Equalization Tax is an apt example. When first imposed, the tax had the desired effect of restricting foreign companies' access to dollar financing. Over time, however, borrowers found they could avoid the tax by simply going to the Eurodollar markets. The longer-run effect of the IET, therefore, was to shift business away from the United States without greatly affecting the total volume of dollar financing. An avowed goal in repealing the IET was to make U.S. markets more competitive with Eurodollar markets.

Not all regulations are bad, of course. Regulatory oversight of financial markets and the willingness of governments to combat panics have greatly stabilized markets and economies for over 50 years. The ongoing question is whether the deregulatory pressures created by Eurodollar markets are improving efficiency by stripping away unwarranted restraints, or whether they are dangerously destabilizing the world economy. Stay tuned.

Investment Banking

Investment bankers are the grease that keeps financial markets running smoothly. They are finance specialists who assist companies in raising money. Other activities include stock and bond brokerage, investment counselling, merger and acquisition analysis, and corporate consulting. Some investment banking companies, such as Merrill Lynch, employ thousands of brokers and have offices all over the world. Others, exemplified by Morgan Stanley and First Boston, specialize in working with companies and are consequently less in the public eye. As to the range of services provided, H. F. Saint said it best in his Wall Street thriller, *Memoirs of an Invisible Man,* "[Investment bankers] perform all sorts of interesting services and acts—in fact any service or act that can be performed in a suit, this being the limitation imposed by their professional ethics."[2]

---

[2] H. F. Saint, *Memoirs of an Invisible Man* (New York: Dell Publishing, 1987), p. 290.

When a company is about to raise new capital, an investment banker's responsibilities are not unlike his fees—many and varied. In a private placement, the investment banker customarily acts as an agent, bringing issuer and potential buyer together and helping them negotiate an agreement. In a public issue, the investment banker's responsibilities are much broader; they vary depending on whether the company registers the securities with the SEC in the traditional manner or uses what is known as a "shelf registration."

Traditional Registration

In this mode, the investment banker begins working with the issuing company very early in the decision process. In most instances, the banker will have worked closely with management for some years and will have built up a working rapport. The first task is to help the company decide what type of security to sell. Then, if it is to be a public issue, the banker will help the company register the issue with the SEC. This usually takes 30 to 90 days. A deterrent to registration for many companies, particularly foreign firms, is the extent of the SEC disclosure requirements. Companies must disclose detailed information about their finances, officers, plans, and so on—information some managements would prefer to keep confidential.

While a traditional registration wends its way toward approval, the investment banker puts together a *selling* and an *underwriting syndicate.* A syndicate is a team of as many as 100 investment banking houses that join forces for a brief time to place the new securities. Each member of the selling syndicate accepts the responsibility for selling a specified portion of the new securities to investors. Members of the underwriting syndicate act, in effect, as wholesalers, purchasing all of the securities from the company at a guaranteed price and attempting to sell them to the public at a higher price. The "Rules of Fair Practice" of the National Association of Securities Dealers prohibit underwriters from selling the securities to the public at a price above the original offer price quoted to the company. If necessary, however, the syndicate may sell at a lower price.

Given the volatility of security prices and the length of time required to go through registration, it may appear that underwriters bear significant risks when they guarantee the company a fixed price. This is not the way the world works, however. The underwriters do not commit themselves to a firm price until just hours before the sale, and if all goes as planned, the entire issue will be sold to the public on the same day. It is the company, not the underwriters, that bears the risk that the terms on which the securities can be sold will change during registration.

The life of a syndicate is a brief one. Syndicates form several months prior to an issue for the purpose of preselling and disband as soon as the securities are sold. Even on unsuccessful issues, the syndicate breaks up several weeks after the issue date, leaving each underwriter to dispose of his unsold shares on his own.

Shelf Registration

In a shelf registration the issuer files a general-purpose registration good for up to two years indicating in broad terms the securities it may issue. Once approved by the SEC, and provided it is updated periodically, the company can put the registration on the "shelf" ready for use as desired. A shelf registration cuts the time lag between the decision to issue a security and receipt of the proceeds from several months to as little as 48 hours.

Because 48 hours is far too little time in which to throw together a syndicate, shelf registrations tend to be "bought deals" in which a single investment house buys the entire issue, hoping to resell it piecemeal at a profit. And because a shelf registration increases the likelihood of competitive bidding among investment banks, the issue costs on shelf registrations are as much as 10 to 50 percent lower than for traditional registrations, depending on the type of security and other factors.[3]

Cost of New Issues

Financial securities impose two kinds of costs on the issuer: annual costs and issue costs. We will consider the more important annual costs later. Issue costs are the costs incurred by the issuer

---

[3]Robert J. Rogowski and Eric H. Sorensen, "Deregulation in Investment Banking, Shelf Registrations, Structure, and Performance," *Financial Management,* Spring 1985, pp. 5–15. See also Sanjai Bhagat, M. Wayne Marr, and G. Rodney Thompson, "The Rule 415 Experiment: Equity Markets," *Journal of Finance,* December 1985, pp. 1385–1402.

and its shareholders on initial sale. For a private placement, the only substantive cost is the fee charged by the investment banker in his or her capacity as agent. On a public issue, there are legal, accounting, and printing fees, plus those paid to the investment banker. The investment banker states his fee in the form of a *spread.* To illustrate, suppose ABC Corporation wants to sell one million new shares using traditional registration procedures and that its shares are presently trading at $20 on the American Stock Exchange. A few hours prior to public sale, the lead investment banker might inform ABC management that "Given the present tone of the markets we can sell the new shares at an issue price of $19 and a spread of $1.50, for a net to the company of $17.50." This means that the investment banker intends to *underprice* the issue $1 per share ($20 market price less $19 issue price) and that he is charging a fee of $1.50 per share, or $1.5 million for his services. This fee will be split among the managing underwriter, or lead bank, and the syndicate members by prior arrangement, according to each bank's importance in the syndicates.

To underprice an issue means to offer the new shares for sale at a price below that prevailing for existing shares. Investment bankers often underprice on the theory that the price of the new shares must be below that of existing shares to induce investors to hold more and because it makes their own job easier. Selling something worth $20 for $19 is a lot easier than selling it for $20. Underpricing is not an out-of-pocket cost to the company, but it is a cost to shareholders. The greater the underpricing, the more new shares a company must issue to raise a given amount of money. And as the number of shares issued goes up, the percentage ownership of existing shareholders goes down.

Empirical studies of issue costs confirm two prominent patterns. First, equity is much more costly than debt. Ballpark figures for larger companies indicate that the cost of a typical-size equity issue, ignoring underpricing, is about 5.5 percent of the gross proceeds, while a comparable figure for debt is only 1.0 percent. Second, issue costs for all security types rise rapidly as issue size declines. Issue costs as a percent of gross proceeds for equity are as low as 3 percent for issues larger than $100 million but rise to over *20 percent* for issues under $500,000. Comparable figures for debt financing are below 0.9 percent for large issues to over 10 percent for very small ones.[4]

Regulatory Changes

Financial market deregulation has ignited a revolution among American financial institutions. In part, deregulation has been the outgrowth of a changing regulatory philosophy, but at least as important has been a wide array of technological and competitive innovations that have made regulation increasingly ineffective.

Prior to the Great Depression, U.S. banks were allowed to engage in commercial and investment banking. In 1933, Congress passed the Glass-Steagall Act to eliminate perceived conflicts of interest between the two activities. Since then, commercial banks have been prohibited from engaging in most securities-trading activity, while investment banks have been prohibited from acting as depository institutions. However, it has become increasingly difficult to draw a clear line of separation between what constitutes commercial banking as opposed to investment banking; we see today a steady encroachment of each type of bank on the other's turf. This trend has prompted many observers to predict that the legal barriers separating the two activities cannot be long maintained in the face of heightening competition. In other countries, most banks, including U.S. multinational banks, are free to engage in investment and commercial banking activities.

The recent savings and loan debacle and the growing financial difficulties among commercial banks have increased pressure on Congress to make fundamental changes in the nation's banking laws. At the time of this writing, February 1991, the majority view appears to be that the laws should be relaxed to allow banks to expand across state lines, to engage in certain investment banking activities, and possibly to be owned by industrial companies. At the other extreme, however, there are some who believe that the risk-

---

[4]W. H. Mikkelson and M. M. Partch, "Valuation Effects of Security Offerings and the Issuing Process," *Journal of Financial Economics,* January/February 1986; Securities and Exchange Commission, "Cost of Flotation of Registered Securities, 1971–1972" (Washington, D.C.: U.S. Government Printing Office, December 1974).

taking ability of commercial banks should be sharply curtailed by allowing them to invest only in government securities and home mortgages. The only certainty at this point is that Congress must do something soon or events will pass them by.

EFFICIENT MARKETS

A recurring issue in raising new capital is that of *timing.* Companies are naturally anxious to sell new securities when prices are high. Toward this end, managers routinely devote considerable time and money to the prediction of future price trends in financial markets.

Concern for proper timing of security issues is natural, but there is a growing perception among academicians and market professionals that attempts to forecast future prices in financial markets will be successful only in exceptional circumstances, and that unless these circumstances exist, there is nothing to be gained by forecasting.

Such pessimism follows from the notion of *efficient markets,* a much debated and controversial topic in recent years. This is not the place for a detailed discussion of efficient markets. However, because the implications of the topic are far-reaching and because the concept is beginning to affect the way financial managers think about their jobs, it merits some attention. The interested reader is referred to the recommended readings at the end of the chapter for more detailed treatments of the topic.

Market efficiency is controversial in large part because many proponents have overstated the evidence supporting efficiency and have misrepresented its implications. To avoid this, let us agree on two things right now. First, market efficiency is not a question of black or white but rather of shades of gray. A market, rather than being efficient or inefficient, is *more* or *less* efficient. Moreover, the degree of efficiency is an empirical question that can be answered only by studying a particular market. Second, market efficiency depends on one's perspective. The New York Stock Exchange can be efficient to a dentist in Des Moines who doesn't know an underwriter from an undertaker; and at the same time, it can be highly *in*efficient to a specialist on the floor of the exchange who has detailed information about buyers and sellers of each stock and up-to-the-second prices.

What Is an Efficient Market?

Market efficiency is a description of how prices in competitive markets respond to new information. The arrival of new information to a competitive market can be likened to the arrival of a lamb chop to a school of flesh-eating piranha, where investors are—plausibly enough—the piranha. The instant the lamb chop hits the water, there is turmoil as the fish devour the meat. Very soon the meat is gone, leaving only the worthless bone behind, and the water returns to normal. Similarly, when new information reaches a competitive market there is much turmoil as investors buy and sell securities in response to the news, causing prices to change. Once prices adjust, all that is left of the information is the worthless bone. No amount of gnawing on the bone will yield any more meat, and no further study of old information will yield any more valuable intelligence.

An efficient market, then, is one in which prices adjust rapidly to new information and in which current prices fully reflect available information about the assets traded. "Fully reflect" means that investors rapidly pounce on new information, analyze it, revise their expectations, and buy or sell securities accordingly. They continue to buy or sell securities until price changes eliminate the incentive for further trades. In such an environment, current prices reflect the cumulative judgment of investors. They *fully reflect* available information.

The degree of efficiency displayed by a particular market depends on the speed with which prices adjust to news and the type of news to which prices respond. It is common to speak of three levels of informational efficiency:

A market is *weak-form* efficient if current prices fully reflect all information about past prices.

A market is *semistrong-form* efficient if current prices fully reflect all publicly available information.

A market is *strong-form* efficient if current prices fully reflect all information public or private.

Extensive tests of many financial markets suggest that with limited exceptions most financial markets are semistrong-form efficient, but not strong-form efficient. This statement needs to be qualified in two respects. First, there is the issue of perspective. The above statement applies to the typical investor, subject to brokerage fees and without special information-gathering equipment. It does *not* apply to market makers. Second, it is impossible to test every possible type and combination of public information for efficiency. All we can say is that the most plausible types of information tested with the most sophisticated techniques available indicate efficiency. This does not preclude the possibility that a market may be inefficient with respect to some as yet untested information source.

Implications of Efficiency

If financial markets are semistrong-form efficient, the following statements are true:

- Publicly available information is not helpful in forecasting future prices.
- In the absence of private information, the best forecast of future price is current price, perhaps adjusted for a long-run trend.
- Without private information, a company cannot improve the terms on which it sells securities by trying to select the optimal time to sell.

Individuals without private information have two choices. They can reconcile themselves to efficiency and quit trying to forecast security prices, or they can attempt to make the market inefficient from their perspective. This involves becoming a market insider by acquiring the best available information-gathering system in hopes of learning about events before others. A variation— usually illegal—is to seek inside information. Advance knowledge that Carl Icahn will attempt to acquire TWA, for example, would undoubtedly be useful in forecasting TWA's future stock price. A

How Rapidly Do Stock Prices Adjust to New Information?

The following graph, Figure 5–3, gives an indication of the speed with which common stock prices adjust to new information. It is a result of what is known as an "event study." In this instance the researcher is studying the impact of acquisition offers on the stock price of the target firm. It is easiest to think of the graph initially as a plot of the daily prices of the target firm's stock from a period beginning 40 days before the announcement of the acquisition offer and ending 40 days after. An acquisition offer is invariably good news to the target firm's shareholders because the offer is at a price well above the prevailing market price of the firm's shares; so we expect to see the target company's stock price rise after the announcement. The question is, How rapidly? The answer evident from the graph is, Very rapidly. We see that the stock price drifts upward prior to the announcement, shoots up dramatically on the announcement day, and then drifts without much direction after the announcement. Clearly, if you read about the announcement in the evening paper and buy the stock the next morning, you will miss out on the major price move. The market will already have responded to the new information.

The upward drift in stock price prior to the announcement is consistent with three possible explanations: (1) insiders are buying the stock in anticipation of the announcement, (2) security analysts are very good at anticipating which firms will be acquisition targets and when the offer will be made, or (3) acquiring firms tend to announce offers after the price stock of the target firm's stock has increased for several weeks. I have my own views, but will leave it to you to decide which explanation is more plausible.

An old Jewish proverb says, "For example is no proof." If the price pattern illustrated by the graph were for just one firm, it would be a curiosity only. To avoid this problem, the researcher has studied the price patterns of 161 target firms involving successful acquisitions that occurred over 15 years ending in 1977. The prices you see are an index composed of the prices of the 161 firms, and the time scale is in "event time," not calendar time. Here the event is the acquisition announcement, defined as day 0, and all other dates are relative to this event date. The pattern observed, therefore, describes general experience, not an isolated event.

How Rapidly Do Stock Prices Adjust to New Information? (concluded)

In recent years, academicians have performed a great number of event studies involving different markets and events, and the preponderance of these studies indicates that financial markets in the United States respond to new, publicly available information within one day or less.

FIGURE 5–3

Time Series of the Mean Price Index of the Shares of 161 Target Firms Involved in Successful Tender Offers

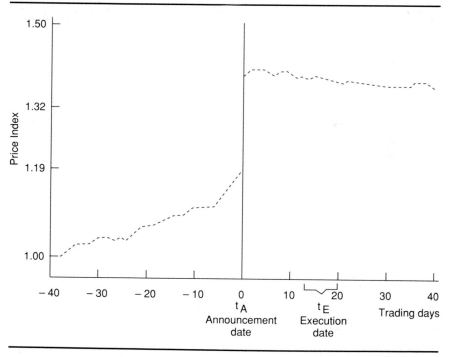

Source: Michael Bradley, "Interfirm Tender Offers and the Market for Corporate Control," *Journal of Business* 53, no. 4 (1980).

third strategy used by some is to purchase the forecasts of prestigious consulting firms, the chief virtue of which appears to be that there will be someone to blame if things go wrong.

As the above comments suggest, market efficiency is a subtle and provocative notion with a number of important implications for investors as well as companies. Our treatment of the topic here has been necessarily brief, but it should be sufficient to suggest that unless executives have inside information or superior information-gathering and analysis systems, there may be little to be gained from trying to forecast prices in financial markets. This conclusion applies to many markets in which companies participate, including those for government and corporate securities, foreign currencies, and commodities.

APPENDIX

USING FINANCIAL MARKETS TO MANAGE CORPORATE RISKS

This appendix looks briefly at the use of forward and option markets to manage certain business risks. The topic merits our consideration for at least three reasons. First, sharp increases in the volatility of foreign exchange rates, interest rates, and commodity prices in recent years have heightened corporate interest in controlling these risks. Second, as companies make increasing use of forward and option markets to manage risk, it is important for executives to appreciate what these markets can and *cannot* do to help avoid unexpected losses. Third, the popularity of forward and option trading is growing rapidly among stock and bond investors, sometimes as a means of controlling portfolio risks and other times as a potent alternative to a day at the track.

In the interest of brevity we will confine our attention here to the use of financial markets to manage foreign exchange risks. If you want to study the topic in more depth, or to learn about similar techniques for managing interest rate and commodity price risks, take a look at *Managing Financial Risks* by Smith, Smithson, and Wilford.[5]

---

[5]C. W. Smith, Jr., C. W. Smithson, and D. Sykes Wilford, *Managing Financial Risk* (New York: Ballinger Publishing Company, 1990).

Forward Markets

Most financial markets are *spot* markets, in which a price is set today for immediate exchange. In a *forward* market, the price is set today, but exchange occurs at some stipulated *future* date. Buying bread at the grocery store is a spot market transaction, while reserving a hotel room, to be billed later, is a forward market transaction. Most assets trading in forward markets also trade spot. To illustrate these markets, on February 7, 1991, the spot price of one German mark in currency markets was $0.6873, meaning that payment of this amount would buy one mark for immediate delivery. In contrast, the 90-day forward rate on the same day was $0.6831, meaning that payment of this slightly lesser amount in 90 days would buy one mark for delivery at that time. A forward transaction typically involves a contract, most likely with a bank, in which the parties set the price today at which they agree to trade marks for dollars in 90 days.

Speculating in Forward Markets

Although our interest in this appendix is on risk avoidance, we will begin at the opposite end of the spectrum by looking at forward market speculation. As will become apparent, speculation—especially the creative use of one speculation to counteract another—is the essence of the risk-management techniques to be described. To demonstrate this important fact, imagine that, struck with an irresistible impulse, you have just remortgaged your home and bet $100,000 on Sugar Ray Leonard to beat Larry Norris in an upcoming fight. Your spouse, having learned of your transgression, threatens serious consequences if you do not cancel the bet immediately, but a brief chat with your bookie suggests that wagers are seldom canceled without a broken kneecap or two. So what do you do? Recognizing that your mother was incorrect, that two wrongs may indeed make one right, you place a second wager—but this time on Norris to beat Leonard. Now no matter who wins, the proceeds from your winning wager will cover the cost of your losing one; and except for the bookie's take, it's just as if you had never made the first bet. You've hedged your bet. Companies use financial market "wagers" analogously to manage unavoidable commercial risks.

For a closer look at forward market speculation, suppose the treasurer of American Merchandising Inc., AMI, believes the dollar price of the German mark will fall dramatically over the next 90 days.[6] Forward

---

[6]My apologies to non-U.S. readers for making the United States the home country throughout this appendix. Please take solace in the fact that Americans need all the help we can get when it comes to understanding exchange rates.

currency markets offer a simple way for the treasurer to bet on his expectations by executing a modest variation on the old buy-low, sell-high strategy. Here he will sell high first and buy low later. Sell marks forward today at $0.6831, wait 90 days as the mark plummets, and then purchase marks in the spot market for delivery on the forward contract. If the treasurer is correct, the forward price at which he sells the marks will exceed the future spot price at which he buys them, and he will profit from the difference. Of course, the reverse is also true. If the mark strengthens relative to the dollar, the forward selling price will be below the spot buying price, and the treasurer will lose money.

Putting this into equation form, the gain or loss on, say, a one million mark forward sale is

$$\text{Gain or loss} = (F - \tilde{S})\text{DM 1 million},$$

where F is the 90-day forward price and $\tilde{S}$ is the spot price 90 days hence. The spot price has a tilde over it as a reminder that it is unknown today.

Figure 5A-1I shows this equation graphically. The treasurer's gamble is a winner when the future spot price is below today's forward rate, and a loser when it is above. We will refer to this and similar position diagrams several times throughout the appendix.

Hedging in Forward Markets

We are now ready to see how currency speculation can reduce risk of loss on cross-border transactions. Whenever a company has assets or liabilities denominated in foreign currencies, it faces the risk that the home currency value of these assets or liabilities will vary due to changing currency values. To illustrate, suppose AMI has just booked a one million mark sale to a German buyer with payment to be received in 90 days. The dollar value of this account receivable is

$$\$ \text{ Value of AMI's receivable} = \tilde{S}(\text{DM 1 million})$$

where $\tilde{S}$ is again the spot exchange rate. AMI faces foreign exchange risk, or exposure, because the dollar value of its German receivable in 90 days depends on the uncertain, future spot rate.

Figure 5A-1 II shows the change in the dollar value of AMI's receivable as the exchange rate changes. If the spot rate remains at $0.6873, the receivable's value will not vary from its current indicated worth, shown as zero gain or loss on the graph. As the price of the mark rises, the dollar value of AMI's receivable rises as well; and as the mark weakens, the dollar value of the receivable declines. Clearly, an unlucky fall in the mark over coming months could turn an expected profit on the German sale into a loss—not exactly a morale booster for the operating folks who worked so hard to make the sale.

To eliminate this risk, suppose AMI's treasurer hedges the receivable "bet" by selling one million marks 90 days forward as before. Adding the gain or loss from the forward sale to the dollar value of the receivable,

$$\underset{\text{forward sale}}{\text{Gain or loss on}} + \underset{\text{receivable}}{\text{\$ value of}}$$

$$(F - \tilde{S}) \text{ DM 1 million} + (\tilde{S}) \text{ DM 1 million}$$
$$= (F) \text{ DM 1 million}$$

The elimination of $\tilde{S}$ from the equation indicates that the treasurer's judicious combination of two opposing bets eliminates AMI's currency exposure. Now, regardless of what happens to the spot rate, AMI will receive the current forward rate times one million marks, or $683,100, in 90 days. The treasurer has executed a *forward market hedge,* the effect of which is to replace the unknown future spot rate with the known forward rate in determining the dollar value of the receivable.

Figure 5A-1 III shows the hedge graphically. The solid, upward-sloping line is the gain or loss on the unhedged receivable from II, while the dotted, downward-sloping line is the position diagram for the forward sale from I. The bold, horizontal line represents the combined effect of the receivable and the forward sale. When both are undertaken, the *net* outcome is independent of the future spot rate. The forward hedge eliminates risk just as opposing bets on the Leonard-Norris bout did.

Instead of manipulating equations to determine the net effect of hedging, it is usually simpler to do the same thing graphically by just adding the position diagram from one bet to that of the other at each exchange rate. For instance, adding the gain on the receivable, denoted by *a* in III, to the loss on the forward sale, *b,* yields the net result, *c.* The fact that the net result at each exchange rate lies on the bold, horizontal line confirms that the hedge eliminates exchange risk.[7]

Hedging in Money and Capital Markets

The treasurer eliminated exchange risk on the AMI's German asset by creating a German mark liability of precisely the same size and maturity. In the jargon of the trader he *covered* the company's *long position* by cre-

---

[7]The hedged position in Figure 5A-1 III appears to result in a loss. Strictly speaking, however, this is not necessarily the case. A hedge involves an expected loss only when the forward rate is below the treasurer's expected *future* spot rate. The figure implicitly assumes that the treasurer's expected future spot rate equals the current spot, which clearly need not be true.

ating an offsetting *short position,* where a long position refers to a foreign-currency asset and a short position corresponds to a foreign-currency liability. By offsetting one against the other, he *squared* the position.

A second way to create a short position in marks is to borrow marks today, promising to repay one million marks in 90 days, and to sell the marks immediately in the spot market for dollars. Then in 90 days, the one million marks received in payment of the account receivable can be used to repay the loan. After the dust settles, such a *money market* hedge enables AMI to receive a known sum of dollars today in return for one million marks in 90 days.

Hedging with Options

Options are for those who tire of Russian roulette—unless of course they are one leg of a hedge. An option is a security entitling the holder to either buy or sell an underlying asset at a specified price and for a specified time. They come in two flavors: A *put* option conveys the right to sell the underlying asset, while a *call* is a right to buy. To illustrate, for a payment of $3,700 on February 7, 1991, you could have purchased *put* options on German marks giving you the right to sell one million German marks for $0.6700 per mark at any time through March 20, 1991. As a matter of semantics, $0.6700 is the option's *exercise,* or *striking,* price, and March 20 is its *maturity date.* The $3,700 purchase price is known as the *premium,* and is payable at purchase.

Figure 5A-2I shows the position diagram for these put options at maturity for differing exchange rates. The lower, dotted line includes the premium, while the solid line omits it. Concentrating first on the solid line, we see that the puts are worthless at maturity when the spot exchange rate exceeds the option's striking price. The right to sell marks for 67 cents each obviously isn't very enticing when they command a higher price in the spot market. In this event, the options will expire worthless, and you will have spent the $3,700 premium for nothing. The outcome is much different, however, when the spot rate is below the striking price at maturity. If the spot exchange rate falls to 65 cents, for instance, the option to sell one million marks at 67 cents is worth $20,000, and this number rises rapidly as the mark sinks further toward zero. In the best of all worlds—provided you're not German—the mark will be worthless, and your puts will garner $670,000—not a bad return on a $3,700 bet.

The position diagram for call options is just the reverse of that for puts. Once again on February 7, call options on one million marks with the same striking price and maturity date as the puts were available for a premium of $19,500. As shown in Figure 5A-2 II, these calls will expire worthless unless the spot price rises above the striking price—the right to buy something for more than its spot price has no value. But once above the striking price, the value of the calls rise penny-for-penny with the spot.

To understand why options appeal to serious speculators, imagine you believe the mark will rise to 70 cents within three months. Using the forward market to speculate on your belief, you can purchase one million marks today for 68.73 cents each and sell them in three months for 70 cents, thereby generating a return of less than 2 percent ([0.70 − 0.6873]/ 0.6873 = 1.8%). Alternatively, you can purchase the call options for $19,500, followed in three months by exercise of the call and immediate sale of the marks for 0.70 cents each, thereby producing a heart-skipping return of 54 percent ([(0.70 − 0.67) × 1 million − 19,500]/19,500 = 54 percent)—a thirty-fold increase relative to the forward market speculation. Of course, the downside risks are equally magnified; thus a fall in the mark to 67 cents would generate a loss of only 2.5 percent in the forward market compared to a 100 percent loss with options.

How might AMI use options to reduce exchange risk on the company's German receivable? Because the receivable makes the company long in marks, the treasurer will want to create an offsetting short position; that is, he will want to purchase put options. Calls would only add to AMI's currency risk.

Analyzing the hedge graphically, Figure 5A-2 III shows the combined effect of AMI's German receivable and purchase of the described put options. As before, the upward-sloping, solid line represents the gain or loss in the dollar value of the receivable, and the bent, dotted line shows the payoff on the puts, including premium. Adding the two together at each exchange rate yields the heavy solid line, portraying AMI's exchange risk after hedging with options.

Comparing the forward market hedge in Figure 5A-1 III with the option hedge, we see that the option works much like an insurance policy, limiting AMI's loss when the mark weakens, while still enabling the company to benefit when it strengthens. The cost of this policy is the option's premium.

Options are especially attractive hedging vehicles in two situations. One is when the hedger has a view about which way currencies will move, but is too cowardly to speculate openly. In this circumstance an option hedge enables the hedger to benefit when her views prove to be correct, but limits her losses to no more than the premium when they are incorrect. Option hedges are also attractive when the exposure is contingent. When a company bids on a foreign contract, its currency exposure obvi-

FIGURE 5A–1

Forward Market Hedge

I. Forward Sale of DM 1 million

II. DM Account Receivable

III. Forward Market Hedge of Receivable

FIGURE 5A–2

Option Market Hedge

I. Put Option on DM 1 million

II. Call Option on DM 1 million

III. Option Market Hedge of Receivable

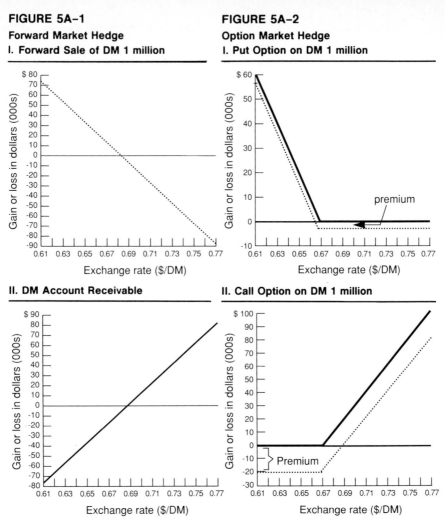

ously depends on whether the bid is accepted. Hedging this contingent exposure in forward markets will result in unintended, and possibly costly, reverse exposure if the bid is not accepted. The worst possible outcome with an option-based hedge, however, is loss of the premium.

Limitations of Financial Market Hedging

Recent initiates to the world of hedging occasionally overestimate the technique's importance, so a few cautionary reflections on the limitations of financial market hedges are in order.

Two basic conditions must hold before commercial risks can be hedged effectively in financial markets. One is that the asset creating the risk—or one closely correlated with it—must trade in financial markets, and must trade in maturities at least equal to that of the cash flows to be hedged. In our example, this means that marks must be a traded currency, and that forward markets, or money markets, must offer mark-denominated instruments with a maturity of at least 90 days.

This condition poses a significant limitation to managing currency exposure; of the world's more than 100 currencies, only *six* trade in public forward or option markets. And although the six traded currencies account for the great percentage of world trade, they do not include the more volatile currencies against which companies would most like to hedge. Had AMI's receivable been denominated in Brazilian cruzeiros or almost any currency other than one of the sacred six, the company would have been unable to hedge the exposure in forward or option markets.

The condition also means that it is difficult to hedge currency exposures beyond a year or two into the future, for the longest forward or option contracts traded in public markets are only nine months. Banks will often quote rates for longer periods for some currencies and in limited volumes, but pricing and volumes become less attractive as the maturity increases. This often leaves money and capital market hedges as the only viable instruments for managing longer-term exposure.[8]

The second necessary condition for effective foreign currency hedging is that the amount and the timing of the foreign cash flow must be known with reasonable certainty. This is not usually a problem when the cash flow is a foreign receivable or payable, but when it is an operating

---

[8]It might appear at first glance that a foreign currency receipt in, say, five years can be hedged by rolling over a sequence of five one-year forward sales, but this is not the case. The first one-year contract eliminates currency exposure in the first year, but the exposure in following years remains because the future forward rates at which the one-year contracts can be rolled over are unknown today.

cash flow, such as expected sales, cost of sales, or earnings, the story is quite different. To demonstrate, suppose the treasurer of an American exporter to Germany anticipates earnings next year of one million marks, and that she wants to lock in the dollar value of these profits by hedging. What should she do? At first glance, the answer appears elementary: just sell one million marks forward for dollars. But on further reflection, is it reasonable to assume that an exporter's profits will be independent of the dollar-mark exchange rate? Clearly, not. For as the mark strengthens, the exporter will become more competitive relative to German rivals, and earnings should rise; conversely, a falling mark should depress earnings. So how many marks should be sold forward to protect expected earnings? It's hard to say—very hard. Given extensive information about the exporter's products, markets, and competitors, we might be able to come up with an estimate in time, but the exercise will not be a trivial one. Moreover, even if we successfully hedge next year's earnings, the whole stream of future earnings from year two out into the indefinite future will remain at risk—talk about losing the forest for the trees. We conclude that hedging operating cash flows in financial markets is a complex, uncertain activity.

Our final caveat about financial market hedging is more philosophical. Empirical studies suggest that foreign exchange, commodity, and debt markets are all "fair games," meaning that the chance of benefiting from unexpected price changes in these markets about equals the chance of losing. If so, companies facing repeated exchange exposures, or those with a number of exposures in different currencies, might justifiably dispense with hedging on the grounds that long-run losses will about equal gains anyway. Financial market hedging according to this philosophy would be warranted only when the company seldom faced currency exposures, when the potential loss was too big for the company to absorb gracefully, or when the elimination of exchange exposure yielded administrative benefits such as more accurate performance evaluation or improved employee morale.

CHAPTER SUMMARY

1. This chapter has examined financial instruments and markets. When raising capital, the financial manager acts much like a marketing manager. The product is claims on the firm's income and assets, and the manager's goal is to package and sell these claims in a manner that yields the highest price to the company.

2. Companies are *not* greatly restricted by law or regulation in their ability to select or design a security. The key questions in designing a new security are: What does the investor want, and what meets the company's needs?

3. Fixed-income securities, such as bonds and most preferred stock, receive a comparatively safe income stream but do not participate in the growth of the firm. As an investment over the last 60-odd years, corporate bonds have done little more than keep up with inflation.

4. Common stock is a residual income security with claim on all income after payment of prior fixed claims. Common stockholders are the principal beneficiaries of company growth. They receive income as dividends and share price appreciation. Since 1926, the average *real* return on common stocks has been about 8.9 percent per year.

5. Private placement of new securities with a small group of knowledgeable institutions is usually faster and more flexible than a public issue.

6. A transaction is said to take place in the Eurodollar market when the currency employed is outside the control of the issuing monetary authority. Eurodollar markets are a free market response to regulated domestic financial markets. Competition from the Eurodollar markets has pressured domestic markets to deregulate or lose business.

7. A sizable body of empirical evidence suggests that financial markets in the United States and other well-developed financial markets are quite efficient. To earn above-average returns, an investor in these markets must have access to private information, or must be among the first to act upon newly available public information.

ADDITIONAL READING

Malkiel, Burton G. *A Random Walk Down Wall Street.* 4th ed. New York: W. W. Norton & Company, Inc., 1985. 377 pages.

A best-selling introduction to personal investing by an individual who knows both the academic and the professional sides of the story. No get-rich-quick schemes, but the straight stuff for the intelligent beginner. Available in paperback.

Stigum, Marcia. *The Money Market.* 3rd ed. Homewood, Ill.: Dow Jones-Irwin, 1989. 725 pages.

The bible of the money markets. When you devote over 700 pages to financial instruments with maturities of one year or less, you can cover the topic in considerable depth. Very well written, especially given the level of detail.

Van Horne, James C. *Financial Market Rates and Flows.* 3rd ed. Englewood Cliffs, N.J.: Prentice Hall, 1990. 340 pages.

A well-written, informative look at the function of financial markets, the flow of funds through markets, market efficiency, interest rates, and interest rate differentials. An excellent summary of empirical studies of financial markets. Intended as a supplement for courses in financial markets and for practitioners interested in issuing or investing in fixed-income securities. Not a bedtime read.

CHAPTER PROBLEMS

1. The return an investor earns on a bond over a period of time is known as the *holding period return,* defined as interest income plus, or minus, the change in the price of the bond over the period, all divided by the beginning bond price.
   a. What is the holding period return on a bond with a par value of $1,000 and a coupon rate of 8 percent if its price at the beginning of the year was $1,050 and its price at the end of the year was $920?
   b. Can you name two reasons the price of the bond might have declined over the year?

2. a. Can a company's bonds be riskier than the same company's common stock? Why, or why not?
   b. Can one company's bonds be riskier than another company's common stock? Why, or why not?

3. Jensen Pharmaceuticals wants to raise $200 million in a new stock issue. The company's investment banker indicates that a sale of new stock will require 5 percent underpricing and a 6 percent spread.
   a. Assuming Jensen's stock price does not change from its current price of $56 per share, how many shares must the company sell and at what price to the public?
   b. How much money will the investment banking syndicates earn on the sale?
   c. Is the 5 percent underpricing a cash flow? Is it a cost? If so, to whom?

4. At the end of 1988, Russell Corporation's stock price was $16.12 per share. A year later it was $26.12. Per share dividends during the year were $0.28 and earnings per share were $1.57.
   a. What rate of return did Russell shareholders earn during 1989?
   b. What was the dividend yield? What was the percentage change in share price?
   c. What proportion of the return earned by shareholders was received as dividends and what proportion was in the form of share price appreciation?

5. A common justification given by management for repurchasing its own company's shares is that the shares were a bargain at the acquisition price. If markets are efficient, can managers expect to get bargains on share repurchases? Why, or why not?

CHAPTER 6

THE FINANCING DECISION

*Equity Capital: The least amount of money
owners can invest in a business
and still obtain credit.*
Michael Sperry

We began our inquiry into the raising of external capital in the last chapter by looking at financial instruments and the markets in which they trade. We continue here by examining the proper choice of a financing instrument by the company.

Selecting the proper financing instrument is a two-step process. The first step is to decide how much external capital is required. Frequently, this is the straightforward outcome of the forecasting and budgeting process described in Chapter 3. Management estimates sales growth, the need for new assets, and the money available internally. Any remaining monetary needs must come from outside sources. Increasingly, however, this is only the start of the exercise. There follows a careful consideration of financial markets and the terms on which the company can raise capital. If management does not believe it can raise the required sums on agreeable terms, a modification of operating plans to bring them within budgetary constraints is initiated.

Once the amount of external capital to be raised has been determined, the second step is to select—or, more accurately, design—the instrument to be sold. This is the heart of the financing decision. As indicated in the last chapter, the company can choose from a tremendous variety of financial securities. The proper choice will provide the company with needed cash on attractive terms. An improper one will result in an excessive cost of funds, undue risk, or an inability to sell the securities.

For simplicity in this chapter, we will frequently consider a single financing choice: The XYZ Company needs to raise $200 million this year. Should it sell bonds or stock? But do not let this focus obscure the complexity of the topic. First, bonds and stocks are just extreme examples of a whole spectrum of possible security types. Fortunately, the conclusions drawn regarding these extremes will apply in modified degree to other instruments along the spectrum. Second, and more important, financing decisions are never one-time events. Instead, the raising of money at any point in time is just one event in an evolving financial strategy. Yes, XYZ Company needs $200 million today but will likely need $150 million in two years and an undetermined amount in future years. Consequently, a major element of XYZ's present financing decision is the effect today's choice will have on the company's future ability to raise capital. Ultimately then, a company's financing strategy is closely intertwined with its long-run competitive goals and the way it intends to manage growth.

This chapter begins by considering a central topic in finance known as OPM: other people's money. We will look at the advantages and disadvantages of OPM in financing operations and will examine how the choice of a financing strategy affects company performance. This will involve a close look at *financial leverage* and at techniques for evaluating alternative financing options. This chapter will conclude by considering financing decisions in light of a company's growth objectives and its access to financial markets. We will see that smaller companies and those that are unable or unwilling to sell new equity may view financial leverage differently from other firms. The appendix to the chapter takes up the related topic of the financing decision and firm value.

FINANCIAL LEVERAGE

In physics, a lever is a device to increase force. In business OPM, or what is commonly called financial leverage, is a device to increase owners' returns. It involves the prudent substitution of fixed-cost debt financing for owners' equity in the *hope* of increasing equity returns. The word *hope* is important here because leverage does not always have the intended effect. If operating profits are below a critical value, financial leverage will reduce, not increase, equity returns. If we think of the increased variability in the return to owners as an increase in risk, we can say that financial leverage is the proverbial two-edged sword: It increases the return to owners in most instances, but it also increases their risk.

Financial leverage also has much in common with operating leverage, defined as the substitution of fixed-cost production methods for variable-cost methods. Consider a proposal to replace three production workers with a new robot. Because a robot cannot be laid off when sales decline, the robot increases fixed costs, but because it is not necessary to pay the robot more for overtime work, it also reduces variable costs. Such an increase in operating leverage has two effects: More sales are required to cover fixed costs, but once break-even is achieved, profits grow more quickly with added sales. Analogously, the substitution of debt for equity financing increases fixed costs in the form of greater required interest and principal payments, but because creditors do not participate in company profits, it also reduces variable costs. Increased financial leverage thus has two effects as well: More operating income is required to cover fixed financial costs, but once break-even is achieved, profits grow more quickly with additional operating income.

To see these effects more clearly, let's look at the influence of financial leverage on ROE. Recall from Chapter 2 that, despite some problems, ROE is the most widely used single measure of financial performance. It is defined as

$$ROE = \frac{\text{Profit after tax}}{\text{Equity}}$$

In Chapter 2 we said that an increase in financial leverage usually increases ROE. Here, we want to explore this linkage more closely. To begin, write profit after tax as

$$\text{Profit after tax} = (\text{EBIT} - jD)(1 - t)$$

where EBIT is earnings before interest and tax, j is the interest rate, D is debt outstanding, and t is the firm's tax rate. This equation reflects the steps an accountant goes through to calculate profit after tax from EBIT.

Then using some basic algebra,[1] we can rewrite ROE as

$$ROE = r + (r - i)D/E$$

where r is the company's *operating return on assets,* defined as

$$r = \text{Operating return on assets} = \frac{\text{EBIT } (1 - t)}{\text{Assets}}$$

i is the aftertax interest rate, defined as

$$i = \text{Aftertax interest rate} = j(1 - t)$$

and E is the firm's equity. Operating return on assets, r, is very similar to ROIC, defined in Chapter 2. It is the return on assets of an all-equity company; you can think of it as the return earned by the company before the effects of financial leverage are considered. Looking at i, recall that because interest is a tax-deductible expense, a company's tax bill declines whenever its interest expense rises; i takes this relationship into account.

The revised expression for ROE is a revealing one. It shows clearly that the impact of financial leverage on ROE depends on the size of r relative to i. If r exceeds i, financial leverage—as measured by D/E—increases ROE. The reverse is also true; if r is less than i, leverage reduces ROE. Leverage improves financial performance when things are going well but worsens it when things are going poorly. Leverage is the classic fair-weather friend.

Figure 6–1 says the same thing graphically. It shows how ROE changes with leverage for three values of r, corresponding to a boom of 18 percent, an expected outcome of 12 percent, and a bust of zero percent. The aftertax interest rate is assumed to be 6 percent. Increasing leverage has two obvious effects: It increases expected ROE *and* it increases the range of possible ROEs.

---

[1]
$$ROE = \frac{(\text{EBIT} - jD)(1 - t)}{E} = \frac{\text{EBIT}(1 - t)}{E} - \frac{jD(1 - t)}{E}$$
$$= r \times \frac{D + E}{E} - i \frac{D}{E} = r + (r - i) \frac{D}{E}$$

FIGURE 6–1
Leverage Increases Expected Return and Risk

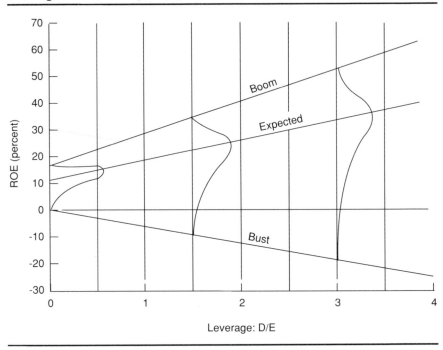

For at least two reasons, it is appropriate to think of the range of possible ROEs as a measure of risk. One is that a greater range of possible outcomes means more uncertainty about what ROE the company will earn and more variability in ROE over time. The second reason is that a greater range of possible ROEs means a greater chance of bankruptcy. Look at the bust line. With zero leverage, the worst the company will do in our example is earn an ROE of zero, but with a debt-to-equity ratio of 4.00, the same level of operating income generates a *loss* of 24 percent on equity. In this situation, operating income is not sufficient to cover interest expense, and a loss results. If the loss is large enough or persistent enough, bankruptcy can occur.

To summarize, *financial leverage increases expected return to shareholders and risk.* The trick is to balance one against the other.

TECHNIQUES FOR EVALUATING FINANCIAL ALTERNATIVES

If management knew the value of r, the financing decision would be easy: Whenever r exceeds i, pile on the debt; whenever r is less than i, finance with equity. What makes life exciting, of course, is that future values of r are unknown and frequently highly uncertain. The financing decision therefore comes down to a comparison of the possible benefits of leverage against the possible costs.

Ideally we would like to be able to calculate precisely what degree of financial leverage would yield a company the greatest net benefit, but this is not presently possible. Instead, the best we can do is to measure in a rough way the increased returns and risks created by debt financing and to offer some broad generalizations about what should be paramount in management's mind when selecting a financing instrument.

For a practical look at the measurement of the risks and returns of debt financing, consider the problem faced by Clark Thompson, financial vice president of Harbridge Fabrics in early 1991. Harbridge Fabrics, a manufacturer of quality cotton and wool fabrics, was trying to decide how best to raise $30 million to finance acquisition of a Spanish manufacturer of cotton materials. After considerable negotiation, a price of $35 million cash had been agreed to. Thompson had determined that $5 million could be financed internally, leaving $30 million to be financed from outside sources. Harbridge's investment bankers indicated that the following two options were possible:

1. Sell 1.5 million new shares of common stock at a net price of $20 per share.
2. Sell $30 million, par value bonds at an interest rate of 12 percent. The maturity would be 20 years, and the bonds would carry an annual sinking fund of $1.5 million.

Looking to the future, Mr. Thompson expected that the addition of the Spanish manufacturer would increase Harbridge's earnings before interest and taxes (EBIT) to $30 million in 1991. Past EBIT levels had been as follows:

	1984	1985	1986	1987	1988	1989	1990	1991F
EBIT ($ millions)	15	10	30	26	5	15	21	30

F = forecast

Mr. Thompson anticipated that Harbridge's need for outside capital in coming years would be substantial, ranging from $5 to $20 million annually. The company had paid annual dividends of 50 cents per share in recent years, and Mr. Thompson believed it was management's intention to continue doing so. Tables 6–1 and 6–2 present Harbridge's recent financial statements.

Range-of-Earnings Chart

Mr. Thompson's first task in analyzing the financing options available to Harbridge should be to measure the impact of the decision on Harbridge's return to shareholders. This could be done by calculating the company's ROE under alternative financing plans. Instead, the common practice is to simplify the procedure somewhat by looking at the decision's impact on earnings per share (EPS) rather than ROE. Because the analysis is virtually the same either way, we will adhere to this convention.

TABLE 6–1
Harbridge Fabrics Income Statement 1990 ($ millions)

Sales	$200
Cost of goods sold	144
Gross profit	56
General and administrative expenses	35
Interest expense	4
Earnings before tax	17
Tax at 34%	6
Earnings after tax	11
Preferred dividends	1
Available for common	$ 10
Number of shares outstanding	5 million
Earnings per share	$2.00

TABLE 6–2
Harbridge Fabrics Balance Sheet 1990 ($ millions)

Assets	
Cash and securities	$ 14
Accounts receivable	32
Inventories	22
Total current assets	68
Net fixed assets	70
Total assets	$138

Liabilities and owners' equity	
Accrued expenses	$ 15
Accounts payable	21
Short-term debt	2
Current portion long-term debt	4
Total current liabilities	42
Long-term debt*	34
Preferred stock†	8
Common stock	13
Retained earnings	41
Total liabilities and owners' equity	$138

*Average interest rate on debt in 1990 was 10%; annual sinking fund requirements were $4 million. Both of these numbers will stay at this level through 1996.

†Dividend rate on preferred stock is 12%; there are no principal repayment requirements on the preferred.

Harbridge Fabrics Partial Pro Forma Income Statement 1991
($ millions except EPS)

	Bust		Boom	
	Bonds	*Stock*	*Bonds*	*Stock*
EBIT	$10.0	$10.0	$40.0	$40.0
Interest expense	7.2	3.6	7.2	3.6
Earnings before tax	2.8	6.4	32.8	36.4
Tax at 34%	1.0	2.2	11.2	12.4
Earnings after tax	1.8	4.2	21.6	24.0
Preferred dividends	1.0	1.0	1.0	1.0
Available for common	0.8	3.2	20.6	23.0
Number of shares (millions)	5.0	6.5	5.0	6.5
EPS	$0.17	$0.50	$4.13	$3.54

To see the effect of financial leverage on Harbridge's EPS we need to look at the company's income statement under the two financing plans. We can save considerable work in doing this by assuming, as is usually the case, that all of the income statement entries from sales down through EBIT are unaffected by the way a company is financed. Then, we can ignore these items and begin with EBIT. The figures at the bottom of the prior page show the bottom portion of a 1991 pro forma income statement for Harbridge under bust and boom conditions. Bust corresponds to a recessionary EBIT of only $10 million, while boom represents a very healthy EBIT of $40 million.

The accounting here is straightforward. Interest expense under the stock financing alternative is 10 percent of the debt outstanding in 1991. Debt outstanding in 1991 equals present short- and long-term debt of $40 million, less the $4 million sinking fund due during 1991, or $36 million. Interest expense under the bond alternative is higher by an amount equal to the interest on the new bonds. Preferred dividends are an aftertax expense, so they are subtracted from earnings after tax. Finally, selling stock increases the number of shares outstanding from 5 to 6.5 million.

Several noteworthy observations emerge from these figures. One involves the tax advantage of debt financing. Provided only that Harbridge has sufficient taxable income, its tax liability is always $1.2 million lower under bond financing than under stock financing. This figure equals 34 percent of the interest expense on the new debt. In effect, the government pays companies a subsidy, in the form of reduced taxes, to encourage the use of debt financing. Letting t be the company's tax rate, and I its interest expense, the subsidy equals tI annually. Frequently known as the *interest tax shield* from debt financing, this subsidy is thought by many to be the chief benefit of debt financing.

A second observation is that common stock financing always produces higher earnings after tax simply because it involves no additional interest expense. The most important thing to observe is the impact of the financing decision on EPS. We concentrate on earnings per share here because it reflects the fact that equity financing will force current owners to share Harbridge's earnings with newcomers, while debt will not. Looking at the boom conditions, we see the expected impact of leverage: EPS with debt financing is a healthy 17 percent higher than with equity financing. Under bust conditions, the reverse is true; stock financing produces a significantly higher EPS. This corresponds to our earlier example when r was less than i.

To display this information more informatively, it is useful to construct a *range-of-earnings chart*. To do so, we need only plot the EBIT-EPS pairs calculated above on a graph and connect the appropriate points with straight lines. Figure 6–2 shows the resulting range-of-earnings chart for Harbridge. It presents the EPS

FIGURE 6–2
Range-of-Earnings Chart for Harbridge Fabrics

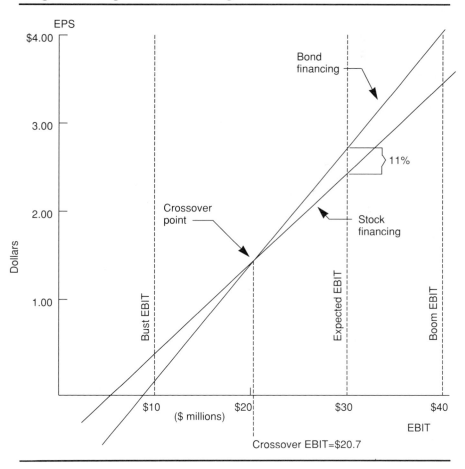

Harbridge will report for any level of EBIT under the two financing plans. Consistent with our boom-bust pro formas, note that the bond financing line passes through an EPS of $4.13 at $40 million EBIT and $0.17 at $10 million EBIT, while the corresponding figures for stock financing are $3.54 and $0.50 respectively.

Mr. Thompson will be particularly interested in two aspects of the range-of-earnings chart. One is the increase in EPS Harbridge will report at the expected EBIT level if the company selects bond financing over stock financing. As shown on the graph, this increase will be 11 percent at an expected EBIT of $30 million. Thompson also will observe that, in addition to an immediate increase in EPS, bond financing also puts Harbridge on a faster growth trajectory. This is represented by the steeper slope of the bond financing line. For each dollar Harbridge adds to EBIT, EPS will rise more with bond financing than with equity financing. Unfortunately, the reverse is also true; for each dollar EBIT declines, EPS will fall more with bond financing than with equity financing.

The second aspect of the range-of-earnings chart that will catch Mr. Thompson's eye is that bond financing does not always yield a higher EPS. If Harbridge's EBIT should fall below a critical crossover value of about $20.7 million, EPS will actually be higher with stock financing than with bond financing. Harbridge's expected EBIT is well above the crossover value, but the historical record presented earlier indicates that EBIT has been quite volatile in past years. In fact, it has been below $20.7 million in four of the seven years for which we have data. A higher EPS with bond financing is clearly not guaranteed.

Coverage Ratios

The primary use of a range-of-earnings chart is to examine the return dimension of financial leverage: What EPS, or ROE, can a company anticipate at expected levels of operating income for the various financing plans under consideration? The risk dimension of leverage is best considered by calculating ratios. Because coverage ratios were treated in Chapter 2, our discussion here will be brief.

The before- and aftertax burdens of Harbridge Fabric's financial obligations appear below. Recall that because we wish to compare these financial obligations to the company's EBIT—a before-tax number—it is necessary to calculate their *before*-tax equivalents. Since Harbridge is in the 34 percent tax bracket, the before-tax burden is about one and one-half times the aftertax burden for all obligations except interest, which is a tax-deductible expense ($[1/(1 - 0.34)] = 1.5$).

Financial Obligations ($ millions)

| | Bonds | | Stock | |
	Aftertax	Before-tax	Aftertax	Before-tax
Interest expense		$7.2		$3.6
Principal payment	$5.5	8.3	4.0	6.1
Preferred dividends	1.0	1.5	1.0	1.5
Common dividends	2.5	3.8	3.3	4.9

Four coverage ratios, corresponding to the progressive addition of each of these financial obligations, appear below for an assumed EBIT of $30 million. To illustrate calculation of these ratios, "times common covered" equals $30 million EBIT divided by the sum of all four financial burdens in before-tax dollars. [For bonds, $1.44 = 30/(7.2 + 8.3 + 1.5 + 3.8)$.]

| | Bonds | | Stock | |
	Coverage	Percent EBIT Can Fall	Coverage	Percent EBIT Can Fall
Times interest earned	4.17	76%	8.33	88%
Times burden covered	1.94	48	3.09	68
Times preferred covered	1.76	43	2.68	63
Times common covered	1.44	31	1.86	46

The column headed "Percent EBIT Can Fall" presents a second way to interpret coverage ratios. It is the percentage amount EBIT can decline from its expected level before coverage equals 1.0. For example, interest expense with bond financing is $7.2 million; so EBIT can fall from $30 million to $7.2 million, or 76 percent, before times interest earned for bond financing equals 1.0. A coverage of 1.0 is critical because any lower coverage indicates that the financial burden under examination cannot be covered out of operating income and another source of cash must be available.

Harbridge's coverage ratios clearly illustrate the added risks inherent in debt financing. For each ratio, coverage is significantly worse with bond financing than with stock financing. Given the instability of Harbridge's operating income over past years, debt financing implies a worrisome increase in the possibility of default.

To put Harbridge's numbers into perspective and to see how coverage has changed in recent years, Table 6–3 presents interest-bearing debt-to-total-asset ratios and times-interest-earned ratios for companies comprising the Standard & Poor's 400 industrial stock averages, and for selected industries from 1984 to 1989. Note the general increase in indebtedness and decline in coverage over these years. Table 6–4 shows the variation in key performance ratios across Standard & Poor's rating categories in the 1987 to 1989 period. Observe that the median times-interest-earned ratio falls steadily from 12.02 for AAA corporations down to 0.75 for CCC corporations.

SELECTING THE APPROPRIATE FINANCING INSTRUMENT

Thompson now has quantitative indicators of the risk and the return to Harbridge from each financing option. The next question is how best to use this information to pick the most appropriate financing instrument. Unfortunately, the state of the art does not allow very specific answers to this question, so we must be content with some rather general advice. Let us begin by placing Harbridge's decision in the proper timeframe.

TABLE 6-3

Times Interest Earned Has Generally Declined and Debt to Total Assets Has Generally Risen over the Years 1984–1989 (Numbers in parentheses are the number of companies in industry sample.)

	1984	1985	1986	1987	1988	1989
Standard & Poor's 400 Industrials:						
Debt to total assets (%)	17	17	18	18	23	22
Times interest earned	4.8	4.2	3.6	4.4	3.8	3.3
Aerospace Defense (10):						
Debt to total assets (%)	6	6	10	9	12	13
Times interest earned	10.8	10.9	7.2	7.5	5.6	3.8
Broadcast Media (4):						
Debt to total assets (%)	19	40	41	47	45	46
Times interest earned	6.7	3.2	2.4	2.2	2.2	1.7
Cosmetics (4):						
Debt to total assets (%)	18	26	27	25	39	27
Times interest earned	4.7	3.1	4.4	6.2	4.7	4.6
Hospital Management (3):						
Debt to total assets (%)	43	44	46	40	39	28
Times interest earned	3.2	2.8	1.6	2.3	2.9	4.5
Household Furnishings and Appliances (7):						
Debt to total assets (%)	11	10	11	12	18	20
Times interest earned	11.1	7.3	9.5	9.2	4.9	3.5
Textile Apparel Manufacturers (5):						
Debt to total assets (%)	16	14	17	15	14	25
Times interest earned	9.4	15.1	16.2	10.4	9.7	8.9

Source: *Standard & Poor's Analysts Handbook: Official Series, 1990.* Annual Edition. © Standard & Poor's Corporation. All rights reserved. Companies in selected industries are those firms represented in the Standard and Poor's 400 industrial stock averages. Generally they are among the largest companies in the industry.

Financial Flexibility

Up to now, we have looked at the financing decision as if it were a one-time event. Should Harbridge Fabrics raise $30 million today by selling bonds or stock? Realistically, such individual decisions are invariably part of a longer-run financing strategy that is shaped in large part by the firm's access to capital markets over time.

At one extreme, if Harbridge has the rare luxury of always being able to raise debt or equity capital on acceptable terms, the decision is straightforward. Thompson can simply select a target capital structure based on long-run risk-return considerations and

TABLE 6–4

Averages of Key Ratios by Standard & Poor's Rating Category (Industrial Long-Term Debt, Three-Year Median Figures, 1987–1989)

	AAA	AA	A	BBB	BB	B	CCC
Times interest earned	12.02	9.13	5.54	3.62	2.29	0.99	0.75
Times interest and rental expense earned	4.79	5.04	3.30	2.22	1.76	1.01	0.73
Cash flow/Total debt (%)	89.1	79.2	48.7	35.7	18.6	6.4	5.2
Operating income/ sales (%)	21.2	16.3	13.5	12.1	13.1	9.8	4.5
Long-term debt/ capitalization* (%)	12.4	18.8	30.1	37.7	50.5	66.1	62.4

*Capitalization = All long-term sources of capital = Total assets − Short-term liabilities.
Note: These figures are not meant to be minimum standards.

then base specific debt-equity choices on transitory market conditions and on the proximity of the company's present capital structure to its target. So if Harbridge's existing debt-to-assets ratio is below target, debt financing would be the obvious choice unless equity were available on unusually attractive terms.

In the more realistic case when continuing access to capital markets is not ensured, the decision becomes more complex. For now Thompson must worry not only about long-run targets and current conditions but also about how today's decision might affect Harbridge's future access to capital markets. This is the notion of *financial flexibility:* the concern that today's decision not jeopardize future financing options or growth opportunities.

Looking at Harbridge, we know that the company anticipates tapping the markets for from $5 to $20 million annually in coming years. And given the company's volatile past earnings and comparatively low coverage ratios, it is possible that selling bonds now will "close off the top," meaning that over the next few years Harbridge may be unable to raise meaningful amounts of additional debt without a proportional increase in equity. ("Top" as used here refers to the top portion of the liabilities side of an American balance sheet. British and Australian balance sheets show equity on top of liabilities, but then they drive on the wrong side too.) Having thus reached its debt capacity, Harbridge could become dependent on the equity market over the next few years for any additional external capital. This is a precarious position, for if equity could not be sold at a reasonable price when needed, Harbridge would be forced to forgo attractive investment opportunities for lack of funds. This could prove very expensive, because the inability to make competitively mandated investments can result in a permanent loss of market position. Consequently, a concern for financing future growth would suggest that Harbridge issue equity now while it is available, thereby maintaining financial flexibility to meet future contingencies.

Market Signaling

Concern for future financial flexibility customarily favors equity financing today. A persuasive counterargument in opposition to equity financing, however, is the stock market's likely response. Mention was made in Chapter 4 that on balance U.S. corporations do not make extensive use of new equity financing, and several possible explanations of this apparent bias were suggested. It is time now to discuss another.

Academic researchers have recently begun to explore the stock market's reaction to various company announcements regarding future financing. And although the results must still be considered preliminary, they make fascinating reading. In one study, Paul Asquith and David Mullins, then of Harvard, were interested in what happens to a company's stock price when it announces a new equity sale.[2] To find out, they performed an event study, similar to the one described in the last chapter, on 531 common stock offerings over the period 1963 to 1981. Defining the event date as the day of first public announcement, Asquith and Mullins found that *over 80 percent* of the industrial firms sampled experienced a decline in stock price on the event date, and that for the sample as a whole, the decline could not reasonably be attributed to random chance. Moreover, the observed decline did not ap-

---

[2]Paul Asquith and David W. Mullins, Jr., "Equity Issues and Offering Dilution," *Journal of Financial Economics,* January/February 1986, pp. 61–89.

pear to be recouped in subsequent trading, but rather remained as a permanent wealth loss to existing owners.

The size of the announcement loss was startling, averaging *over 30 percent* of the size of the new issue. To put this number into perspective, a 30 percent loss means that Harbridge Fabrics could expect to suffer a permanent loss in the market value of existing equity of about $9 million the day it announced a $30 million equity issue.

To complete the picture, similar studies of debt announcements have *not* observed the adverse price reactions found for equity financing. Further, it appears that equity announcements work both ways. That is, a company's announcement of its intention to repurchase some of its shares is greeted by a significant *increase* in stock price.

Why do these price reactions occur? No one is yet certain, but several tentative explanations exist. One, suggested most often by executives and market professionals, attributes the observed price reactions to dilution. According to this reasoning, a new equity issue slices the corporate pie into more pieces and reduces the portion of the pie owned by existing shareholders. It is natural, therefore, that the shares owned by existing shareholders will be worth less. Conversely, when a company repurchases its shares each remaining share represents ownership of a larger portion of the company and hence is worth more. Others, including yours truly, remain unconvinced by this reasoning, pointing out that while an equity issue may be analogous to slicing a pie into more pieces, the pie is also a larger one by virtue of the equity issue. And there is no reason to expect that a smaller slice of a larger pie is necessarily worth less. Nor is there any reason to expect remaining shareholders necessarily to gain from a share repurchase. True, each post-repurchase share represents a larger percentage ownership claim, but the repurchase also reduces the size of the company.

A more intriguing explanation involves what is known as market signaling. Suppose, plausibly enough, that Harbridge Fabric's top management knows much more about their company than do outside investors, and consider again Harbridge's range-of-earnings chart, Figure 6–2. Begin by reflecting on which financing option you would recommend if, as Harbridge's financial vice president, you were highly optimistic about the company's future.

After thorough analysis of the market for Harbridge's products and its competitors, you were confident that EBIT could only grow over the next decade, most likely at a rapid rate. If you have been awake the last few pages, you will know that the logical choice in this circumstance is debt financing. Debt produces higher EPS today and puts the company on the steeper growth trajectory.

Now reverse the exercise and consider which financing option you would recommend if you were concerned about Harbridge's prospects, fearing that future EBIT might well decline. In this scenario, equity financing is the clear winner because of its superior coverage and higher EPS at low operating levels.

But if those who know the most about a company finance with debt when the future looks bright, and with equity when it looks grim, what does an equity announcement tell investors? Right. It signals the market that management is concerned about the future and has opted for the safe financing choice. Is it any wonder then that stock price falls on the announcement and that many companies are consequently reluctant to even mention the E-word, much less to sell it?

The market signal conveyed by a share repurchase announcement is just the reverse. Top management is optimistic about their company's future prospects, and perceives that current stock price is inexplicably low, so low that share repurchase constitutes an irresistible bargain. A repurchase announcement, therefore, signals good news to investors and stock price rises.

I find market signaling stories such as these highly plausible, but whether they will stand up to further inquiry, only time will tell. Nonetheless, regardless of what explanation one favors, it does appear that the stock price reaction to new equity announcements is usually large and negative.

The Financing Decision and Sustainable Growth

When selecting a financing instrument, we have suggested so far that management should be cognizant of the need to maintain financial flexibility and of the decision's effect on stock price. Concern for financial flexibility customarily weighs in favor of equity financing, while concern for stock price favors debt. How then does management strike a balance between these opposing concerns?

Don't Talk to Deere & Company about Market Signaling

The experiences of Deere & Company, the world's largest farm equipment manufacturer, in the late 1970s and early 1980s provide a vivid object lesson for much of this chapter. Among the lessons illustrated are the value of financial flexibility, the use of finance as a competitive weapon, and the power of market signaling.

Beginning in 1976, rising oil prices, high and rising inflation rates, and record high interest rates sent the farm equipment industry into a severe tailspin. Financially much more conservative than its principal rivals, Massey Ferguson and International Harvester, Deere chose this moment to use its superior balance-sheet strength as a competitive weapon. While competitors retrenched under the burden of high interest rates and heavy debt loads, Deere borrowed liberally to finance a major capital investment program and to support financially distressed dealers. The strategy saw Deere's three-company market share rise from 38 percent in 1976 to 49 percent by 1980—such was the value of Deere's superior financial flexibility.

But by late 1980, with borrowing capacity dwindling and the farm equipment market still depressed, Deere faced the difficult choice of curtailing its predatory expansion program or issuing new equity into the teeth of an industry depression. On January 5, 1981, the company announced a $172 million equity issue, and watched the market value of its existing shares immediately fall $241 million. So powerful was the announcement effect that Deere's existing shareholders lost more value than Deere stood to raise from the issue.

Despite the negative market response, Deere management was so convinced of the long-run virtues of their strategy that they gritted their teeth, issued the equity, and used the proceeds to reduce indebtedness. Deere thus regained the borrowing capacity and the financial flexibility necessary to continue expanding, while its rivals remained mired in financial distress.

Although the farm equipment business has been slow to recover, Deere's strategy appears to be bearing fruit in recent years. The company still has a dominant market share, and after suffering losses in 1986, earned a 15 percent return on equity in 1989. Meanwhile, Deere's stock price has risen from the low 20s in 1986 to over $75 in 1990.

The answer for many companies is to place the financing decision within the broader context of managing growth.

Recall from Chapter 4 that when a company is unable or unwilling to sell new equity, its sustainable growth rate is

$$g^* = P \, R \, A \, \hat{T}$$

where P, R, A, and $\hat{T}$ are profit margin, retention ratio, asset turnover, and financial leverage, respectively. P and A in this equation are determined on the operating side of the business. The financial challenge is to develop dividend, financing, and growth strategies that enable the firm to expand at the target rate without resorting to common-stock financing. For these companies, the chief appeal of leverage is not increased ROE, but an increased sustainable growth rate, while the principal disadvantages are the risk of closing off the top and the heightened chance of bankruptcy. Managements in these firms do not view the financing choice as a stand-alone decision, but rather as one aspect of the broader issue of managing growth.

SELECTING A MATURITY STRUCTURE

When a company elects to raise debt capital, the next question is what maturity should the debt have? Should the company take out a 1-year loan, sell 7-year notes, or market 30-year bonds? Looking at the firm's entire capital structure, *the minimum risk maturity structure occurs when the maturity of liabilities equals or exceeds that of assets* for, in this configuration, cash generated from operations over coming years should be sufficient to repay existing liabilities as they mature. In other words, the liabilities will be self-liquidating. If the maturity of liabilities is less than that of assets, the company incurs a refinancing risk because some maturing liabilities will have to be paid off from the proceeds of newly raised capital. And as noted in an earlier chapter, the rollover of maturing debt is not an automatic feature of capital markets. When the maturity of liabilities is greater than that of assets, cash provided by operations should be more than sufficient to repay existing liabilities as they mature. This provides an extra margin of safety, but it also means that the firm may have excess cash in some periods.

Academic Views of the Debt-Equity Choice

Rather than study the impact of financial leverage on company risk and return as we have done, the usual academic perspective is to examine the impact of leverage on the market value of the firm. Fundamentally, these are not conflicting approaches because a capital structure that effectively balances risk against return in the long-run interests of the company should also increase firm value.

Academicians usually begin by demonstrating that in properly functioning markets with no taxes and no bankruptcy costs, the increased risk to equity from debt financing just counterbalances the increased expected return, so that leverage has no effect on firm value. They then relax the no taxes, no bankruptcy assumptions to demonstrate that the capital structure decision ultimately involves a prudent balancing of the tax advantage of debt financing against the increased chance of bankruptcy. At low levels of indebtedness, the tax advantage predominates, so that increases in leverage produce higher market values. But beyond some prudent range, the increasing probability of bankruptcy begins to outweigh the tax advantage and firm value falls with further increases in leverage.

To date, academic research has yielded two benefits: It has greatly clarified our thinking about the financing decision, and it has proven useful in understanding and interpreting the recent rise in major financial restructurings. However, it has been of only modest help to financial executives charged with developing practical financing strategies. The principal difficulty has been that, by assuming the continuous availability of debt and equity capital to firms, academicians have assumed away a major part of the problem as it really exists. As a result, academic treatments of the topic tend to involve one-time, debt-equity choices without consideration for future financing flexibility. See the appendix to this chapter for more on the ties between the financing decision and firm value, and Chapter 9 for a look at corporate restructuring.

If maturity matching is minimum-risk, why do anything else? Why allow the maturity of liabilities to be less than that of assets? Companies mismatch either because long-term debt is unavailable on acceptable terms or because management anticipates that mismatching will reduce total borrowing costs. For example, if management believes that interest rates will decline in the future, an obvious strategy is to use short-term debt now and hope to roll it over into longer-term debt at lower rates in the future. Of course, efficient markets advocates criticize this strategy on the grounds that management has no reason to believe it can forecast future interest rates in an efficient market.

Inflation and Financing Strategy

An old saying in finance is that it's good to be a borrower during inflation because the borrower repays the loan with depreciated dollars. It is important to understand, however, that this saying is correct only when the inflation is *unexpected.* When creditors expect inflation, the interest rate they charge rises to compensate them for the expected decline in the purchasing power of the loan principal. This means that it is not necessarily advantageous to borrow during inflation. In fact, if inflation unexpectedly declines during the life of a loan, inflation can work to the disadvantage of the borrower.

APPENDIX

THE FINANCING DECISION AND FIRM VALUE

Our purpose here is to study the relation between a company's capital structure and its market value. As noted in Chapter 2, many academicians and consultants recommend that managers work to increase the market value of their firm. With this in mind, we are interested in whether financial leverage affects firm value, and if so, what capital structure maximizes value.

Our strategy will be to begin with an idealized world of no taxes and no bankruptcy. Once this foundation is firmly established, we will add progressive doses of reality in the form of taxes and bankruptcy. While other potentially influential forces might also be considered, taxes and bankruptcy are thought to be among the more pervasive, and their review will provide a useful overview of the subject.[3] Although this line of inquiry will not enable us to specify precisely how much debt a particular company should have, it will enable us to identify several important factors management should consider when making financing decisions.

No Taxes or Bankruptcy

When once asked how many slices he would like his pizza cut into, Yogi Berra is said to have replied, "You'd better make it six; I don't think I'm hungry enough to eat eight." Absent taxes and bankruptcy, a company's financing decision can be likened to slicing Yogi's pizza; for no matter how you slice up claims to the firm's earnings, it is still the same firm with the same earning power, and hence, the same market value. In this world, the benefits of increased return to shareholders from higher leverage are precisely offset by the increased risks, so that market value is unaffected by leverage.

Here is an example demonstrating this apparently extreme position. You have an extra $1,000 in your pocket (clearly a hypothetical example) and plan to start a small business that you believe will generate earnings before interest and tax of $400 per year into the indefinite future. To keep things simple, we will suppose your company plans to distribute all of its earnings every year as a dividend. The left column of Table 6A–1 shows the bottom portion of a pro forma income statement for the enterprise. Note that both the company's earnings and your total income equal $400.

A $400 annual income on a $1,000 investment implies a 40 percent annual return. Not bad. But your brother-in-law, the real estate broker, has sung the praises of debt financing for years. So just to see what difference it might make, you talk to a local banker who affirms that an interest-only loan for $800 can be arranged, but that in view of such high leverage, a 15 percent interest rate will be required. A revised pro forma assuming debt financing appears in the second column from the left in Table 6A–1. Your company's earnings are down with debt financing but so too is your investment. With an $800 loan, you need to invest only $200 in equity, and a $280 annual income on a $200 investment produces an expected return of 140 percent (280/200 = 140%). Wow!

---

[3]See Thomas E. Copeland and J. Fred Weston, *Financial Theory and Corporate Policy,* 3rd ed. (Reading, Mass.: Addison-Wesley, 1988), Chapters 13 and 14, for a more complete review of the possible links between capital structure and firm value.

TABLE 6A–1

In the Absence of Taxes, Debt Financing Affects Neither Income nor Firm Value. In the Presence of Taxes, Prudent Debt Financing Increases Income and Firm Value

	No Taxes		Corporate Taxes at 40%	
	No Debt Financing	80% Debt Financing	No Debt Financing	80% Debt Financing
Corporate Income				
EBIT	$400	$400	$400	$400
Interest expense	0	120	0	120
Earnings before tax	400	280	400	280
Corporate tax	0	0	160	112
Earnings after tax	400	280	240	168
Personal Income				
Dividends received	400	280	240	168
Interest received	0	120	0	120
Total income	$400	$400	$240	$288
Personal Taxes at 33%				
Total income	400	400	240	288
Personal tax	0	0	80	96
Income after tax	$400	$400	$160	$192

But you have studied enough finance to know that the expected return to equity almost always rises with debt financing, so this result is not especially surprising. Moreover, a moment's reflection should convince you that it is incorrect to compare returns on two investments with different risk. If the return on investment A is greater than the return on investment B *and* they have the same risk, A is the better choice. But if A has higher return *and* higher risk—as in the present case—all bets are off. Poker players and fighter pilots might prefer investment A despite its higher risk, while we more timid souls might reach the opposite conclusion.

To make a fair comparison of the two financing schemes, we need to set their risks equal. We can do this by concentrating on the $800 remaining in your pocket when you take advantage of the bank loan. In particular, let us assume that you will lend this $800 to some worthy borrower at an interest rate of 15 percent. (The fact that your $800 loan and the bank's bear the same interest rate is confirmation that the two loans are equally risky.)

If you prefer, another way to think about equalizing the risks is to imagine you deposit the $800 left in your pocket in the bank at a 15 percent interest rate and that the bank loans the same $800 to your company. This way the entire $1,000 invested in the business is yours, as in the all-equity case, except now you are calling $800 of your investment debt.

With the risks now equal, we can decide which financing scheme is better by looking only at their prospective returns. Recall that with all-equity financing, your annual return is 40 percent. If you opt for debt financing, you will receive a $280 annual dividend from the business and $120 in interest on your loan, for a total of $400 (0.15 × $800 = $120). This, of course, is precisely the same total income you would receive with all-equity financing, and the same 40 percent return on your $1,000 investment.

So what have we proven? We have shown that, with risks held equal and ignoring taxes and bankruptcy costs, the way a business is financed does not affect the total return to owners. And if total return is unaffected, so too is the value of the business. Firm value is independent of financing.

Here is a more intuitive way to say the same thing. Companies typically *own* physical assets, such as trucks and buildings, and *owe* paper liabilities such as stocks and bonds. Our argument is essentially that a company's physical assets are the real creators of value and that simply reshuffling paper claims to the income produced by these assets does not add value. The company is worth no more with one set of paper claims than another. The only exception to this proposition would occur if the reshuffling of claims somehow changed the income produced by the assets, and in the absence of taxes and bankruptcy, this does not occur. Firm value in this hypothetical world is, therefore, independent of financial leverage.

Corporate Taxes but Still No Bankruptcy

Let us now repeat our saga in a more interesting world that includes corporate taxes. If you finance your new business entirely with your own money, the third column from the left in Table 6A–1 shows your firm's pro forma income statement, assuming a 40 percent corporate tax rate. Your company's income, and your total personal income, are now $240, which implies a 24 percent return on investment.

Finally, the right column in Table 6A–1 shows your business's pro forma income statement and your total personal income when you use 80 percent debt financing at 15 percent interest. The return on your $200 investment in the business is now 84 percent ($168/200 = 84\%$), but we know this is not comparable to the "all-equity" return of 24 percent because it is much riskier. Assuming as before that you set the risks equal by lending your remaining $800 at 15 percent interest, your total income will be $288 ($168 + $120), yielding an expected return of 28.8 percent. Contrary to the no-taxes case, use of financial leverage now increases your total income by $48 annually and your risk-equivalent return from 24 to 28.8 percent. The business is now a better investment, and hence more valuable, when financed with debt.

Why does debt financing increase the value of the business? Look at the tax bill. When financed solely with equity, the company owes $160 in taxes, but with 80 percent debt financing, taxes fall to only $112, a reduction of $48. Three parties share the fruits of your company's success: creditors, owners, and the taxman. Our example shows that debt financing, with its tax-deductible interest expense, reduces the taxman's take in favor of the owners'.

The bottom portion of Table 6A–1 is for suspicious readers who think these results might hinge on the omission of personal taxes. There, you will note that imposition of a 33 percent personal tax on income reduces the annual aftertax advantage of debt financing from $48 to $32, but does not eliminate it. Because many investors, such as mutual funds and pension funds, do not pay personal taxes, the convention is to dodge the problem of defining an appropriate personal tax rate by concentrating on earnings after corporate, but before personal, taxes. We will gratefully follow that convention here.

I should note that our findings of a tax-law bias in favor of debt financing is largely an American result. In most other industrialized countries, corporate and personal taxes are at least partially integrated, meaning that dividend recipients receive at least partial credit on their personal tax bills for corporate taxes paid on distributed profits. As in our no-tax example, financial leverage does not affect firm value when corporate and personal taxes are fully integrated.

In the presence of American-style corporate taxes, then, the reshuffling of paper claims to include more debt *does* create value—at least from the shareholders' perspective, if not from that of the U.S. Treasury—because it increases the income available to private investors. The amount of the increase in annual income to shareholders created by debt financing equals the corporate tax rate times the interest expense, or what we referred to earlier as the *interest tax shield*. In our example, annual company earnings increase $48 per year, which equals the tax rate of 40 percent times the interest expense of $120.

To say the same thing in symbols, if V_L is the value of your company when levered and V_U is the value of the company *unlevered*, our example says that

$$V_L = V_U + \text{Value } [tI]$$

where t is the corporate tax rate, I is annual interest expense in dollars, and Value $[tI]$ represents the value today of all future interest tax shields. In the next chapter, we will refer to this last term as the *present value* of future tax shields. In words then, our equation says the value of a levered company equals the value of the same company unlevered plus the present value of the interest tax shields.

Taken at face value, this equation, and our example, suggest a disquieting conclusion: that the value of a business is maximized when it is financed entirely with debt. Fortunately there is more to our story.

But before proceeding it is worth reflecting for a moment on the practical implications of our example and the above equation for company financing. The equation tells us that not all companies can benefit from interest tax shields. Certainly if a company is losing money, it has no taxable income to shield and hence sees no benefit from debt financing. Similarly, a company that is in danger of incurring losses over the life of the debt financing will find the tax benefits of leverage less appealing than will a company with robust profits. A similarly disposed group of companiés are those that, although profitable, are already shielding all or most of their income from taxes through the use of various tax credits, accelerated depreciation, and other legitimate tax reduction or deferral techniques. We should thus expect companies such as these to use less debt financing than other enterprises facing predictable future tax liabilities.

Taxes and Bankruptcy

We have seen that the tax deductibility of interest increases after tax income to owners, and thereby increases firm value. Corporate bankruptcy creates a second link between the financing decision and income that works in opposition to interest tax shields.

A number of events can push a company into bankruptcy. For present purposes, let us agree that a company is bankrupt when the market value of its assets is equal to or less than its liabilities, or equivalently, when the market value of equity falls to zero. Once in bankruptcy, a company's fate is in the hands of a bankruptcy judge and a multitude of attorneys, each representing an aggrieved creditor or class of investors and each determined to pursue the best interests of his client until justice is served, or until the money runs out. The logic of what should happen in bankruptcy is straightforward. The court first determines whether the company is worth more to its creditors dead or alive. If dead, the court oversees the company's liquidation and distributes the proceeds to creditors. If alive, creditors and owners reorganize the business under court supervision and it continues to operate.

This is what should happen. What actually happens is more like a high stakes card game in which the only certain winners are attorneys. Depending on their luck, owners of a bankrupt firm stand a chance of coming away with nothing, and senior managers can suddenly find themselves with ample time to polish their resumes.

Changing Attitudes Toward Bankruptcy

Although not entirely relevant to the topic at hand, it is interesting to note that attitudes toward bankruptcy have changed dramatically in recent years. Bankruptcy used to be seen as a black hole where companies were clumsily dismembered for the benefit of creditors, and shareholders lost everything. Due in part to a liberalization of the law, bankruptcy today is seen increasingly as a quiet refuge where the courts keep creditors at bay while management works on its problems. Manville Corporation was the first company to see the virtues of bankruptcy in August 1982, when, although solvent by any conventional definition, it declared bankruptcy in anticipation of massive product liability suits involving asbestos. Continental Airlines followed in September 1983, using bankruptcy protection to abrogate what it considered ruinous labor contracts. And more recently, A H Robbins and Texaco have found bankruptcy an inviting haven while wrestling with product liability suits and a massive legal judgment, respectively. In all of these instances, the companies expect to emerge from bankruptcy healthier and more valuable than when they entered. Because financial leverage plays no part in these dramas, however, we will focus attention on the costs of bankruptcy rather than any possible benefits.

The Probability of Bankruptcy

The expected cost of bankruptcy to a company depends on two things: the probability bankruptcy will occur, and the cost if it does occur. Looking first at the probability of occurrence, it should come as no surprise to hear that raising financial leverage increases the probability of bankruptcy. To illustrate, suppose some unforeseen economic event causes the market value of a company's assets to fall from $10 billion to $5 billion. If the firm has $4 billion of debt outstanding, equity will equal $1 billion, and it will avoid bankruptcy. If it has $6 billion in debt, however, equity vanishes and bankruptcy awaits.

Because companies in volatile, unpredictable economic environments are more likely to suffer such unforeseen declines in firm value, one obvious conclusion is that high-risk companies are wise to use less debt financing than other firms with more stable operating environments. This is a major reason that high-technology companies, such as Hewlett-Packard and IBM, employ comparatively little debt financing, while public utilities use much more.

The Cost of Bankruptcy

To some companies, bankruptcy is little more than a pothole along the road of corporate life, while to others it is a complete disaster. A key factor determining the cost of bankruptcy to an individual company is what can be called "the resale value" of its assets. Two simple examples will illustrate the concept. Suppose ACE Corporation's principal asset is an apartment complex, and that due to local overbuilding and overly aggressive use of debt financing, ACE has been forced into bankruptcy. Because apartment complexes are readily salable, the likely outcome will be the sale of the complex to a new owner and distribution of the proceeds to creditors. The cost of bankruptcy in this instance will be correspondingly modest, consisting of the obvious legal, appraisal, and court costs, plus whatever price concessions are necessary to sell the apartments. In substance, because bankruptcy has little impact on the operating income generated by the apartment complex, bankruptcy costs are modest.

Note that the cost of bankruptcy does *not* include the difference between what ACE and its creditors originally thought the apartments were worth and their value just prior to bankruptcy. This loss is due to overbuilding, not bankruptcy, and is incurred by the firm regardless of how it is financed, or whether it declares bankruptcy. Even all-equity financing, while it may avoid bankruptcy, will not eliminate this loss.

At the other extreme, consider Moletek, a genetic engineering firm, whose chief assets are a brilliant research team and attractive growth opportunities. If Moletek stumbles into bankruptcy, the costs are likely to be very high. Selling the company's assets individually in a liquidation will generate little cash because most of the assets are intangible. It will also be difficult to realize value by keeping the company intact, either as an independent company or in the hands of a new owner, for in such an unsettled environment, it will be hard to retain key employees and to raise funds necessary to exploit growth opportunities. In essence, because bankruptcy adversely affects Moletek's operating income, bankruptcy costs are likely to be large.

In addition to bankruptcy costs themselves, companies may also incur costs of *financial distress* as the probability of bankruptcy increases. Internally, these costs include lost profit opportunities as the company cuts back investment, research and development, and advertising to conserve cash. Externally, they include lost sales as potential customers become concerned about future parts and service availability, and increased costs as suppliers become reluctant to make long-run commitments and to provide trade credit.

In sum, our brief review of bankruptcy costs suggests that they vary with the nature of a company's assets. If the resale value of the assets is high either in liquidation or when sold intact to new owners, bankruptcy costs are correspondingly modest. Such firms should be expected to make liberal use of debt financing. Conversely, when resale value is low because the assets are largely intangible and would be difficult to sell intact, bankruptcy costs are comparatively high. Companies matching this profile should use more conservative financing.

Concluding Comments

Figure 6A–1 summarizes the results of our musings about debt financing and firm value. It shows the value of a typical firm as a function of financial leverage, denoted by the ratio of debt to firm value. At modest debt levels, the tax shield benefits outweigh the expected cost of bankruptcy, and value rises with leverage. But at higher debt levels, bankruptcy costs predominate, and value declines with further increases in leverage. The object of the exercise is to position the firm at the optimal capital structure, $(D/V)^*$, where value is maximized.

Beyond identifying the main costs and benefits of debt financing, our present line of inquiry is not especially helpful in pinpointing the precise location of $(D/V)^*$ for an individual firm. It does, however, suggest that managers consider the following three firm-specific issues when making financing choices:

FIGURE 6A–1
The Market Value of a Company Increases and then Decreases as Financial Leverage Rises

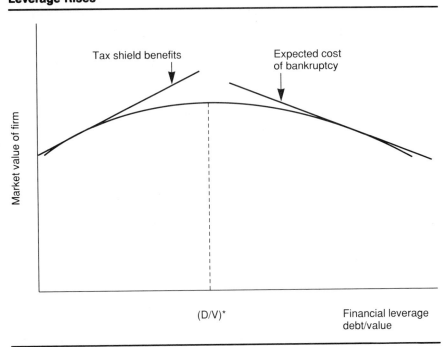

1. The ability of the company to utilize additional interest tax shields over the life of the debt.
2. The increased risk of bankruptcy created by added leverage.
3. The cost to the firm if bankruptcy were to occur.

A final observation: The perspective throughout this appendix has been that of shareholders; yet it is ultimately management, not shareholders, who make financing decisions. This distinction is an important one because there is reason to believe that the costs and benefits of leverage to managers differ systematically from those to shareholders. In particular, managers appear to incur much higher costs in bankruptcy, in the form of disrupted lives and careers, than do shareholders. And they probably see fewer benefits of debt financing as well. Indeed, because the tax shield advantages of debt accrue to shareholders, not to managers, the chief benefit of leverage to managers may be nothing more than a higher sustainable growth rate. As a result, unless burdened by sustainable-growth problems, managers may be much more conservative in their use of debt financing than shareholders would prefer.

CHAPTER SUMMARY

1. This chapter studied the corporate financing decision and, in particular, the advantages and disadvantages of financial leverage.
2. For businesses that are unable or unwilling to raise new equity, debt financing increases growth. It enables the business to acquire assets that are otherwise unattainable, and it increases the firm's sustainable growth rate. For businesses with access to new equity, the chief benefit of debt financing is that it increases the expected return on equity.
3. The principal disadvantages of debt financing are increased variability of income and of return on equity and increased bankruptcy risk.
4. Coverage ratios are useful for evaluating the added risk of debt financing, while a range-of-earnings chart is useful for looking at the return dimensions of the decision.
5. Because money from external sources is not always available on agreeable terms, a major concern in most financing decisions is the impact of today's choice on tomorrow's options. Decisions that constrain a company's future ability to raise capital reduce financial flexibility.
6. When management announces a new equity issue, it appears to signal investors that it is concerned about the company's future prospects. In most instances, this results in a stock price decline. The mean decline equals about 30 percent of the new issue. Repurchase announcements have a positive effect on stock price, and debt announcements have little or no impact.

ADDITIONAL READING

Asquith, Paul, and David W. Williams, Jr. "Signaling with Dividends, Stock Repurchases, and Equity Issues." *Financial Management,* Autumn 1986, pp. 27–44.
   A well-written summary of recent empirical work on measuring the capital market's reaction to major equity-related decisions. An excellent introduction–overview of market signaling.

Donaldson, Gordon. "New Framework for Corporate Debt Capacity." *Harvard Business Review,* March/April 1962, pp. 117–31.

Old, but still one of the best practical discussions of the financing decision.

Meyers, Stewart C. "The Search for Optimal Capital Structure." *Midland Corporate Finance Journal,* Spring 1983, pp. 6–16.

A nontechnical review of what we think we know about the impact of financial leverage on firm value and its implications for corporate decision making, written by one of the leading contributors to the topic.

Piper, Thomas R. and Wolf A. Weinhold. "How Much Debt Is Right for Your Company?" *Harvard Business Review,* July/August 1982, pp. 106–14.

A practical, well-balanced look at the financing decision with particular emphasis on flexibility.

CHAPTER PROBLEMS

1. Suppose you own a business and your goal is to maximize return on equity.
   a. Looking at the equation in the chapter relating ROE to operating return on assets, under what condition(s) would you want to maximize debt financing?
   b. Under what condition(s) would you be indifferent to how the business is financed?
   c. Is maximizing ROE an appropriate goal? Why, or why not?
2. As the financial vice president for Target Company, you have the following information:

Expected net income after tax next year before consideration of new financing	$100 million
Interest due next year on existing debt	$ 43 million
Sinking fund payments due next year on existing debt	$ 30 million
Tax rate	40%
Common shares outstanding today	50 million

   a. Calculate Target's times-interest-earned ratio for next year assuming it raises $200 million of new debt at an interest rate of 10 percent.
   b. Calculate Target's times-burden-covered ratio for next year assuming annual sinking fund payments on the new debt equal $40 million.
   c. Calculate next year's earnings per share assuming Target raises the $200 million of new debt.
   d. Calculate next year's times-interest-earned ratio, times-burden-covered ratio, and earnings per share if Target sells 5 million new shares priced to net the company $40 per share instead of raising new debt.
   e. Looking at earnings per share and coverage with debt financing and with equity financing, what do you think Target should do, and why?
3. XYZ Company management believes it has a window of opportunity over the next five years to capture a significant share of a new market. Once the market reaches maturity, about five years

from now, it will be much more difficult to increase market share. To take full advantage of this opportunity XYZ will need to raise significant amounts of money from external sources.

    Would you advise XYZ to maintain a conservative capital structure involving modest amounts of debt or an aggressive capital structure characterized by higher levels of debt? Explain your reasoning.

4. ABC, Inc. is a well-diversified company competing in a number of mature, stable markets. Operating cash flows are large relative to new investment requirements.
    a. As an ABC shareholder would you recommend that the company adopt a conservative capital structure involving modest amounts of debt or an aggressive one characterized by higher debt levels? Why?
    b. Might you feel differently if you were a senior manager at ABC who owned few shares and did not participate in any stock option plans? Why, or why not?
5. Explain how each of the following changes will affect Harbridge Fabric's range-of-earnings chart, Figure 6–2. Which changes would make debt financing more attractive, which less attractive?
    a. An increase in the interest rate on new debt.
    b. An increase in Harbridge's stock price.
    c. Increased uncertainty about Harbridge's future earnings.
    d. Increased common stock dividends.
    e. An increase in the amount of debt Harbridge already has outstanding.

PART 4

EVALUATING INVESTMENT OPPORTUNITIES

CHAPTER 7

DISCOUNTED CASH
FLOW TECHNIQUES

A nearby penny is worth a distant dollar.
Anonymous

The chief determinant of what a company will become is the investments it makes today. The generation and evaluation of creative investment proposals is far too important a task to be left to finance specialists; instead it is the ongoing responsibility of all managers throughout the organization. In well-managed companies, the process starts at a strategic level with senior management specifying the businesses in which the company will compete and determining the means of competition. Operating managers then translate these strategic goals into concrete action plans involving specific investment proposals. A key aspect of this process is the financial evaluation of investment proposals, or what is frequently called *capital budgeting.* The achievement of an objective requires the outlay of money today in expectation of increased future income. It is necessary to decide, first, whether the anticipated future income is large enough, given the risks, to justify the current expenditure, and second, whether the proposed investment is the most cost-effective way to achieve the objective. This and the following chapter address these questions.

FIGURES OF MERIT

The financial evaluation of any investment opportunity can be broken down into three discrete steps:

1. Estimate the relevant cash flows.
2. Calculate a figure of merit for the investment.
3. Compare the figure of merit to an acceptance criterion.

221

A figure of merit is a number summarizing an investment's economic worth. A common figure of merit is the rate of return. Like the other figures of merit to be discussed, the rate of return translates the complicated cash inflows and outflows associated with an investment into a single number summarizing its economic worth. An acceptance criterion, on the other hand, is a standard of comparison that helps the analyst determine whether an investment's figure of merit is attractive enough to warrant acceptance. It's like a fisherman who must throw back all fish shorter than 10 inches. To the fisherman, the length of the fish is the relevant figure of merit, and 10 inches is the acceptance criterion.

Although figures of merit and acceptance criteria may appear difficult on first exposure, the first step, estimating the relevant cash flows, is the most challenging in practice. Unlike the basically mechanical problems encountered in calculating figures of merit and acceptance criteria, estimating relevant cash flows is more in the nature of an art form, often requiring thorough understanding of a company's markets, competitive position, and long-run intentions. Difficulties range from commonplace concerns with depreciation, financing costs, and working capital investments to more arcane questions of shared resources, excess capacity, and contingent opportunities. And pervading the whole topic is the fact that many important costs and benefits cannot be measured in monetary terms, and so must be evaluated qualitatively.

The plan in this chapter is initially to set aside questions of relevant cash flows and acceptance criteria in order to concentrate on figures of merit. Later in the chapter, we will return to the estimation of relevant cash flows. Acceptance criteria will be addressed in the following chapter under the general heading, "Risk Analysis in Investment Decisions."

To begin our discussion of figures of merit, let's consider a simple numerical example. Pacific Rim Resources, Inc., is contemplating construction of a container loading pier in Seattle. The company's best estimate of the cash flows associated with constructing and operating the pier for a 10-year period appears in Table 7–1.

Figure 7–1 presents the same information in the form of a *cash flow diagram,* which is nothing more than a graphical display of the pier's costs and benefits distributed along a time line. De-

TABLE 7–1
Cash Flows for Container Loading Pier ($ millions)

Year	0	1	2	3	4	5	6	7	8	9	10
Cash flow	(40)	7.5	7.5	7.5	7.5	7.5	7.5	7.5	7.5	7.5	17

FIGURE 7–1
Cash Flow Diagram for Container Loading Pier

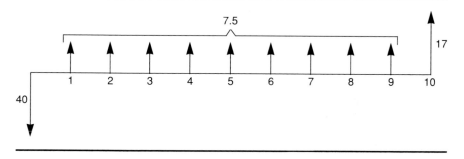

spite its simplicity, I find that many common mistakes can be avoided by preparing such a diagram for even the most elementary investment opportunities. We see that the pier will cost $40 million to construct and is expected to generate cash inflows of $7.5 million annually for 10 years. In addition, the company expects to salvage the pier for $9.5 million at the end of its useful life, bringing the 10th year cash flow to $17 million.

The Payback Period and the Accounting Rate of Return

Pacific's management wants to know whether the anticipated benefits from the pier justify the $40 million cost. As we will see shortly, a proper answer to this question must reflect *the time value of money*. But before addressing this topic, let's consider two commonly used, back-of-the-envelope type figures of merit that despite their popularity suffer from some glaring weaknesses. One, known as the *payback period,* is defined as the time the company must wait before recouping its original investment. For an investment with a single cash outflow followed by uniform annual inflows

$$\text{Payback period} = \frac{\text{Investment}}{\text{Annual cash inflow}}$$

The pier's payback period is thus 5⅓ years, meaning the company will have to wait this long to recoup its original investment (5⅓ = 40/7.5).

The second widely used, but nonetheless deficient, figure of merit is the accounting rate of return, defined as

$$\text{Accounting rate of return} = \frac{\text{Average annual cash inflow}}{\text{Total cash outflow}}$$

The pier's accounting rate of return is 21.1 percent [(7.5 × 9 + 17)/10)/40].

The problem with the accounting rate of return is its insensitivity to the timing of cash flows. For example, a postponement of all of the cash inflows from Pacific's container loading pier to year 10 obviously reduces the value of the investment but does not affect the accounting rate of return. In addition to ignoring the timing of cash flows, the payback period is also insensitive to all cash flows occurring beyond the payback date. Thus an increase in the salvage value of the pier from $9.5 million to $90.5 million clearly makes the investment more attractive. Yet, it has no effect on the payback period; nor does any other change in cash flows in years 6 through 10.

In fairness to the payback period, I should add that, although it is clearly an inadequate figure of investment merit, it has proved to be useful as a rough measure of investment risk. In most settings, the longer it takes to recoup an original investment, the greater the risk. This is especially true in high-technology environments where management can forecast only a few years into the future. Under these circumstances, an investment that does not promise to pay back within the forecasting horizon is equivalent to a night in Las Vegas without the floor show.

The Time Value of Money

An accurate figure of merit must reflect the fact that a dollar today is worth more than a dollar in the future. This is the notion of the time value of money, and it exists for at least three reasons. One is that inflation reduces the purchasing power of future dollars relative to current ones; another is that in most instances the uncertainty surrounding the receipt of a dollar increases as the date of receipt recedes into the future. Thus the promise of $1 in 30 days is usually worth more than the promise of $1 in 30 months, simply because it is likely to be more certain.

A third reason money has a time value involves the notion of *opportunity costs*. By definition, the opportunity cost of any investment is the return one could earn on the next best alternative. A dollar today is worth more than a dollar in one year because the dollar today can be productively invested and will grow into more than a dollar in one year. Waiting to receive the dollar until next year carries an opportunity cost equal to the return on the foregone investment.

Compounding and Discounting

Because money has a time value, we cannot simply combine cash flows occurring at different dates as is done in calculating the payback period and the accounting rate of return. To adjust investment cash flows for their differing time value, we need to use the ideas of compounding and discounting. Everyone who has ever had a bank account knows intuitively what compounding is. Suppose you have a bank account paying 10 percent annual interest, and you deposit $1 at the start of the year, what will it be worth at the end of the year? Obviously, $1.10. Now, suppose you leave the dollar in the account for two years, what will it be worth then? This is a littler harder, but most of us realize that, because you earn interest on your interest, the answer is $1.21. Compounding is the process of determining the future value of a present sum. The simple cash flow diagrams on the next page summarize the exercise.

Discounting is just compounding turned on its head: It is the process of finding the present value of a future sum. Yet despite the obvious similarities, many persons find discounting somehow mysterious. And as luck would have it, the convention has become to use discounting rather than compounding to analyze investment opportunities.

Here is how discounting works. Suppose you can invest money to earn a 10 percent annual return and that you are promised $1 in one year; what is the value of this promise today? Clearly, it is worth less than $1, but the exact figure is probably not something that pops immediately to mind. In fact, the answer is $0.909. This

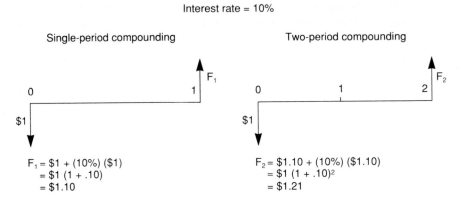

Interest rate = 10%

Single-period compounding

Two-period compounding

$F_1 = \$1 + (10\%) (\$1)$
$= \$1 (1 + .10)$
$= \$1.10$

$F_2 = \$1.10 + (10\%) (\$1.10)$
$= \$1 (1 + .10)^2$
$= \$1.21$

is the *present value* of $1 to be received in one year because if you had $0.909 today, you could invest it at 10 percent interest, and it would grow into $1 in one year [$1.00 = 0.909(1 + 0.10)].

Now, if we complicate matters further and ask the value of one dollar to be received in two years, intuition fails most of us completely. We know the answer must be less than $0.909, but beyond that things are a fog. In fact, the answer is $0.826. This sum, invested for two years at 10 percent interest, will grow, or compound, into $1 in two years. The following cash flow diagrams illustrate these discounting problems. Note the formal similarity to compounding. The only difference is that in compounding we know the present amount and we seek the future sum, whereas in discounting we know the future sum and seek the present amount.

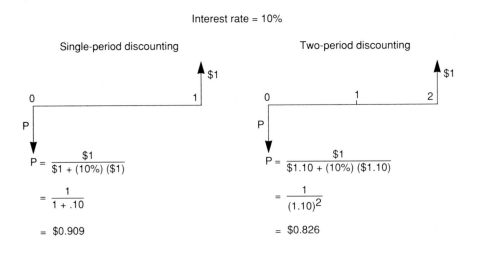

Interest rate = 10%

Single-period discounting

Two-period discounting

$P = \dfrac{\$1}{\$1 + (10\%) (\$1)}$

$= \dfrac{1}{1 + .10}$

$= \$0.909$

$P = \dfrac{\$1}{\$1.10 + (10\%) (\$1.10)}$

$= \dfrac{1}{(1.10)^2}$

$= \$0.826$

Present Value Tables

How did I know the answers to the discounting problems? I could have used the formulas appearing below the cash flow diagrams, or I could have used one of several brands of pocket calculators, or a computer spreadsheet, but I did none of these. I looked up the answers in Appendix A at the end of the book. I might well have used a calculator or a computer if my sole purpose were to solve the problems posed, but because I also want to offer an intuitive explanation of compounding and discounting, I used the less elegant Appendix A. Appendix A, known as a present value table, shows the present value of $1 to be received at the end of any number of periods from 1 to 50, and at interest rates ranging from 1 to 50 percent per period. The present values appearing in the table are generated from repeated application of the above formulas for differing time periods and interest rates. It might be useful to consult Appendix A for a moment to confirm the present values mentioned above.

As a matter of semantics, the interest rate in present value calculations is frequently called the *discount rate*. It can be interpreted two ways. If a company already has cash in hand, the discount rate is the rate of return that could be earned on alternative investments. In other words, it is the company's *opportunity cost of the capital*. If a firm must raise the cash by selling securities, the discount rate is the rate of return expected by buyers of the securities. In other words, it is the investors' *opportunity cost of capital*. As we will see in the next chapter, the discount rate is frequently used to adjust the investment cash flows for risk and is hence also known as a *risk-adjusted* discount rate.

Appendix B at the end of the book is a close cousin to Appendix A. It shows the present value of $1 to be received at the end of *each period* for anywhere from 1 to 50 periods, and at discount rates ranging from 1 to 50 percent per period. To illustrate both appendixes, suppose the Cincinnati Reds sign a promising new catcher to a contract promising $500,000 per year for four years. Let us calculate what the contract is worth today if the ballplayer has investment opportunities yielding 15 percent per year.

The cash flow diagram for the contract is as follows.

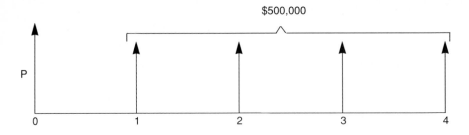

To find the present value, P, using Appendix A, we must find the present value at 15 percent of each individual payment. The arithmetic is

Present value of contract $=$ $0.870 \times \$500,000 + 0.756 \times \$500,000$
$+ 0.658 \times \$500,000 + 0.572 \times \$500,000$
$= \$1,428,000$

A much simpler approach is to recognize that since the dollar amount is the same each year, Appendix B can be used. Consulting Appendix B, we learn that the present value of $1 per period for four periods at a 15 percent discount rate is $2.855. Thus, the present value of $500,000 per period is

Present value of contract $= 2.855 \times \$500,000 = \$1,428,000$

Although the baseball player will receive a total of $2 million over the next four years, the present value of these payments is barely over $1.4 million. Such is the power of compound interest.

Equivalence

The important fact about the present value of future cash flows is that the present sum is *equivalent* in value to the future cash flows. It is equivalent because if you had the present value today, you could transform it into the future cash flows simply by investing it at the discount rate. To confirm this important fact, the following table shows the cash flows involved in transforming $1,428,000 today into the baseball player's contract of $500,000 per year for four years. We begin by investing the present value at 15 percent interest. At the end of the first year, the investment has grown to over $1.6 million, but the first $500,000 salary payment reduces the principal to just over $1.1 million. In the second year the investment grows to over $1.3 million, but the second salary installment brings the principal down to just over $800,000. And so it goes until at the end of four years the $500,000 salary payments just exhaust the account. Hence, from the baseball player's perspective, $1,428,000 today is equivalent in value to $500,000 per year for four years because he can readily convert the former into the latter by investing it at 15 percent.

Year	Beginning-of-Period Principal	Interest at 15 percent	End-of-Period Principal	Withdrawal
1	$1,428,000	$214,200	$1,642,200	$500,000
2	1,142,200	171,330	1,313,530	500,000
3	813,530	122,030	935,560	500,000
4	435,560	65,334	500,894	500,000

The Net Present Value

Now that you have mastered compounding, discounting, and equivalence, let's use these concepts to analyze the container pier investment. More specifically, let us use Appendixes A and B to replace the future cash flows appearing in Figure 7–1 with a single cash flow of equivalent worth occurring today. Because all cash flows will then be in current dollars, we will have eliminated the time dimension from the decision and can proceed to a direct comparison of present value cash inflows against present value outflows.

Here is how it works in practice. Assuming Pacific has other investment opportunities yielding 10 percent, the present value of the cash inflows for the pier investment is as follows

$$\begin{array}{l} \text{Present value} \\ \text{of cash inflows} \end{array} = 5.759 \times \$7.5 + 0.386 \times \$17$$

$$= \$49.755 \text{ million}$$

In this calculation, 5.759 is the present value of $1 per year for nine years at a discount rate of 10 percent, and 0.386 is the present value of $1 in year 10 at the same discount rate.

The cash flow diagrams below provide a schematic representation of this calculation. The present value calculation transforms the messy original cash flows into two cash flows of equivalent worth, each occurring at time zero. And our decision becomes elementary. Should Pacific invest $40 million today for a stream of future cash flows with a value today of $49.755 million? Yes, obviously. Paying $40 million for something worth $49.755 million makes sense.

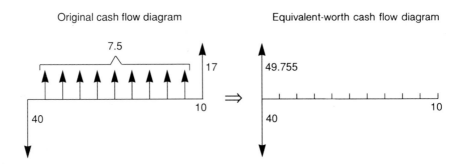

What we have just done is calculate the pier's *net present value,* or NPV, an important figure of investment merit.

$$NPV = \frac{\text{Present value of}}{\text{cash inflows}} - \frac{\text{Present value of}}{\text{cash outflows}}$$

The NPV for the container pier is $9.755 million.

The declaration that an investment's NPV is $9.755 million may not generate a lot of enthusiasm around the water cooler; so it might be informative to offer a more intuitive definition of the concept. An investment's NPV measures how much richer you will become by undertaking the investment. Thus Pacific's wealth rises $9.755 million when it builds the pier because it pays $40 million for an asset worth $49.755 million. Because more wealth is customarily preferred to less, it is safe to conclude that all investments with a positive NPV are attractive because they increase wealth; all investments with a negative NPV are unattractive because they destroy wealth; and all investments with a zero NPV are marginal because they leave wealth unchanged.

In symbols,
when

NPV > 0, accept the investment.
NPV < 0, reject the investment.
NPV = 0, the investment is marginal.

The Profitability Index

The net present value is a perfectly respectable figure of investment merit, and if all you want is one way to analyze investment
opportunities, feel free to skip ahead to "Determining the relevant
cash flows." On the other hand, if you want to be able to communicate with people who use different, but equally acceptable, figures
of merit, and if you want to reduce the work involved in analyzing
certain types of investments, you will need to slog through a few
more pages.

A second time-adjusted figure of investment merit popular in
government circles is the *profitability index* (PI), or what is sometimes called the *benefit-cost ratio,* defined as

$$PI = \frac{\text{Present value of cash inflows}}{\text{Present value of cash outflows}}$$

The container pier's PI is 1.24 ($49.755/$40). Obviously, an investment is attractive when its PI exceeds 1.0 and is unattractive when
its PI is less than 1.0.

The Internal Rate of Return

Without doubt the most popular figure of merit among executives
is a close cousin to the NPV known as the investment's *internal
rate of return* or IRR. To illustrate the IRR and to show its relation
to the NPV, let's follow the fanciful exploits of the Seattle area
manager of Pacific Rim Resources as he tries to win approval for
the container pier investment. After determining that the pier's
NPV is positive at a 10 percent discount rate, the manager forwards his analysis to the company treasurer with a request for approval. The treasurer responds that she is favorably impressed

with the manager's methodology, but that in today's high-interest-rate environment, she feels a discount rate of 12 percent is more appropriate. So the Seattle manager calculates a second NPV at a 12 percent discount rate and finds it to be $5.434 million, still positive but considerably lower than the original $9.7 million ($5.434 million = 5.328 × $7.5 million + 0.322 × $17 million − $40 million). Confronted with this evidence, the treasurer reluctantly agrees that the project is acceptable and forwards the proposal to the chief financial officer. (That the NPV falls as the discount rises here should come as no surprise, for all of the pier's cash inflows occur in the future, and a higher discount rate reduces the present value of future flows.)

The chief financial officer, being even more conservative than the treasurer, also praises the methodology but argues that with all the risks involved and the difficulty raising money, an 18 percent discount rate is called for. Doing his calculations a third time, the dejected Seattle manager now finds that at an 18 percent discount rate the NPV is −$4.481 million. Because the NPV is now negative, the chief financial officer, betraying his former career as a bank loan officer, gleefully rejects the proposal. The manager's efforts prove unproductive, but in the process he has helped us to understand the IRR.

Table 7–2 summarizes the manager's calculations. From these figures, it is apparent that something critical happens to the investment merit of the container pier as the discount rate increases from 12 to 18 percent. Somewhere within this range the NPV changes from positive to negative, and the investment changes from acceptable to unacceptable. The critical discount rate at which this change occurs is the investment's IRR.

TABLE 7–2
NPV of Container Pier at Differing Discount Rates

Discount Rate	NPV
10%	$ 9.755 million
12	5.434
	← ———— IRR = 15%
18	−4.481

Formally, an investment's IRR is defined as

IRR = Discount rate at which the investment's NPV equals zero

The IRR is yet another figure of merit. The corresponding acceptable criterion against which to compare the IRR is the opportunity cost of capital to the firm. If the investment's IRR exceeds the opportunity cost of capital, the investment is attractive, and vice versa. If the IRR equals the cost of capital, the investment is marginal.

In symbols, if K is the percentage cost of capital, then

IRR > K, accept investment.
IRR < K, reject investment.
IRR = K, investment is marginal.

You will be relieved to learn that in most, but regrettably not all, instances the IRR and the NPV yield the same investment recommendations. That is, in most instances, if an investment is attractive based on its IRR, it will also have a positive NPV, and vice versa. Figure 7–2 illustrates the relation between the container pier's NPV and its IRR by plotting the information in Table 7–2. Note that the pier's NPV = 0 at a discount rate of about 15 percent; so this by definition is the project's IRR. At capital costs below 15 percent, the NPV is positive and the IRR also exceeds the cost of capital; so the investment is acceptable on both counts. When the cost of capital exceeds 15 percent, the reverse is true, and the investment is unacceptable according to both criteria.

Figure 7–2 suggests several informative ways to interpret an investment's IRR. One is that the IRR is a break-even return in the sense that at capital costs below the IRR the investment is attractive, but at capital costs greater than the IRR it is unattractive. A second, more important interpretation is that the IRR is the rate at which money remaining in an investment grows, or compounds. As such, an IRR is comparable in all respects to the interest rate on a bank loan or a savings deposit. This means you can compare the IRR of an investment directly to the cost of the capital to be invested. We cannot say the same thing about other simpler measures of return such as the accounting rate of return because they do not properly incorporate the time value of money.

FIGURE 7–2
NPV of Container Pier at Different Discount Rates

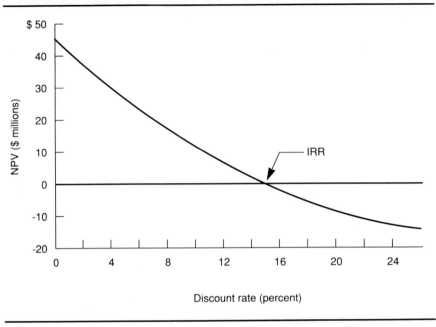

Discount rate (percent)

Calculating an Investment's IRR

The IRR has considerably more intuitive appeal to most executives than the NPV or the PI. The statement that an investment's IRR is 45 percent is more likely to get the juices flowing than one indicating the investment's NPV is $12 million, or that its PI is 1.41. The IRR is, however, usually harder to calculate; it is frequently necessary to search for the IRR by trial and error or, as the computer people would say, iteratively.

The first step in this trial and error process is to pick a likely IRR, selected in any fashion you like, and to test it by calculating the investment's NPV at the chosen rate. If the resulting NPV is zero, you're through. If it is positive, this is usually a signal that you need to try a higher discount rate. Conversely, if the NPV is negative you need to try a lower one. This trial-and-error process continues until you find a discount rate for which the NPV equals zero.

The Container Pier Investment Is Economically Equivalent to a Bank Account Paying 15 Percent Annual Interest

To confirm that an investment's IRR is equivalent to the interest rate on a bank account, suppose that instead of building the pier, Pacific Rim Resources were to put the $40 million cost of the pier in a bank account earning 15 percent annual interest. The table below demonstrates that Pacific could then use this bank account to replicate precisely the cash flows from the pier and that, just like the investment, the account would run dry in 10 years. In other words, the fact that the pier's IRR is 15 percent means that the investment is economically equivalent to a bank saving account yielding this rate.

	($ millions)			
Year	Beginning-of-Period Principal	Interest Earned at 15%	End-of-Period Principal	Withdrawals = Investment Cash Flows
1	40.0	6.0	46.0	7.5
2	38.5	5.8	44.3	7.5
3	36.8	5.5	42.3	7.5
4	34.8	5.2	40.0	7.5
5	32.5	4.9	37.4	7.5
6	29.9	4.5	34.4	7.5
7	26.9	4.0	30.9	7.5
8	23.4	3.5	26.9	7.5
9	19.4	2.9	22.3	7.5
10	14.8	2.2	17.0	17.0

To see how this works in practice, let's calculate the container pier's IRR. From Table 7–2 and Figure 7–2 we know that the IRR must be somewhere between 12 and 18 percent because 12 percent yields a positive NPV and 18 percent a negative one. So let's try 15 percent. Using Appendixes A and B

$$NPV = 4.772 \times \$7.5 + 0.247 \times \$17 - \$40 \stackrel{?}{=} 0$$
$$- 0.01 \stackrel{?}{=} 0$$

For practical purposes, the NPV is zero at a discount rate of 15 percent; therefore this is the project's IRR. Further, if Pacific's opportunity cost of capital is less than 15 percent, we know the pier is acceptable; otherwise, it is not. The need to solve for an investment's IRR iteratively was a meaningful limitation before the advent of computers and pocket calculators, but this is no longer a significant barrier to its use. Today you simply punch in the appropriate cash flows, and let the electronics search for the IRR.

Bond Valuation

Investors regularly use discounted cash flow techniques to value bond investments. Here is an example. Suppose ABC Corporation bonds have an 8 percent coupon rate paid annually, a par value of $1,000, and nine years to maturity. What is the most an investor should pay for an ABC bond if she wants a return of at least 14 percent on her investment? The cash flow diagram is as follows.

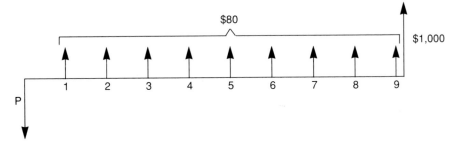

We want to find P such that it is equivalent in value to the future cash receipts discounted at 14 percent. Taking the present value of the receipts:

$$P = \$80 \times 4.946 + \$1,000 \times 0.308$$
$$= \$703.68$$

Thus we know that when the investor pays $703.68 for the bond, her return over nine years will be 14 percent. When she pays more, her return will fall below 14 percent.

Suppose now that we know a bond's price and want to learn the return we will earn by holding the bond to maturity. In the jargon of the trade, we want to know the bond's *yield to maturity*. To illustrate, suppose a $1,000 par value bond pays a 10 percent annual coupon, matures in seven years, and is selling presently for $639.54. What is its yield to maturity, or equivalently its IRR? Let's begin by trying a discount rate of 12 percent.

$$\text{NPV} = 4.564 \times \$100 + 0.452 \times \$1,000 - \$639.54 \overset{?}{=} 0$$
$$268.85 \neq 0$$

Clearly, 12 percent is too low a discount rate. Suppose we try 25 percent.

$$\text{NPV} = 3.161 \times \$100 + 0.210 \times \$1,000 - \$639.54 \overset{?}{=} 0$$
$$-113.44 \neq 0$$

The NPV is now negative, so 25 percent is too high. Let's try 20 percent.

$$\text{NPV} = 3.605 \times \$100 + 0.279 \times \$1,000 - \$639.54 \overset{?}{=} 0$$
$$-0.04 = 0$$

Because NPV is approximately zero, we know the bond's yield to maturity, or IRR, is about 20 percent.

Mutually Exclusive Alternatives and Capital Rationing

Before turning to the determination of relevant cash flows in investment analysis, we should consider briefly two common occurrences that often complicate investment selection. We begin by looking at *mutually exclusive alternatives*.

Frequently there is more than one way to accomplish an objective, and the investment problem is to select the best alternative. In this case, the investments are said to be mutually exclusive. Examples of mutually exclusive alternatives include the choice of whether to build a concrete structure or a wooden one, whether to drive to work or take the bus, and whether to build a 40-story building or a 30-story one. Even though each option gets the job done and may be attractive individually, it does not make economic sense to do more than one. If you decide to take the bus to work, also driving to work could prove a difficult feat. When confronted with mutually exclusive alternatives then, it is not enough to de-

The IRR of a Perpetuity

An annuity is a stream of cash flows having the same value each year. A perpetuity is an annuity that lasts forever. Many preferred stocks are perpetuities, as are some British and French government bonds. They have no maturity date and promise the holder a constant annual dividend or interest payment forever. Let us use Appendix B to calculate the approximate present value of a perpetuity yielding $1 per year forever. Begin by noting that at a discount rate of say 15 percent, the present value of $1 per year for 50 years is $6.661. Think of it; although the holder will receive a total of $50, the present value of this stream is less than $7. Why? Because if the investor put $6.661 in a bank account today yielding 15 percent per year, he could withdraw approximately $1 in interest each year *forever* without touching the principal. ($15\% \times \$6.661 = \$0.999$). Consequently, $6.661 today is approximately equivalent in value to $1 per year forever.

This suggests the following very simple formula for the present value of a perpetuity. Letting A equal the annual receipt, r the discount rate, and P the present value,

$$P = \frac{A}{r}$$

$$\text{and } r = \frac{A}{P}$$

As an example, suppose a share of preferred stock sells for $480 and promises an annual dividend of $82 forever. Then its IRR is 17.1 percent (82/480). Because the equations are so simple, perpetuities are often used to value long-lived assets.

cide if each option is attractive individually, you must determine which is best. Mutually exclusive investments are in contrast to independent investments where the capital budgeting problem is simply to accept or reject a single investment.

When investments are independent, all three of the figures of merit introduced above, the NPV, PI, and IRR, will generate the same investment decision, but this is no longer true when the investments are mutually exclusive. In all of the examples above we have implicitly assumed independence.

A second complicating factor in many investment appraisals is known as *capital rationing.* So far we have implicitly assumed that sufficient money is available to enable the company to undertake all attractive opportunities. In contrast, under capital rationing the decision maker has a fixed investment budget that may not be exceeded. Such a limit on investment capital may be imposed externally by investors' unwillingness to supply more money, or it may be imposed internally as part of the company's budgeting-control system. In either case, the investment decision under capital rationing requires the analyst to *rank* the opportunities according to their investment merit and to accept only the best.

Both mutually exclusive alternatives and capital rationing require a ranking of investments, but here the similarity ends. With mutually exclusive investments, money is available but for technological reasons only certain investments can be accepted, whereas under capital rationing, a lack of money is the complicating factor. Moreover, even the criteria used to rank the investments differ in the two cases, so that the best investment among mutually exclusive alternatives need not be best under conditions of capital rationing. The appendix to this chapter discusses these technicalities, and indicates which figures of merit are appropriate under which conditions.

DETERMINING THE RELEVANT CASH FLOWS

Calculating a figure of merit requires an understanding of the time value of money and equivalence, and it necessitates a modicum of algebra. But these difficulties pale to insignificance compared to those arising in the estimation of an investment's relevant cash flows—the former require only technical competence, whereas the latter calls for the exercise of judgment and perspective.

Two principles govern the determination of relevant cash flows. Both are obvious when stated in the abstract but can be very difficult to apply in practice. They are

1. *The cash flow principle:* Because money has a time value, record investment cash flows when they actually occur, not

when the accountant using accrual concepts says they occur.

2. *The with-without principle:* Imagine two worlds, one in which the investment is made and one in which it is rejected. All cash flows that are different in these two worlds are relevant to the decision, and all those that are the same are irrelevant.

The following examples illustrate the practical application of these principles to commonly recurring cash flow estimation problems.

Depreciation

Accountants' treatment of depreciation is reminiscent of the Swiss method of counting cows: count the legs and divide by four. It gets the job done but not always in the most direct manner.

The physical deterioration of assets over time is an economic fact of life that must be included in investment evaluation. We do it whenever we forecast that an asset's salvage value will be less than its original cost. An asset acquired for $1 million and salvaged 10 years later for $10,000 is clearly forecasted to depreciate over its life. Having included depreciation in this manner, it would clearly be double-counting to follow the accountant and also subtract an annual amount called depreciation from operating income.

And here our story would end were it not for the tax man. Although annual depreciation is a noncash charge and hence irrelevant for investment analysis, annual depreciation does affect a company's tax bill, and taxes are relevant. So we need to use the following two-step procedure: (1) Use standard accrual accounting techniques, including the treatment of depreciation as a cost, to calculate taxes due, then (2) add depreciation back to income after tax to calculate the investment's aftertax cash flow (ATCF). ATCF is the correct measure of an investment's operating cash flow. To illustrate, assume that the container loading pier considered earlier in the chapter will generate an annual income before depreciation and taxes of $9.8 million, that annual depreciation will be $3 million, and that Pacific Rim Resources is in the 34 percent tax bracket. Then, aftertax cash flow is $7.5 million, as shown in the following table.

Operating income	$9.8 million
Less: Depreciation	3.0
Earnings before tax	6.8
Less: Tax at 34%	2.3
Earnings after tax	4.5
Plus: Depreciation	3.0
Aftertax cash flow	$7.5 million

Another way to say the same thing is

$$\text{Aftertax cash flow} = \text{Operating income} - \text{Taxes}$$
$$\$7.5 = \$9.8 - \$2.3$$

This formulation shows clearly that aftertax cash flow treats depreciation as irrelevant except for its role in determining taxes.

Working Capital

In addition to increases in fixed assets, many investments, especially those for new products, require increases in working-capital items, such as inventories and receivables. According to the with-without principle, changes in working capital that are the result of an investment decision are relevant to the decision. In some instances they are the largest cash flows involved.

There are two unique features of working-capital investments. One is that such investments are reversible in the sense that at the end of the project's life, the liquidation of working capital generates cash inflows. The second unique feature is that many investments requiring working-capital increases also generate *spontaneous sources of cash* in the form of increased trade credit, accrued taxes, and the like, which partially offset the working-capital investment. The proper treatment of these spontaneous sources is to subtract them from the increases in current assets when calculating the project's working-capital investment.

To illustrate, suppose XYZ Corporation is considering a new product investment that, in addition to an increase in plant and equipment, will require a $3 million investment in inventories and accounts receivable. Partially offsetting this buildup in current assets, management also anticipates that accounts payable, accrued wages, and accrued taxes will rise by $1 million as a result of the

---

Depreciation as a Tax Shield

Here is yet another way to view the relation between depreciation and aftertax cash flows.

The recommended way to calculate an investment's aftertax cash flow is to add depreciation to profit after tax. In symbols,

$$\text{ATCF} = (R - C - D)(1 - T) + D$$

where R is revenue, C is cash costs of operations, D is depreciation, and T is the firm's tax rate. Combining the depreciation terms, this expression can also be written as

$$\text{ATCF} = (R - C)(1 - T) + TD$$

where the last term is known as the *tax shield from depreciation.*

This expression is interesting in several respects. First, it shows unambiguously that, were it not for taxes, annual depreciation would be irrelevant for estimating an investment's aftertax cash flow. Thus if T is zero in the expression, depreciation disappears entirely. Second, the expression demonstrates that aftertax cash flow rises with depreciation. The more depreciation a profitable company can claim, the higher its aftertax cash flow. On the other hand, if a company is not paying taxes, added depreciation has no value.

Third, the expression is useful for evaluating a class of investments known as replacement decisions in which a new piece of equipment is being considered as a replacement for an old one. In these instances, cash operating costs and depreciation may vary among equipment options but not revenues. Setting R equal to zero above, it is apparent that the relevant aftertax cash flows for replacement decisions depend on differing operating costs after taxes and on differences in depreciation tax shields.

---

new product. So the net increase in working capital is $2 million. Management has agreed to analyze the proposed investment over a 10-year horizon and feels that all of the working capital investment will be recovered at the end of 10 years as the company sells off inventory, collects receivables, and pays off trade creditors. The cash flow associated only with the working capital portion of this investment is shown in the following diagram.

If money had no time value, these offsetting cash flows would cancel one another out, but because money does have a time value, we need to include it in our analysis.

Allocated Costs

The proper treatment of depreciation and working capital in investment evaluation is comparatively straightforward. Now things get a bit trickier. According to the with-without principle, those cash flows that do not change as a result of an investment are irrelevant for the decision. For example, many companies allocate overhead costs to departments or divisions in proportion to the amount of direct labor expense incurred by the department. Suppose a department manager in such an environment has the opportunity to invest in a laborsaving asset. From the department's narrow perspective, there are two benefits to such an asset: (1) a reduction in direct labor expense and (2) a reduction in the overhead costs allocated to the department. Yet from the total company perspective and from the correct economic perspective, only the reduction in direct labor is a benefit because the overhead costs are unaffected by the decision. They are just reallocated from one cost center to another.

Now consider a subtler example. Suppose a company is considering a new product investment that, if undertaken, will increase sales by 5 percent over the next 10 years. The point at issue is whether corporate expenses not directly associated with the new product, such as the president's salary, legal department expenses, and accounting department expenses, are relevant to the decision. A narrow interpretation of the with-without principle suggests that if the president's salary will not change as a result of the investment, it is not relevant. Nor are legal and accounting department expenses, if they will not change. Yet we observe that over time, as companies grow, presidents' salaries tend to increase; and we observe that presidents of large companies tend to have higher salaries than those of small companies. This suggests that, although we may be unable to see a direct cause-effect tie between such expenses and increasing sales, there is a longer-run relation between the two. Consequently, such costs may well be relevant to the decision.

Sunk Costs

A sunk cost is one that has already been incurred and that according to the with-without principle is not relevant for present decisions. This seems easy enough, but consider some examples. Suppose you purchased some common stock a year ago at $100 per share and that it is presently trading at $70. Even though you believe the stock is fairly priced at $70, would you be prepared to admit your mistake and sell it now, or would you be tempted to hold it in hopes of recouping your original investment? The with-without principle says the $100 price is sunk and hence irrelevant, except for possible tax effects, so sell the stock. Yet natural human reluctance to admit a mistake and the daunting prospect of having to justify our mistake to a skeptical spouse frequently muddy our thinking.

Suppose the R&D department of a company has devoted 10 years and $10 million to perfecting a new, long-lasting light bulb. Their original estimate was a development time of two years at a cost of $1 million, and every year since they have progressively extended the development time and increased the cost. Now they are estimating only one more year and an added expenditure of only $1 million. Since the present value of the benefits from such a light bulb is only $4 million, there is considerable feeling in the company that the project should be killed and whoever had been approving the budget increases throughout the years should be fired.

In retrospect, it is clear the company should never have begun work on the light bulb. Even if successful, the cost will be well in excess of the benefits. Yet at any point along the development process, including the current decision, it may have been perfectly rational to continue work. Past expenditures are sunk, so the only question at issue is whether the anticipated benefits exceed the *remaining* costs required to complete development. Past expenditures are relevant only to the extent that they influence one's assessment of whether the remaining costs are properly estimated. So if you believe the current estimates, the light bulb project should be continued for yet another year.

Excess Capacity

For technological reasons, it is frequently necessary to acquire more capacity than required to accomplish an objective, and a question arises of how to handle the excess. For example, suppose a company is considering the acquisition of a hydrofoil boat to provide passenger service across a lake, but that effective use of the hydrofoil will require construction of two very expensive special-purpose piers. Each pier will be capable of handling 10 hydrofoils, and for technical reasons it is impractical to construct smaller piers. If the full cost of the two piers must be borne by the one boat presently under consideration, the boat's NPV will be large and negative, suggesting rejection of the proposal; yet if only one-tenth of the pier costs is assigned to the boat, its NPV will be positive. How should the pier costs be treated?

The proper treatment of the pier costs depends on the company's future plans. If the company does not anticipate acquiring any additional hydrofoils in the future, the full cost of the piers is relevant for the present decision. On the other hand, if this boat is but the first of a contemplated fleet of hydrofoils, then it is appropriate to consider only a fraction of the pier's costs. More generally, the problem faced by the company is that of defining the investment. The relevant question is not should the company acquire a boat, but should it enter the hydrofoil transportation business. The broader question forces the company to look at the investment over a longer time span and to consider explicitly the number of boats to be acquired.

The reverse situation also arises. A company has excess capacity of some sort and is considering an investment that will utilize the unused resources. In this case, the question is what cost, if any, to assign to the excess capacity. As an example, a prominent producer of canned foods was considering the addition of a new product line that would utilize some presently underemployed canning facilities. Some company executives argued that, since the facilities had already been paid for, their cost was sunk and consequently irrelevant. Others argued that the canning capacity was a scarce resource and should be assigned a cost. What cost should be assigned to the excess capacity?

The answer again depends upon future plans. If there are no alternative uses for the canning facilities now or in the future, no costs are involved in its use. On the other hand, if the company is likely to have need for the facilities in the future, there is an opportunity cost associated with their use by the new product line.

Financing Costs

Financing costs are relevant in investment evaluation. Care must be taken, however, not to double-count them. As the next chapter will clarify, the most common discount rate used in calculating any of the recommended figures of merit equals the annual percentage cost of capital to the company. It would obviously be double-counting to subtract financing costs from an investment's annual cash inflows *and* to expect an investment to generate a return greater than the cost of the capital. The standard procedure, therefore, is to reflect the cost of money in the discount rate and to ignore all financing costs when estimating an investment's cash flows. We will revisit this problem in the next chapter.

APPENDIX

MUTUALLY EXCLUSIVE ALTERNATIVES AND CAPITAL RATIONING

We noted briefly in the chapter that the presence of mutually exclusive alternatives or capital rationing complicates investment analysis. The purpose of this appendix is to demonstrate how investments should be analyzed in these cases.

Two investments are mutually exclusive if accepting one precludes further consideration of the other. The choices between building a steel or a concrete bridge, of laying a 12-inch pipeline instead of an 8-inch one, or of driving to Boston instead of flying are all mutually exclusive alternatives. In each case, there is more than one way to accomplish a task, and the objective is to choose the best. Mutually exclusive investments stand in contrast to independent investments, where each opportunity can be analyzed on its own without regard to other investments.

When investments are independent and the decision is simply to accept or reject, the NPV, the PI, and the IRR are equally satisfactory figures of merit. You will reach the same investment decision regardless of the figure of merit used. When investments are mutually exclusive, the world is not so simple. Let's consider an example. Suppose Petro Oil and Gas company is considering two alternative designs for new service stations and wants to evaluate them using a 10 percent discount rate. As shown in the cash flow diagrams in Figure 7A–1, the inexpensive option involves a present investment of $522,000 in return for an anticipated $100,000 per year for 10 years; the expensive option costs $1.1 million, but because of its greater customer appeal, is expected to return $195,000 per year for 10 years.

Table 7A–1 presents the three figures of merit for each investment. All of the figures of merit signal that both options are attractive: the NPVs are positive, the PIs are greater than 1.0, and the IRRs exceed Petro's opportunity cost of capital. If it were possible, Petro should make both investments but because they are mutually exclusive, this does not make technological sense. So rather than just accepting or rejecting the investments, Petro must rank them and select the better one. When it comes to ranking the alternatives, however, the three figures of merit no longer give the same signal, for although the inexpensive option has a higher PI and a higher IRR, it has a lower NPV than the expensive one.

To decide which figure of merit is appropriate for mutually exclusive alternatives, we need only remember that the NPV is a direct measure of

FIGURE 7A–1
Cash Flow Diagrams for Alternative Service Station Designs

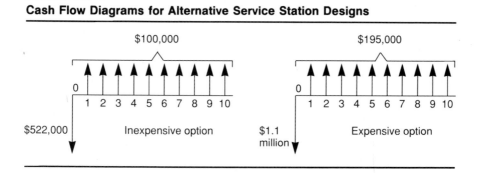

TABLE 7A–1
Figures of Merit for Service Station Designs

	NPV at 10 Percent	PI at 10 Percent	IRR
Inexpensive option	$92,500	1.18	14%
Expensive option	98,275	1.09	12%

the anticipated increase in wealth created by the investment. Since the expensive option will increase wealth by $98,275, as opposed to only $92,500 for the inexpensive option, the expensive option is clearly superior.

The problem with the PI and the IRR for mutually exclusive alternatives is basically that they are insensitive to the scale of the investment. As an extreme example, would you rather have an 80 percent return on a $1 investment or a 50 percent return on a $1 million investment? Clearly, when investments are mutually exclusive, scale is relevant, and this leads to the use of the NPV as the appropriate figure of merit.

What Happened to the Other $578,000?

Some persons feel the preceding reasoning is incomplete because we have said nothing about what Petro can do with the $578,000 it would save by choosing the inexpensive option. It would seem that if this saving could be invested at a sufficiently attractive return, the inexpensive option might prove to be superior after all. We will address this concern in the section titled Capital Rationing. For now, it is sufficient to say that the problem arises only when there are fixed limits on the amount of money Petro has available for investment. When the company can raise sufficient money to make all investments promising positive NPVs, the best use of any money saved by selecting the inexpensive option will be to invest in zero NPV opportunities. And because zero NPV investments do not increase wealth, any money saved by selecting the low-cost option does not alter our decision.

Unequal Lives

The Petro Oil and Gas example conveniently assumed that both service station options had the same 10-year life. This, of course, is not always the case. When the alternatives have different lives, a simple comparison of NPVs is usually inappropriate. Consider the problem faced by a company trying to decide whether to build a wooden bridge or a steel one.

The wooden bridge has a initial cost of $125,000, requires annual maintenance expenditures of $15,000, and will last 10 years.

The steel bridge costs $200,000, requires $5,000 annual maintenance, and will last 40 years.

Which is the better buy? At a discount rate of, say, 15 percent, the present value cost of the wooden bridge over its expected life of 10 years is $150,190 ($125,000 + 5.019 × $15,000). This compares to a figure for the steel bridge over its 40-year life expectancy of $233,210 ($200,000 + 6.642 × $5,000). So if the object is to minimize the cost of the bridge, a simple comparison of present values would suggest that the wooden structure is a clear winner. However, this obviously overlooks the difference in the life expectancy of the two bridges, assuming implicitly that if the company builds the wooden bridge, it will not need a bridge after 10 years.

When comparing mutually exclusive alternatives having differing service lives, it is necessary to examine each over the same *common investment horizon*. For example, suppose our company believes it will need a bridge for 20 years, that due to inflation, the wooden bridge will cost $200,000 to reconstruct at the end of 10 years, and that the salvage value of the steel bridge in 20 years will be $90,000. The cash flow diagrams for the two options are thus

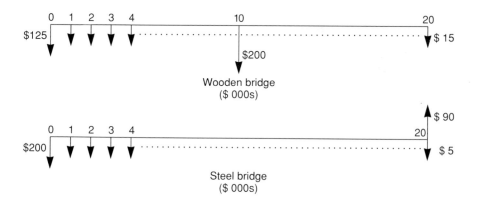

Wooden bridge
($ 000s)

Steel bridge
($ 000s)

Now the present value cost of the wooden bridge is $268,285 ($125,000 + 6.259 × $15,000 + 0.247 × $200,000), and that of the steel bridge is $225,805 ($200,000 + 6.259 × $5,000 − 0.061 × $90,000). Compared over a common 20-year horizon, the steel bridge has the lower present value cost.

Capital Rationing

Implicit in our discussion to this point has been the assumption that investment capital is readily available to companies at a cost equal to the discount rate. The other extreme is *capital rationing*. Under capital rationing, the company has a fixed investment budget, which it may not exceed. As was true with mutually exclusive alternatives, capital rationing requires us to rank investments rather than simply to accept or reject them. Despite this similarity, however, you should understand that the two conditions are fundamentally different. With mutually exclusive alternatives, the money is available but, for technological reasons, the firm cannot make all investments. Under capital rationing, it may be technologically possible to make all investments, but there is not enough money. This difference is more than semantic, for as the following example illustrates, the nature of the ranking process differs fundamentally in the two cases.

Suppose Sullivan Electronics Company has a limited investment budget of $200,000 and that management has identified the four independent investment opportunities appearing in Table 7A–2. According to the three figures of merit, all investments should be undertaken, but this is impossible because the total cost of the four investments exceeds Sullivan's budget. Looking at the investment rankings, the NPV criterion ranks A as the best investment, followed by B, C, and D in that order, while the PI and IRR rank C best, followed by D, B, and A. So we know that A is either the best investment or the worst.

To make sense of these rankings, we need to remember that the underlying economic objective in evaluating investment opportunities is to increase wealth. Under capital rationing, this means the company should undertake that *bundle* of investments that generates the highest *total* NPV. How is this to be done? One way is to look at every possible bundle of investments having a total cost less than the budget con-

TABLE 7A–2

Four Independent Investment Opportunities under Capital Rationing (Capital Budget = $200,000)

Investment	Initial Cost	NPV at 12 Percent	PI at 12 Percent	IRR
A	$200,000	$10,000	1.05	14.4%
B	120,000	8,000	1.07	15.1
C	50,000	6,000	1.12	17.6
D	80,000	6,000	1.08	15.5

straint and to select the bundle with the highest *total* NPV. A short cut is to rank the investments by their PI and work down the list, accepting investments until either the money runs out or the PI drops below 1.0. This suggests that Sullivan should accept projects C, D, and $7/12$ of B, for a total NPV of \$16,670 [6,000 + 6,000 + $7/12 \times 8,000$]. Only $7/12$ of B should be undertaken because the company has only \$70,000 remaining after accepting C and D.

Why is it incorrect to rank investments by their NPV under capital rationing? Because under capital rationing, we are interested in the payoff per dollar invested, not simply in the payoff itself. The Sullivan example illustrates the point. Investment A has the largest NPV, equal to \$10,000, but it has the smallest NPV per dollar invested. Since investment dollars are limited under capital rationing, we must look at the benefit per dollar invested when ranking investments. This is what the PI does.

Two other details warrant mention. In the above example, the IRR provides the same ranking as the PI, and although this is usually the case, it is not always so. It turns out that when the two rankings differ, the PI ranking is the correct one. Why the rankings differ and why PI is superior are not worth explaining here. It is sufficient to remember that if you rank by IRR rather than PI, you might occasionally be in error, but that in the grand sweep of life, it probably doesn't matter much. A second detail is that when fractional investments are not possible—when it does not make sense for Sullivan Electronics to invest in $7/12$ of project B—then rankings according to any figure of merit are unreliable, and one must resort to the tedious method of looking at each possible bundle of investments in search of the highest total NPV.

The Problem of Future Opportunities

Implicit in the above discussion is the assumption that, as long as an investment has a positive NPV, it is better to make the investment than to let the money sit idle. However, under capital rationing, this may not be true. To illustrate, suppose that the financial executive of Sullivan Electronics believes that within six months company scientists will develop a new product costing \$200,000 and having an NPV of \$60,000. In this event, the company's best strategy is to forgo all of the investments presently under consideration and to save its money for the new product.

This example illustrates that investment evaluation under capital rationing involves more than a simple appraisal of current opportunities; it also involves a comparison between current opportunities and future prospects. The difficulty with this comparison, at a practical level, is that it is unreasonable to expect a manager to have anything more than a vague impression of what investments are likely to arise in the future. Consequently, it is impossible to decide with any assurance whether it is better to invest in current projects or to wait for brighter future opportunities. This means that practical investment evaluation under capital rationing necessarily involves a large degree of subjective judgment.

A Decision Tree

Mutually exclusive investment alternatives and capital rationing complicate an already confusing topic. To provide a summary and overview, Figure 7A–2 presents a capital budgeting decision tree. It indicates the figure or figures of merit that are appropriate under the various conditions discussed in the chapter. For example, following the lowest branch in the tree, we see that when evaluating investments under capital rationing that are independent and that can be acquired fractionally, ranking by

FIGURE 7A–2
Capital Budgeting Decision Tree

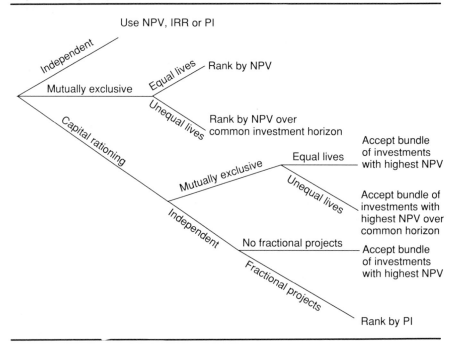

the PI is the appropriate technique. To review your understanding of the material, see if you can explain why the recommended figures of merit are appropriate under the various conditions indicated whereas the others are not.

CHAPTER SUMMARY

1. This chapter has examined the use of discounted cash flow techniques in investment appraisal.
2. The three steps in financial evaluation of investment opportunities are: (*a*) estimate the relevant cash flows, (*b*) calculate a figure of merit, and (*c*) compare it with an acceptance criterion. The first step is the hardest in practice.
3. Money has a time value because risk customarily increases with the futurity of an event, because inflation reduces the purchasing power of future cash flows, and because waiting for future cash flows involves a lost opportunity to make interim investments.
4. The payback period and the accounting rate of return ignore the time value of money and, hence, are inferior figures of merit. The payback period, however, is a useful indicator of investment risk.
5. Cash flows at two dates are equivalent if it is possible to transform the near-term cash flow into the later cash flow by investing it at the prevailing interest rate. Discounting uses equivalence to convert a messy stream of future receipts and disbursements into equal value cash flows occurring today.
6. A valid figure of merit is the net present value, defined as the difference between the present value of cash inflows and of outflows. Projects with a positive net present value are acceptable.
7. A second popular, valid figure of merit is the internal rate of return, defined as the discount rate that makes the investment's NPV equal zero. It is also the rate at which money left in a project is compounding and is therefore comparable to the interest rate on a bank loan. Investments with an internal rate of return greater than the cost of capital are acceptable.
8. The guiding principles in deciding what cash flows are relevant for an investment decision are the with-without principle and the cash flow principle.
9. Recurring problems in determining relevant cash flows involve depreciation, working capital changes, allocated costs, sunk costs, temporarily excess capacity, and financing costs.

ADDITIONAL READING

Bierman, Harold, Jr. and Seymour Smidt. *The Capital Budgeting Decision: Economic Analysis of Investment Projects.* 7th ed. New York: MacMillan, 1988.

   This textbook has more of a finance orientation than *Principles of Engineering Economy,* described below, and is somewhat harder to follow.

Grant, Eugene L., et al. *Principles of Engineering Economy.* 8th ed. New York: Wiley & Sons, 1990. 608 pages.

   Everything you ever wanted to know about discounted cash flow techniques and more. A very solid, understandable treatment containing many practical examples.

CHAPTER PROBLEMS

1. Answer the following questions assuming the interest rate is 14 percent:
   a. What is the present value of $1,000 in 5 years?
   b. What is the present value of $1,000 in 10 years? Why does the present value fall as the number of years increases?
   c. How much is a bond worth that has 10 years to maturity, a $1,000 par value, and a 10 percent coupon rate? Assume interest is paid annually.
   d. What will be the value in 20 years of $10 invested today? [**Hint:** Present value = PVF × future value, where PVF is the present value factor from the tables for an appropriate interest rate and time period. So, future value = (1/PVF) × present value.]
   e. About how long will it take for a $1 investment to triple in value?
   f. What will be the value in 6 years of $10 invested at the end of each year for the next 6 years?
   g. A couple wants to save $100,000 over the next 18 years for their child's college education. What uniform annual amount must they deposit at the end of each year to achieve their objective?
2. You purchase a piece of land for $100,000, hold it for 10 years, and sell it for $260,000. What was your approximate rate of return, ignoring taxes and transaction costs?
3. What was your approximate rate of return in problem 2 if you were required to pay annual property taxes of $1,500 and a sales commission in year 10 equal to 8 percent of the selling price?
4. A $100,000 investment promises an aftertax cash flow of $20,000 for 10 years.
   a. What is the investment's accounting rate of return?
   b. What is the investment's payback period?
   c. What is the investment's net present value at an 18 percent discount rate?
   d. What is the investment's profitability index at a discount rate of 18 percent?
   e. What is the investment's approximate internal rate of return?

    f. Assuming the required rate of return on the investment is 18 percent, which of the above figures of merit indicate the investment is attractive? Which indicate it is unattractive?

5. City Meats is contemplating purchase of a meat slicer. The following information is known about the slicer.

Initial cost	$100,000
Expected life	6 years
Expected salvage value	$10,000
Annual depreciation for tax purposes	$15,000
Expected annual cost savings	$30,000
Tax rate	40%
Minimum required rate of return	15%

    What advice would you offer City Meats?

6. An individual wants to borrow $10,000 from a bank and to repay it in five equal annual end-of-year payments including interest. If the bank wants to earn a 14 percent rate of return on the loan, what should the payments be? You may ignore default risk.

7. Times are tough for April Novelties. If they engage in a new year-long promotional campaign costing $10 million in present value terms, their annual aftertax cash flow over the next 5 years will be only $100,000. If they do not invest in the campaign, they expect aftertax cash flow to be −$3 million annually for the same period.

    Assuming the company has decided to stay in the novelty business, is this investment worthwhile when the discount rate is 10 percent?

8. Sanderson Electronics has made a long-run commitment to produce semiconductor chips of a specific type. Two designs are to be evaluated for their production. Design Y involves a present investment of $60,000. Estimated annual profits after tax for 15 years are $10,000. Design Z involves a present investment of $120,000. Estimated profits after tax for 20 years are $22,000. Assuming zero salvage value and straight-line depreciation, what recommendation would you give the company when the discount rate is 12 percent? You may assume Design Z is worth its book value at the end of year 15. [You may want to read the chapter appendix before trying this problem.]

9. In 1987, Vincent Van Gogh's painting *Sunflowers* (not reputed to be one of his best) sold at auction, net of fees, for $36 million. In 1889, 98 years earlier, the same painting sold for $125. Calculate the rate of return to the seller on this investment, ignoring all taxes and costs. What does this suggest about the merit of fine art as an investment? [You will need a business calculator or a computer to answer this question.]

CHAPTER 8

RISK ANALYSIS IN INVESTMENT DECISIONS

A man's gotta make at least one bet a day,
else he could be walking around lucky
and never know it.
Jimmy Jones, Horse trainer

All interesting financial decisions involve considerations of risk as well as return. By their nature, business investments require the expenditure of a known sum of money today in anticipation of uncertain future benefits. Consequently, if the discounted cash flow techniques discussed in the last chapter are to be useful in evaluating such investments, we must incorporate risk effects into the analysis. Two such effects are important: At the practical level, risk increases the difficulty of estimating relevant cash flows, while at the conceptual level, risk itself enters as an important determinant of investment value. A simple example will illustrate the latter point. If two investments promise the same return but have differing risks, most of us will prefer the lower risk alternative. In the jargon of economics, we are risk-averse.

Risk aversion among individuals and corporations creates the recognizable pattern of investment risk and return shown in Figure 8–1. For low-risk investments, such as government securities, the figure shows that the anticipated return is modest, but as risk increases, so too must the anticipated return. I say "must" here because the risk-return pattern shown is more than wishful thinking. Unless higher-risk investments promise higher returns, you and I as risk-averse investors will never hold them.

This risk-return trade-off is fundamental to much of finance. Over the past two decades, researchers have demonstrated that under idealized conditions, and with risk defined in a specific way, the risk-return trade-off is a straight-line one as depicted in the figure. The line is known as the Market Line and represents the combinations of risk and return one can expect in a properly functioning economy.

The details of the Market Line need not detain us here. What is important is the realization that knowledge of an investment's anticipated return is not enough to determine its worth. Instead, investment evaluation is a two-dimensional task involving a balancing of risk against return. The appropriate question when evaluating investment opportunities is not, "What's the rate of return," but rather "Is the return sufficient to justify the risk?" The investments represented by points A and B in Figure 8–1 illustrate this point. Investment A has a higher expected return than B; nonetheless, B is the better investment. Despite its modest return, B lies above the Market Line, meaning that it promises a higher return for its risk than available alternatives, whereas investment A lies below the Market Line, meaning that alternative investments are available that promise a higher return for the same risk.

This chapter examines the incorporation of risk into investment evaluation with particular emphasis on risk-adjusted discount rates and the cost of capital. After defining terms, we will estimate the cost of capital to Russell Corporation, the apparel company discussed in earlier chapters, and we will examine the limitations of the cost of capital as a risk-adjustment mechanism. The chapter con-

FIGURE 8–1
The Risk-Return Trade-Off

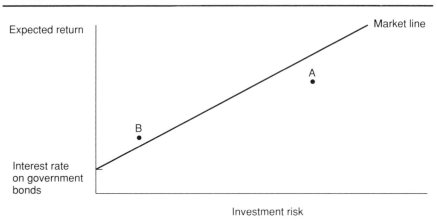

cludes with a look at several important pitfalls to avoid when evaluating investments. An appendix considers diversification and what is known as β-risk as they affect investment appraisal.

You should know at the outset that the topics in this chapter are not simple, for the addition of a whole second dimension to investment analysis in the form of risk introduces a number of complexities and ambiguities. The results of the chapter, therefore, will be a general road map for how to proceed and an appreciation of available techniques rather than a detailed set of answers. But look on the bright side. If investment decisions were simple, there would be less demand for well-educated managers and aspiring financial writers.

RISK DEFINED

Intuitively, investment risk is concerned with the range of possible outcomes from an investment; the greater this range, the greater the risk. Figure 8–2 extends this intuitive notion. It shows the pos-

FIGURE 8–2

Illustration of Investment Risk: Investment A Has a Lower Expected Return and a Lower Risk than B

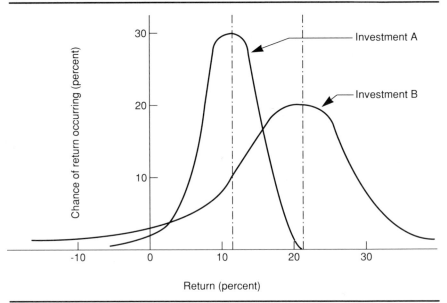

sible rates of return that might be earned on two investments in the form of bell-shaped curves. According to the figure, the expected return on investment A is about 12 percent, and the corresponding figure for investment B is about 22 percent.

A statistician would define "expected return" as the probability-weighted average of possible returns. To take a simple example, if three returns are possible—8, 12, and 18 percent—and if the chance of each occurring is 40, 30, and 30 percent, respectively, the investment's expected return is

Expected return $= 0.40 \times 8\% + 0.30 \times 12\% + 0.30 \times 18\% = 12.2\%$

Risk refers to the bunching of possible returns about an investment's expected return. If there is considerable bunching, as with investment A, the investment is low risk. With investment B there is considerably less clustering of returns about the expected return, so it has higher risk. Borrowing again from statistics, one way to measure this clustering tendency is to calculate a probability-weighted average of the deviations of possible returns from the expected return. One such average is the standard deviation of returns. The details of calculating an investment's standard deviation of returns need not concern us here.[1] It is sufficient to know that risk corresponds to the dispersion in possible outcomes, and that there exist techniques to measure this dispersion.

---

[1]To illustrate calculation of the standard deviation of returns, the differences between the possible returns and the expected return in the above example are $(8\% - 12.2\%)$, $(12\% - 12.2\%)$, and $(18\% - 12.2\%)$. Because some of these differences are positive and others negative, they would tend to cancel one another out if we added them directly. So we square them to ensure the same sign, calculate the probability-weighted average of the squared deviations, and then find the square root.

$$\text{Standard deviation} = [0.4(8\% - 12.2\%)^2 + 0.3(12\% - 12.2\%)^2 + 0.3(18\% - 12.2\%)^2]^{1/2}$$
$$= 4.1\%$$

The probability-weighted average difference between the investment's possible returns and its expected return is 4.1 percentage points. In symbols,

$$\sigma_i = \left[\sum_{i=1}^{n} p_i(r_i - \bar{r})^2 \right]^{1/2}$$

where σ_i is the investment's standard deviation of returns, p_i is the probability the ith return will occur, r_i is ith return, $\bar{r}$ is the expected return, n is the number of different returns which might occur, and $\sum$ indicates that the n squared deviations should be added together.

ESTIMATING INVESTMENT RISK

Having now defined risk in at least a general way, let us next consider how we might estimate the amount of risk present in a particular investment opportunity. In some business situations, an investment's risk can be calculated objectively from scientific or historical evidence. This is true, for instance, of oil and gas development wells. Once an exploration company has found a field and mapped out its general configuration, the probability that a development well drilled within the boundaries of the field will be commercially successful can be determined with reasonable accuracy.

Sometimes history can be a guide. A company that has opened 500 fast-food restaurants across the country should have a good idea about the expected return and risk of opening the 501st. Similarly, if you are thinking about buying IBM stock, the historical record of annual returns to IBM shareholders and the variability of these returns is an important starting point when estimating future risk and return on IBM shares.

These are the easy situations. More often, business ventures are one-of-a-kind investments for which the estimation of risk must be largely subjective. When a company is contemplating a new product investment, for example, there is frequently little technical or historical experience on which to base an estimate of investment risk. In this situation, risk appraisal depends on the perceptions of the managers participating in the decision, on their knowledge of the economics of the industry, and on their understanding of the investment's ramifications.

Sensitivity Analysis and Simulation

Two previously mentioned techniques, sensitivity analysis and simulation, are useful when investment risk must be estimated subjectively. Although neither technique provides an objective measure of investment risk, both help the executive to think systematically about the sources of risk and their impact on project return. Reviewing briefly, an investment's IRR or NPV depends upon a number of economic factors, such as selling price, quantity sold, useful life, and so on, many of which are not known with certainty. Sensitivity analysis involves a determination of how the investment's figure of merit varies with changes in one of these uncertain factors. One commonly used approach is to calculate three returns corresponding to an optimistic, a pessimistic, and a most likely forecast of the uncertain factor. This provides some indication of the range of possible outcomes.

Simulation is an extension of sensitivity analysis in which the analyst assigns a probability distribution to each uncertain factor, specifies any interdependence among the factors, and asks a computer repeatedly to select values for the factors according to their probability of occurring. For each set of values chosen, the computer calculates the investment's return. The result is a graph, such as Figure 8–2, plotting project return against frequency of occurrence. The chief benefits of sensitivity analysis and simulation are that they force the analyst to think systematically about the individual economic determinants of investment risk, they indicate the sensitivity of the investment's return to each of these determinants, and they provide information about the range of possible returns.

An Example of Sensitivity Analysis

A number of software programs are commercially available for analyzing investment opportunities on a personal computer. A standard option on many is the ability to analyze the sensitivity of the results to changes in key assumptions. Below is representative output from such an analysis.

Relative Impact of Key Variables on Net Present Value
(Investment NPV = $212,597)

A 1% Increase in:	Increases NPV by:	% Increase
Sales growth rate	$2,240	1.33
Operating profit margin	3,462	2.05
Capital investment	−1,249	−0.74
Working capital investment	−1,143	−0.68
Discount rate	−4,996	−2.96

INCLUDING RISK IN INVESTMENT EVALUATION

Once you have an idea of the amount of risk inherent in an investment, the final step is to incorporate this information into your evaluation of the opportunity. Speaking broadly, there are two ways to do this: by fiddling with the investment's cash flows, or by fiddling with its discount rate. The former uses what are known as *certainty equivalents.*

A certainty equivalent is a risk-free, or certain, sum of money that has the same value to the analyst as a risky cash flow. If you would just as soon receive $10 as a lottery ticket offering a 50–50 chance at $25 or nothing, $10 is your certainty equivalent of the lottery ticket.

To evaluate risky investments using certainty equivalents, the first step is to replace each risky cash flow with its certainty equivalent. Having thus accounted for risk, the second step is to evaluate the investment as if it were risk free. This means using a risk-free discount rate, such as the government borrowing rate, to calculate the investment's NPV or PI. Or if the IRR is used, it means comparing the certainty equivalent IRR to a risk-free interest rate to determine the investment's acceptability.

Certainty equivalents seldom are used in industry, primarily because there is no practical, objective way to estimate them. When you are making personal investment decisions, it might be possible to estimate certainty equivalents based on your own subjective feelings about risk. But when an executive analyzes an investment on behalf of his company, there is no practical way to determine what certainty equivalents are appropriate. This makes risk assessment almost entirely a matter of personal opinion.

Risk-Adjusted Discount Rates

The more common way to incorporate risk into investment appraisal is to adjust the discount rate. Instead of replacing risky cash flows with their certainty equivalents, the analyst discounts the expected value of the risky cash flows at a discount rate that includes a premium for risk. Alternatively, the analyst compares an investment's IRR, based on expected cash flows, to a required rate of return that again includes a risk premium. The size of the premium naturally increases with the perceived risk of the investment.

To illustrate the use of risk-adjusted discount rates, consider a $10 million investment promising risky cash flows having an expected value of $2 million annually for 10 years. What is the investment's NPV when the risk-free interest rate is 8 percent and management has decided to use a 6 percent risk premium to compensate for the uncertainty of the cash flows?

The cash flow diagram for the investment appears below. At a 14 percent risk-adjusted discount rate, the project's NPV is

$$NPV = -\$10 \text{ million} + \$2 \text{ million} (5.216)$$
$$= \$432,000$$

where 5.216, from Appendix B, equals the present value of $1.00 per year for 10 years at 14 percent interest. Because the investment's NPV is positive, it is attractive even after adjusting for risk. An equivalent approach is to calculate the investment's IRR, using expected cash flows, and compare it to the risk-adjusted rate. Because the project's IRR of 15.1 percent exceeds 14 percent, we again conclude that the investment is attractive despite its risk.

Note how the risk-adjusted discount rate reduces the investment's appeal. If the investment were riskless, its NPV at an 8 percent discount rate would be $3.4 million, but because a higher risk-adjusted rate is deemed appropriate, NPV falls by almost $3 million.

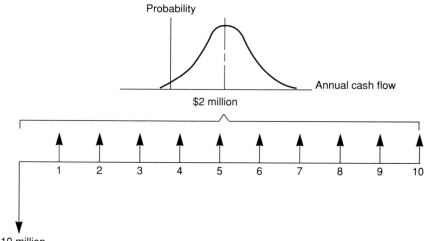

Two things make risk-adjusted discount rates superior to certainty equivalents in practical application. One is that most executives have at least a rough idea of how an investment's required rate of return should vary with risk. Stated differently, they have a basic idea of the position of the Market Line in Figure 8–1. For instance, they know from the historical data in Table 5–1 that over many years common stocks have yielded an average annual return that is about 7.2 percent higher than the return on government bonds. If the present return on government bonds is 8.0 percent, then it is plausible to expect an investment that is about as risky as common stocks to yield a return of about 15.2 percent. Similarly, executives know that, if an investment promises a return of 40 percent, unless the risk is extremely high the investment is likely to be attractive. Granted, such reasoning is imprecise; nonetheless, it does lend some objectivity to risk assessment.

THE COST OF CAPITAL

The second attraction of risk-adjusted discount rates involves the cost of capital. When creditors and owners invest money in a company, they incur an opportunity cost equal to the return they could have earned on alternative investments. This opportunity cost is the firm's cost of capital; it is the minimum rate of return the company can earn on existing assets and still meet the expectations of its capital providers. The cost of capital is a risk-adjusted discount rate, and because we can at least estimate the cost of capital for individual companies, it introduces a welcome degree of objectivity into the risk-adjustment process. In the following paragraphs we will define the cost of capital more precisely, estimate Russell Corporation's cost of capital, and discuss its use as a risk-adjustment factor.

The Cost of Capital Defined

Suppose we want to estimate the cost of capital to the XYZ Corporation, and we have the following information:

	XYZ Liabilities and Owners' Equity	Opportunity Cost of Capital
Debt	$100	10%
Equity	$200	20%

We will discuss the origins of the opportunity costs of capital in a few pages. For now just assume we know that, given alternative investment opportunities, creditors expect to earn at least 10 percent on their loans and shareholders expect to earn at least 20 percent on their ownership of XYZ shares. With this information, we need answer only two simple questions to calculate XYZ's cost of capital:

1. *How much money must XYZ earn annually on existing assets to meet the expectations of creditors and owners?*

   The creditors expect a 10 percent return on their $100 loan, or $10. However, because interest payments are tax-deductible, the effective aftertax cost to a profitable company in the 50 percent tax bracket is only $5. The owners expect 20 percent on their $200 investment, or $40. So in total, XYZ must earn $45 [$45 = (1 − 0.5)(10%) $100 + (20%) $200].

2. *What rate of return must the company earn on existing assets to meet the expectations of creditors and owners?*

   There is a total of $300 invested in XYZ on which the company must earn $45, so the required rate of return is 15 percent $45/$300). This is XYZ's cost of capital.

   Let's repeat the above reasoning using symbols. The money XYZ must earn annually on existing capital is

$$(1 - t)K_D D + K_E E$$

where t is the tax rate, K_D is the expected return on debt or the cost of debt, D is the amount of debt in XYZ's capital structure, K_E is the expected return on equity or the cost of equity, and E is the amount of equity in XYZ's capital structure. Similarly, the annual return XYZ must earn on existing capital is

$$K_W = \frac{(1 - t)\ K_D D + K_E E}{D + E} \qquad (8\text{-}1)$$

where K_w is the cost of capital.

From the above example,

$$15\% = \frac{(1 - 50\%) \times 10\% \times \$100 + 20\% \times \$200}{\$100 + \$200}$$

In words, a company's cost of capital is the cost of the individual sources of capital, weighted according to their importance in the firm's capital structure. The subscript w appears in the cost-of-capital expression to denote that the cost of capital is a weighted-average cost. To demonstrate, one third of XYZ's capital is debt and two thirds is equity, so its cost of capital is one third the cost of debt plus two-thirds the cost of equity.

$$15\% = 1/3 \times 5\% + 2/3 \times 20\%$$

The Cost of Capital and Stock Price

An important tie exists between a company's cost of capital and its stock price. To see the linkage, ask yourself what happens when XYZ Corporation earns a return on existing assets greater than its cost of capital. Because the return to creditors is fixed by contract, the excess return accrues entirely to shareholders. And because the company can earn more than shareholders' opportunity cost of capital, XYZ's stock price will rise as new investors are attracted by the excess return. Conversely, if XYZ earns a return below its cost of capital, shareholders will not receive their expected return, and stock price will fall. The price will continue to decline until the prospective return to new investors again equals equity investors' opportunity cost of capital. Another definition of the cost of capital, therefore, is the return a firm must earn on existing assets to keep its stock price constant. Finally, from the perspective of creating shareholder value we can say that management creates value when it earns returns above its cost of capital and destroys value when it earns returns below its cost of capital.

Russell's Cost of Capital

To use the cost of capital as a risk-adjusted discount rate in investment evaluation, we must be able to measure it. This involves assigning values to the quantities on the right side of Equation 8–1.

To illustrate the process, let's estimate Russell Corporation's cost of capital at year-end 1989.

The Weights

We begin by measuring the weights, D and E. There are two common ways to do this, only one of which is correct: Use the *book values* of debt and equity appearing on the company's balance sheet, or use the *market values*. By "market value," I mean the price of the company's bonds and common shares in securities markets multiplied by the number of each security type outstanding. As shown in Table 8–1, the book values of Russell's debt and equity at the end of fiscal year 1989 were $219.8 million and $402.2 million, respectively. The figure for debt includes only interest-bearing debt because other liabilities are spontaneous sources which are treated as part of working capital in the investment's cash flows. The table also indicates that the market values of Russell's debt and equity on the same date were $215.0 million and $1,055.2 million, respectively.

The market value of Russell's debt is about equal to its book value because most of the debt is either short term or recently issued. Russell's debt is not publicly traded, so $215.0 million is my estimate of the price at which it would have traded given its quality, coupon rate, and maturity. The market value of Russell's equity is its price per share at year-end of $26.12 times 40.4 million common shares outstanding. The market value of equity exceeds the book value by over two-to-one because investors are optimistic about Russell's future prospects.

TABLE 8–1
Book and Market Values of Russell's Debt and Equity (December 31, 1989)

| Source | Book Value | | Market Value | |
	Amount ($ millions)	Percent of Total	Amount ($ millions)	Percent of Total
Debt	$219.8	35.3%	$ 215.0	16.9%
Equity	402.2	64.7	1,055.2	83.1
Total	$622.0	100.0%	$1,270.2	100.0%

To decide whether book weights or market weights are appropriate for measuring the cost of capital, consider the following analogy. Suppose that 10 years ago you invested $20,000 in a portfolio of common stocks which, through no fault of your own, is now worth $50,000. After talking to stockbrokers and investment bankers, you feel that a reasonable return on the portfolio, given present market conditions, is 15 percent. Would you be satisfied with a 15 percent return on the original $20,000 cost of the portfolio, or would you expect to earn 15 percent on the current $50,000 market value? Obviously, the current market value is relevant for decision making; the original cost is sunk and therefore irrelevant. Similarly, Russell owners and creditors have investments worth $1,055.2 million and $215.0 million, respectively, on which they expect to earn competitive returns. Thus the market values of debt and equity are appropriate for measuring the cost of capital.

The Cost of Debt
This is an easy one. High-quality bonds of a maturity similar to Russell's were yielding a return of approximately 9.5% percent in December 1989, and the company's tax rate is about 37 percent. Consequently, the aftertax cost of debt to Russell was 6.0 percent $[(1 - 37\%) \times 9.5\%]$. Some persons are tempted to use the coupon rate on the debt rather than the prevailing market rate in this calculation. But again the coupon rate is a sunk cost. Moreover, because we want to use the cost of capital to evaluate new investments, we want the cost of new debt.

The Cost of Equity
Estimating the cost of equity is as hard as debt was easy. With debt, or preferred stock, the company promises the holder a specified stream of future payments. Knowing these promised payments and the current price of the security, it is a simple matter to calculate the expected return. This is what we did in the last chapter when we calculated the yield to maturity on a bond. With common stock, the situation is more complex. Because the company makes no promises about future payments to shareholders, there is no simple way to calculate the return expected.

The following cash flow diagrams illustrate the problem, looking first at the cash flows to a bond investor and then to a stock investor. Finding K_D is a simple discounted cash flow problem. Finding K_E would be just as simple except we do not know the future cash receipts expected by shareholders. This calls for some ingenuity.

Investor's Cash Flow Diagram for a Bond

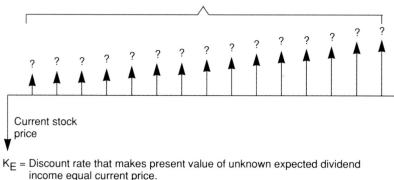

K_D = Discount rate that makes present value of cash inflows equal to current price.

Investor's Cash Flow Diagram for Common Stock

K_E = Discount rate that makes present value of unknown expected dividend income equal current price.

Assume a Perpetuity

One way out of this dilemma recalls the story of the physicist, the chemist, and the economist trapped at the bottom of a 40-foot pit. After failing with a number of schemes based on their knowledge of physics and chemistry for extracting themselves from the pit, the two finally turn to the economist in desperation and ask if his professional training might suggest a method of escape. "Why, yes," he replies, "The problem is really quite elementary . . . Simply assume a ladder." Here our "ladder" is an assumption about the future payments shareholders expect. From this heroic beginning the problem really does become quite elementary. To illustrate, suppose equity investors expect to receive an annual dividend of $d per share forever. The cash flow diagram then becomes

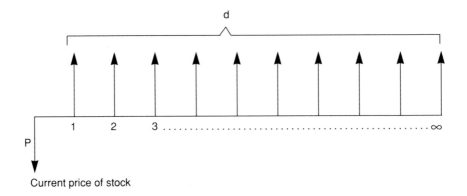

Current price of stock

Because we know P and have assumed a future payment stream, all that remains is to find the discount rate that makes the present value of the payment stream equal the current price. From the last chapter we know that the present value of such a perpetuity, at a discount rate of K_E, is

$$P = \frac{d}{K_E}$$

and solving for the discount rate,

$$K_E = \frac{d}{P}$$

In words, if you are willing to assume that investors expect a company's stock to behave like a perpetuity, the cost of equity capital is simply the dividend yield.

Perpetual Growth
A somewhat more plausible but still tractable assumption is that shareholders expect a per share dividend next year of $d, and that they expect this dividend to grow at the rate of g percent per annum forever. In this case the cash flow diagram becomes

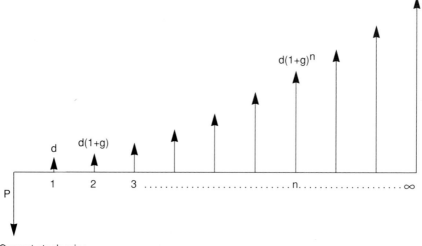

Current stock price

Fortunately, it turns out that this discounted cash flow problem also has an unusually simple solution. Without boring you with the arithmetic details, the present value of the assumed payment stream, at a discount rate of K_E, is

$$P = \frac{d}{K_E - g}$$

and solving for the discount rate,

$$K_E = \frac{d}{P} + g$$

This equation says that, if the perpetual growth assumption is correct, the cost of equity capital equals the company's dividend yield (d/P), plus the growth rate in dividends. This is known as the perpetual growth equation for K_E.

The problem with the perpetual growth estimate of K_E is that it is only as good as the assumption on which it is based. For *mature* companies, like railroads, electric utilities, and steel mills, it may be reasonable to assume that observed growth rates will continue indefinitely. And in these cases the perpetual growth equation yields a plausible estimate of the cost of equity capital. Moreover, we can meaningfully apply the equation to the economy as a whole and say that with an average dividend yield of about 5 percent, and an average nominal dividend growth rate of 8 percent, the cost of equity capital to the typical firm is about 13 percent. The equation is not applicable to Russell, however, because Russell's growth rate is well above one that could be sustained in perpetuity.

Let History Be Your Guide
A second, and generally more fruitful, approach to estimating the cost of equity capital looks at the structure of expected returns on risky investments. In general, the expected return on any risky asset is composed of three factors:

$$\begin{array}{c} \text{Expected return} \\ \text{on risky asset} \end{array} = \begin{array}{c} \text{Risk-free} \\ \text{interest rate} \end{array} + \begin{array}{c} \text{Inflation} \\ \text{premium} \end{array} + \begin{array}{c} \text{Risk} \\ \text{premium} \end{array}$$

The equation says that the owner of a risky asset should expect to earn a return from three sources. The first is compensation for the opportunity cost incurred in holding the asset. This is the risk-free interest rate. The second is compensation for the declining purchasing power of his investment over time. This is the inflation premium. The third is compensation for bearing risk. This is the risk premium. Fortunately, we do not need to treat the first two terms as separate factors because together they equal the expected return on a default-free bond such as a government bond. In other words, owners of government bonds expect a return from the first two sources but not the third. Consequently,

$$\begin{array}{c} \text{Expected return} \\ \text{risky asset} \end{array} = \begin{array}{c} \text{Interest rate on} \\ \text{government bond} \end{array} + \begin{array}{c} \text{Risk} \\ \text{premium} \end{array}$$

Since we can readily determine the government bond interest rate, the only challenge is to estimate the risk premium.

When the risky asset is a common stock, it is useful to let history be our guide and recall from Table 5–1 that on average over the period 1926 to 1990 the annual return on common stocks exceeded that on government bonds by 7.2 percent. As a reward for bearing the added risk, common stockholders earned a 7.2 percent higher annual return than government bondholders. Treating this as a risk premium, and adding it to a 1990 government bond rate of

8.0 percent yields an estimate of 15.2 percent as the cost of equity capital for the typical company.

What is the logic of treating the 7.2 percent historical excess return as a risk premium? It is essentially that over a long enough time the return investors receive and what they expect to receive should approximate one another. For example, suppose investors expect a 20 percent excess return on common stocks but the actual return keeps turning out to be 3 percent. Then two things should happen: Investors should lower their expectations, and selling on the part of disappointed investors should increase subsequent realized returns. Eventually expectations and reality should come into rough parity.

We now have an estimate of the cost of equity capital to an average-risk company. In the appendix to this chapter, we discuss a technique for modifying this estimate to reflect the risk of a specific firm. For now, let us do this more informally. Because Russell has created retail brand recognition and a well-defined market niche in a basic industry, it probably has somewhat less business risk than the average firm. And its relatively modest reliance on debt financing probably gives it a somewhat below-average financial risk as well. Together, I believe that Russell is somewhat less risky than the average share of stock. Let us, therefore, use 15.0 percent as an estimate of Russell's cost of equity capital.

Calculation of Russell's Cost of Capital

All that remains is the figure work. Table 8–2 presents our estimate of Russell's cost of capital in tabular form. Russell's weighted-average cost of capital is 13.5 percent. This means that in

TABLE 8–2
Calculation of Russell Corporation's Cost of Capital

Source	Amount ($ millions)	Percent of Total	Cost After Tax	Weighted Cost
Debt	$ 215.0	16.9%	6.0%	1.0%
Equity	1,055.2	83.1	15.0	12.5
			Cost of capital =	13.5%

1989 Russell had to earn at least this percentage return on the market value of existing assets to meet the expectations of creditors and shareholders and to maintain share price.

In equation form:

$$K_W = \frac{(1 - 0.37)(6.0\%)(\$215.0 \text{ million}) + (15.0\%)(\$1,055.2 \text{ million})}{\$215.0 \text{ million} + \$1.055.2 \text{ million}}$$

$$= 13.5\%$$

The Cost of Capital in Investment Appraisal

The fact that the cost of capital is the return a company must earn on *existing assets* to meet creditor and shareholder expectations is an interesting detail, but we are after bigger game here: We want to use the cost of capital as an acceptance criterion for *new investments.*

Are there any problems in applying a concept derived for existing assets to new investments? Not if one critical assumption holds: The new investment must have the same risk as existing assets. If it does, the new investment is essentially a "carbon copy" of existing assets, and the cost of capital is the appropriate risk-adjusted discount rate. If it does not, we must proceed more carefully.

The Market Line in Figure 8–3 clearly illustrates the importance of the equal-risk assumption. It emphasizes that the rate of return anticipated by risk-averse individuals rises with risk. This means, for example, that management should demand a higher expected return when introducing a new product than when replacing aged equipment because the new product is presumably riskier and, therefore, warrants a higher return. The figure also shows that a company's cost of capital is but one of many possible risk-adjusted discount rates, the one corresponding to the risk of the firm's existing assets. We conclude that the cost of capital is an appropriate acceptance criterion only when the risk of the new investment equals that of existing assets. For other investments, the cost of capital is inappropriate, but even when inappropriate itself, the cost of capital frequently serves as an important, practical touchstone about which further adjustments are made.

FIGURE 8–3
An Investment's Risk-Adjusted Discount Rate Increases with Risk

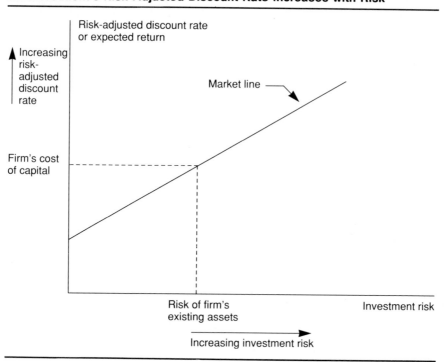

Multiple Hurdle Rates

Many companies adjust for differing levels of investment risk by using multiple hurdle rates, each rate applying to a different level of risk. For example, Russell might use the following array:

Type of Investment	Discount Rate (%)
Replacement or repair	9.0
Cost reduction	10.0
Expansion	13.5
New product	17.5

Investments to expand capacity in existing products are essentially carbon-copy investments, so their hurdle rate equals Russell's cost of capital. Other types of investments have a higher or lower hurdle rate, depending on their risk relative to expansion investments. Replacement or repair investments are the safest because virtually all of the cash flows are well known from past experience. Cost-reduction investments are somewhat riskier because the magnitude of potential savings is uncertain. New product investments are the riskiest type because both revenues and costs are uncertain.

Multiple hurdle rates are consistent with risk aversion and with the Market Line, but the amount by which the hurdle rate should be adjusted for each level of risk is largely arbitrary. Whether the hurdle rate for cost-reduction investments should be three percentage points or five percentage points below Russell's cost of capital cannot be determined objectively.

Rather than assign a different discount rate to each type of investment, some multidivision companies assign a different discount rate to each division. A potential advantage of this approach is that, if a division competes against one or several single-product firms, the cost of capital of these competitors can be used as the division's hurdle rate for new investment. An offsetting disadvantage of divisional hurdle rates is the implicit assumption that all investments made by the division have the same business risk.

FOUR PITFALLS

We come now to a moment of truth. Having convinced you of the power of discounted cash flow techniques in investment appraisal, should I quit while ahead; or should I risk undermining your enthusiasm for the subject by acknowledging the existence of several pitfalls in the practical application of these techniques? In the interest of full disclosure, I will gingerly mention four such pitfalls. The first two are easily avoided once you become aware of them; the last two, however, are more problematic.

The Fallacy of the Marginal Cost of Capital

Some persons look at Equation 8–1 and naively conclude that it is possible to reduce a company's weighted-average cost of capital by using more of the cheap source of financing, debt, and less of the expensive source, equity. In other words, they conclude that increasing leverage will reduce the cost of capital. This reasoning, however, evidences an incomplete understanding of leverage. As observed in the last chapter, increasing leverage increases the risk borne by shareholders. And because they are risk-averse, shareholders react by demanding a higher return on their investment. Thus, K_E, and to a less extent K_D, rises as leverage increases. This means that increasing leverage affects a company's cost of capital in two opposing ways: Increasing use of cheap debt reduces K_W, but the rise in K_E and K_D that accompanies added leverage increases it.

To review this reasoning, ask yourself how you would respond to a subordinate who made the following argument in favor of an investment. "I know the company's cost of capital is 15 percent and the IRR of this carbon-copy investment is only 10 percent. But at the last directors' meeting we decided to finance this year's investments with new debt. Since new debt has a cost of only about 6 percent after tax, it is clearly in our shareholders' interest to invest 6 percent money to earn a 10 percent return."

The subordinate's reasoning is incorrect. Financing with debt means increasing leverage and increasing K_E. Adding the change in K_E to the 6 percent interest cost means the true marginal cost of the debt is well above the interest cost.

The Total Firm Perspective versus the Equity Perspective

Any corporate investment that is partially financed with debt can be analyzed from either of two perspectives: from that of the firm making the investment, or from that of the firm's equity owners. As the following example demonstrates, these two perspectives are functionally equivalent in the sense that when properly applied they typically lead to the same investment decision—but woe be to him who confuses the two.

ABC Enterprises has a capital structure composed of 40 percent debt, costing 5 percent after tax, and 60 percent equity, costing 20 percent. Its weighted-average cost of capital is therefore

$$K_W = 5\% \times 0.40 + 20\% \times 0.60 = 14\%$$

The company is considering an average-risk investment costing $100 million and promising an aftertax cash flow of $14 million a year in perpetuity. If undertaken, ABC plans to finance the investment with $40 million in new borrowings and $60 million in equity. Should ABC make the investment?

The Total Firm Perspective

The figure on the left at the top of the next page shows the investment's cash flows from the viewpoint of the firm. Applying our now-standard approach, the investment is a perpetuity with a 14 percent internal rate of return. Comparing this return to ABC's weighted-average cost of capital, also 14 percent, we conclude that the investment is marginal. Undertaking it will neither increase nor decrease shareholder wealth.

The Equity Perspective

The figure on the right shows the same investment from the owners' viewpoint. Because $40 million of the initial cost will be financed by debt, the equity outlay is only $60 million. Similarly, because $2 million after tax must be paid to creditors each year as interest, the residual cash flow to equity will be only $12 million. The investment's internal rate of return from the equity perspective is therefore 20 percent.

Does the fact that the return is now 20 percent mean the investment is suddenly an attractive one? Clearly, not. Because the equity cash flows are leveraged, they are riskier than the original cash flows and, hence, require a higher risk-adjusted discount rate. Indeed, the appropriate acceptance criterion for these equity cash flows is ABC's cost of equity capital, or 20 percent. (Remember the discount rate should reflect the risk of the cash flows to be discounted.) Comparing the project's 20 percent return to equity with ABC's cost of equity, we again conclude that the investment is only marginal.

Cash Flow Diagrams for ABC Enterprise's Investment

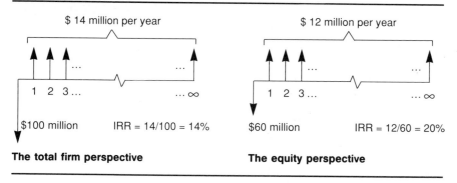

The total firm perspective

The equity perspective

It is not an accident that the total firm and the equity perspectives yield the same result since the weighted-average cost of capital is defined to ensure that each supplier of capital receives a return equal to her opportunity cost. Thus we know that an investment by ABC earning 14 percent, from the total firm perspective, will earn just enough to service the debt and generate a 20 percent return on invested equity. Problems arise only when you mix the two perspectives, using K_E to discount firm cash flows or, more commonly, using K_W to discount equity cash flows.

Which perspective is better? Some of my best friends use the equity perspective, but I believe the firm perspective is easier to apply in practice. The problem with the equity perspective is that both the return to equity and the appropriate risk-adjusted discount rate vary with the amount of leverage used. The IRR to equity on ABC Enterprise's investment is 20 percent with $40 million of debt financing, but jumps to 95 percent with $90 million of debt, and rises to *infinity* with all-debt financing.

The interdependency between the means of financing and the risk-adjusted discount rate is easily handled in a classroom, but when real money is on the line, we often become so enthralled by the return-enhancing aspect of debt that we forget that the required rate of return rises as well. Moreover, even when we remember that leverage increases risk as well as return, it is devilishly hard to estimate exactly how much the cost of equity should change with leverage.

I recommend that you avoid unnecessary complications by using the total firm perspective whenever possible. Assess the economic merit of the investment without regard to how it will be financed or how you will divvy up the spoils. If the investment meets this fundamental test, you can then turn to the nuances of how best to finance it.

Inflation

Pitfall number two involves the improper handling of inflation. Too often managers ignore inflation when estimating an investment's cash flows but inadvertently include it in their discount rate. The effect of this mismatch is to make companies overly conservative in their investment appraisal, especially with regard to long-lived assets. Table 8–3 illustrates the point. A company with a 15 percent cost of capital is considering a $10 million, carbon-copy investment. The investment has a four-year life and is expected to increase production capacity by 10,000 units annually. Because the product sells for $900, the company estimates that annual revenues will rise $9 million ($900 × 10,000 units) which, after subtracting production costs, yields an increase in annual aftertax cash flows of $3.3 million. The IRR of the investment is calculated to be 12.1 percent, which is below the firm's cost of capital.

Did you spot the error? By assuming a constant selling price and constant production costs over four years, management has implicitly estimated real, or constant dollar, cash flows, whereas the cost of capital as calculated earlier in the chapter is a nominal one. It is nominal because both the cost of debt and the cost of equity include a premium for expected inflation.

The key to capital budgeting under inflation is always to compare like to like. When cash flows are in nominal dollars, use a nominal discount rate. When cash flows are in real, or constant, dollars, use a real discount rate. The bottom portion of Table 8–3 illustrates a proper evaluation of the investment. After including a 5 percent annual increase in selling price and in variable production costs, the expected nominal cash flows from the investment are as shown. As one would expect, the nominal cash flows exceed the constant-dollar cash flows by a growing amount in each year.

TABLE 8–3

When Evaluating Investments under Inflation, Always Compare Nominal Cash Flows to a Nominal Discount Rate or Real Cash Flows to a Real Discount Rate ($ millions)

A. Incorrect Investment Evaluation Comparing Real Cash Flows to a Nominal Discount Rate

	1989	1990	1991	1992	1993
Aftertax Cash Flow	($10.0)	$3.3	$3.3	$3.3	$3.3

$$IRR = 12.1\%$$
$$K_w = 15\%$$
Decision: Reject

B. Correct Investment Evaluation Comparing Nominal Cash Flows to a Nominal Discount Rate

	1989	1990	1991	1992	1993
Aftertax Cash Flow	($10.0)	$3.5	$3.8	$4.0	$4.3

$$IRR = 20.0\%$$
$$K_w = 15\%$$
Decision: Accept

The IRR of these flows is 20%, which now exceeds the firm's cost of capital.[2]

Real Options

The third pitfall involves the possible omission of important managerial options inherent in many corporate investment opportunities. These options seldom arise in simple textbook illustrations because most textbooks, in their emphasis on the mechanical dimensions of investment appraisal, implicitly assume that management has no control over the outcome of an investment once undertaken. Instead, simple textbook examples implicitly assume that, after having selected their favorite investments, managers stand idly by as Dame Fate rolls the dice.

---

[2]An alternative approach would have been to calculate the firm's real cost of capital and compare it to a real IRR. But, because this approach is more work and is fraught with potential errors, I recommend working with nominal cash flows and a nominal discount rate instead.

Such passivity may be an appropriate assumption when the investments under review are stocks and bonds, but it can be dangerously inappropriate in other instances when managers have the ability to alter a project during its life. Examples of what are often called *real options,* in recognition of their formal equivalence to stock options, include the option to abandon an investment if cash flows do not meet expectations, the option to modify the scale of operations as demand varies, the option to alter the mix of inputs as raw materials prices change, and the option to make follow-on investments if the initial investment is successful. In each case, management can change the nature or the scope of the investment in response to information not known at the time of the original decision. The importance of such real options in valuing certain investments can be appreciated by noting that a pure R&D investment could never be justified if it were not for the option such expenditures give management to exploit positive research results with follow-on investments.

Here is an example of how real options affect the value of an investment. General Design Corporation is considering investing $100 million to develop a new line of high-speed semiconductors based on a newly emerging diamond film technology. Panel A of Table 8–4 shows that the investment's anticipated life is five years and that annual cash flows are expected to be $60 million if the project succeeds and −$40 million if it fails. Management pegs the chance of success at only 50 percent. If General Design requires an 8 percent return on low-risk investments, 15 percent on moderate-risk investments, and 25 percent on high-risk ones, what should the company do?

The Option to Abandon
Calculating expected cash flows and discounting at a 25 percent rate reflecting the venture's high risk, the net present value is large and negative, −$73 million. The diamond film project is clearly unacceptable. But on reflection is it likely that General Design will passively incur losses for five years if the technology is found to be unworkable early on? Assuming more realistically that management has the option to abandon the venture after two years at a salvage value of, say, $20 million, the revised cash flows appear in

TABLE 8–4
General Design's Diamond Film Project ($ millions)

PANEL A: Stage 1, Ignoring Option to Abandon
                Probability of Success = 50%
Expected Aftertax Cash Flows

Year	0	1	2	3	4	5
Success	($100)	60	60	60	60	60
Failure	($100)	−40	−40	−40	−40	−40
Expected	($100)	10	10	10	10	10
NPV @ 25% =	($73)					

PANEL B: Stage 1, Including Option to Abandon
                Probability of Success = 50%
Expected Aftertax Cash Flows

Year	0	1	2	3	4	5
Success	($100)	60	60	60	60	60
Failure	($100)	−40	−40	20	0	0
Expected	($100)	10	10	40	30	30
NPV @ 25% =	($43)					

PANEL C: Stage 2, The Option to Expand
                Probability of Success (Assuming Stage 1 Successful) = 90%
Expected Aftertax Cash Flows

Year	0	1	2	3	4	5	6	7
Success			($500)	300	300	300	300	300
Failure			($500)	−200	−200	100	0	0
Expected			($500)	250	250	280	270	270
NPV @ 25% = $130								

              TOTAL NPV @ 25% (Stage 1 + 0.50 × Stage 2) = $ 22

Panel B of Table 8–4. Note that the abandonment option is worth $30 million, bringing the NPV up to −$43 million.

The Option to Grow

A chief attraction of many new technology investments is that success today creates the opportunity to make highly profitable follow-on investments tomorrow, investments that are possible only because management took an intelligent gamble today. In this vein, suppose General Design believes that initial success in diamond films will open the door to a stage-2, follow-on investment in two years that is precisely five times the size of today's stage-1 investment.

The probability assigned to a stage-2 success is critical. In management's eyes, if the stage-2 investment were made today, it would probably be no more likely to succeed than would stage 1; after all, stage 2 is the same technology, only five times as large. If made today, then, stage 2's NPV would just be five times as negative as stage 1's. But management does not have to make a decision on stage 2 today. It has the option to defer a decision until the initial results from stage 1 are in, and will consequently be able to make a more informed choice. Supposing stage 2 will be undertaken only if stage 1 succeeds and that the chance of a stage-2 success in this event is 90 percent, Panel C in Table 8–4 shows that the NPV of stage 2 at time zero is $130 million. Because General Design stands only a 50 percent chance of making the stage-2 investment, its expected NPV is half this amount, or $65 million. Adding the expected NPVs of both stages, the total NPV is now a healthy $22 million; and this ignores any stage-3 or stage-4 investments that might logically follow a stage-2 success. Proper consideration of the options embedded in General Design's investment transform it from a clunker into a winner.

The moral should be clear: Failure to recognize and value these and other real options implicit in many corporate investments will make executives inappropriately timid in the face of high-risk, high-payoff opportunities.

Excessive Risk Adjustment

Our last pitfall is a subtle one concerning the proper use of risk-adjusted discount rates in investment appraisal. Adding an increment to the discount rate to adjust for an investment's risk makes intuitive sense. You need to be aware, however, that as you apply this discount rate to more-distant cash flows, the arithmetic of the discounting process compounds the risk adjustment. Table 8–5 illustrates the effect. It shows the present value of $1.00 in one year and in 10 years, first at a risk-free discount rate of 5 percent, and then at a risk-adjusted rate of 10 percent. Comparing these present values, note that addition of the risk premium knocks a modest 4.3 cents off the value of a dollar in one year, but a sizable 22.8 cents

TABLE 8–5

Use of a Constant Risk-Adjusted Discount Rate Implies that Risk Increases with the Remoteness of a Cash Flow (Risk-Free Rate = 5%; Risk-Adjusted Rate = 10%)

	Present Value of $1	
	Received in One Year	Received in 10 Years
Risk-free	0.952	0.614
Risk-adjusted	0.909	0.386
Reduction in present value due to risk	0.043	0.228

off in 10 years. Clearly, use of a constant risk-adjusted discount rate is appropriate only when the risk of a cash flow grows as the cash flow recedes further into the future.

For many, if not most, business investments the assumption that risk increases with the remoteness of a cash flow is quite appropriate, but as will be seen by looking again at General Design's diamond film project, this is not always the case.

Recall that General Design is contemplating a possible two-stage investment. The first stage, costing $100 million, is attractive chiefly because it gives management the option to make a much more lucrative follow-on investment. Because both stages depend on a new, untested diamond film technology, the discount rate used throughout the analysis was General Design's high-risk hurdle rate of 25 percent.

Given the speculative nature of this investment, many executives would argue that it is entirely appropriate to use a high risk-adjusted discount rate throughout. But is it really? The investment clearly involves high risk, but because most of the risk will be resolved in the first two years, use of a constant risk-adjusted discount rate is overly conservative.

To see the logic, suppose you are at time 2, that stage 1 has been successful, and the company is about to launch stage 2. Because the stage-2 cash flows are now relatively certain, their value *at time 2* is their expected values, as shown in Panel C of Table 8–4, *discounted at 15 percent,* the rate applicable to moderate-risk investments. This amounts to $330 million.

As seen from the present, therefore, General Design's decision to invest in stage 1 gives it a 50 percent chance at a follow-on investment worth $330 million in two years. And because the next two years are high risk, we can find the present value of stage 2 today by discounting the $330 million time-2 value to the present at 25 percent.

$$\begin{array}{l} \text{Expected present value} \\ \text{of stage-2 investment} \end{array} = 0.50 \times \$330 \text{ million} \times 0.640$$

$$= \$106 \text{ million}$$

Adding this sum to the stage-1 NPV of −$43 million yields a total NPV of $63 million. Explicit recognition of the two risk phases in General Design's investment adds another $41 million to its present worth.

To recap, whenever you encounter an investment with two or more distinct risk phases, be careful about using a constant risk-adjusted discount rate, for although such investments may be comparatively rare, they are also frequently the type of opportunities companies can ill-afford to waste.

A CAUTIONARY NOTE

An always-present danger when using analytic or numerical techniques in business decision making is that the "hard facts" will assume exaggerated importance compared to more qualitative issues and that the manipulation of these facts will become a substitute for creative effort. It is important to bear in mind that numbers and theories don't get things done, people do. And the best of investments will fail unless capable workers are committed to their success. As Barbara Tuchman put it in another context, "In military as in other human affairs will is what makes things happen. There are circumstances that can modify or nullify it, but for offense or defense its presence is essential and its absence fatal."[3]

---

[3]Barbara W. Tuchman, *Stilwell and the American Experience in China 1911–1945* (New York: Bantam Books, 1971), pp. 561–62.

APPENDIX

DIVERSIFICATION AND β-RISK

In the chapter, we observed that the expected rate of return on a risky asset can be written as

$$\begin{array}{c} \text{Expected return} \\ \text{on risky asset} \end{array} = \begin{array}{c} \text{Interest rate on} \\ \text{government bonds} \end{array} + \text{Risk premium}$$

where the interest rate on government bonds is itself the sum of a risk-free interest rate and an inflation premium. We noted too that when the risky asset in question is a typical company's common stock, one measure of the risk premium is the *excess* return earned by common shareholders relative to government bondholders over a long period. Here we want to discuss the risk premium in more detail and relate it to risk measures that include the effects of diversification.

We can repeat the equation above in symbols by letting i equal the prevailing interest rate on government bonds, R_m, the average annual return on a well-diversified portfolio of common stocks over a long period, and i_b, the average annual return on government bonds over the same period.

$$\begin{array}{c} \text{Expected return on typical} \\ \text{company's common stock} \end{array} = i + (R_m - i_b)$$

In late 1990, the interest rate on government bonds was about 8.0 percent. Using the figures in Table 5–1, the average annual return earned by investors in the 500 stocks comprising the Standard & Poor's 500 stock index over the period 1926 to 1990 was 12.1 percent, whereas the average annual return on government bonds over the same period was 4.9 percent. This suggests a risk premium $(R_m - i_b)$, of 7.2 percent, and an expected return on a typical company's stock, given prevailing interest rates of 15.2 percent $(15.2\% = 8.0\% + 7.2\%)$.

The above equation provides an estimate of a typical company's cost of equity capital, where by "typical" I mean a company having average risk.[4] However, if we want to use this equation to estimate the cost of capi-

---

[4] Careful study of this topic will reveal that estimating an equity risk premium is not quite as simple as implied here. The most complete discussion of the topic of which I am aware is Chapter 8 in *Stocks, Bonds, Bills and Inflation, 1991 Yearbook*, Ibbotson Associates, Chicago, 1991, where it is observed that 7.2 percent is an estimate of the "long-horizon" equity risk premium suitable for valuing cash flows projected over a long period. A short-horizon equity risk premium would substitute the short-term government bill rate for the long-term bond rate, yielding a premium of 8.4 percent $(12.1\% - 3.7\%)$. Also, for technical reasons relating to the method used to average annual risk premiums and to the distinction between expected and realized returns on the part of bondholders, it is likely that 7.2 percent is a modest overestimate of the true risk premium. See the *1991 Yearbook* for more complete details.

tal of an *atypical* company, or if we want to estimate the expected return on any other kind of risky asset, we must modify the equation to reflect the particular risk of the company or asset in question. The following equation includes the necessary modification. Letting R_j equal the expected rate of return on risky asset j,

$$
\begin{array}{c}
\text{Expected} \\
\text{return on} \\
\text{risky asset } j
\end{array}
=
\begin{array}{c}
\text{Interest rate} \\
\text{on government} \\
\text{bonds}
\end{array}
+
\begin{array}{c}
\text{β-risk of} \\
\text{asset } j
\end{array}
\times
\begin{array}{c}
\text{Risk} \\
\text{premium}
\end{array}
$$

$$R_j = i + \beta_j \,(R_m - i_b) \tag{8A-1}$$

β_j is known as the asset's β-risk, or its *volatility.* We will talk more about the calculation of β_j in a few paragraphs. For now, think of it as simply the risk of asset j relative to that of the common stock portfolio, m.

$$\beta_j = \frac{\text{Risk of asset } j}{\text{Risk of portfolio } m}$$

If the risk of asset j is equal to that of a typical company's common stock, $\beta_j = 1.0$ and the equation is just as before. If the asset is of above-average risk, β_j exceeds 1.0, and if it is of below-average risk, β_j is less than 1.0.

In recent years, β-risk has become an important factor in security analysis, so much so that many stock brokerage companies and investment advisors regularly publish the βs for virtually all publicly traded common stocks. Table 8A–1 presents βs for a representative sample of firms, as well as industry-average βs. Recalling that a β of 1.0 is typical, or average, note that the range for company βs in the table is from a high of 1.85 for Applied Biosystems, Inc. to a low of 0.34 for Duke Power, a utility company. Also note that Russell's β is 0.98, indicating that Russell's common stock is of about average risk.

With knowledge of a company's β it becomes easy to use Equation 8A–1 to estimate a company's cost of equity capital. For example, Russell's cost of equity in 1989 according to this equation was

$$
\begin{aligned}
R_j &= i + \beta_j \,(R_m - i_b) \\
&= 8.0\% + 0.98 \,(12.1\% - 4.9\%) \\
&= 15.1\%
\end{aligned}
$$

In contrast, Applied Biosystem's cost of equity was

$$8.0\% + 1.85 \,(12.1\% - 4.9\%) = 21.3\%$$

and that of DukePower was

$$8.0\% + 0.34 \,(12.1\% - 4.9\%) = 10.5\%$$

TABLE 8A–1
Representative Industry and Company Betas

Industry Betas		Company Betas	
Industry	Beta	Company	Beta
Aircraft	0.99	Amdahl	1.50
Apparel	1.26	American Brands	1.01
Banks	0.87	American Elect. Power	0.51
Computers—micro	1.29	American Express	1.35
Electronc components	1.37	AT&T	0.79
Farm machinery	0.88	Applied Biosystems Inc.	1.85
Food	0.98	Bank of America	1.21
Gold and precious metals	0.55	Brunswick Corp.	1.51
Motion pictures	1.44	Caterpillar	1.06
Motor vehicles	1.04	Citicorp	1.25
Publishing	1.16	Coca Cola	0.90
Textile	1.09	Control Data	1.11
Utilities—electric	0.53	Duke Power	0.34
		General Electric	1.15
		General Motors	1.10
		Idaho Power & Light	0.47
		IBM	0.74
		Nat'l Semiconductor	1.37
		Russell Corp.	0.98
		Textronix Inc.	0.91
		Westinghouse	1.21
		Xerox	1.07

Source: Selected industry betas reprinted by permission of Vestek Systems, San Francisco, from *Investment Data Book,* November 1990. Selected company betas reprinted by permission of Merrill Lynch, Pierce, Fenner and Smith, Inc. from *Security Risk Evaluation,* December 1990.

At a conceptual level, Equation 8A–1 is quite important, for it tells us the rate of return we should expect on any risky asset and how that return varies with the asset's β-risk. Looking at Figure 8–1, another way to say the same thing is that Equation 8A–1 is the equation of the Market Line. To determine the appropriate risk-adjusted discount rate for any risky asset, all we need to do is calculate the asset's β, plug this value into Equation 8A–1, and calculate the expected return on the asset. This expected return, denoted by R_j, is the correct risk-adjusted discount rate for investment evaluation.

Diversification

To understand β-risk more fully, we need to take a slight detour and talk about risk in general. Below is information about two very simple risky investments, purchase of an ice cream stand and an umbrella shop. For simplicity, we will consider only two possible states for tomorrow's weather, sun or rain. Purchase of an ice cream stand is clearly a risky undertaking since the investor stands to make $600 if it is sunny tomorrow but will lose $200 if it rains. The umbrella shop is also risky since the investor will lose $300 if tomorrow is sunny but will make $500 if it rains.

Yet despite the fact that these two investments are risky when viewed in isolation, they are not risky when viewed as members of a portfolio containing both investments.

Ice Cream Stand

Weather	Probability	Outcome	Weighted Outcome
Sun	0.40	$600	$240
Rain	0.60	–200	–120
		Expected outcome	$120

Umbrella Shop

Weather	Probability	Outcome	Weighted Outcome
Sun	0.40	–$300	–$120
Rain	0.60	500	300
		Expected outcome	$180

Portfolio: Ice Cream Stand and Umbrella Shop

Weather	Probability	Outcome	Weighted Outcome
Sun	0.40	$300	$120
Rain	0.60	300	180
		Expected outcome	$300

In a portfolio, the losses and gains from the two investments counterbalance one another in each state, so that regardless of tomorrow's weather, the outcome is a riskless $300. The expected outcome from the portfolio is the sum of the expected outcomes from each investment in the portfolio, but the risk of the portfolio is zero.

This is an extreme example, but it does illustrate an important fact. When you own a portfolio of assets, the relevant measure of risk is not the asset's risk in isolation but rather its risk as part of the portfolio. And as the example demonstrates, the difference between these two perspectives can be substantial.

An asset's risk in isolation is greater than its portfolio risk whenever the asset's cash flows and the portfolio's cash flows are less than perfectly correlated. In this commonplace situation, some of the asset's cash flow variability is offset by variability in the portfolio's cash flows, and the effective risk borne by the investor is reduced. Look again at the ice cream stand-umbrella shop example. The ice cream stand cash flows are highly variable, but because they are perfectly inversely correlated with those from the umbrella shop, cash flow variability for the two investments disappears. An "averaging out" process occurs when assets are added to a portfolio that reduces risk.

Because most business investments are dependent to some extent on the same underlying business cycle, it is highly unusual to find investment opportunities with perfectly inversely correlated cash flows as in the ice cream-umbrella example. However, the described diversification effect still exists. Whenever investment cash flows are less than perfectly positively correlated—whenever individual investments are unique in some respects—an investment's risk in a portfolio context is less than its risk in isolation.

Let us refer to an asset's risk in isolation as its *total risk* and to its risk as part of a portfolio as its *nondiversifiable risk*. This is the risk remaining after the rest has been diversified away in the portfolio. The part that is diversified away is known as the asset's *diversifiable risk* (surprise!). Then, for any risky asset j

$$\frac{\text{Total risk}}{\text{of asset } j} = \frac{\text{Nondiversifiable}}{\text{risk of asset } j} + \frac{\text{Diversifiable}}{\text{risk of asset } j}$$

From the above discussion, we know that the portion of an asset's total risk that is nondiversifiable depends on the correlation of the returns on the asset and on the portfolio. When the correlation is high, nondiversifiable risk is a large fraction of total risk, and vice versa. To say the same thing in symbols, let σ_j equal asset j's total risk and ρ_{jm} equal a scale factor reflecting the degree to which asset j's returns correlate with those of portfolio m. Then,

$$\text{Nondiversifiable risk of asset } j = \rho_{jm}\sigma_j$$

(ρ and σ are lowercase Greek symbols for rho and sigma, respectively. The equation would perhaps appear less daunting had I used a and b instead, but ρ and σ have become standard notation in the literature.)

Studying this expression, the scale factor ρ_{jm} can have any value between +1.00 and −1.00. At one extreme, when the returns on asset j and portfolio m are perfectly positively correlated, $\rho_{jm} = 1.00$, and nondiversifiable risk equals total risk. In this case, there are no benefits from diversification. At the other extreme, when the returns on asset j and portfolio m are perfectly negatively correlated, as in the ice cream-umbrella stand example, $\rho_{jm} = -1.00$, and nondiversifiable risk is negative. This means that addition of an appropriate amount of asset j to the portfolio will eliminate risk entirely. For most business investments, ρ_{jm} is in the range 0.5 to 0.8, meaning that 20 to 50 percent of an investment's total risk can be diversified away.

Measuring Beta

We are now ready to reconsider beta risk. Recall that β_j was described as the ratio of two risks and defined as

$$\beta_j = \frac{\text{Risk of asset } j}{\text{Risk of portfolio } m}$$

When diversification is possible, we now know that the relevant measure of asset j's risk is its nondiversifiable risk. Consequently,

$$\beta_j = \frac{\rho_{jm}\sigma_j}{\rho_{mm}\sigma_m}$$

This expression says that the beta risk of asset j is the ratio of asset j's nondiversifiable risk to the nondiversifiable risk of the analyst's portfolio. However, a moment's reflection should convince you that ρ_{mm} equals 1.00 because any asset's or any portfolio's return must be perfectly positively correlated with itself. Thus,

$$\beta_j = \frac{\rho_{jm}\sigma_j}{\sigma_m} \tag{8A-2}$$

If you have studied a little statistics, it will come as no surprise to learn that σ_j and σ_m are commonly defined to be the *standard deviation* of returns for asset j and portfolio m, respectively, and ρ_{jm} is the *correlation coefficient* between these returns.

Using these definitions and the above equation, the betas appearing in Table 8A–1 were calculated as follows. First, for each stock calculate the monthly return to investors, including price appreciation and dividends, over the past five years. Then calculate the average monthly return and the standard deviation of returns about this average. The latter is σ_j. Second, go through the same exercise for a broad portfolio of common stocks such as the Standard & Poor's 500 stock averages. This generates σ_m. Third, calculate the correlation coefficient, ρ_{jm}, between the monthly returns for stock j and the portfolio. Fourth, plug these numbers into Equation 8A–2 to calculate the stock's β. Or if you know a little regression analysis, just regress r_j on r_m. The slope of this line is β_j.

Using Beta in Investment Evaluation

Beta can be used two ways in investment evaluation. As already suggested, one way is to use the beta of the company's common stock to calculate the firm's cost of equity and its weighted average cost of capital.

A more direct approach is to calculate the beta of an individual investment and plug it into Equation 8A–1 to calculate the investment's risk-adjusted discount rate. This reduces risk adjustment to a totally mechanical, objective exercise. The approach has obvious conceptual appeal, but a number of problems must be solved before it can be applied in practice. The most serious is that there is usually no objective way to estimate an investment's beta. Some researchers have experimented with using the betas of publicly traded, single-product companies engaged in the same business as the proposed investment as surrogates for the investment's beta. But this has proved to be a complicated, imprecise exercise. One difficulty is that a company's beta depends on leverage as well as on business risk. So before using a company beta as a surrogate for an investment's beta, it is necessary to eliminate the effect of leverage. This can be done, but the process is complex and of unknown accuracy. A second difficulty pervading all applications is that the real object of interest is the beta that will prevail in future years. But because this is unknown, we must calculate a historical beta and assume it will hold in the future. Empirical studies of beta over time suggest that this is a reasonable, but not infallible, assumption.

The bottom line in practice is that beta is useful for estimating a company's cost of equity capital. However, the calculation of project betas is still no more than a glimmer in the eyes of Ph.D. students.

Beta Risk and Conglomerate Diversification

Some executives have seized on the idea that diversification reduces risk as a justification for conglomerate diversification. Even when merger promises no increase in profitability, it is said to be beneficial because the resulting diversification reduces the risk of company cash flows. Because shareholders are risk-averse, this reduction in risk is said to increase the value of the firm.

Such reasoning is at best incomplete. If shareholders wanted the risk-reduction benefits of such a conglomerate merger, they could have achieved them much more simply by just owning shares of the two independent companies in their own portfolios. Shareholders are not dependent on company managements for such benefits. Executives intent on acquiring other firms must look elsewhere to find a rationale for their actions.

CHAPTER SUMMARY

1. The purpose of this chapter has been to incorporate risk into investment evaluation with particular emphasis on risk-adjusted discount rates and the cost of capital.

2. Investments involve a trade-off between risk and return. The appropriate question when evaluating investment opportunities is not, What's the rate of return? but rather Is the return sufficient to justify the risk?

3. Risk refers to the range of possible outcomes for an investment. Sometimes risk can be calculated objectively, but usually risk estimation must be subjective.

4. The most popular, practical technique for incorporating risk into investment decisions uses a risk-adjusted discount rate in which the analyst adds a premium to the discount rate reflecting the perceived risk of the project.

5. The cost of capital is a risk-adjusted discount rate suitable for a firm's average risk, or carbon-copy, investments. It is the average cost of individual capital sources, weighted by their relative importance in the firm's capital structure. Average risk investments yielding returns above the cost of capital increase stock price.

6. Estimating the cost of equity is the most difficult step in measuring the cost of capital. For most businesses the best estimate is the current cost of government borrowing plus a risk premium based on historical experience of about 7.2 percent. If the equity is above or below average risk, it is necessary to adjust the risk premium accordingly.

7. It is also necessary to raise or lower the discount rate relative to the cost of capital, depending on whether a specific project is above or below average risk for the business.

8. Leveraged investments can be analyzed from the perspective of the firm making the investment or from that of the equity owner. Used properly, the two perspectives customarily yield the same investment decisions, but for practical reasons, I recommend the firm perspective.

9. Under inflation one must always use nominal cash flows and a nominal discount rate, or real cash flows and a real discount rate. Never mix the two.
10. Do not overlook real options, such as the option to abandon or the option to expand, when evaluating corporate investment opportunities.
11. A constant risk-adjusted discount rate should not be used to evaluate investments with two or more distinct risk phases. To evaluate such investments, begin with the most distant phase and use a risk-adjusted rate that is appropriate to each phase.
12. Proper technique is never a substitute for thought or leadership. People, not analysis, get things done.

ADDITIONAL READING

Brealey, Richard, and Stewart Myers. *Principles of Corporate Finance.* 3rd ed. New York: McGraw-Hill, 1988. 889 pages.
  A leading graduate text. Very well written, almost lively. Part 3, Risk, is especially good.
Hodder, James E., and Henry E. Riggs. "Pitfalls in Evaluating Risky Projects." *Harvard Business Review,* January/February 1985, pp. 128–35.
  A thorough discussion of inflation and excessive risk adjustment in capital budgeting.
Mullins, David W., Jr. "Does the Capital Asset Pricing Model Work?" *Harvard Business Review,* January/February 1982, pp. 105–14.
  A practical look at the concepts discussed in the appendix to this chapter, including beta risk, the Market Line, and diversification.
Myers, Stewart C. "Finance Theory and Financial Strategy." *Midland Corporate Finance Journal,* Spring 1987, pp. 6–13.
  A nontechnical look at the integration, or lack thereof, of strategic planning and finance theory. Especially good on challenges to the use of discounted cash flow techniques in strategic decision making. Covers the four pitfalls mentioned in this chapter.

CHAPTER PROBLEMS

1. How will an increase in financial leverage affect a firm's cost of equity capital? Why?
2. Under what conditions might an investment promising an IRR of 9 percent be superior to one promising 11 percent?
3. Under what conditions might a company rationally accept an investment promising a return below its weight-average cost of capital?
4. Looking at Figure 8–1, explain why a company should reject investment opportunities lying below the Market Line and accept those lying above it.
5. What is the expected net present value of the following investment opportunity? What does the expected NPV suggest about the merit of this investment?

Probability	Net Present Value
20%	−100
40	10
10	150
30	200
100%	

6. You have the following information about the Landau Corporation, a highly profitable enterprise:

Tax rate	50%
Cost of equity capital	16%
Book value of equity	$20 million
Market value of equity	$50 million
Market value of debt	$50 million
Coupon rate on debt	6%
Book value of debt	$60 million
Yield to maturity on debt	8%
Stock price per share	$12

Landau is considering an average risk investment costing $10 million and yielding an annual aftertax cash flow of $1 million in perpetuity.

a. What is the internal rate of return on this investment?

b. What is Landau's weighted-average cost of capital?

c. Would you expect this investment to create shareholder value or to destroy it? Why?

7. An investment opportunity costs $100 million, will last 10 years, and promises an annual aftertax cash flow equal to $20.7 million. It will be financed with 80 percent debt yielding 8 percent. The debt will be repaid in 10 equal, end-of-year payments.

a. What is the IRR of this investment from the total firm perspective?

b. What is the IRR of the investment from an equity perspective?

c. Assuming the investment is average risk and that the decision maker's weighted average cost of capital is 18 percent, is this an attractive opportunity?

8. Calculate the internal rate of return on an investment costing $20 that promises to pay $1.00 *this* year if you expect this amount to grow at 5 percent per year forever.

9. Use the perpetual growth formula to estimate a firm's cost of equity capital when its current dividend per share is $1.00, its current stock price is $20, and you expect the dividends per share to grow at 5 percent per year forever.

10. An investment with an expected life of three years costs $50 million today and promises *real* cash flows of $18.7 million per year.

a. What is the real rate of return on this investment?

b. If you expect the inflation rate to equal 10 percent per year for the next three years, what nominal cash flows does the investment promise?

c. What is the nominal rate of return on the investment?

d. If the nominal weighted average cost of capital is 20 percent, approximately what is the real weighted average cost of capital?

e. Is this investment attractive? Why, or why not?

CHAPTER 9

BUSINESS VALUATION AND
CORPORATE RESTRUCTURING

"Morality is all right, but what about dividends?"
Kaiser Wilhelm II

Aptly billed as The Battle of the Media Titans, the 1989 struggle between Time Inc. and Paramount Communications is one the corporate world will not soon forget. It began on March 4, 1989, when Time, venerable publishers of *Fortune, Time, Sports Illustrated,* and *People* magazines, announced its intention to merge with Warner Communications in a friendly exchange of shares. Subject only to shareholder approval, the merger would create a $10 billion media-communications giant with important global stakes in magazines, books, films, records, music, and cable television.

After struggling for a decade with mediocre financial performance, increasingly restive shareholders, and growing takeover rumors, Time CEO, J. Richard Munro, saw the Warner marriage as just the elixir his company needed to get it moving again. But before the merger could be put to a shareholder vote, Martin Davis, chief executive of Paramount Communications, jabbed a stick in the spokes of Time's plan by offering $175 a share in cash—later increased to $200—for all of Time's shares. With Time's stock trading around $110 a share just before the merger announcement, $200 amounted to an 82 percent premium to shareholders.

Munro and his board were less than pleased by Paramount's move. Over two years of behind-the-scenes planning and negotiation had already gone into the Warner deal, and in their eyes, a Time-Warner combination made more economic sense than a link up with Paramount. There was also the fact that Paramount's bid threatened to transform Time executives from rulers of their own

$10 billion kingdom to mere minions in Davis's empire. Munro was determined to avoid Paramount's clutches. Yet with a $175 cash bid on the table, there appeared to be little chance Time shareholders would approve the Warner merger.

Faced with an imminent shareholder revolt, Time's board hastily scrapped the proposed stock swap in favor of an outright purchase of Warner stock for approximately $14 billion in cash and securities. Although an acquisition of Warner would saddle the combined companies with over $12 billion of new debt and create significant tax liabilities for Warner shareholders, it had one luminous advantage over a stock swap: It did not require shareholder approval. Time's board could rebuff Paramount and acquire Warner whether the shareholders liked it or not—which they immediately proceeded to do.

Then all hell broke loose. Shareholders howled in protest, Paramount filed suit in Delaware court to block the acquisition, and editorial writers across the country joined the fray, some extolling Time management for standing up to the fast-buck, takeover crowd, and others rebuking management for trampling on fundamental shareholder rights. "Who does Dick Munro think he works for anyway," was a common refrain of the shareholder-rights crowd.

Paramount's lawsuit to block Time's acquisition of Warner ended in total defeat. In his opinion sanctioning Time's acquisition—an opinion unanimously upheld on appeal—Chancellor William T. Allen concluded that it didn't matter that shareholders might have preferred the Paramount bid. In his chilling words, "The corporation law does not operate on the theory that directors . . . are obligated to follow the wishes of a majority of shares. In fact, directors, not shareholders, are charged with the duty to manage the firm."[1] If shareholders don't like it, let them sell their shares.

Although it is premature to pass judgment on the ultimate wisdom of Time's acquisition of Warner, several winners and losers are already clearly discernable. Steve Ross, CEO of Warner

---

[1] Bill Saporito, "The Inside Story of Time Warner," *Fortune,* November 20, 1989, pp. 206–7.

and co-CEO of the combined companies, received a 10-year contract paying him *$193 million* at the close of the deal for deferred compensation due him at Warner, an annual salary of $1.2 million, a minimum bonus of 0.4 percent of Time-Warner's earnings before tax and depreciation, and options on 1.8 million shares of Time-Warner stock at a minimum exercise price of $150 a share. Finally, after 10 years Ross stands to collect $750,000 annually for five years as an advisor. Warner shareholders were also apparent winners. Relating the $70 a share acquisition price to Warner's stock price one week prior to the merger announcement, shareholders pocketed an extra $4.1 billion from the acquisition. Investment bankers and attorneys representing the combatants also had little to complain about after divvying up fees totaling at least $73.5 million.[2] At the other end of the spectrum, Time shareholders lost at least $3.4 billion in ready cash as Time shares sank to $141 immediately after the court decision, drifted clear down to $66 in late 1990, and are presently trading around $100 a share almost two years later. $200 a share cash in 1989 looks better with every passing month.

If the Time-Warner-Paramount ménage à trois were an isolated event, we might reasonably dismiss it as just another colorful episode in what has proven to be an unusually colorful decade. Evidence indicates, however, that the battle of the media titans is but one example of a phenomenon that has significantly affected the corporate landscape and in the process raised fundamental questions about American corporate governance. Known broadly as "corporate restructuring," this phenomenon encompasses a number of maneuvers intended to alter fundamentally a company's asset composition, capital structure, or ownership. In addition to friendly mergers and hostile acquisitions, corporate restructuring includes purchase or sale of operating divisions, large repurchases of common stock, major changes in financial leverage, and leveraged buyouts, or LBOs. An LBO is characterized by extensive use of the acquired entity's excess cash and borrowing power to help finance the acquisition.

---

[2]"The Inside Story of Time Warner," pp. 178, 194.

Indications of the popularity of corporate restructuring among U.S. companies appear in the data on share repurchases and cash acquisitions in Figure 4–2, and in the sharp increases in debt levels in certain industries apparent in Table 6–3. Recent merger and acquisition statistics tell a similar tale, although activity has declined noticeably since late 1989. From 1979 through 1988, the number of mergers, acquisitions, and leveraged buyouts involving U.S. companies grew at an annual rate of over 12 percent, reaching a high in 1986 of almost 4,500. Moreover, the reported value of transactions increased a whopping 27 percent per annum to over $235 billion in 1988. Then, from 1988 through 1990, the number of transactions fell 10 percent and aggregate value dropped by almost one third.[3] In addition, many other companies not represented in these figures have initiated various restructurings that did not involve a change in ownership.

Time's battle with Paramount and many other restructurings pose several important questions to executives, and indeed, to all students of finance. In terms of the Time-Paramount struggle, these questions include:

1. Why did Paramount go after Time? Did Paramount CEO Martin Davis have reason to believe Time was worth much more than $110 a share? If so, what analysis led to this conclusion?
2. If Davis was willing to pay as much as $200 per share for Time stock, why was the price not long before Paramount's bid only $110? Does the stock market misprice companies this much, or is something else at work?
3. If Time stock really was worth much more than $110, why didn't Time management—who presumably knew more about their own company than Davis did—realize this fact? And if they did, why didn't they take actions to ensure that the added value was reflected in Time's stock price?

[3]Data for 1980 through 1989 are from "Ten-Year Merger Completion Record 1980–1989," *Mergers & Acquisitions,* May/June 1990, p. 57. 1990 data are from "Quarterly Profile," *Mergers & Acquisitions,* March/April 1991, p. 103.

4. Who really controls America's corporations, and who should control them? Is it the shareholders who collectively bear the residual risk, or is it the managers who at least nominally work for shareholders?

The purpose of this chapter is to answer these questions and, in the process, to examine the financial dimensions of business valuation and corporate restructuring. At bottom, ours is a simple, three-part story. First, whenever a company's business or financial strategy becomes ill-suited to its marketplace, the firm's market value will suffer, and when the decline in value becomes pronounced, a restructuring may be necessary to refocus the business in a new, more profitable direction. Financially, then, corporate restructuring is simply a redeployment of company resources in pursuit of enhanced market value. Second, restructuring activity burgeoned during the 1980s, not because managers suddenly uncovered many more value-enhancing opportunities, but because shareholders used the threat of hostile takeover to force recalcitrant managements to execute restructurings they would otherwise have avoided. Many recent restructurings can thus be thought of as preemptive actions intended to lessen the threat of hostile takeover. Third, as the Time-Paramount struggle suggests, a recent combination of sympathetic court decisions, protective state laws, and draconian acquisition defenses appear to have so shielded incumbent managers from hostile attack that the era of forced restructuring may well be over. Mergers, acquisitions, and various other restructurings will certainly continue but at a much more traditional pace, and more often than not they will be management, not shareholder, inspired. Whether this is good news or bad depends on who you believe should control America's corporations—management or owners.

The chapter begins with a look at the techniques available for valuing all or part of a business. An important and useful topic in its own right, business valuation also sets the stage for consideration of the premium an acquirer might be willing to pay to purchase controlling interest in a company. Attention then turns to three of the more controversial possible benefits of restructuring, which we will consider under the headings tax shields, incentive effects, and controlling free cash flow. The chapter closes with another look at the Time-Paramount battle and the questions posed above.

VALUING A BUSINESS

You will be relieved to learn that in many respects business valuation is just an application of the concepts discussed in earlier chapters.

Market Value—Again

George Bernard Shaw once observed that "Economists know the price of everything and the value of nothing." And in a very real sense he is correct since to an economist the value of an asset is nothing more than the price at which informed buyers and sellers are willing to trade it. The question of whether an asset has value beyond its selling price is one economists are content to leave to philosophers.

If value is synonymous with selling price, an obvious indicator of the worth of a company is its market value—the aggregate price at which its equity and debt trade in financial markets. Thus, when Time Inc. announced its intention to acquire Warner Communications in June 1989, the market value of Warner's equity was $59.25 per share times 166.4 million shares outstanding, or $9.9 billion. Adding the market value of Warner's liabilities, similarly determined, yields the market value of the company.

The story does not end here, however, for there are many instances in which market prices are inadequate or unavailable, and it is necessary to think about the determinants of value more carefully. These include:

1. The entity being valued is privately held, or a division of a public company, and market prices do not exist.
2. The company's securities are publicly traded, but so infrequently and in such modest volume that market prices are unreliable indicators of value.
3. The company's securities are actively traded, but the goal is to find bargains. By comparing an independent estimate

of value against market price, the analyst hopes to discover securities that are undervalued.

4. The analyst intends to gain control of the company and to increase market value by altering the way the firm does business.

When speaking of control, it is important to note that ownership of a company's shares and control of the company are two vastly different things. Unless a shareholder owns or can influence at least 51 percent of a company's voting stock, he or she is just along for the ride. As a minority shareholder, an investor has virtually no say in any substantive issue facing the company, including how the business is to be run or what dividends should be paid. Further, in most large, publicly held corporations no shareholder group owns enough stock to exercise voting control, and effective control devolves to incumbent management. More on how this works and the opportunities it creates for Boone Pickens and friends later.

Liquidation and Going-Concern Values

If securities prices are not always appropriate or available, how else might one value a business? In broadest terms, there are two choices: to value a company in liquidation or as a going concern. *Liquidation value* is the cash generated by terminating a business and selling its assets individually, while *going-concern value* is the present worth of expected future cash flows generated by a business. In most instances we will naturally be interested in a business's going-concern value.

It will be helpful at this point to define an asset's *fair market value* (FMV) as the price at which the asset would trade between two rational individuals, each in command of all of the information necessary to value the asset and neither under any pressure to trade. Estimating FMV is the first step in most valuation problems.

Usually, the FMV of a business is the *higher* of its liquidation value and its going-concern value. Figure 9–1 illustrates the relationship. When the present value of expected future cash flows is low, the business is worth more dead than alive, and FMV equals

FIGURE 9–1

The Fair Market Value of a Business Is Usually the Higher of Its Liquidation and Its Going-Concern Value

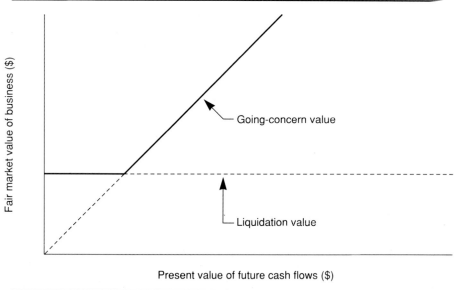

the company's liquidation value. At higher levels of expected future cash flows, liquidation value becomes increasingly irrelevant, and FMV depends almost entirely on going-concern value. It can also occur that some of a company's assets, or divisions, are worth more in liquidation while others are more valuable as going concerns. In this case, the firm's FMV is a combination of liquidation and going-concern values as they apply to individual assets.

An exception to Figure 9–1 occurs when the individuals controlling the company—perhaps after reflecting on their alternative employment opportunities and the pleasures afforded by the corporate yacht—choose not to liquidate, even though the business is worth more dead than alive. Then, because minority investors cannot force liquidation, the FMV of a minority interest can fall below the liquidation value. This is illustrated in Figure 9–2. Additional latent value exists, but because minority owners cannot get their hands on it, the value has no effect on the price they are willing to pay for the shares. As seen by minority shareholders, the

FIGURE 9–2
**When the Individuals Controlling the Business Refuse to Liquidate,
Fair Market Value Can Fall below Liquidation Value**

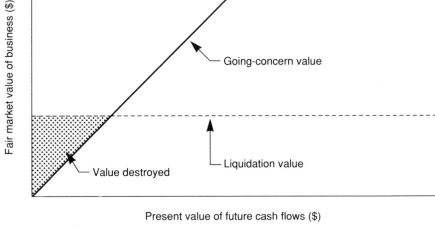

Present value of future cash flows ($)

individuals controlling the business are destroying value by refus-
ing to liquidate. We will consider other instances in which price, as
determined by minority investors, does not reflect full value later
in the chapter.

ESTIMATING GOING-CONCERN VALUE

Having reviewed business valuation in the large, let's turn now to
the more specific task of estimating a company's going-concern
value. For simplicity, we will begin by considering the value of a minority interest in a privately held firm.

The most direct way to estimate going-concern value, if not always the most practical, is to think of the target company as if it
were nothing more than a large, capital-expenditure opportunity.
Just as with any piece of capital equipment, investing in a company requires the expenditure of money today in anticipation of

future benefits. And the central issue is both cases is whether tomorrow's benefits justify today's costs.

Valuing Equity

Building on our earlier discussion of evaluating investment opportunities in Chapters 7 and 8, we can determine whether future benefits justify current costs, at least conceptually, by calculating the present value of expected future cash flows to equity. Thus

FMV of Equity = PV [Expected future cash flows to equity]

This formula says that the maximum price a minority investor should pay for the equity of a business equals the present value of expected future cash flows to the investor, discounted at an appropriate, risk-adjusted rate. No surprises here, I trust.

Let's consider a simple (simplistic?) example. The diagram below shows the relevant cash flows for a company that is expected to distribute common dividends of $50 million annually for the next five years and $75 million annually during the following five. At the end of the 10th year we assume the equity can be sold for 20 times year-10 dividends.

Cash Flow Diagram: Expected Future Cash Flows to Equity

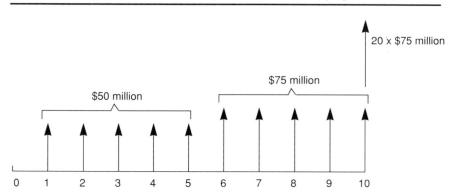

As in any other application of risk-adjusted discount rates, the discount rate employed should reflect the risk of the cash flows being discounted. Here, the cash flows are to equity investors of

the target firm. So the appropriate discount rate is the target's cost of equity capital. Assuming this is 18 percent, and using the present value factors in Appendices A and B, the estimated FMV of equity is

$$V_E = \$50 \text{ million}(3.127) + \$75 \text{ million}(3.127)(0.437) +$$
$$\$75 \text{ million}(20)(0.191)$$
$$= \$545.34 \text{ million}$$

So you now see how simple it is. Once you know all future dividends, the cost of equity capital, and the selling price at some distant future date, valuing a company's equity is almost trivial.

Valuing the Firm

One conclusion from our earlier discussion of investment analysis is that the investment decision should be separated from the financing decision whenever possible. First, decide if the investment makes economic sense regardless of how it is financed; then decide how best to finance it. Techniques that treat the two decisions simultaneously unnecessarily complicate the issue. Unfortunately, the equity approach to business valuation does precisely this, for the cash flows to equity and the cost of equity both depend on the way the business is financed. Thus, the calculated FMV reflects both the value of the business and its financing.

A second approach to estimating going-concern value circumvents this problem by calculating the FMV of the firm rather than the FMV of equity. Once the value of the firm is known, it is then relatively easy to estimate the value of equity.

Applying the capital budgeting analogy again, the FMV of the firm equals the present value of expected aftertax cash flows available for distribution to owners *and* creditors, discounted at an appropriate risk-adjusted rate.

FMV of firm = PV [Expected aftertax cash flows to
owners and creditors]

where the term in brackets can be written as

EBIT(1−Tax rate) + Depreciation − Investment

Under certain conditions described below, this expression is known as the firm's *free cash flow*, or FCF. The logic of using FCF goes like this. EBIT, *earnings before interest and taxes*, is the income earned by the company without regard to how it is financed; so EBIT(1−Tax rate) is income after tax, excluding any effects of debt financing. Adding depreciation yields aftertax cash flow from operations. If management were prepared to run the company into the ground, it could distribute this cash flow in the form of dividends and interest payments. In the conventional case, however, where some income is retained to make new investments, only the difference between operating cash flow and investment is available for distribution. (Investment in this equation is interpreted broadly to mean all acquisitions of new property, plant, and equipment, as well as all increases in working capital.)

Because the cash flow being discounted here accrues to the firm, not to equity, the appropriate risk-adjusted discount rate in the above formula is the target firm's *weighted-average* cost of capital. As with capital expenditure analysis, this approach reflects the benefits of the particular capital structure employed by the firm in the discount rate, not the cash flows.

Once the FMV of the firm is known, the FMV of equity can be easily deduced by recalling that

$$\text{Value of equity} = \text{Value of firm} - \text{Value of liabilities}$$

Fortunately, the value of a company's liabilities is usually relatively easy to estimate and depends on the nature of the liabilities and the change in interest rates since the liabilities were incurred. In fact, if the liabilities are reasonably short term and interest rates have not changed dramatically, a plausible estimate of the FMV of liabilities might be just their book value.

An Example
Suppose you have the opportunity to purchase 100,000 shares of AT&P Railroad common stock, and it is necessary to estimate an appropriate price. AT&P has 1 million shares of common stock outstanding. You have already concluded that AT&P's weighted-average cost of capital is about 12 percent and that the market value of the company's liabilities is roughly $500 million.

Now comes a practical problem. Our equation for the FMV of a firm says FMV equals the present value of all future cash flows to owners and creditors. But because AT&P expects to be in business for many years to come, finding its FMV will apparently require estimating hundreds of annual cash flows extending out into the far-distant future—a clearly unreasonable task.

The standard way around this problem is to divide the future into two periods. During the first, near-term period of, say, 5 to 15 years, estimate the annual cash flows individually as the equation suggests. Then, for the second, more-distant period, forget the individual cash flows and estimate instead a terminal value representing the worth at the end of the first period of all subsequent cash flows. If the first period is, say, five years, our valuation equation then becomes

$$\text{FMV of firm} = \text{PV}\{\text{FCF 5 years}\} + \text{PV}\{\text{Terminal value in fifth year}\}$$

Railroading, at least as practiced by AT&P, appears to be a declining business, for although the company has large annual depreciation charges, investment is quite modest. You believe this situation will continue for the next six years, and have estimated the free cash flows appearing in Table 9–1. As noted in the table, the present value of these free cash flows is $634 million.

Beginning in the seventh year, you believe management will have to raise investment up to equal annual depreciation charges, so that free cash flow in subsequent years will just equal EBIT(1 −

TABLE 9–1
Free Cash Flow for AT&P Railroad ($ in millions)

Year	EBIT	EBIT(1 − T)	+ Depreciation	− Investment	= Free Cash Flow
1	100	64	160	50	174
2	98	63	170	50	183
3	96	61	170	60	171
4	95	61	160	70	151
5	96	61	150	90	121
6	95	61	140	110	91
			Present value of FCF years 1–6 @ 12% =		$634
7	95	62.22	140	140	62.22

Tax rate). And you believe that free cash flow from this date forward into the indefinite future will grow at 2 percent per year.

Your estimate that free cash flow in years seven and beyond will grow at a constant rate is quite convenient, because it means we can use the perpetual growth equation described in the last chapter to calculate AT&P's terminal value. Recall that the present value of a perpetually growing cash flow stream can be written as next year's receipt divided by the difference between the discount rate and the growth rate. For AT&P

$$\text{Terminal value in year 6} = \frac{\text{FCF in year 7}}{K_w - g}$$

$$= \frac{\$62.22}{0.12 - 0.02}$$

$$= \$622.2 \text{ million}$$

And discounting the terminal value back to the present,

$$\text{Terminal value @ year 0} = \$622.20(0.507)$$
$$= \$315 \text{ million}$$

Adding the present value of the free cash flows for the first six years to that of the terminal value, and subtracting the value of liabilities,

$$\text{FMV}_{\text{equity}} = \$634 \text{ million} + \$315 \text{ million} - \$500 \text{ million}$$
$$= \$449 \text{ million}$$

Finally, if AT&P's equity is worth $449 million and it has 1 million shares outstanding, its value per share is $449; so your 100,000 share purchase should cost about $44.9 million ($449 × 100,000).

As this example suggests, the proper selection of a forecast horizon and a terminal value is critical to the successful application of discounted cash flow approaches to business valuation. Because most tractable terminal value estimates implicitly assume that the firm is a constant-growth, or a no-growth, perpetuity from that date forward, it is important to extend the near-term forecast horizon far enough into the future that this assumption plausibly applies. For example, the forecast horizon for AT&P was six years because annual free cash flows were expected to vary erratically over this period, after which an assumption of perpetual growth became plausible. When valuing a rapidly growing business, this philosophy suggests estimating how long the company can be expected to sustain its supernormal growth before reaching maturity, and setting the forecast horizon at this date.

Free Cash Flow

A fundamental conclusion from our discussion of investment analysis in earlier chapters was that companies should undertake only those investments promising returns in excess of capital costs. When a firm follows this optimal investment strategy, the cash flow in the firm valuation formula above is properly referred to as *free cash flow*. It is the cash flow available for distribution to owners and creditors after undertaking all worthwhile investment opportunities. Up to now, I have used the term under the implicit assumption that AT&P follows an optimal investment strategy, but as we shall soon see, such an assumption is not always warranted.

Problems with Present Value Approaches to Valuation

If you are a little hesitant at this point about your ability to apply these discounted cash flow techniques to anything but simple textbook examples, welcome to the club. While DCF approaches to business valuation are conceptually correct, and even rather elegant, they are devilishly difficult to apply in practice. Valuing a business may be conceptually equivalent to any other capital expenditure decision, but there are several fundamental differences in practice. They include

1. The typical investment opportunity has a finite—usually brief—life, while the life expectancy of a company is indefinite.
2. The typical investment opportunity promises stable or perhaps declining cash flows over time, while the ability of a company to reinvest earnings customarily produces a growing cash flow.

3. The cash flows from a typical investment belong to the owner, while the cash flows generated by a company go to the owner only when management chooses to distribute them. If management decides to invest in Mexican diamond mines rather than pay dividends, there is little a minority owner can do other than sell out.

As the problems in the accompanying boxes demonstrate, these practical differences introduce potentially large errors into the valuation process and can make the resulting FMV estimates quite sensitive to small changes in the discount rate and the growth rate employed.

The Problem of Growth and Long Life

In many investment decisions involving long-lived assets, it is common to circumvent the problem of forecasting far-distant cash flows by ignoring all flows beyond some distant horizon. The justification for this practice is that the present value of far-distant cash flows will be quite small. When the cash flow stream is a growing one, however, growth offsets the discounting effect, and even far-distant cash flows can contribute significantly to present value. Here is an example.

At a discount rate of 10 percent, the present value of $1 per year for 20 years is $8.51. Using the perpetuity equation, the present value of $1 per year forever, at the same discount rate, is $10 ($1/0.10). Hence, ignoring all cash flows beyond the 20th year reduces the calculated present value of this perpetuity by only about 15 percent ($8.51 versus $10). But things change when the income stream is a growing one.

The present value at a 10 percent discount rate of $1 per year, growing at the rate of 6 percent per annum, for 20 years is $13.08. Using the perpetual growth equation, the present value of $1 per year, growing at 6 percent per annum forever, is $25 ($1/[0.10 − 0.06]). Therefore, ignoring growing cash flows beyond the 20th year reduces the present value by 48 percent ($13.08 versus $25).

The Sensitivity Problem

Use the perpetual growth equation and a 10 percent discount rate to calculate the fair market value of a company with free cash flows next year of $1 million, growing at 5 percent per year indefinitely.

Assuming the discount rate and the growth rate could each be in error by as much as one percentage point, what are the maximum and minimum possible FMVs for the company? What does this suggest about the accuracy of present value approaches to valuation?

Answer: FMV at a 10 percent discount rate and a 5 percent growth rate is $20 million ($1 million/[0.10 − 0.05]). The maximum is $33.3 million ($1 million/[0.09 − 0.06]) and the minimum is $14.3 million ($1 million/[0.11 − 0.04]). It is difficult to charge very high fees for advising a client that a business is worth somewhere between $14.3 and $33.3 million.

Comparables

Granting that present value approaches to business valuation are conceptually correct but difficult to apply, what are the alternatives? One popular technique involves comparing the target company to similar, publicly traded firms. Imagine shopping for a used car. The moment of truth comes when the buyer finds an interesting car, looks at the asking price, and ponders what to offer the dealer. One strategy, analogous to a present value approach, is to estimate the value of labor and raw materials in the car, add a markup for overhead and profit, and subtract an amount for depreciation. A more productive approach is comparison shopping. Develop an estimate of fair market value by comparing the subject car to similar autos that have recently sold or are presently available. If three, similar-quality 1982 T-Birds have sold recently for $3,000 to $3,500, the buyer has reason to believe the target T-Bird has a similar value. Of course, comparison shopping provides no information about whether 1982 T-Birds are really worth $3,000 to $3,500 in any fundamental sense; it only indicates the going rate. However, in many instances this is sufficient. (Another tactic recommended by some is to skip the valuation process entirely and proceed directly to bargaining by asking the dealer what he wants for the car, and responding, "B——————t, I'll give you half that." This probably works better for cars than companies, but don't rule it out entirely.)

Use of comparables in business valuation requires equal parts of art and science. First, it is necessary to decide which publicly traded companies are most similar to the target and then to determine what the share prices of the publicly traded companies imply for the FMV of the firm in question. The discounted cash flow valuation equations just considered offer a useful starting point. They suggest that comparable companies should offer similar future cash flows and similar business and financial risks. The risks should be similar so that roughly the same discount rate would apply to all of the firms.

In practice, these guidelines suggest we begin our search for comparables by considering firms in the same, or closely related, industries with similar growth prospects and capital structures. With luck, the outcome of this exercise will be several, more or less comparable, publicly traded companies. Considerable judgment will then be required to decide what the comparables imply as a group for the fair market value of the target.

Table 9–2 offers a quick look at the use of comparables to value our friend from earlier chapters, the Russell Corporation. It goes without saying that if I were being paid by the hour to value Russell and you were being similarly compensated to read about it, we would both proceed much more thoroughly and deliberately; nonetheless, the table should give you a general idea of how the comparables approach is applied in practice.

The valuation date is December 31, 1989, and the chosen comparables are the other four textile-apparel manufacturers represented along with Russell in the S&P 500 Stock Averages. Russell is, of course, publicly traded itself, so at the end of this exercise we will be able to compare our estimated value with the actual market price to get some idea of the accuracy of the comparables approach.

The first set of numbers in Table 9–2 looks at Russell's returns, risk, and growth relative to the comparable firms. The numbers suggest that Russell is in the middle of the pack. Its return on invested capital and return on equity are below three of the four

TABLE 9–2

Using Comparable Public Companies to Value Russell Corporation
(December 31, 1989)

	Russell Corp	Oshkosh B'Gosh	Liz Claiborne	V F Corp	Hartmarx Corp
Comparison of Russell with Comparable Companies; Returns, Risks, and Growth Rates					
Return on invested capital	11.4%	29.5	25.9	13.3	5.6
Return on equity	16.1%	29.1	27.0	21.5	1.1
Liabilities-to-total capital	44.2%	20.9	27.9	56.6	60.4
5-year growth in earnings	18.3%	23.9	31.5	7.1	(16.0)
Indicators of Value					
Price/earnings		15.4x	12.8	11.7	22.2
MV firm/EBIT (1−Tax rate)		15.5x	14.2	14.3	26.5
MV equity/BV equity		4.5x	3.5	2.3	1.1
MV firm/BV firm		3.8x	2.8	1.6	1.0

My Estimated Indicator of Value for Russell

Price/earnings	12.0x
MV firm/EBIT (1−Tax rate)	14.5x
MV equity/BV equity	3.0x
MV firm/BV firm	2.4x

Implied Value of Russell Common Stock per Share

Price/earnings	$18.84
MV firm/EBIT (1−Tax rate)	18.92
MV equity/BV equity	29.85
MV firm/BV firm	34.94
MEAN =	$25.64
Actual Stock Price =	$26.13

MV = Market value
BV = Book value
The market value of debt is assumed to be equal to the book value throughout.

Sources: Standard & Poor's *Daily Stock Price Record*, New York Stock Exchange and Over the Counter, October, November, December 1989. Standard & Poor's *Stock Reports*, New York Stock Exchange and Over the Counter, August 1990. Copyright Standard & Poor's Corporation. All rights reserved.
To ensure consistency across firms, all data in this table are from the above sources. As a result, some of the ratios for Russell Corporation differ from those reported in Chapters 1 and 2.

comparable companies, but its liabilities-to-capital ratio and its growth in net income over the past five years are about average.

The second set of numbers in the table shows four possible *indicators of value* for the comparable firms. Speaking broadly, each indicator expresses how much investors are paying per dollar of current income, or per dollar of invested capital, for each comparable. Thus the first indicator says that one dollar of Hartmarx income costs $22.20, while one dollar of V F Corporation income is priced at $11.70. Similarly, the last indicator tells us that Oshkosh B'Gosh is selling for a hefty 3.8 times its book value of assets, while Hartmarx's market value just equals book value. Indicators one and three focus on equity values, and are thus affected by the way the business is financed, while the other two indicators concentrate on the value of the firm.

Reflecting on how Russell Corporation stacks up against the other firms in terms of returns, risk, and growth, the valuation challenge is now to decide what indicators of value are appropriate for Russell. The third set of numbers in Table 9–2 are my necessarily subjective estimates. In coming to these estimates, I anticipated that Russell would be valued most like Liz Claiborne and V F Corporation. Liz Claiborne's numbers are better than Russell's, but they are also in the high-fashion end of the business, implying greater business risk. V F Corporation has better returns but lower historical growth. Conversely, I was inclined to place little weight in Hartmarx's numbers because unlike Russell, or any of the other firms, Hartmarx is clearly having financial difficulties. Earnings in 1989 were less than half the 1988 figure, and the price-to-earnings ratio is high, not because investors are optimistic about future growth, but because they do not believe the company's poor 1989 performance fairly represents its long-run capabilities.

The bottom set of numbers in the table presents the share prices for Russell's stock implied by the chosen indicators of value. To illustrate the calculation of these prices, I have estimated in the third indicator of value that the market value of Russell's equity should be three times book value. The book value of Russell's equity in 1989 was $402 million, so the implied market value is $1.2 billion, or $29.85 per share. The other three share prices are calculated similarly. The results range from share prices of about $19 to

$35 with a mean of $25.64. This compares to an actual price on the valuation date of $26.13.

Lack of Marketability

An important difference between owning stock in a publicly traded company and a private one is that the publicly traded shares are more liquid. They can be sold quickly for cash without significant loss of value. Because liquidity is a valued attribute of any asset, it is necessary to reduce the FMV of a private company estimated by reference to publicly traded comparables. Without boring you with details, a representative lack of marketability discount is on the order of 25 percent.[4] Of course, if the purpose of the valuation is to price an initial public offering of common stock, the shares will soon be liquid, and no discount is required.

A second possible adjustment when using the comparables approach to valuation is a premium for control. Quoted prices for public companies are invariably for a minority interest in the firm, while valuations of private companies often involve transactions in which operating control passes from seller to buyer. Because control is valuable, it is necessary in these instances to add a premium to the estimated value of the target firm to reflect the value of control. We will consider the premium for control in greater detail below.

CORPORATE RESTRUCTURING

Having now reviewed the basics of business valuation, let's see what they tell us about mergers, acquisitions, and other forms of corporate restructuring.

We have noted on several occasions that buying a minority interest in a company differs fundamentally from buying control. With a minority interest, the investor is a passive observer; with control, she is able to restructure the corporation and perhaps increase its value significantly. Indeed, the two situations are so dis-

---

[4]Shannon P. Pratt, *Valuing a Business: The Analysis and Appraisal of Closely Held Companies,* 2nd ed. (Homewood, Ill.: Dow Jones-Irwin, 1988).

parate that it is appropriate to speak of stock as selling in two separate markets: the market in which you and I trade claims on future company cash flows, and the market in which Paramount, Time, and other acquiring firms and individuals trade the right to control the firm. The latter—*the market for control*—involves a two-in-one sale. In addition to claims on future cash flows, the buyer in this market also gains the privilege of structuring the company as he or she wishes. Because shares trading in the two markets are really different assets, they naturally sell at different prices.

The Premium for Control

Figure 9–3 illustrates this two-tier market. From the perspective of minority investors, the fair market value of a company's equity, m, is the present value of cash flows to equity, given current manage-

FIGURE 9–3

FMV of a Corporation to Investors Seeking Control May Exceed FMV to Minority Investors

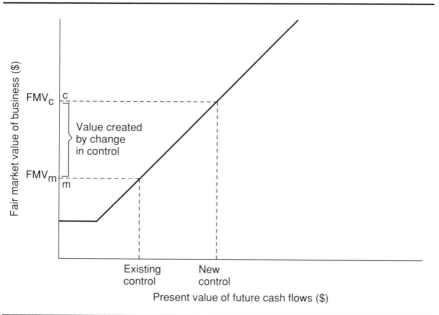

ment. To a corporation or individual seeking control, however, the FMV is c, which may be well above m. The difference, $c - m$, is the value of control. It is the maximum premium over the minority FMV an acquirer should pay to gain control. It is also the expected increase in shareholder value created by the change in control. When an acquirer pays FMV_c for a target, all of the increased value will be realized by existing shareholders, while at any lower price part of the increased value accrues to the acquirer.

What Price Control?

After determining the FMV_m of a target, the acquirer's next task is to decide how large a control premium he can afford to pay. The following simple equation suggests one useful approach when the target is privately held.

$$FMV_c = FMV_m + \text{Enhancements}$$

where c refers to a controlling interest and m to a minority interest. It says the value of controlling interest in a business equals the FMV of the business under present stewardship, plus whatever enhancements to value the new buyer envisions. If the buyer intends no changes in the business now or in the future, the enhancements are zero, and no premium over FMV_m can be justified. On the other hand, if the buyer believes current leadership is squandering shareholders' money on ill-advised schemes and delusions, enhancements can be quite large.

Table 9–3 presents the average premiums paid in mergers and acquisitions in the years 1984 through the third quarter of 1990. These numbers are down from a whopping 70.7 percent in 1981. Evidently, acquirers believe the changes they contemplate will significantly increase the value of the acquired firm.

Putting a price tag on the value enhancements resulting from a change in control is a straightforward undertaking conceptually. Make a detailed list of all the ways free cash flow will be increased and/or business and financial risks reduced as a result of the acquisition; estimate the magnitude and timing of these changes; calculate the present value of each; and sum.

$$\text{Enhancements} = PV \ [\text{All value increasing changes} \\ \text{due to acquisition}]$$

TABLE 9–3
Average Premiums Paid in Mergers and Acquisitions 1984–Third Quarter 1990

Year	Number of Transactions*	Average Premium over Stock Price One Month before Announcement
1984	405	37.0%
1985	392	42.3
1986	450	36.4
1987	380	37.9
1988	404	42.7
1989	371	36.6
1990 (Q3)	298	27.5

*Number of transactions revealing price, enabling acquisition premium to be calculated.

Source: "Control Premiums in Mergers and Acquisitions," *Mergers & Acquisitions,* January/February 1991, p. 70.

Controlling Interest in a Publicly Traded Company

If we are willing to assume that the preacquisition stock price of the target firm reasonably approximates its FMV_m—or at least that we are unable to detect when the approximation is unreasonable—this formula can also be used to value controlling interest in a publicly traded company:

$$FMV_c = \text{Market value of business} + \text{Enhancements}$$

A particular virtue of this formula for valuing acquisition candidates is that it forces attention on the specific improvements anticipated from the acquisition and the maximum price one should pay for them. This perspective reduces the possibility that an exuberant buyer will become carried away during spirited bidding and overpay.

The Battle for Free Cash Flow

We conclude (or at least I conclude) that the best way to value a public company for acquisition purposes is to add the present value of all benefits attributable to the acquisition to the target's current market value. "So," you ask perceptively, "what types of benefits might motivate an acquisition, or other form of restruc-

Avoiding Dilution in Earnings per Share

A popular alternative approach to determining how much one company can afford to bid for another looks at the impact of the acquisition on the acquirer's earnings per share (EPS). Popularity is about all this approach has to recommend it, for it grossly oversimplifies the financial effects of an acquisition, and it rests on an inappropriate decision criterion.

Suppose the following data apply to an acquiring firm, A, and its target, T, in an exchange-of-shares merger; that is, A will give T's shareholders newly printed shares of A in exchange for their shares of T.

	Co. A	Co. T	Merged Company
Earnings ($ millions)	100	20	130
Number of shares (millions)	20	40	26
Earnings per share ($)	5.00	0.50	5.00 (minimum)
Stock price ($)	70	5	
Market value of equity ($ millions)	1,400	200	

The suggested decision criterion is that, at a minimum, A should avoid dilution in EPS. If earnings of the merged firm are forecasted to be $130 million, the figures above indicate that A can issue as many as 6 million shares without suffering dilution ([$130 million/$5.00] − 20 million). At $70 per share, this implies a maximum price of $420 million for T ($70 × 6 million), or a 110 percent premium ([420 − 200]/200). It also suggests a maximum exchange ratio of 0.15 shares of A for each share of T (6 million/40 million).

The obvious shortcomings of this simplistic approach are, first, that earnings are not the cash flows that determine value and, second, that it is grossly inappropriate to base an acquisition decision on only one year's results. Doing so is comparable to making investments because they promise to increase next year's profits. If T's growth prospects are sufficiently bright, it may be perfectly reasonable to sacrifice near-term EPS in anticipation of long-run gains. Business valuation is tough in practice, but there is no reason to use flawed techniques just because they are tractable.

turing?" The list is truly a lengthy one, ranging from anticipated savings in manufacturing, marketing, distribution, or overhead to better access to financial markets to enhanced investment opportunities. And while neither space nor patience warrant a complete listing, three possible enhancements are sufficiently common and controversial to merit review. I will refer to them as *tax shields, incentive effects,* and *controlling free cash flow.*

Tax Shields
Many acquisitions and other restructurings appear to be motivated by the desire to make more extensive use of depreciation and interest tax shields. As noted in Chapter 6, the tax deductibility of depreciation and interest expenses reduces a company's tax bill, and hence may add value. Investment manager Warren Buffett puts it more directly when he observes, "If you can eliminate the government as a 46 percent partner," the business will be far more valuable.

Consider the following restructuring of Mature Manufacturing, Inc. (2M). Pertinent data for 2M, a mature, publicly traded company, appear below.

Mature Manufacturing, Inc. ($ in millions)

Annual EBIT	25
Market value of equity	200
Long-term debt	0
Fixed plant and equipment	100
Annual depreciation	10

Global Investing Corp. believes 2M management may be interested in a leveraged buyout (LBO) and has approached them with a proposal to form a new corporation, called NEWCO, to purchase all of 2M's equity. Because 2M's cash flows are very stable, Global figures it can finance most of the purchase price by borrowing $190 million on a 10-year loan at 10 percent interest. The loan will be interest only for the first five years. In addition, Global believes its auditors will allow NEWCO to write up the book value of 2M's fixed plant and equipment to a fair market value of $160 million on acquisition. This will generate an additional $6 million in annual depreciation for the next 10 years. The value of the anticipated tax shields to NEWCO, discounted at a 12 percent rate, is shown below.

Year	Increase in Interest Expense	Increase in Depreciation	Tax Shield @ 34% Tax Rate
1	$19.00	$6.00	$ 8.50
2	19.00	6.00	8.50
3	19.00	6.00	8.50
4	19.00	6.00	8.50
5	19.00	6.00	8.50
6	19.00	6.00	8.50
7	15.89	6.00	7.44
8	12.46	6.00	6.28
9	8.70	6.00	5.00
10	4.56	6.00	3.59
		PV @ 12% =	$43.81 million

The figures suggest that NEWCO can bid up to $243.81 million—a 22 percent premium—to purchase 2M. Global's equity investment will be as high as $53.81 million ($243.81 million value of firm − $190 million value of liabilities), implying a postacquisition debt-to-assets ratio of 78 percent. This, believe it or not, is conservative financing by LBO standards. LBOs are indeed aptly named.

Note that if increased tax shields are the objective, an LBO is not the only way to attain them. 2M can generate much the same effect by simply issuing debt and distributing the proceeds to owners as a large dividend, or by a share repurchase. This was Colt Industries' strategy in 1986 when they floated a large debt issue to finance distribution of a special $85 per share dividend. To put this number in perspective, Colt's stock traded for only $67 just prior to announcement of the restructuring. After recapitalization, Colt faced a negative net worth of $1 billion and $1.6 billion in long-term debt. But what's to fear from a mountain of debt as long as you have the cash flow to service it? And if you don't, your creditors have so much at stake in your company they are more likely to behave like partners than policemen.

Nor must a leveraged buyout necessarily involve a takeover. Many LBOs are initiated by incumbent management who team up with outside investors to purchase all of the company's stock and take it private. Management risks its own money in return for a sizable equity position in the restructured company.

The pros and cons of financial leverage were examined in Chapter 6, where we concluded that capital structure policy involves a judicious balancing of the tax and growth benefits of debt financing against the increased expected cost of bankruptcy. Restructurings involving extensive increases in financial leverage are implicitly saying that many companies have overestimated the cost side of this equation. The current recession is proving that a number of companies have been overly optimistic in this regard, although the great majority of LBOs continue to perform satisfactorily.

Incentive Effects

Tax shield enhancements are clearly just a game: To the extent that shareholders win, "we, the people" (in the form of the U.S. Treasury) lose. And if this were the only gain to restructuring, the phenomenon would not command serious public attention. Best that we eliminate the tax benefits of restructuring and get back to producing goods and services instead of stocks and bonds.

The other two potential enhancements are relevant only to shareholder-inspired restructurings and are not so easily dismissed. Both involve free cash flow and both are premised on the view that there is a constant tug-of-war in many public corporations between shareholders and incumbent management for control of the company. When shareholders have the upper hand, companies are run to maximize shareholder value; but when management is in the driver's seat, increasing value is only one of a number of competing corporate goals. After over 50 years on the losing end of this tug-of-war, the emergence of the hostile raider in the mid-1980s enabled shareholders to gain the ascendancy, if only briefly. While in command, shareholders forced companies to restructure as a means of gaining control of free cash flows. According to this view, the hostile acquisitions and restructurings of the past half-dozen years were a boon not only to shareholders but to the entire economy. To the extent that shareholders can force management to increase firm value, the economy's resources are allocated more efficiently. Let us explore this reasoning in more detail below.

Before restructuring, the life of a senior manager at Mature Manufacturing, Inc. may well have been an enviable one. With very stable cash flows, a mature business, and no debt, management had no pressing reason to improve performance. They could pay themselves and their employees generously, make sizable corporate contributions to charity, and, if the president were so inclined, sponsor an Indy race car or an unlimited hydroplane. Alternatively, if they wanted to grow, the company could buy growth by sacrificing profitability. This might involve making some uneconomic investments, but, hey, as long as cash flows are strong, almost anything is possible.

As Samuel Johnson once observed, "The certainty of hanging in a fortnight focuses the mind wonderfully." Restructuring can have a similar consequence, for it fundamentally changes the world of 2M senior executives. Because they have probably invested much of their own resources in equity of the restructured company, management's own material well-being is tied closely to that of the business. Moreover, the huge debt-service burden restructuring frequently creates forces management to generate healthy cash flows or face bankruptcy—no more "corpocracy" at 2M. The carrot of ownership and the stick of possible financial ruin create significant incentives for management to maximize free cash flow and to spend it for the benefit of owners.

Controlling Free Cash Flow

Many of the past decade's hostile takeovers occurred in mature or declining industries. Because investment opportunities in these industries are low, affected businesses often have large free cash flows. At the same time, industry decline creates real concern in the minds of executives about the continued survival of their organization. And although the proper strategy from a purely economic perspective is to shrink or terminate the business, management may take another tack. Out of a deep commitment to the business and concern for employees, the community, and their own welfare, managers may continue to fight the good fight by reinvesting in the business, despite the poor returns. The purpose of restructuring in these instances is brutally basic: to wrest control of free cash flow away from management and put it in the hands of owners.

The Board of Directors

One piece of the puzzle remains: How does incumbent management gain control of the firm in the first place? In theory, managers should be incapable of acting in opposition to owners for at least two reasons. First, if a company competes in highly competitive markets, management has very little discretion; it must maximize profits or be driven from the industry. Second, all corporations have boards of directors with the power to hire and fire management and the responsibility to represent owners' interests.

Theory, however, differs from reality. Most corporations operate in less than perfectly competitive markets, and most corporate boards are not an effective, independent shareholder voice. Primarily because of the vagaries of the proxy process for shareholder voting, most directors are more closely affiliated with incumbent management than with owners. Many are inside directors, others have significant ties to the enterprise other than ownership, and in most instances, directors are more beholden to incumbent management than to shareholders for their seat on the board. Consequently, while the board may aid management in running the company, it is seldom an independent voice for shareholders. Or as one professional director put it, "The most important skill a board member can have is the ability to yawn with his mouth shut."

The Time-Paramount Battle

The Time-Paramount skirmish should no longer seem quite so mystifying. Time's premerger price of $110 was the value of a share to minority investors, given Richard Munro's stewardship, while the $200 price offered by Paramount included a sizable premium for control. Clearly, neither price was necessarily incorrect or irrational.

LBOs and Company Performance

Preliminary evidence on the effect of leveraged buyouts on company performance and on returns to investors has recently begun to surface. In the best study to date, Steven Kaplan of the University of Chicago examined 48 large management buyouts executed between 1980 and 1986.[5] (A management buyout is an LBO in which prebuyout management plays an active role in taking the company private.)

Looking first at changes in operating return on assets, Kaplan found that, relative to overall industry performance, the median buyout firm increased his measure of operating return on assets a healthy 36.1 percent in the two years following the buyout. A similar look at capital expenditures revealed that the typical buyout firm reduced its ratio of capital expenditures to assets—relative to its industry—by a statistically insignificant 5.7 percent over the same period. Reflecting both improved operating performance and reduced investment, Kaplan found that the typical buyout firm increased an industry-adjusted measure of free cash flow to total assets an enormous 85.4 percent in the two years following the buyout. Evidently, the carrot of increased ownership and the stick of heavy debt service really do focus management's attention.

---

[5]Steven Kaplan, "The Effects of Management Buyouts on Operating Performance and Value," *Journal of Financial Economics,* October 1989, pp. 217–54.

Martin Davis apparently bid for Time for several reasons, some offensive, some defensive. Like many observers, Davis believed that Time management was not realizing full value from their unique franchises such as *Sports Illustrated* and HBO. In company with Time and Warner executives, he also perceived that the combination of a major communications company with a major entertainment company promised important synergistic benefits. In particular, Time was strong in several major entertainment distribution channels, but owned very few entertainment products, while both Warner and Paramount had plenty of prod-

LBOs and Company Performance (concluded)

The investment figures are equally impressive. Of the 48 firms in his sample, Kaplan was able to find post-buyout valuation data on 25, either because they issued stock to the public, repurchased stock, were liquidated, or were sold. Recognizing that these 25 may be the cream of the crop, he found that the median, market-adjusted return to all sources of capital, measured from the buyout date to the valuation date, was 28 percent. The median time between the buyout date and the valuation date was 2.6 years. Because Kaplan found it difficult to identify a common stock portfolio that had the same risk as the equity portion of the MBOs, he was unable to report market-adjusted returns to equity. The median, unadjusted return to equity, however, was a staggering 785.6 percent. Is it any wonder that plenty of money has been available to finance leveraged buyouts?

These data are clearly preliminary. Moreover, they were generated during one of the longest business expansions in American economic history and are coincident with one of the strongest stock markets in history; so there is no guarantee that such performance will ever be repeated. Nonetheless, the data do suggest that LBOs are not just tax gimmicks. Rather, the increased managerial incentives accompanying buyouts appear sufficiently powerful to cause noticeable improvements in operating performance and in shareholder value. The data also pose a significant challenge to those who argue that management alone should control America's corporations.

uct, but lacked Time's distribution muscle. A link-up between Time and either Warner or Paramount thus appeared to benefit both parties. And, finally, Davis may have bid for Time simply to throw a monkey wrench into the merger, thereby damaging a chief competitor.

Paramount's decision to bid $200 a share for Time was the result of valuation studies performed by the firm's investment advisors, Morgan Stanley. The studies paralleled the techniques described in this chapter, concentrating in particular on the value of possible enhancements attributable to a Time acquisition and on the likely price of certain Time properties if sold individually. There was speculation during the heat of the battle that Paramount was prepared to bid at least $220 a share and possibly higher for Time, but because of the company's unwillingness to negotiate, we will never know for certain.

The primary objective of Time's management team in rebuffing Paramount appears to have been organizational survival. On at least two occasions management could have sold the business at a price well above market value, but chose instead to remain independent. Security analysts—using the valuation tools described above—had been arguing for several years prior to the Warner acquisition that Time's *breakup value* was well above its market price, meaning that more value could be realized for shareholders by breaking up the firm and selling it piecemeal than by continuing to run it as in the past. Yet management chose to do precisely the opposite by merging with Warner, and thus retaining its independence. Then three months after the merger announcement, management rebuffed Paramount's takeover bid, and its implied loss of independence, in favor of the Warner acquisition. In addition to walking away from a considerable pile of cash, the rejection of Paramount's offer is rendered doubly hard to comprehend when one learns that Paramount was second only to Warner on Time's own list of merger candidates.

It is, of course, possible that Time management may yet be vindicated, and that the Warner acquisition will prove to be a long-run bonanza for shareholders. But after almost two years there is still no evidence to this effect, and the clock continues to tick. In the absence of evidence to the contrary, the most likely supposition is that Time's management and its board were less single-minded and less ruthless in managing shareholders' money than they would have been in managing their own.

In essence, management saw Time first and foremost as a venerable business at risk, and only secondarily as a financial investment responsible for generating competitive returns for its owners. Shareholders and possibly Martin Davis reversed these priorities, saying in effect that a corporation's fundamental purpose is to create value for its owners and that continued survival is contingent on the achievement of this objective.

As debate topics go, the question of whether management should have broader social responsibilities than simply creating shareholder value is among the more intriguing. Like many important societal questions, however, the issue has tended to be resolved more on the basis of power than of logic. Throughout most of this century, incumbent management has retained the power to interpret its responsibilities broadly and to treat shareholders as only one of several constituencies possessing a claim on the corporation. The balance of power shifted briefly in shareholders' favor during the era of the hostile takeover, but more recently has swung back in management's favor. The battle is not over, however; having tasted the fruits of corporate control, a growing number of institutional investors are choosing to fight rather than switch when management ignores their views. Today's weapon of choice, the proxy contest, is cumbersome and biased toward incumbent management, but may yet provide the means by which activist owners can at least discipline management's exercise of corporate control.

CHAPTER SUMMARY

1. The topic of this chapter has been corporate restructuring, defined loosely as any major episodic change in capital structure or ownership including mergers, acquisitions, leverage buyouts, divestitures, and stock repurchases.
2. The motivations fueling corporate restructurings are to be found in the study of business valuation—the art of valuing all or part of a business.
3. For publicly traded firms, the market *value of equity* is the price per share of common stock times the number of shares outstanding. The *market value of the firm* equals the market value of equity plus the market value of liabilities similarly calculated.
4. An asset's *fair market value* (FMV) is an abstract ideal defined as the price at which the asset would trade among two rational individuals, each in command of all information necessary to value the asset and neither under any pressure to trade.
5. The FMV of a business is usually the higher of its liquidation value or its going-concern value, where liquidation value is the cash generated by selling the business's assets individually and

going-concern value is the present worth of expected future cash flows generated by the business.

6. Three techniques for estimating the going-concern value of equity are: (1) estimate the present value of expected cash flows to equity, (2) estimate the present value of cash flows to the firm and subtract the value of liabilities, and (3) infer the value of equity from the prices at which the shares of comparable, publicly traded firms trade.

7. The price of common stock in public markets is for a minority interest. A buyer is justified in paying a premium above the minority value to gain control of a firm if he believes that in so doing he can enhance its value. The maximum justifiable premium equals the present value of all value-increasing changes contemplated by the buyer.

8. Free cash flow equals the operating cash flow available to the firm after financing all worthwhile investment opportunities. Three common and controversial benefits motivating restructurings appear to be (1) increased interest tax shields from debt financing, (2) increased incentive effects from increasing management's ownership of the company, and (3) owner control of free cash flow.

9. There appears to be an ongoing tug-of-war between shareholders and incumbent management for control of a number of America's corporations. Shareholder advocates argue that takeovers are good for the economy because they provide a means to oust ineffective management and discipline management to pay more attention to increasing shareholder value. Management advocates argue that excess shareholder control forces the pursuit of short-run payoffs to the detriment of long-run performance.

ADDITIONAL READING

Copeland, Tom; Tim Koller; and Jack Murrin. *Valuation: Measuring and Managing the Value of Companies.* New York: John Wiley, 1990. 428 pages.

 Written by three McKinsey & Company consultants, this is a well-written, practical, how-to discussion of business valuation. Part III, Applying Valuation, is especially well done, with whole chapters devoted to multinational business valuation and valuing banks. You can spend $60,000 and let McKinsey do a valuation for you, or spend $60 and learn how to do it yourself.

Hickman, Kent, and Glenn H. Petry. "A Comparison of Stock Price Predictions Using Court Accepted Formulas, Dividend Discount, and P/E Models." *Financial Management,* Summer 1990, pp. 74–85.

One of the few studies I know of that attempts to assess the empirical accuracy of alternative valuation models. The authors conclude that the comparables approaches they tested provided much more reliable estimates of value than the discounted cash flow models did.

Jensen, Michael C. "The Corporate Takeover Controversy: Analysis and Evidence." *Midland Corporate Finance Journal,* Summer 1986, pp. 6–32.

Harry Truman's proverbial "one-armed economist"; none of this "on the one hand but then on the other hand" from Mike Jensen. This article is a cogent, tightly reasoned, provocative review of the empirical literature on corporate takeovers and a strong statement in support of the virtues of an unfettered market for corporate control.

Pratt, Shannon P. *Valuing a Business: The Analysis and Appraisal of Closely Held Companies,* 2nd ed. Homewood, Ill.: Dow Jones-Irwin, 1988.

A detailed road map of how to value a closely held company. A wealth of practical detail on sources of data and applied valuation approaches. Far less sophisticated than Tom Copeland's book described above. Relevant primarily for valuing small firms.

CHAPTER PROBLEMS

1. Below is a four-year forecast for Maternity Modes.

	($ millions)			
	1993	*1994*	*1995*	*1996*
Earnings before interest and taxes	100	130	170	210
Capital expenditures	150	90	100	110
Changes in working capital	20	50	(10)	10
Depreciation	25	30	50	60

  a. Assuming all of Maternity Modes' investments have positive
     NPVs and that the company's tax rate is 40 percent, calculate
     estimated free cash flow in each year.
  b. What does a negative free cash flow imply? Does it mean that
     the company is destroying value in that year, or might another
     interpretation be possible?
  c. Estimate the fair market value of Maternity Modes at the end
     of 1992. Assume that after 1996, earnings before interest and
     tax will remain constant at $210 million, depreciation will
     equal capital expenditures in each year, and working capital
     will not change. Maternity Modes' weighted-average cost of
     capital is 14 percent.
  d. Estimate the fair market value per share of Maternity Modes'
     equity at the end of 1992 if the company has 50 million shares
     outstanding and the market value of its liabilities on the valu-
     ation date equals $300 million.
  e. Now, let's try a different terminal value. Estimate the fair
     market value of Maternity Modes at the end of 1992 under the
     following assumptions:
     • Free cash flows in years 1993 through 1996 remain as above.
     • EBIT after 1996 grows 4 percent per year forever.
     • To support the perpetual growth in EBIT, capital expendi-
       tures in 1997 exceed depreciation by $20 million, and this
       difference grows 4 percent per year forever.

- Similarly, working capital increases $10 million in 1997, and this amount grows 4 percent per year forever.
  f. Finally, let's try a third terminal value. Estimate the fair market value of Maternity Modes at the end of 1992 under the following assumptions:
  - Free cash flows in years 1993 through 1996 remain as above.
  - At year-end 1996, Maternity Modes has reached maturity, and its equity sells for a "typical" multiple of 1996 net income. Use eight as a typical multiple.
  - At year-end 1996, Maternity Modes has $200 million of liabilities outstanding at an average interest rate of 10 percent.
2. The following information is available about International Multiproducts, Inc. (IMI).

Stock price	$16 per share
Common shares outstanding	10 million
Current liabilities	$30 million
Market value of long-term liabilities	$100 million
Weighted average cost of capital	12 percent

A competitor is confident that by liquidating IMI's new "pet fragrances cosmetics line" and selling the industrial hosiery division, free cash flow can be increased $6 million a year for the next 20 years. In addition, they estimate that an immediate, special dividend of $25 million can be financed by the sale of the hosiery division. Assuming no change in IMI's cost of capital, what is the top price per share the rival would be justified in offering to gain control of IMI? What premium does this represent?

3. A capital goods manufacturer has decided to expand into a related business. Management estimates that to build and staff a facility of the desired size and to attain capacity operations would cost $250 million in present value terms. Alternatively, the company could acquire an existing firm or division with the desired capacity. One such opportunity is the division of another company. The book value of the division's assets is $140 million and its earnings before interest and tax are presently $30 million. Publicly traded comparable companies are selling in a narrow range around 13 times current earnings. These companies have debt-to-asset ratios averaging 40 percent with an average interest rate of 10 percent.

a. Using a tax rate of 34 percent, estimate the minimum price the owner of the division should consider for its sale.
b. What is the maximum price the acquirer should be willing to pay?
c. Does it appear that an acquisition is feasible? Why, or why not?
d. Would a 30 percent decline in stock prices to an industry average price-to-earnings ratio of 9.1 change your answer to *c?* Why, or why not?
e. Referring to the $250 million price tag as the replacement value of the division, what would you predict would happen to acquisition activity when market values of companies and divisions fall below their replacement values?

APPENDIX A
Present Value of $1 Discounted at Discount Rate k, for n Years

Period (n)	1%	2%	3%	4%	5%	6%	7%	8%	9%	10%	11%	12%
1	0.990	0.980	0.971	0.962	0.952	0.943	0.935	0.926	0.917	0.909	0.901	0.893
2	0.980	0.961	0.943	0.925	0.907	0.890	0.873	0.857	0.842	0.826	0.812	0.797
3	0.971	0.942	0.915	0.889	0.864	0.840	0.816	0.794	0.772	0.751	0.731	0.712
4	0.961	0.924	0.885	0.855	0.823	0.792	0.763	0.735	0.708	0.683	0.659	0.636
5	0.951	0.906	0.863	0.822	0.784	0.747	0.713	0.681	0.650	0.621	0.593	0.567
6	0.942	0.888	0.837	0.790	0.746	0.705	0.666	0.630	0.596	0.564	0.535	0.507
7	0.933	0.871	0.813	0.760	0.711	0.665	0.623	0.583	0.547	0.513	0.482	0.452
8	0.923	0.853	0.789	0.731	0.677	0.627	0.582	0.540	0.502	0.467	0.434	0.404
9	0.914	0.837	0.766	0.703	0.645	0.592	0.544	0.500	0.460	0.424	0.391	0.361
10	0.905	0.820	0.744	0.676	0.614	0.558	0.508	0.463	0.422	0.386	0.352	0.322
11	0.896	0.804	0.722	0.650	0.585	0.527	0.475	0.429	0.388	0.350	0.317	0.287
12	0.887	0.788	0.701	0.625	0.557	0.497	0.444	0.397	0.356	0.319	0.286	0.257
13	0.879	0.773	0.681	0.601	0.530	0.469	0.415	0.368	0.326	0.290	0.258	0.229
14	0.870	0.758	0.661	0.577	0.505	0.442	0.388	0.340	0.299	0.263	0.232	0.205
15	0.861	0.743	0.642	0.555	0.481	0.417	0.362	0.315	0.275	0.239	0.209	0.183
16	0.853	0.728	0.623	0.534	0.458	0.394	0.339	0.292	0.252	0.218	0.188	0.163
17	0.844	0.714	0.605	0.513	0.436	0.371	0.317	0.270	0.231	0.198	0.170	0.146
18	0.836	0.700	0.587	0.494	0.416	0.350	0.296	0.250	0.212	0.180	0.153	0.130
19	0.828	0.686	0.570	0.475	0.396	0.331	0.277	0.232	0.194	0.164	0.138	0.116
20	0.820	0.673	0.554	0.456	0.377	0.312	0.258	0.215	0.178	0.149	0.124	0.104
25	0.780	0.610	0.478	0.375	0.295	0.233	0.184	0.146	0.116	0.092	0.074	0.059
30	0.742	0.552	0.412	0.308	0.231	0.174	0.131	0.099	0.075	0.057	0.044	0.033
40	0.672	0.453	0.307	0.208	0.142	0.097	0.067	0.046	0.032	0.022	0.015	0.011
50	0.608	0.372	0.228	0.141	0.087	0.054	0.034	0.021	0.013	0.009	0.005	0.003

APPENDIX A *(concluded)*

Discount rate (k)

Period (n)	13%	14%	15%	16%	17%	18%	19%	20%	25%	30%	35%	40%	50%
1	0.885	0.877	0.870	0.862	0.855	0.847	0.840	0.833	0.800	0.769	0.741	0.714	0.667
2	0.783	0.769	0.756	0.743	0.731	0.718	0.706	0.694	0.640	0.592	0.549	0.510	0.444
3	0.693	0.675	0.658	0.641	0.624	0.609	0.593	0.579	0.512	0.455	0.406	0.364	0.296
4	0.613	0.592	0.572	0.552	0.534	0.515	0.499	0.482	0.410	0.350	0.301	0.260	0.198
5	0.543	0.519	0.497	0.476	0.456	0.437	0.419	0.402	0.320	0.269	0.223	0.186	0.132
6	0.480	0.456	0.432	0.410	0.390	0.370	0.352	0.335	0.262	0.207	0.165	0.133	0.088
7	0.425	0.400	0.376	0.354	0.333	0.314	0.296	0.279	0.210	0.159	0.122	0.095	0.059
8	0.376	0.351	0.327	0.305	0.285	0.266	0.249	0.233	0.168	0.123	0.091	0.068	0.039
9	0.333	0.308	0.284	0.263	0.243	0.225	0.209	0.194	0.134	0.094	0.067	0.048	0.026
10	0.295	0.270	0.247	0.227	0.208	0.191	0.176	0.162	0.107	0.073	0.050	0.035	0.017
11	0.261	0.237	0.215	0.195	0.178	0.162	0.148	0.135	0.086	0.056	0.037	0.025	0.012
12	0.231	0.208	0.187	0.168	0.152	0.137	0.124	0.112	0.069	0.043	0.027	0.018	0.008
13	0.204	0.182	0.163	0.145	0.130	0.116	0.104	0.093	0.055	0.033	0.020	0.013	0.005
14	0.181	0.160	0.141	0.125	0.111	0.099	0.088	0.078	0.044	0.025	0.015	0.009	0.003
15	0.160	0.140	0.123	0.108	0.095	0.084	0.074	0.065	0.035	0.020	0.011	0.006	0.002
16	0.141	0.123	0.107	0.093	0.081	0.071	0.062	0.054	0.028	0.015	0.008	0.005	0.002
17	0.125	0.108	0.093	0.080	0.069	0.060	0.052	0.045	0.023	0.012	0.006	0.003	0.001
18	0.111	0.095	0.081	0.069	0.059	0.051	0.044	0.038	0.018	0.009	0.005	0.002	0.001
19	0.098	0.083	0.070	0.060	0.051	0.043	0.037	0.031	0.014	0.007	0.003	0.002	0
20	0.087	0.073	0.061	0.051	0.043	0.037	0.031	0.026	0.012	0.005	0.002	0.001	0
25	0.047	0.038	0.030	0.024	0.020	0.016	0.013	0.010	0.004	0.001	0.001	0	0
30	0.026	0.020	0.015	0.012	0.009	0.007	0.005	0.004	0.001	0	0	0	0
40	0.008	0.005	0.004	0.003	0.002	0.001	0.001	0.001	0	0	0	0	0
50	0.002	0.001	0.001	0.001	0	0	0	0	0	0	0	0	0

APPENDIX B Present Value of an Annuity of $1 for *n* Years, Discounted at Rate *k*

Period (n)		Discount rate (k)										
	1%	2%	3%	4%	5%	6%	7%	8%	9%	10%	11%	12%
1	0.990	0.980	0.971	0.962	0.952	0.943	0.935	0.926	0.917	0.909	0.901	0.893
2	1.970	1.942	1.913	1.886	1.859	1.833	1.808	1.783	1.759	1.736	1.713	1.690
3	2.941	2.884	2.829	2.775	2.723	2.673	2.624	2.577	2.531	2.487	2.444	2.402
4	3.902	3.808	3.717	3.630	3.546	3.465	3.387	3.312	3.240	3.170	3.102	3.037
5	4.853	4.710	4.580	4.452	4.329	4.212	4.100	3.993	3.890	3.791	3.696	3.605
6	5.795	5.601	5.417	5.242	5.076	4.917	4.767	4.623	4.486	4.355	4.231	4.111
7	6.728	6.472	6.230	6.002	5.786	5.582	5.389	5.206	5.033	4.868	4.712	4.564
8	7.652	7.325	7.020	6.733	6.463	6.210	5.971	5.747	5.535	5.335	5.146	4.968
9	8.566	8.162	7.786	7.435	7.108	6.802	6.515	6.247	5.995	5.759	5.537	5.328
10	9.471	8.983	8.530	8.111	7.722	7.360	7.024	6.710	6.418	6.145	5.889	5.650
11	10.368	9.787	9.253	8.760	8.306	7.887	7.499	7.139	6.805	6.495	6.207	5.938
12	11.255	10.575	9.954	9.385	8.863	8.384	7.943	7.536	7.161	6.814	6.492	6.194
13	12.134	11.348	10.635	9.986	9.394	8.853	8.358	7.904	7.487	7.103	6.750	6.424
14	13.004	12.106	11.296	10.563	9.899	9.295	8.745	8.244	7.786	7.367	6.982	6.628
15	13.865	12.849	11.939	11.118	10.380	9.712	9.108	8.559	8.061	7.606	7.191	6.811
16	14.718	13.578	12.561	11.652	10.838	10.106	9.447	8.851	8.313	7.824	7.379	6.974
17	15.562	14.292	13.166	12.166	11.274	10.477	9.763	9.122	8.544	8.022	7.549	7.102
18	16.398	14.992	13.754	12.659	11.690	10.828	10.059	9.372	8.756	8.201	7.702	7.250
19	17.226	15.678	14.324	13.134	12.085	11.158	10.336	9.604	8.950	8.365	7.839	7.366
20	18.046	16.351	14.877	13.590	12.462	11.470	10.594	9.818	9.129	8.514	7.963	7.469
25	22.023	19.523	17.413	15.622	14.094	12.783	11.654	10.675	9.823	9.077	8.422	7.843
30	25.808	22.396	19.600	17.292	15.372	13.765	12.409	11.258	10.274	9.427	8.694	8.055
40	32.835	27.355	23.115	19.793	17.159	15.046	13.332	11.925	10.757	9.779	8.951	8.244
50	39.196	31.424	25.730	21.482	18.256	15.762	13.801	12.233	10.962	9.915	9.042	8.304

APPENDIX B *(concluded)*

Discount rate (k)

Period (n)	13%	14%	15%	16%	17%	18%	19%	20%	25%	30%	35%	40%	50%
1	0.885	0.877	0.870	0.862	0.855	0.847	0.840	0.833	0.800	0.769	0.741	0.714	0.667
2	1.668	1.647	1.626	1.605	1.585	1.566	1.547	1.528	1.440	1.361	1.289	1.224	1.111
3	2.361	2.322	2.283	2.246	2.210	2.174	2.140	2.106	1.952	1.816	1.696	1.589	1.407
4	2.974	2.914	2.855	2.798	2.743	2.690	2.639	2.589	2.362	2.166	1.997	1.849	1.605
5	3.517	3.433	3.352	3.274	3.199	3.127	3.058	2.991	2.689	2.436	2.220	2.035	1.737
6	3.998	3.889	3.784	3.685	3.589	3.498	3.410	3.326	2.951	2.643	2.385	2.168	1.824
7	4.423	4.288	4.160	4.039	3.922	3.812	3.706	3.605	3.161	2.802	2.508	2.263	1.883
8	4.799	4.639	4.487	4.344	4.207	4.078	3.954	3.837	3.329	2.925	2.598	2.331	1.922
9	5.132	4.946	4.772	4.607	4.451	4.303	4.163	4.031	3.463	3.019	2.665	2.370	1.948
10	5.426	5.216	5.019	4.833	4.659	4.494	4.339	4.192	3.571	3.092	2.715	2.414	1.965
11	5.687	5.453	5.234	5.029	4.836	4.656	4.486	4.327	3.656	3.147	2.752	2.438	1.977
12	5.918	5.660	5.421	5.197	4.988	4.793	4.611	4.439	3.725	3.190	2.779	2.456	1.985
13	6.122	5.842	5.583	5.342	5.118	4.910	4.715	4.533	3.780	3.223	2.799	2.469	1.990
14	6.302	6.002	5.724	5.468	5.229	5.008	4.802	4.611	3.824	3.249	2.814	2.478	1.993
15	6.462	6.142	5.847	5.575	5.324	5.092	4.876	4.675	3.859	3.268	2.825	2.484	1.995
16	6.604	6.265	5.954	5.668	5.405	5.162	4.938	4.730	3.887	3.283	2.834	2.489	1.997
17	6.729	6.373	6.047	5.749	5.475	5.222	4.988	4.775	3.910	3.295	2.840	2.492	1.998
18	6.840	6.467	6.128	5.818	5.534	5.273	5.033	4.812	3.928	3.304	2.844	2.494	1.999
19	6.938	6.550	6.198	5.877	5.584	5.316	5.070	4.843	3.942	3.311	2.848	2.496	1.999
20	7.025	6.623	6.259	5.929	5.628	5.353	5.101	4.870	3.954	3.316	2.850	2.497	1.999
25	7.330	6.873	6.464	6.097	5.766	5.467	5.195	4.948	3.985	3.329	2.856	2.499	2.000
30	7.496	7.003	6.566	6.177	5.829	5.517	5.235	4.979	3.995	3.332	2.857	2.500	2.000
40	7.634	7.105	6.642	6.233	5.871	5.548	5.258	4.997	3.999	3.333	2.857	2.500	2.000
50	7.675	7.133	6.661	6.246	5.880	5.554	5.262	4.999	4.000	3.333	2.857	2.500	2.000

GLOSSARY

accelerated depreciation Any *depreciation*[1] that produces larger deductions for depreciation in the early years of a project's life.

acceptance criterion Any minimum standard of performance in investment analysis (cf. *hurdle rate*).

accounting income An economic agent's *realized income* as shown on financial statements (cf. *economic income*).

accounting rate of return A figure of investment merit, defined as average annual cash inflow divided by total cash outflow (cf. *internal rate of return*).

accounts payable (payables, trade payables) Money owed to suppliers.

accounts receivable (receivables, trade credit) Money owed by customers.

accrual accounting A method of accounting in which *revenue* is recognized when earned and expenses are recognized when incurred without regard to the timing of cash receipts and expenditures (cf. *cash accounting*).

acid test (quick ratio) A measure of *liquidity*, defined as *current assets* less inventories divided by *current liabilities*.

aftertax cash flow Total cash generated by an investment annually, defined as profit after tax plus depreciation, or equivalently, operating income after tax plus the tax rate times depreciation.

allocated costs Costs systematically assigned or distributed among products, departments, or other elements.

annuity A level stream of cash flows for a limited number of years (cf. *perpetuity*).

asset turnover ratio A broad measure of asset efficiency, defined as net sales divided by total assets.

---

[1]Words in italics are defined elsewhere in the glossary.

bankruptcy   A legal condition in which an individual's or company's assets are assumed by a federal court official and used to pay off creditors.

bearer securities   Any securities that are not registered on the books of the issuing corporation. Payments are made to whoever presents the appropriate coupon. Bearer securities facilitate tax avoidance.

benefit-cost ratio   *Profitability index.*

β-risk (systematic risk, nondiversifiable risk)   Risk that cannot be diversified away.

bond   Long-term publicly issued debt.

bond rating   An appraisal by a recognized financial organization of the soundness of a *bond* as an investment.

book value   The value at which an item is reported in financial statements (cf. *market value*).

book value of equity   The value of *owners' equity* as shown on the company's balance sheet (cf. *market value of equity*).

break-even analysis   Analysis of the level of sales at which a firm or product will just break even.

breakup value   The value one could realize by dividing a multibusiness company into a number of separate enterprises and disposing of each individually.

business risk   Risk due to uncertainty about investment outlays, operating cash flows, and salvage values without regard to how investments are financed (cf. *financial risk*).

call option   Option to buy an asset at a specified exercise price on or before a specified maturity date (cf. *put option*).

call provision   Provision describing terms under which a bond issuer may redeem bond in whole or in part prior to maturity.

capital   The amount invested in a venture (cf. *capitalization*).

capital budget   List of planned investment projects.

capital consumption adjustment   Adjustment to historical-cost depreciation to correct for understatement during inflation.

capital rationing   Fixed limit on capital that forces company to choose among worthwhile projects.

capital structure   The composition of the liabilities side of a company's balance sheet. The mix of funding sources a company uses to finance its operations.

capitalization The sum of all long-term sources of financing to the firm, or equivalently, total assets less current liabilities.

cash accounting A method of accounting in which changes in the condition of an organization are recognized only in response to the payment or receipt of cash (cf. *accrual accounting*).

cash budget A plan or projection of cash receipts and disbursements for a given period of time (cf. *cash flow forecast, cash flow statement, pro forma forecast*).

cash cow Company or product that generates more cash than can be productively reinvested.

cash flow The amount of cash generated or consumed by an activity over a certain period of time.

cash flow cycle The periodic transformation of cash through *working capital* and fixed assets back to cash.

cash flow forecast A financial forecast in the form of a *sources and uses statement*.

cash flow from operations Cash generated or consumed by the productive activities of a firm over a period of time; defined as profit after tax plus *noncash charges* minus noncash receipts.

cash flow principle Principle of investment evaluation stating that only actual movements of cash are relevant and that they should be listed on the date they move.

cash flow statement A report of the sources of cash to a business and the uses to which the cash was put over an accounting period.

certainty-equivalent A guaranteed amount of money that a decision maker would trade for an uncertain cash flow.

close off the top Financial jargon meaning to foreclose the possibility of additional debt financing.

collection period A ratio measure of control of *accounts receivable*, defined as accounts receivable divided by credit sales per day.

common shares *Common stock.*

common-size financial statements Device used to compare financial statements, frequently of companies of disparate size, whereby all balance sheet entries are divided by total assets and all income statement entries are divided by net sales.

common stock (common shares) Securities representing an ownership interest in a firm.

comparables   A method for estimating the *fair market value* of a closely held business by comparing it to one or more comparable, publicly traded firms.

compounding   The growth of a sum of money over time through the reinvestment of interest earned to earn more interest (cf. *discounting*).

conglomerate diversification   Ownership of operations in a number of functionally unrelated business activities.

constant-dollar accounting   System of inflation accounting in which historical-cost items are restated to adjust for changes in the general purchasing power of the currency (cf. *current-dollar accounting*).

constant purchasing power   The amount of a currency required over time to purchase a stable basket of physical assets.

consumer price index (CPI)   An index measure of inflation equal to the sum of prices of a number of assets purchased by consumers weighted by the proportion each represents in a typical consumer's budget.

contribution to fixed cost and profits   The excess of *revenue* over *variable costs*.

control ratio   Ratio indicating management's control of a particular current asset or liability.

conversion ratio   Number of shares for which a *convertible security* may be exchanged.

conversion value   Market value of shares investor would own if he or she converted one convertible security.

convertible security   Financial security that can be exchanged at the holder's option for another security or asset.

corporate restructuring   Any major episodic change in a company's capital or ownership structure.

correlation coefficient   Measure of the degree of comovement of two variables.

cost of capital (opportunity cost of capital, hurdle rate, weighted-average cost of capital)   Return on new, average-risk investment that a company must expect in order to maintain share price. A weighted average of the cost to the firm of individual sources of capital.

cost of debt   *Yield to maturity* on debt; frequently after tax, in which event it is one minus the tax rate times the yield to maturity.

cost of equity   Return equity investors expect to earn by holding shares in a company. The expected return foregone by equity investors in the next best, equal-risk opportunity.

cost of goods sold (cost of sales)   The sum of all costs required to acquire and prepare goods for sale.

coupon rate   The interest rate specified on interest coupons attached to bonds. Annual interest received equals coupon rate times the *par value* of the bond.

covenant (protective covenant)   Provision in a debt agreement requiring the borrower to do, or not do, something.

coverage ratio   Measure of financial leverage relating annual operating income to annual burden of debt (cf. *times-interest-earned ratio, times-burden-covered ratio*).

cumulative preferred stock   *Preferred stock* containing the requirement that any unpaid preferred dividends accumulate and must be paid in full before common dividends may be distributed.

current asset   Any asset that will turn into cash within one year.

current-dollar accounting   System of inflation accounting in which historical-cost items are restated to adjust for changes in the price of specific item (cf. *constant-dollar accounting*).

current liability   Any liability that is payable within one year.

current portion of long-term debt   That portion of long-term debt that is payable within one year.

current ratio   A measure of *liquidity,* defined as current assets divided by current liabilities.

days' sales in cash   A measure of management's control of cash balances, defined as cash divided by sales per day.

debt (liability)   An obligation to pay cash or other goods or to provide services to another.

debt capacity   The total amount of debt a company can prudently support, given its earnings expectations and equity base.

debt-to-assets ratio   A measure of *financial leverage,* defined as debt divided by total assets (cf. *debt-to-equity ratio*).

debt-to-equity ratio   A measure of *financial leverage,* defined as debt divided by shareholders' equity.

default   To fail to make a payment when due.

default premium   The increased return on a security required to compensate investors for the risk the company will default on its obligation.

deferred tax liability   An estimated amount of future income taxes that may become payable from income already earned but not yet recognized for tax-reporting purposes.

delayed call   Provision in a security that gives the issuer the right to call the issue but only after a period of time has elapsed (cf. *call provision*).

depreciation   The reduction in the value of a long-lived asset from use or obsolescence. The decline is recognized in accounting by a periodic allocation of the original cost of the asset to current operations (cf. *accelerated depreciation*).

dilution   The reduction in any per share item (such as earnings per share or book value per share) due to an increase in the number of shares outstanding either through new issue or conversion of outstanding securities.

discount rate   Interest rate used to calculate the *present value* of future cash flows.

discounted cash flow   The method of evaluating long-term projects that explicitly takes into account the time value of money.

discounted cash flow rate of return   *Internal rate of return.*

discounting   Process of finding the present value of future cash flows (cf. *compounding*).

diversifiable risk   That risk that is eliminated when an asset is added to a diversified portfolio (cf. β-*risk*).

diversification   The process of investing in a number of differing assets.

dividend payout ratio   A measure of the level of dividends distributed, defined as dividends divided by earnings.

earnings (income, net income, net profit, profit)   The excess of revenues over all related expenses for a given period.

earnings per share (EPS)   A measure of each common share's claim on earnings, defined as earnings available for common divided by the number of common shares outstanding.

earnings yield   *Earnings per share* divided by stock price.

EBIT   Abbreviation for earnings before interest and taxes.

economic income   The amount an economic agent could spend during a period of time without affecting his or her wealth (cf. *accounting income*).

efficient market   A market in which asset prices instantaneously reflect new information.

equity (owners' equity, net worth, shareholders' equity)   The ownership interests of common and preferred stockholders in a company; on a balance sheet, equity equals total assets less all liabilities.

equivalence   Equality of value of two cash flows occurring at different times if the cash flow occurring sooner can be converted into the later cash flow by investing it at the prevailing interest rate.

Eurodollar   Originally a U.S. dollar in Europe, now any currency outside the control of its issuing monetary authority. The Eurodollar market is any market in which transactions in such currencies are executed.

expected return   Average of possible returns weighted by their probability.

fair market value (FMV) (intrinsic value)   An idealized *market value* defined as the price at which an asset would trade between two rational individuals, each in command of all of the information necessary to value the asset and neither under any pressure to trade.

figure of merit   A number summarizing the investment worth of a project.

Financial Accounting Standards Board (FASB)   Official rule-making body in accounting profession.

financial flexibility   The ability to raise sufficient capital to meet company needs under a wide variety of future contingencies.

financial leverage   Use of debt to increase the expected return and the risk to equity (cf. *operating leverage*).

first-in, first-out (FIFO)   A method of inventory accounting in which the oldest item in inventory is assumed to be sold first (cf. *last-in, first-out*).

Fisher effect   Proposition that the nominal rate of interest should approximately equal the real rate of interest plus a premium for expected inflation (cf. *real amount, nominal amount*).

fixed cost   Any cost that does not vary over the observation period with changes in volume.

fixed-income security   Any security that promises an unvarying payment stream to holders over its life.

forcing conversion   Strategy in which a company forces owners of a convertible security to convert by calling the security at a time when its call price is below its conversion value (cf. *call provision, convertible security*).

foreign exchange exposure   The risk that an unexpected change in exchange rates will impose a loss of some kind on the exposed party. With **transaction exposure,** the loss is to reported income; with **accounting exposure,** the loss is to net worth; and with **economic exposure,** the loss is to the market value of the entity.

forward contract   A contract in which the price is set today for a trade occurring at a specified future date.

forward market   A market in which prices are determined for trade at a specified future date.

free cash flow   The *cash flow* available to a company after financing all worthwhile investments. It is defined as operating income after tax plus depreciation less investment. The presence of large free cash flows is said to be attractive to a corporate raider.

frozen convertible (hung convertible)   *Convertible security* that has been outstanding for several years and whose holders cannot be forced to convert because its *conversion value* is below its call price (cf. *forcing conversion*).

funds   Any means of payment. Along with cash flow, "funds" is one of the most frequently misused words in finance.

gains to net debtors   Increase in debtor's wealth due to decline in purchasing power of liabilities.

general creditor   Unsecured creditor.

going-concern value   The *present value* of a business's expected future *aftertax cash flows*. The going-concern value of *equity* is the present value of cash flows to equity, while the going-concern value of the firm is the present value of cash flows to all providers of capital.

gross margin percentage   Revenue minus cost of goods sold divided by revenue.

hedge   A strategy to offset investment risk. A perfect hedge is one that eliminates all possibility of gain or loss due to future movements of the hedged variable.

historical-cost depreciation   *Depreciation* based on amount originally paid for asset.

hurdle rate   Minimum acceptable rate of return on investment (cf. *acceptance criterion, cost of capital*).

income   *Earnings.*

income statement (profit and loss statement)   A report of a company's revenues, associated expenses, and resulting *income* for a period of time.

inflation premium   The increased return on a security required to compensate investors for expected inflation.

insolvency   The condition of having debts greater than the realizable value of one's assets.

internal rate of return (IRR)   *Discount rate* at which project's *net present value* equals zero. Rate at which funds left in a project are *compounding* (cf. *rate of return*).

internal sources   Cash available to a company from *cash flow from operations.*

inventory turnover ratio   A measure of management's control of its investment in inventory, defined as *cost of goods sold* divided by ending inventory, or something similar.

inventory valuation adjustment   Adjustment to historical-cost financial statements to correct for the possible understatement of inventory and *cost of goods sold* during inflation.

investment bank   A financial institution specializing in the original sale and subsequent trading of company securities.

investment value   Value of a *convertible security* based solely on its characteristics as a fixed-income security and ignoring the value of the conversion feature.

junk bond   Any *bond* rated below investment grade.

last-in, first-out (LIFO)   A method of inventory accounting in which the newest item in inventory is assumed to be sold first (cf. *first-in, first-out*).

leveraged buyout (LBO)   Purchase of a company financed in large part by company borrowings.

liability   An obligation to pay an amount or perform a service.

liquid asset   Any asset that can be quickly converted to cash without significant loss of value.

liquidation   The process of closing down a company, selling its assets, paying off its creditors, and distributing any remaining cash to owners.

liquidation value   The cash generated by terminating a business and selling its assets individually. The liquidation value of equity is the proceeds of the asset sale less all company liabilities.

liquidity   The extent to which a company has assets that are readily available to meet obligations (cf. *acid test, current ratio*).

liquidity ratio   Any ratio used to estimate a company's *liquidity* (cf. *acid test, current ratio*).

mark-to-market accounting   The practice of adjusting the carrying value of traded assets and liabilities appearing on a business's balance sheet to their recent market values.

market for control   The active, competitive trading of controlling interests in corporations, effected by the purchase or sale of sizable blocks of common stock.

market line (securities market line)   Line representing relationship between *expected return* and β-*risk*.

market value   The price at which an item can be sold (cf. *book value*).

market value of equity   The price per share of a company's *common stock* times the number of shares of common stock outstanding (cf. *book value of equity*).

market value of firm   The market value of *equity* plus the market value of the firm's liabilities.

monetary asset   Any asset having a value defined in units of currency. Cash and accounts receivable are monetary assets; inventories and plant and equipment are physical assets.

multiple hurdle rates   Use of different *hurdle rates* for new investments to reflect differing levels of risk.

mutually exclusive alternatives   Two projects that accomplish the same objective, so that only one will be undertaken.

net income   *Earnings.*

net monetary creditor   Economic agent having *monetary assets* in excess of *liabilities.*

net monetary debtor   Economic agent having *monetary assets* less than *liabilities.*

net present value (NPV)   *Present value* of cash inflows less present value of cash outflows. The increase in wealth accruing to an investor when he or she undertakes an investment.

net profit   *Earnings.*

net sales   Total sales revenue less certain offsetting items such as returns and allowances and sales discounts.

net worth   *Equity,* shareholders' equity.

nominal amount   Any quantity not adjusted for changes in purchasing power of the currency due to inflation (cf. *real amount*).

noncash charge   An expense recorded by an accountant not matched by a cash outflow during the accounting period.

nondiversifiable risk   β-*risk, systematic risk.*

operating leverage   Fixed operating costs that tend to increase the variation in profits (cf. *financial leverage*).

opportunity cost   Income forgone by an investor when he or she chooses one action opposed to another. Expected income on next best alternative.

opportunity cost of capital   *Cost of capital.*

option   See *call option, put option.*

option premium   The amount paid per unit by an option buyer to the option seller for an option contract.

over-the-counter (OTC) market   Informal market in which securities not listed on organized exchanges trade.

owners' equity   *Equity.*

paid-in capital   That portion of *shareholders' equity* that has been paid in directly, as opposed to earned profits retained in the business.

par value   An arbitrary value set as the face amount of a security. Bondholders receive par value for their bonds on maturity.

payables period   A measure of a company's use of trade credit financing, defined as accounts payable divided by purchases per day.

payback period   A crude figure of investment merit and better measure of investment risk, defined as the time an investor must wait to recoup his or her initial investment.

perpetual growth equation   An equation representing the *present value* of a *perpetuity* growing at the rate of *g* percent per annum as next year's receipts divided by the difference between the *discount rate* and *g.*

perpetuity   An *annuity* that lasts forever.

plug   Jargon for the unknown quantity in a pro forma forecast.

portfolio Holdings of a diverse group of assets by an individual or a company.

position diagram A graph relating the value of an investment position on the vertical axis to the price of an underlying asset on the horizontal axis.

preferred stock A class of stock, usually fixed-income, that carries some form of preference to income or assets over *common stock* (cf. *cumulative preferred stock*).

premium for control The premium over and above the existing *market value* of a company's *equity* an acquirer is willing to pay to gain control of the company.

present value The present worth of a future sum of money.

price-to-earnings ratio (P/E ratio) Amount investors are willing to pay for $1 of a firm's current earnings. Price per share divided by earnings per share over the most recent 12 months.

principal The original, or face, amount of a loan. Interest is earned on the principal.

private placement The raising of capital for a business through the sale of securities to a limited number of well-informed investors rather than through a public offering.

pro forma statement A financial statement prepared on the basis of some assumed future events.

profit center An organizational unit within a company that produces revenue and for which a profit can be calculated.

profit margin The proportion of each sales dollar that filters down to *income,* defined as income divided by *net sales.*

profitability index (benefit-cost ratio) A figure of investment merit, defined as the *present value* of cash inflows divided by present value of cash outflows.

profits *Earnings.*

protective covenant *Covenant.*

public issue (public offering) Newly issued securities sold directly to the public (cf. *private placement*).

purchasing power parity A theory stating that foreign exchange rates should adjust so that, in equilibrium, commodities in different countries cost the same amount when prices are expressed in the same currency.

put option   Option to sell an asset at a specified exercise price on or before a specified maturity date (cf. *call option*).

quick ratio   *Acid test.*

range-of-earnings chart   Graph relating *earnings per share* (EPS) to earnings before interest and taxes (EBIT) under alternative financing options.

rate of return   Yield obtainable on an asset.

ratio analysis   Analysis of financial statements by means of ratios.

real amount   Any quantity that has been adjusted for changes in the purchasing power of the currency due to inflation (cf. *nominal amount*).

realized income   The earning of income related to a transaction as distinguished from a paper gain.

residual income security   A security that has last claim on company income. Usually the beneficiary of company growth.

residual profits   An alternative to *return on investment* as a measure of *profit center* performance, defined as *income* less the annual cost of the capital employed by the profit center.

retained earnings (earned surplus)   The amount of earnings retained and reinvested in a business and not distributed to stockholders as dividends.

return on assets (ROA)   A measure of the productivity of assets, defined as *income* divided by total assets. A superior but less common definition includes interest expense and preferred dividends in the numerator.

return on equity (ROE)   A measure of the productivity or efficiency with which shareholders' equity is employed, defined as *income* divided by *equity*.

return on invested capital (ROIC)   A fundamental measure of the earning power of a company that is unaffected by the way the company is financed. It is equal to earnings before interest and tax times one minus the tax rate, all divided by *debt* plus *equity*.

return on investment (ROI)   The productivity of an investment or a profit center, defined as *income* divided by *book value* of investment or *profit center* (cf. *return on assets*).

revenues   *Sales.*

rights of absolute priority   Specification in bankruptcy law stating that each class of claimants with a prior claim on assets in liquidation will be paid off in full before any junior claimants receive anything.

risk-adjusted discount rate (cost of capital, hurdle rate)   A *discount rate* that includes a premium for risk.

risk aversion   An unwillingness to bear risk without compensation of some form.

risk-free interest rate   The interest rate prevailing on a default-free bond in the absence of inflation.

risk premium   The increased return on a security required to compensate investors for the risk borne.

sales (revenue)   The inflow of resources to a business for a period from sale of goods or provision of services (cf. *net sales*).

secured creditor   A creditor whose obligation is backed by the pledge of some asset. In liquidation, the secured creditor receives the cash from the sale of the pledged asset to the extent of his or her loan.

Securities and Exchange Commission (SEC)   Federal government agency that regulates securities markets.

semistrong-form efficient market   A market in which prices instantaneously reflect all publicly available information.

senior creditor   Any creditor with a claim on income or assets prior to that of *general creditors.*

sensitivity analysis   Analysis of effect on a plan or forecast of a change in one of the input variables.

shareholders' equity   *Equity, net worth.*

shelf registration   SEC program under which a company can file a general-purpose prospectus describing its possible financing plans for up to two years. This eliminates time lags for new public security issues.

simulation (Monte Carlo simulation)   Computer-based extension of *sensitivity analysis* that calculates the probability distribution of a forecast outcome.

sinking fund   A fund of cash set aside for the payment of a future obligation. A bond sinking fund is a payment of cash to creditors.

solvency   The state of being able to pay debts as they come due.

sources and uses statement   A document showing where a company got its cash and where it spent the cash over a specific period of time. It is constructed by segregating all changes in balance sheet accounts into those that provided cash and those that consumed cash.

spontaneous sources of cash   Those liabilities such as accounts payable and accrued wages that arise automatically, without negotiation, in the course of doing business.

spot market   A market in which prices are determined for immediate trade.

spread   Investment banker jargon for difference between the issue price of a new security and the net to the company.

standard deviation of return   A measure of variability. The square root of the mean squared deviation from the *expected return.*

statement of changes in financial position   A financial statement showing the sources and uses of working capital for the period.

stock   *Common stock.*

stock option   A contractual privilege sometimes provided to company officers giving the holder the right to purchase a specified number of shares at a specified price within a stated period of time.

striking price (exercise price)   The fixed price for which a stock can be purchased in a call contract or sold in a put contract (cf. *call option, put option*).

strong-form efficient market   A market in which prices instantaneously reflect all information public or private.

subordinated creditor   A creditor holding a debenture having a lower chance of payment than other liabilities of the firm.

sunk cost   A previous outlay that cannot be changed by any current or future action.

sustainable growth rate   The rate of increase in sales a company can attain without changing its profit margin, assets-to-sales ratio, debt-to-equity ratio, or dividend payout ratio. The rate of growth a company can finance without excessive borrowing or issuing new stock.

tax shield   The reduction in a company's tax bill caused by an increase in a tax-deductible expense, usually depreciation or interest. The magnitude of the tax shield equals the tax rate times the increase in the expense.

times burden covered   A *coverage ratio* measure of *financial leverage,* defined as earnings before interest and taxes divided by interest expense plus principal payments grossed up to their before-tax equivalents.

times interest earned   A *coverage ratio* measure of *financial leverage,* defined as earnings before interest and taxes divided by interest expense.

trade payables   *Accounts payable.*

transfer price   An internal price at which units of the same company trade goods or services among themselves.

underwriting syndicate   A group of *investment banks* that band together for a brief time to guarantee a specified price to a company for newly issued securities.

unrealized income   Earned income for which there is no confirming transaction. A paper gain.

variable cost   Any expense that varies with sales over the observation period.

volatility   β-*risk.*

warrant   A security issued by a company granting the right to purchase shares of another security of the company at a specified price and for a stated time.

weak-form efficient market   A market in which prices instantaneously reflect information about past prices.

weak-form efficient market   Cost of capital.

weighted-average cost of capital   *Cost of capital.*

with-without principle   Principle defining those cash flows that are relevant to an investment decision. It states that if there are two worlds, one with the investment and one without it, all cash flows that differ in these two worlds are relevant and all cash flows that are the same are irrelevant.

working capital (net working capital)   The excess of current assets over current liabilities.

working capital cycle   The periodic transformation of cash through current assets and current liabilities and back to cash (cf. *cash flow cycle*).

yield to maturity   The *internal rate of return* on a bond when held to maturity.

CHAPTER 1
SUGGESTED ANSWERS

1. Because a primary goal of the accountant is to measure earnings, not cash provided. Earnings are seen as a fundamental indicator of viability, while cash provided is not.

   Many financial analysts would argue that accountants over-emphasize earnings and should devote more attention to cash accounting. Accountants have responded recently by requiring companies to include cash flow statements as part of their annual reports.

   A balanced perspective is that over the long run successful companies must be both profitable and solvent, that is, they must have the cash available to pay their bills when due. This means that one must pay attention to both earnings and cash flows.

2. a.

	1991 Books of Account	
	Reporting Purposes	Tax Purposes
Net sales	$2,000	$2,000
Cost of goods sold	1,000	1,000
Gross profit	1,000	1,000
General, selling, administrative expenses	400	400
Depreciation	20	80
Operating income	580	520
Nonoperating expense	100	100
Income before tax	480	420
Provision for taxes @ 40%	192	
Taxes due @ 40%		168
Net income	288	252
Accrued taxes*	224	0
Gross fixed assets	1,600	1,600
Accumulated depreciation	220	580

*Accrued taxes = $200 + '91 taxes accrued − '91 taxes paid

b. Cash flow from operations = net income ± noncash items.
Using reporting data:

Cash flow from operations = \$288 + depreciation +
increase in accrued taxes
= \$288 + \$20 + \$24 = \$332

Using tax data:
Cash flow from operations = \$252 + \$80 + 0 = \$332

3. APL Corporation Cash Flows from Operating Activities 1991

Net income	\$84
Adjustment to reconcile net income to net cash provided by operating activities	
Depreciation	40
Accrued taxes	20
Changes in current assets and liabilities:	
Accounts receivable	(50)
Inventories	20
Accounts payable	10
Accrued wages	(30)
Net cash flows from operations	\$94

4. a. **R & E Supplies, Inc.** Sources and Uses Statement 1987–1990

Sources of cash:

Decrease in cash and securities	\$ 259
Increase in accounts payable	2,205
Increase in current portion long-term debt	40
Increase in accrued wages	13
Increase in retained earnings	537
Total	\$3,054

Uses of cash:

Increase in accounts receivable	\$1,543
Increase in inventories	1,148
Increase in prepaid expenses	4
Increase in net fixed assets	159
Decrease in long-term debt	200
Total	\$3,054

b. Insights:
 i. R & E is making extensive use of trade credit to finance a buildup in current assets. The increase in accounts payable equals almost three fourths of total sources of cash. Increasing accounts receivable and inventories account for almost 90 percent of the uses of cash.
 ii. External financing is a use of cash for R & E, meaning that it is repaying its loans. A restructuring involving less accounts payable and more bank debt appears appropriate.

5. *a.* Balance sheet: property, plant, and equipment up $1 million, cash down $1 million. Income statement: no immediate change. Cash flow statement: purchase of property, plant, and equipment ($1 million). This will reduce net increase (decrease) in cash and cash balance at end of year $1 million.
 b. Balance sheet: property, plant, and equipment up $1 million, cash down $400,000, bank loan up $600,000. Income statement: no immediate impact. Cash flow statement: purchase of property, plant, and equipment ($1 million), bank borrowings $600,000. These entries will reduce net increase (decrease) in cash, and cash balance at end of year $400,000.
 c. Balance sheet: cash up $100,000, accounts receivable down $100,000. Income statement: no change, $100,000 of revenue was recognized when sale originally made. Cash flow statement: change in accounts receivable $100,000; remember a reduction in an asset account is a source of cash.
 d. Balance sheet: shareholders' equity down $10 million, cash down $10 million. Income statement: no immediate change, throughout the year interest earned will decline because the $10 million is no longer invested and per share numbers will increase because fewer shares are outstanding. Cash flow statement: repurchase of common shares ($10 million).

6. The General Secretary has confused accounting profits with economic profits. Earning $40 million on a $500 million equity investment is a return of only 8 percent. This is too low a return for the company to continue attracting new equity investment necessary for firm growth.

7. *a.*

Company	*A*	*B*	*C*
End of year cash balance	$5 million	$1 million	$4 million

b. It appears that company C retired more debt than it issued, repurchased more stock than it issued, or some combination of these two.

c. I'd prefer to own company A. A appears to be a growing company as evidenced by the sizable net cash used in financing activities, and its negative net cash flows from operations may well be due to increasing accounts receivable and inventories that naturally accompany sales growth. Company B appears not to be growing, so its negative net cash flows from operations are probably due to losses or to increasing receivables and inventories relative to sales, a trend denoting poor management of current assets.

d. I don't think there is necessarily any cause for concern. It appears company C is a mature, slow-growth company that is returning its unneeded operating cash flows to investors in the form of debt repayment, share repurchase, dividends, or some combination of these. This is a perfectly viable strategy.

CHAPTER 2
SUGGESTED ANSWERS

1. *a.* (1) Liabilities-to-equity ratio = 50/(80 − 50) = 167%
   (2) Assets-to-equity ratio = 80/(80 − 50) = 267%
   (3) Liabilities-to-assets ratio = 50/80 = 62.5%
   (4) Times interest earned = 10/5 = 2 times
   (5) Times burden covered = 10/(5 + 2/(1 − .40)) = 1.2 times
   b. (1) % decline in EBIT for times burden covered to fall to 1.00
       = [10 − (5 + 2/(1 − 0.40)]/10 = 16.7%.
       (2) % decline in EBIT before failing to cover common dividends: 1.00 = [10 − (5 + (2 + 0.40 × 5)/(1 − 0.40))]/10 = −16.7%.
       In 1990, the before-tax burden of interest, sinking fund, and dividends exceeded EBIT. The company fell 16.7% short of covering these burdens as it was, and must have sold assets or raised money from external sources to pay its dividend.
2. A/E = 2.5; $(L + E)/E$ = L/E + 1 = 2.5; L/E = 150%, where A is assets, E is equity, and L is liabilities.
3. Introducing the new calibrator will reduce the division's profit margin, but this is not a valid reason for opposing introduction. Thus the asset turnover on the new calibrator may be very high, more than offsetting the reduced profit margin.
4. The argument is *not* convincing. If simply maximizing ROE were the goal, this could be achieved by shrinking a firm down to the one activity that generates the highest ROE. The proper perspective is to undertake activities promising returns in excess of costs.
5. *a.* ROE = 54/400 = 13.5%, ROA = 54/500 = 10.8%, ROIC = 100(1 − 0.40)/500 = 12%.
   b.

EBIT	$100
Interest expense	40
Earnings before tax	60
Tax @ 40%	24
Earnings after tax	$ 36

   ROE = 36/100 = 36%, ROA = 36/500 = 7.2%
   ROIC = 100(1 − 0.40)/500 = 12%

c. The increased ROE does not necessarily imply that ABC is a better company because it has been achieved by increasing financial risk. The reduced ROA does not imply that ABC is a worse company. It simply reflects the higher interest expense accompanying higher borrowing. ROIC reflects the fundamental earning power of ABC's assets independent of how the company is financed, and, hence, is unaffected by the recapitalization.

6.

Assets	
Cash	$ 98,630
Accounts receivable	328,767
Inventory	400,000
Total current assets	$ 827,397
Net fixed assets	172,603
Total assets	$1,000,000
Liabilities and Owners' Equity	
Accounts payable	$ 54,795
Short-term debt	358,904
Total current liabilities	$ 413,698
Long-term debt	186,382
Shareholders' equity	400,000
Total liabilities and equity	$1,000,000

CHAPTER 3
SUGGESTED ANSWERS

1.

	October	November	December
Cash receipts:			
Sales for cash	$ 40,000	$ 16,000	$ 16,000
Collection of credit sales	320,000	160,000	64,000
Total receipts	360,000	176,000	80,000
Cash disbursements:			
Payment for credit purchases	180,000	400,000	100,000
Wages	60,000	60,000	60,000
Principal payment			70,000
Interest payment			30,000
Dividends			100,000
Taxes		60,000	
Total disbursements	240,000	520,000	360,000
Net receipts (disbursements)	120,000	(344,000)	(280,000)
Determination of cash needs:			
Beginning cash	100,000	220,000	(124,000)
Net receipts (disbursements)	120,000	(344,000)	(280,000)
Ending cash	220,000	(124,000)	(404,000)
Minimum cash desired	50,000	50,000	50,000
Cash surplus (deficit)	$170,000	($174,000)	($454,000)

Quite obviously the treasurer had better concern herself with
where to borrow money. Raycore will need almost half a million
dollars by the end of December.

2. *a.*

Raycore Drilling
Income Statement
September 30–December 31, 1991
($ thousands)

Net sales	$360
Cost of goods sold @ 65%	234
Gross profit	126
Selling and administrative expenses	180
Interest	30
Depreciation	10
Net profit before tax	(94)
Tax @ 33%	(31)
Net profit after tax	$(63)

Balance Sheet
December 31, 1991
($ thousands)

Assets

Cash		$ 50
Accounts receivable		64
Inventory		546
Total current assets		660
Gross fixed assets	$300	
− Accumulated depreciation	60	
Net fixed assets		240
Total assets		$900

Liabilities

Bank loan	$454
Accounts payable	80
Miscellaneous accruals	20
Current portion long-term debt	50
Taxes payable	9
Total current liabilities	613
Long-term debt	280
Shareholders' equity	7
Total liabilities and shareholders' equity	$900

Comments:
Inventory is estimated as follows:

Beginning inventory Sept. 30	$600
+ 4th quarter purchases	180
− 4th quarter cost of goods sold	234
Ending inventory Dec. 31	$546

Taxes payable is estimated as follows:

Taxes payable Sept. 30	$100
− payments	60
+ 4th quarter taxes accrued	(31)
Taxes payable Dec. 31	$ 9

Shareholders' equity is estimated as follows:

Equity Sept. 30	$170
− Dividends	100
+ 4th quarter profits	(63)
Equity Dec. 31	$ 7

b. The loan estimates are equal, as they should be.

c. The pro formas indicate clearly that the 4th quarter will be a disaster for Raycore. The company will lose $63,000, equity will fall to $7,000, and the total debt-to-assets ratio will jump to 99 percent. It is clearly time to rethink the $100,000 dividend planned for December. None of this is evident from the cash budget.

3.

Raycore Drilling
Cash Flow Forecast
4th Quarter 1991
($ thousands)

Sources of cash:	
Cash from operations:	
Profit after tax	$(63)
Depreciation	10
Increases in liabilities or reductions in assets:	
Bank loan	454
Cash	50
Accounts receivable	256
Inventory	54
Total sources	$761
Uses of cash:	
Dividends	$100
Decreases in liabilities or increases in assets:	
Accounts payable	500
Current portion long-term debt	20
Taxes payable	91
Long-term debt	50
Total uses	$761

4. When the plug is a liability account, a negative value implies that the company can loan money to the bank rather than borrow money from the bank. In other words, the company will have excess cash above its desired minimum. You can show this on the balance sheet by setting the bank loan to zero and adding the absolute value of the plug to cash.

5.

L. M. Wilson, Inc.
Pro Forma Income Statement and Balance Sheet
December 31, 1991

Net sales		$120
Cost of goods sold		84
Gross profit		36
General selling expenses		5
Depreciation		5
Interest expense		5
Profit before tax		21
Tax at 34%		7
Profit after tax		14
Dividends paid @ 50%		7
Additions to retained earnings		$ 7
Assets		
Cash		$ 4
Accounts receivable		24
Inventories		30
Total current assets		58
Gross fixed assets	$170	
Accumulated depreciation	75	
Net fixed assets		95
Total assets		$153
Liabilities and Shareholders' Equity		
Accounts payable		$ 6
Bank loan		plug
Total current liabilities		6 + plug
Long-term debt		50
Common stock		20
Retained earnings		42
Total liabilities and shareholders' equity		$118 + plug

Plug = $153 − $118 = <u>$35 million</u>

a. If Wilson's inventory turn falls to 2.4 times,
   Ending inventory = cost of goods sold/inventory turnover
   $$\$35 = 84/2.4$$
   So inventories will increase $6 million, and the plug will rise by a like amount to <u>$41 million</u>.

b. Eliminating the dividend will add $7 million to retained earnings and will reduce the plug by a like amount; so the plug will fall to <u>$34 million</u>.

CHAPTER 4
SUGGESTED ANSWERS

1. *a.*

	1986	*1987*	*1988*	*1989*	*1990*
Sustainable growth rate (%)	9.55	11.61	9.59	7.22	3.65

    b. Jamesway's actual growth rate in every year has exceeded its sustainable growth rate the prior year. Sales are increasing at an unsustainably rapid pace.

    c. Jamesway has coped with rapid growth principally by increasing financial leverage. Assets/beginning-of-period equity has risen from 2.36 times in 1986 to 2.81 in 1990.

    d. Repurchasing stock worsens Jamesway's growth problems by reducing equity and further increasing financial leverage. Let's hope the price was really attractive.

    e. Reducing future expansion will lessen the company's growth problems by lowering actual growth.

2. *a.*

	1986	*1987*	*1988*	*1989*
Sustainable growth rate (%)	46	40	26	32
Actual growth rate (%)	46	30	12	19

    b. The company's growth rate in sales has fallen considerably below its sustainable growth rate.

    c. It has used some of the excess cash flow to reduce its indebtedness. Financial leverage has fallen from 2.1 in 1986 to 1.9 in 1989. It has also allowed asset turnover to fall from 2.5 times in 1985 to 1.7 in 1989, due possibly to a build-up in excess cash and securities.

CHAPTER 5
SUGGESTED ANSWERS

1. *a.* Holding period return = $(80 - 130)/1,050 = -4.8\%$.
   b. Investor perceptions of the bond's risk may have increased, or market interest rates may have risen. As will be demonstrated in Chapter 7, bond prices and interest rates vary inversely.
2. *a.* It would be most unusual for a company's bonds to be riskier than its common stock because bondholders have priority over stockholders for receipt of annual payments as well as for cash distributions in liquidation.
   b. Yes, certainly. The bonds of a bankrupt company may well be riskier than the common stock of a healthy firm.
3. *a.*

Stock price	$56.00
−5% underpricing	2.80
Issue price	$53.20
−6% spread	3.19
Net to company	$50.01

Number of shares = $200 million/$50.01 = ~~399,920~~ shares $3,999,200$

b. Investment bankers' revenue = $3.19 × ~~399,920~~ = ~~$1,275,745~~ $12,757,448$ $3,999,200$

c. Underpricing is not a cash flow. It is, however, an opportunity cost to current owners because it means that more shares must be sold to raise $200 million and each share will represent a smaller ownership stake in Jensen.

4. *a.* Return on Russell stock = $(0.28 + 26.12 - 16.12)/16.12$
   = $\underline{63.8}$ %.
   b. Dividend yield = $0.28/16.12 = \underline{1.7\%}$, percentage change in share price = $(26.12 - 16.12)/16.12 = \underline{62.0\%}$.
   c. Proportion of return in form of dividends = $1.7\%/63.8\% = \underline{2.7\%}$. Proportion attributable to stock price appreciation = $62\%/63.8\% = \underline{97.2\%}$.

   Historically for stocks in general, these proportions have been about equal.

5. Equity markets are, at best, semistrong-form efficient. If managers have more or better information about their firm's prospects, as they should, managers may well be able to detect when their shares are underpriced.

CHAPTER 6
SUGGESTED ANSWERS

1. *a.* When the expected operating return on assets, *r*, exceeds the aftertax cost of borrowing, *i*, maximizing debt maximizes ROE. If expected *r* does not exceed *i*, you are in the wrong business. You could earn at least *i* by lending money.
   b. When *r* = *i*, ROE is unaffected by changes in the debt-to-equity ratio.
   c. Maximizing ROE is a dumb goal because it also maximizes the financial risks borne by owners. The objective should be to find a prudent middle ground.
2. *a.* If net income after tax = $100 million, income before tax = 100/(1 − 0.40) = $167 million and EBIT = $167 + $43 = $210 million.
   Times interest earned = 210/(43 + 20) = 3.3 times
   b. Times burden covered = 210/(43 + 20 + (30 + 40)/(1 − 0.4)) = 1.2 times
   c. Earnings per share = (210 − 63)(1 − 0.4)/50 = $1.76
   d. Times interest earned = 210/43 = 4.9 times
   Times burden covered = 210/(43 + 30/(1 − 0.4)) = 2.3 times
   Earnings per share (210 − 43)(1 − 0.4)/(50 + 5) = $1.82
   e. Target's earnings per share next year are expected to be higher with equity financing than with debt. Target is below the crossover point on the range-of-earnings chart. This suggests that Target should consider equity financing. One reason equity financing looks attractive is that Target's stock is selling at over 20 times next year's earnings.
3. This problem illustrates the importance of flexibility in financing decisions. Over the next five years XYZ will be dependent on the capital markets to make critical investments that are not postponable. A failure to make these investments for lack of funding will be very costly. This suggests that XYZ maintain a conservative capital structure to ensure the availability of needed financing. An aggressive capital structure risks closing of the top and, hence, future flexibility.
4. *a.* ABC has modest business risk, more internally generated cash than it needs, and no need for outside financing. It can there-

fore support a more aggressive capital structure without undo risk. In particular, if it does close off the top, there is no great loss since it does not anticipate a need for external financing anyway.

b. Yes, I might well feel differently as a manager. A principal attraction of debt financing is the tax shield benefits that accrue to owners. But I own few shares. A principal risk of debt financing is the need to cede a measure of operating control to creditors if the firm fails to meet the terms of its loans. As a manager, I will bear much of this cost. So on balance I will be more inclined than shareholders to prefer a conservative capital structure.

5. a. An increase in the interest rate would lower the debt financing line in the range-of-earnings chart. This would reduce the EPS advantage of debt or increase the disadvantage if EBIT is below the crossover point. It would also increase the crossover EBIT. Both changes would reduce the attractiveness of debt financing.

b. An increased stock price will reduce the number of shares issued to raise needed capital, which will increase EPS at all income levels for the equity line. Raising the equity line will improve EPS with equity financing relative to debt and will increase the crossover EBIT. Both changes will make equity more attractive.

c. The range-of-earnings chart will be unchanged, but increased uncertainty will increase the probability that EBIT will fall below the crossover point. This will make equity more attractive.

d. Increased common dividends will not affect the range-of-earnings chart. It will reduce the times-common-covered ratio and will hence make debt marginally more attractive.

e. An increase in the amount of debt already outstanding will increase interest expense and lower EPS for all financing options. This will lower both the debt and the equity financing lines in the range-of-earnings chart by the same amount, but will not affect the attractiveness of debt relative to equity. Interest coverage obviously falls as existing debt rises, which makes additional debt financing riskier.

CHAPTER 7
SUGGESTED ANSWERS

1. *a.* $1,000 × 0.519 = $519.

   b. $1,000 × 0.270 = $270. The present sum is less because the money has more time to grow into $1,000.

   c. Value of bond = $100 × 5.216 + $1,000 × 0.270 = $791.60.

   d. Future value = (1/PVF) Present value = (1/0.073) $10 = $136.99.

   e. $3 = (1/PVF) $1; PVF = 0.333. Examining the 14% column in Appendix A, the present value factor equals 0.333 when *n* is *between 8 and 9 years.*

   f. The present value $10 per year for 6 years is 3.889 × $10 = $38.89. The future value of this sum is (1/0.456) $38.89 = $85.29.

   g. The present value of $100,000 in 18 years is $100,000 × 0.95 = $9,500. Letting *X* equal the uniform annual amount to be deposited, $9,500 = X(6.467), X = $1,469 per year.

2. Try 8%, $260,000 × 0.463 − $100,000 $\overset{?}{=}$ 0; $20,380 ≠ 0.
   Try 10%. $260,000 × 0.386 − $100,000 $\overset{?}{=}$ 0; $360 ≈ 0.
   Rate of return is about 10%.

3. Try 8%. $260,000 (1 − 0.08) × 0.463 − $1,500 × 6.71 − $100,000 $\overset{?}{=}$ 0.
   $684.60 ≈ 0. Rate of return is about 8%. (The exact return, using a computer, is 8.07%.)

4. *a.* Accounting rate of return = $20,000/$100,000 = 20%.

   b. Payback period = 100,000/20,000 = 5 years.

   c. NPV = $20,000 × 4.494 − $100,000 = −$10,120.

   d. PI = ($20,000 × 4.494)/$100,000 = 0.90.

e. 18% is too high because the NPV is negative at this rate; so let's try 15%: $20,000 \times 5.019 - \$100,000 \stackrel{?}{=} 0$; $380 \approx 0$. Return is <u>just above 15%</u>.

f. The accounting rate of return indicates that the investment is attractive. The NPV, PI, and IRR indicate it is unattractive. The payback period is ambiguous.

5. Calculating the investment's aftertax cash flow

Expected annual savings	$30,000
− Depreciation	15,000
Increased income before tax	15,000
− Tax @ 40%	6,000
Increased income after tax	9,000
+ Depreciation	15,000
Aftertax cash flow	$24,000

NPV $= \$24,000 \times 3.784 + \$10,000 \times 0.432 - \$100,000 = \underline{-\$4,864}$. Meat slicer does not earn a return of 15%. Financial analysis suggests rejecting this investment.

6. Let X equal the end-of-year payment. $\$10,000 = X(3.433)$; $X = \underline{\$2,912.90}$. With this annual payment the NPV on the loan from the bank's perspective is 0, so its IRR is 14%.

7. Applying the with-without principle,

Year	Cash Flows with Investment	Cash Flows without Investment	With-Without Cash Flows
0	−$10 million	0	−$10 million
1–5	$100,000	−$3 million	$3.1 million

NPV $= \$3.1 \times 3.791 - \$10 = + \underline{\$1.75 \text{ million}}$. Therefore, spend the $10 million. Spending $10 million avoids an annual loss of $3 million, and this is a benefit.

8. These are mutually exclusive alternatives and can be evaluated over a 15-year horizon.

Design Y annual depreciation:	$ 4,000
Aftertax cash flow:	14,000

NPV = \$14,000 × 6.811 − \$60,000 = \$35,354.

Design Z annual depreciation:	$ 6,000
Aftertax cash flow:	28,000
Salvage value $\frac{5}{20}$ of initial cost	30,000

NPV = \$28,000 × 6.811 + \$30,000 × 0.183 − \$120,000 = \$76,198.
I'd rather be \$76,198 richer than \$35,354 richer; take design Z.

9. The IRR is 13.7 percent. \$125 invested for 98 years at 13.7% will become \$36 million. This is an attractive return, but given that we have ignored insurance, security systems, and climate control equipment, it's not unusually high given the risks involved.

CHAPTER 8
SUGGESTED ANSWERS

1. Increasing financial leverage raises the risk borne by owners and, hence, raises the return they require on the firm's equity. Thus, increases in financial leverage increase the cost of equity capital.
2. The most direct answer is that the 9 percent investment might be low risk and so above the Market Line, while the 11 percent investment is high risk and below the Market Line.
3. When the investment is below average risk for the firm yet above the Market Line.
4. When an investment lies below the Market Line it is possible to make equal-risk investments promising higher expected returns. Conversely, investments above the Market Line promise expected returns above those available on equal-risk, ready alternatives.
5. The investment's expected net present value is:

Probability	NPV	Weighted NPV
20%	−100	−20
40	10	4
10	150	15
30	200	60
	Expected NPV =	$59

A positive expected NPV suggests the investment is acceptable.

6. *a.* Using the perpetuity equation, IRR = $1 million/$10 million = 10%.
   b. The weighted-average cost of capital is

$$K_w = \frac{(1 - 0.50) \times 8\% \times 50 + 16\% \times 50}{50 + 50}$$
$$= 10\%$$

   c. Because IRR = K_w, this investment neither creates nor destroys shareholder value.

7. *a.* NPV = −$100 million + $20.7 million (present value annuity factor, $r\%$, 10 years) = 0

(present value annuity factor, $r\%$, 10 years) = 4.831
Consulting Appendix B for 10 years, $r \simeq \underline{\underline{16\%}}$.

b. Annual interest and principal payment necessary to amortize an $80 million, 10-year loan at 8% is:

$$\text{NPV} = \$80 \text{ million} - \$X(6.710) = 0$$
$$V = \$11.9 \text{ million}$$

So equity cash flows are −$20 million at time 0, and $8.8 million per year for 10 years. IRR is: NPV = −$20 million + $8.8 million (PV annuity factor, $r\%$, 10 years) = 0.

(PV annuity factor, $r\%$, 10 years) = 2.273
Consulting Appendix B for 10 years, $r \simeq \underline{\underline{35\%}}$.

c. The IRR from the entity perspective is below the weighted-average cost of capital, so the investment is unattractive. The high IRR from the equity perspective just reflects the high financial leverage.

8. If the investment pays $1.00 this year, growing at 5 percent, it will pay $1.05 next year. Using the perpetual growth formula

$$\$20 = \$1.05/(r - 5\%)$$
$$r = 10.25\%$$

9. The arithmetic is the same as in problem 8.

$$K_E = \$1.05/\$20 + 5\% = 10.25\%$$

10. *a.* NPV = −$50 million + $18.7 million (PV annuity factor, $r\%$, 3 years) = 0
(PV annuity factor, $r\%$, 3 years) = 2.674
$$r \simeq 6\%$$

b. Year 1 = $20.6 million, year 2 = $22.6 million, year 3 = $24.9 million.

c. Using a computer: IRR = 16.6%.

d.
$$\text{real } K_w \simeq \text{ nominal } K_w - \text{Inflation rate}$$
$$\simeq 20\% - 10\%$$
$$\simeq 10\%$$

e. The investment is unattractive. The real IRR is less than the real K_w; alternatively, the nominal IRR is less than the nominal K_w.

CHAPTER 9
SUGGESTED ANSWERS

1. *a.*

	($ millions)			
	1993	*1994*	*1995*	*1996*
EBIT (1 − Tax rate)	$ 60	$78	$102	$126
+ Depreciation	25	30	50	60
− Capital expenditures	150	90	100	110
− Changes in working capital	20	50	−10	10
= Free cash flow	−$ 85	−$32	$ 62	$ 66

b. A negative free cash flow does not necessarily imply that the company is destroying value. It simply means that capital expenditures and increases in working capital exceed operating cash flow that year. The capital expenditures will presumably add to EBIT and to free cash flow in following years.

c. FMV of Maternity Modes = PV{FCF, '93–'96}
$$+ \text{ PV \{Terminal value\}}$$
PV{FCF, '93–'96} = −$18.3 million
Terminal value = EBIT(1 − Tax rate)/0.14
$$= \$126/0.14 = \$900 \text{ million}$$
PV{Terminal value} = $900 million × 0.592
$$= \$532.9 \text{ million}$$
FMV of Maternity Modes = $514.6 million

d. FMV of equity = $514.6 − $300 = $214.6 million
FMV of equity per share = $214.6/50 = $4.29

e. Terminal value = FCF in 1997/(0.14 − 0.04)
FCF in 1997 = $210(1.04)(1−0.40)−20−10
$$= \$101.4$$
Terminal value = $1,014
PV{Terminal value} = $598.2
FMV of Maternity Modes = −$18.3 + $598.2
$$= \$580.0 \text{ million}$$

f.   Terminal value = Value of equity + Value of
                              liabilities
            Value of equity = 8 × Net income in 1996
        Net income in 1996 = (EBIT − Interest)(1−Tax rate)
                           = (210 − 0.10 × 200)(1−0.4)
                           = $114 million
            Value of equity = $912.0
             Terminal value = $912 + $200 = $1,112.0
         PV{Terminal value} = $658.4
FMV of Maternity Modes = −$18.3 + 658.4
                           = $640.1 million

2.   FMV with control = Market value of IMI
                             + Enhancements
        Market value of IMI = $16 × 10 + $30 + $100
                           = $290 million
             Enhancements = $25 + $6 × 7.469 = $69.8
            FMV with control = $359.8
   FMV equity with control = $359.8 − $30 − $100 = $229.8
   FMV of equity per share = $229.8/10 = $22.98
                 Premium = $22.98 − $16 = $6.98 = 43.6%

3. a. EBIT = $30 million

As a stand-alone company, typical debt would be 0.40 × $140 million = $56 million. At a 10% interest rate, interest expense would be $5.6 million.

Therefore, profit before tax = $30 − $5.6 = $24.4 million.

   Profit after tax = $24.4(1 − 0.34) = $16.1 million.

Therefore the value of the division's equity relative to the comparables is $16.1 × 13 = $209.35 million. Adding liabilities, value of division = $209.35 + $56 = $265.35 million. This should be the owner's minimum acceptable price.

b. From the acquirer's perspective, this is essentially a "make-or-buy" decision. Because the acquirer can "make" a like operation for a present value cost of $250 million, he should not pay more than this to "buy" the division.

c. An acquisition does not appear feasible; the owner's minimum price exceeds the buyer's maximum.

d. Redoing the answer to (*a*) at a 9.1 price-to-earnings ratio, the value of the division's equity = $16.1 × 9.1 = $146.55, and adding liabilities, the value of the division is now $146.55 + $56 = $202.55. Because the owner's minimum price is now less than the buyer's maximum, an acquisition is now possible.

e. The answer to (*d*) suggests that acquisition activity will increase when market value falls below replacement value. In this situation, companies find it less expensive to "buy" assets than to "make" them. This is essentially the logic of James Tobin's *q-ratio*, defined as the market value of a company/ replacement value of its assets.

INDEX